INDIAN POLITICS AND INTERNATIONAL RELATIONS

ESWARAN SRIDHARAN

Indian Politics *and* International Relations

UNDEREXPLORED ISSUES AND APPROACHES

permanent black

Published by

PERMANENT BLACK

"Himalayana", Mall Road, Ranikhet Cantt,
Ranikhet 263645

perblack@gmail.com

Distributed by

ORIENT BLACKSWAN PRIVATE LTD

Bangalore Bhopal Bhubaneshwar Chandigarh Chennai
Ernakulam Guwahati Hyderabad Jaipur Kolkata
Lucknow Mumbai New Delhi Patna
www.orientblackswan.com

ISBN 978-81-7824-702-1

Typeset in Adobe Garamond Pro
by Guru Typograph Technology, Crossings Republic, Ghaziabad
Printed and bound by Manipal Technologies Limited, Manipal

MIX
Paper | Supporting responsible forestry
FSC™ C043100

Contents

Preface and Acknowledgements

In this selection of twelve of my earlier-published papers, five were published in refereed academic journals; three were published in refereed academic journals and later included, after minor revision, in edited volumes; and four first appeared in edited academic books. Together, they cover two broad areas: first, key underexplored issues and approaches in Indian politics, political economy, and political sociology; and second, likewise as regards aspects of India's foreign relations and with a focus on international relations theory in the analysis. My motivation for putting together this collection is that it addresses relatively under-researched issues in the light of theory and data which remain relevant for scholars and students of Indian politics and foreign policy. Let me briefly explain what these papers are essentially about and why they are important.

In Part I, the first paper, "The Fragmentation of the Indian Party System 1952–1999: Seven Competing Explanations", takes a long-range historical view of the evolution of the Indian party system in the second half of the twentieth century, from a one-party hegemonic (Congress) system to a highly fragmented multi-party system resulting in coalition and/or minority governments since 1989, identifying seven competing explanations for the fragmentation of the party system. This paper sets the stage for understanding the Indian party system in the twenty-first century.

The second paper, "Democracy Within Parties and the Accommodation of Diversity: Comparing India and the United States", compares intra-party democracy (an under-researched issue in India) in both the United States and India with respect to the representation of social diversity in the electoral and legislative arena, placing the discussion in the broader comparative literature on intra-party democracy. This is topical today in the context of both the intra-party dynamics in the major Indian parties as well as those in the two American parties.

The third paper, "Does India Need to Switch to Proportional Representation? The Pros and Cons", addresses a debate that never seriously took place when choosing the first-past-the-post system – that is, whether the proportional representation system would better suit a very heterogeneous country with small parties and dispersed minorities in terms of better representation and more protection against possible brute majoritarianism.

The fourth paper (co-authored with Adnan Farooqui), "Is the Coalition Era Over in Indian Politics?", addresses the question of whether the emergence of a single-party majority government in 2014 meant the end of the coalition politics of 1989–2014 and the start of a new party system. This paper argues that, due to the role of pre-electoral coalitions – an under-studied phenomenon – coalition politics did not disappear in 2014 when producing a majority government: this is of increased relevance after the 2024 election.

The fifth paper, "Cross-State Learning in Service Delivery in India's Federal System", is an analysis of how, over the two decades since the late 1990s, policies on governance and development have been diffused across states due to inter-state learning, borrowing, and emulation of policies; and what the incentives, drivers, and mechanisms of such inter-state learning, borrowing, and emulation are – this being of increased relevance, given inter-state competition in development.

The sixth paper, "The Growth and Sectoral Composition of India's Middle Class: Its Impact on the Politics of Economic Liberalization", combines economic and sociological analysis. It goes beyond purely economistic accounts of the middle class and focuses on the sectoral composition of that class – how much of it is in the government/public sector and how much in the private sector – and how this then shapes the politics of economic liberalisation. The subject is of continuing relevance today, both conceptually and policy-wise.

In Part II, which begins with the seventh paper, "Where is India Headed? Possible Future Directions in Indian Foreign Policy", I offer an analysis of India's emergence as a rising power/emerging economy and its prospects for moving from middle power to great power status in the context of international relations theory and changing power hierarchies in the world. This paper is strongly conceptual, apart from being based on empirical data, and therefore relevant in the context of India's continuing and much-debated ascent.

The eighth paper (co-authored with Aashik Jain), "Foreign Assistance in India's Foreign Policy", is an account of India's little-recognised emergence as a new donor in international development and the role of aid in its foreign policy since the late 1990s.

The ninth paper, "Economic Co-operation and Security: Theory, India and Pakistan", is a conceptually and theoretically grounded analysis of possible scenarios for conflict resolution/co-operation-building between India and Pakistan. In integrating security and political economy by combining data and insights from international relations theory, deterrence theory, and international political economy, this paper too remains relevant today.

The tenth paper, "International Relations Theory and the India–Pakistan Conflict", is an analysis of the India–Pakistan conflict that combines deterrence theory and broader international relations theory.

The eleventh paper, "Indo–Sri Lanka Relations: Geopolitics, Domestic Politics or Something More Complex?", is an analysis of the domestic, geopolitical, and other factors in Indo–Sri Lankan relations since the eruption of the Sinhala–Tamil conflict in the island. The essay integrates domestic politics and international relations, going to the roots of state identity and its role as a policy driver in India. It argues that neither domestic politics nor geopolitics or a combination explain Indian policy but that something more complex has driven policy.

The final paper, "Eastward Ho? Indian Foreign Policy in the Indo-Pacific in the Context of Trade Integration and Security Rivalries", analyses the strategic consequences of the economic integration of Asia with China bulking large and the economic consequences of the lack of security consensus in Asia. It explores challenges to India's Act East foreign policy in the light of this evolving Asian architecture.

This being a selection of papers published in a range of journals and edited volumes, I would like to acknowledge the original publishers and thank them for permissions to republish.

My thanks to Taylor & Francis for permission to publish the following three papers which first appeared in UK-based Routledge journals and one that first appeared in an edited Routledge book: "Is the Coalition Era Over in Indian Politics?" (with Adnan Farooqui), *The Round Table: The Commonwealth Journal of International Affairs*, December 2014; "Cross-state Learning in Service Delivery in India's Federal System", *Commonwealth and Comparative Politics*, March 2020; "International Relations Theory and the India-Pakistan Conflict", *India Review*, vol. 4, no. 3, April 2005; "The Growth and Sectoral Composition of India's Middle Class: Its Impact on the Politics of Economic Liberalisation", in Amita Baviskar and Raka Ray, eds, *Elite and Everyman: The Cultural Politics of the Indian Middle Classes* (Routledge, 2011)

I thank the Policy Studies Organization of Washington, D.C., for permission to publish "Foreign Assistance in India's Foreign Policy" (with Aashik Jain), *Indian Politics and Policy*, vol. 1, no. 2, 2018.

I thank Oxford University Press for permission to publish the following four book chapters and one journal article: "The Fragmentation of the Indian Party System 1952–1999: Seven Competing Explanations", in Zoya Hasan, ed., *Parties and Party Politics in India* (New Delhi: Oxford University Press, 2002); "Democracy Within Parties and the Accommodation of Diversity: Comparing India and the United States", in K. Shankar Bajpai, ed., *Democracy and Diversity: India and the American Experience* (New Delhi: Oxford University Press, 2007); "Economic Co-operation and Security: Theory, India and Pakistan", in E. Sridharan, ed., *International Relations Theory and South Asia: Security, Political Economy, Domestic Politics, Identities and Images*, vol. 2 (New Delhi: Oxford University Press, 2011); "Indo–Sri Lanka Relations: Geopolitics, Domestic Politics or Something More Complex?", in Sumit Ganguly, ed., *Engaging the World: Indian Foreign Policy since 1947* (New Delhi: Oxford University Press, 2016); "Where is India Headed? Possible Future Directions in Indian Foreign Policy", *International Affairs*, 93:1 (2017).

I thank Orient BlackSwan for permission to publish the following two chapters from edited volumes: "Does India Need to Switch to Proportional Representation? The Pros and Cons", in Sudha Pai, ed., *Constitutional and Democratic Institutions in India: A Critical Analysis* (New Delhi: Orient BlackSwan, 2019); and "Eastward Ho? Indian Foreign Policy in the Indo–Pacific in the Context of Trade Integration and Security Rivalries", in E. Sridharan, ed., *Eastward Ho? India's Relations with the Indo-Pacific* (New Delhi: Orient BlackSwan, 2021).

I would like to thank Adnan Farooqui and Aashik Jain for their consent to include a paper each that I co-authored with them.

I acknowledge the support of the Ford Foundation for two multi-year projects between 2000 and 2015, one on coalition politics in India, which resulted in two edited volumes; and the other on international relations theory and South Asia which resulted in three edited volumes.

I thank the World Bank which funded some of this research as a consultancy, and the Navajbai Ratan Tata Trust which funded some of this research on international relations which resulted in an edited volume.

I thank the International Development Research Centre, Ottawa, and the Asia Foundation which funded some of the research here. Some of the papers in this volume were the outputs of these projects, either directly or as spin-offs.

I would like to thank the Center for the Advanced Study of India, University of Pennsylvania, particularly Francine Frankel, Devesh Kapur, and Tariq Thachil, and the Governing Council, past and present, of the University of Pennsylvania Institute for the Advanced Study of India (UPIASI) for broadbased, long-term support.

I would like to thank Kamla Pande for her careful copy-editing and reformatting of these papers; Jacqueline Massey of UPIASI for reformatting the many tables in Excel; and UPIASI staffers Tishya Sethi and Ruchika Ahuja for general support.

Last, but not least, I express my gratitude to Divya Raina and Tarini Sridharan for their affection, for which no words are adequate.

1

The Fragmentation of the Indian Party System, 1952–1999

Seven Competing Explanations

Introduction

THIS PAPER AIMS at providing a long-range overview of the process of fragmentation of the Indian party system at the national level over the half-century since independence in 1947 and the first general elections in 1952 to the thirteenth general elections in 1999, and also the evolution of alliances and trends towards reconsolidation into a less fragmented system with fewer poles. It describes and analyses the process of fragmentation of the one party-dominated national party system, dominated by the encompassing centrist umbrella-type Indian National Congress (henceforth Congress) party. This process has resulted in an evolving national party system, still in flux, in which no party has achieved a parliamentary majority for the last five general elections (1989, 1991, 1996, 1998, 1999), necessitating minority and/or coalition governments, even while party systems at the state level have become bipartisan or bipolar, hence *less* fragmented, in more and more states.

The paper is an overview of the party system and focuses on parties' electoral record and hence their position in the party system rather than on their social bases or organisational dynamics. It describes this evolving fragmentation at the electoral and legislative levels in terms of the shifts in vote share, seat shares, and evolution of electoral alliances at both the national and state levels, since the national party system is an aggregate of the state-level party systems. It also assesses competing explanations for these shifts to uncover their underlying logic.

There are, broadly speaking, two classes of explanations for the configuration of party systems in the comparative literature. One can be called the social cleavage theory of party systems, and the other the political-systemic theory of party systems, of which the most elaborate are the electoral rules theories of party systems.[1] The social cleavage theory postulates that the party system will reflect the principal cleavages in society, as for example between capital and labour in ethno-culturally homogeneous industrialised societies having parties positioned on a Left-Right spectrum. The political-systemic theory, particularly the electoral rules theory, postulates that the larger political system's and, more specifically,

[1] Seymour Martin Lipset and Stein Rokkan, *Party Systems and Voter Alignments* (New York: Free Press, 1967) for the classic statement of the social cleavage theory of party systems; and Stefano Bartolini and Peter Mair, *Identity, Competition and Electoral Availability: The Stabilisation of European Electorates, 1885–1985* (Cambridge: Cambridge University Press, 1990) for a modified version which argues essentially that social cleavages do not translate automatically into party systems but offer easy mobilisation opportunities. Much the same is argued by Rajni Kothari in his "Caste and Modern Politics", in Sudipta Kaviraj, ed., *Politics in India* (New Delhi: Oxford University Press, 1997), p. 58, when he says: "Those who complain of 'casteism in politics' are really looking for a sort of politics which has no basis in society . . . Politics is a competitive enterprise . . . and its process is one of identifying and manipulating existing and emerging allegiances in order to mobilise and consolidate positions", thus making the social cleavage theory of party systems appear somehow natural. For recent works within the electoral rules theory of party systems, see Arend Lijphart, *Electoral Systems and Party Systems* (New York: Oxford University Press, 1994); Rein Taagepera and Matthew Soberg Shugart, *Seats and Votes* (New Haven, CT: Yale University Press, 1989); Bernard Grofman and Arend Lijphart, *Electoral Laws and Their Political Consequences* (New York: Agathon Press, 1986); and older classics, Maurice Duverger, *Political Parties: Their Organisation and Activity in the Modern State* (New York: Wiley, 1963); Douglas Rae, *The Political Consequences of Electoral Laws* (New Haven, CT: Yale University Press, 1967).

electoral system's rules, principally, the size of constituencies (number of representatives elected from each constituency), the structure of the ballot (choosing a party list, an individual candidate or a mix of the two), and the decision rule or electoral formula (proportional representation, first-past-the-post, variants of each) create varying disproportionalities between votes and seats, and, hence, incentives for the coalescing or splitting of political forces, which will be reflected in the number, relative weight, and ideological positioning of political parties.[2] For example, a very proportional system consisting of large, multi-member constituencies conduces to a low effective threshold of representation and hence to even small parties getting elected and playing a role in government formation in, typically, multi-party coalitions, such as in Israel and the Netherlands.[3] In such a system, small parties would not have much incentive to merge with larger parties at the cost of ideological compromise, whereas the opposite would hold true in a first-past-the-post system. We will discuss competing explanations of the evolution of the Indian party system in the later part of the paper, some of which will fall into one or other broad category of explanations outlined. However, before this it is logically necessary to lay out the patterns of fragmentation in the unavoidable minimum detail.

The Evolution of the Pattern of Fragmentation of the Party System 1967–1989

Congress Hegemony 1952–1967

The first four general elections to the Lok Sabha, 1952, 1957, 1961, and 1967, coincided with elections to all the state assem-

[2] Taagepera and Shugart, in *Seats and Votes*, emphasise ballot structure, district magnitude, and electoral formula as the basic variables. Arend Lijphart emphasises in addition a derivative variable, effective threshold of representation, and assembly size, and considers the special cases of presidentialism and *apparentement* linking of party lists.

[3] See Lijphart, *Electoral Systems and Party Systems,* op. cit., p. 22, Table 2.2.

blies. In the first three of these, the Congress party won an over two-thirds majority of seats in the Lok Sabha on the basis of only a plurality of votes of 44–48 per cent (Table 1.1).

It also won a majority of seats in the state assemblies of all the then existing states from 1952 to 1962, again on the basis of mostly a plurality of votes against a fragmented opposition that varied from state to state. The only exceptions were Jammu and Kashmir, Nagaland, and Kerala dominated by the National Conference, Independents, and in alternation with the then united Communist Party of India-led coalition, respectively. In three Congress-dominated states it fell a little short of a majority: in Orissa (1952–7), Madhya Pradesh (1962), and pre-1956 (Presidency), Madras (1952).

The Bipolarisation of State Party Systems 1967–1989

The 1967 election marks a break, with the Congress winning only 283 seats on the basis of its lowest ever vote share until then (40.8 per cent), and losing power in eight out of sixteen states. The 1971 elections saw a restoration of two-thirds Congress majority in the Lok Sabha with 43.7 per cent votes and 352 seats. However, from the vantage point of the year 2000, the post-1967 period represents a secular decline in Congress strength nationally and in state after state. In the "exceptional" post-Emergency elections of 1977, the Congress faced a temporarily united opposition consisting of the Janata Party formed just before the elections, and having a seat adjustment with Jagjivan Ram's Congress for Democracy, and the CPI-M, thus consisting of virtually the entire opposition except for the CPI and the DMK. The Congress was trounced, plunging to its lowest-till-then vote and seats figure of 34.5 per cent and 154 seats respectively. The Janata Party won a majority (295 seats, of which the Jana Sangh component was the single largest at 99 seats) on the basis of 41.3 per cent of the vote. This was a Congress-like victory in reverse, that is, a catch-all umbrella party winning a seat majority on the basis of a vote plurality, but not, however, against a fragmented opposition.

In 1980, another Congress restoration took place following the disintegration of the Janata Party, again a near two-thirds majority of 353 seats (out of 542 seats) on the basis of a plurality of 42.7 per cent. The 1984 elections, another "exceptional" election, following the assassination of Prime Minister Indira Gandhi, saw the highest ever Congress vote share (48.1 per cent) and 415 seats. The 1989 elections marked another turning point with the Congress crashing to 39.5 per cent and 197 seats against an opposition electoral "alliance", consisting of seat adjustments, of the National Front coalition (of the Janata Dal and regional and minor parties) supported by the BJP and the Left parties that resulted in a large number of one-on-one contests with the Congress.

The post-1967 period also saw *a very important delinking of parliamentary and state assembly elections since 1971, and a suspension in organisational elections within the Congress from 1972 to 1992,* hand in hand with a centralisation of power at the top of the party apparatus. It also saw the emergence of anti-Congress alliances, then of a principal opposition party to the Congress in state after state, in most states, representing a consolidation of the non-Congress space at the state level. The Index of Opposition Unity (IOU), rose in state after state over 1967–89.[4] This is particularly so if one considers opposition coalitions – and first party plus its pre-electoral allies – as a single party for the purposes of the IOU. In other words, a consolidation of the non-Congress opposition, state by state, broadly in tandem with such consolidation in the state assembly elections, took place over the period, leading even to the displacement of the Congress as one of the two leading parties or

[4] A measure of the fragmentation of the opposition space represented by the percentage share of the largest non-Congress (in todays terms, non-ruling party) vote in the total opposition vote. The higher the IOU the less fragmented the opposition space.

Table 1.1: Elections to the Lok Sabha 1952–1999

	1952	*1957*	*1962*	*1967*	*1971*	*1977*
Total Seats	489	494	494	520	518	542
Contested	479	482	491	515	517	540
Uncontested	10	12	3	5	1	2
Indian National Congress (INC) (INCI) in 1980	364 (479) 45.0%	371 (490) 47.8%	361 (488) 44.7%	283 (516) 40.8%	352 (441) 43.7%	154 (492) 34.5%
Bharatiya Janata Party (BJP) (BLD) in 1977 (BJS) till 1971	 3(94) 3.1%	 4(130) 5.9%	 14(196) 6.4%	 35(251) 9.4%	 22(160) 7.4%	295 (405) 41.3%
Janata Dal (United)(JDU) in 1999, (JD) 1989–98, (SWA) till 1971	 –	 – 7.9%	 18(173) 8.7%	 44(178) 3.1%	 8(56)	 -
Communist Party of India (CPI)	16(49) 3.3%	27(110) 8.9%	29(137) 9.9%	23(106) 5.0%	23(87) 4.7%	7(91) 2.8%
Communist Party of India Marxist (CPIM)	–	–	–	19(62) 4.4%	25(85) 5.1%	22(53) 4.3%
Lok Dal (LKD) (JPS) in 1980, (INCO) till 1977	–	–	–	–	16(238) 10.4%	3(19) 1.7%
Samajwadi Party (SP) in 1991, (JP) till 1989	–	–	–	–	–	–
Bahujan Samaj Party (BSP)	–	–	–	–	–	–
Praja Socialist Party (PSP) (KMPP) in 1952	9(145) 5.8%	19(189) 10.4%	12(168) 6.8%	13(109) 3.1%	2(63) 1.0%	–
Samyukta Socialist Party (SSP) (SOC) till 1962	12(254) 10.6%	–	6(107) 2.7%	23(122) 4.9%	3(93) 2.4%	–

Table 1.1 (*Contd.*)

Table 1.1 (*Contd.*)

1980	*1984*	*1989*	*1991*	*1996*	*1998*	*1999*
542	542	543	543	543	543	543
529a	541	528b	521c	543	539	543
1	1	1	–	–	–	–
353	415	197	232	140	141	114
(492)	(517)	(510)	(492)	(529)	(474)	(453)
42.7%	48.1%	39.5%	36.5%	28.8%	25.9%	28.3%
			120	161	179	182
	2(229)	86(226)	(468)	(471)	(384)	(339)
–	7.4%	11.5%	20.1%	20.3%	25.5%	23.8%
		142				
–	–	(243)	59(307)	46(196)	6(190)	21(60)
		17.7%	11.8%	8.1%	3.2%	3.1%
11(48)	6(66)	12(50)	14(42)	12(43)	9(58)	4(54)
2.6%	2.7%	2.6%	2.5%	2.0%	1.8%	1.5%
36(63)	22(64)	33(64)	35(60)	32(75)	32(71)	33(72)
6.1%	5.7%	6.5%	6.2%	6.1%	5.2%	5.4%
41(294)	3(174)	0(117)	0(78)	–	–	–
9.4%	5.6%	0.2%	0.1%	–	–	–
31(432)	10(219)	0(156)	5(345)	17(111)	20(164)	26(151)
19.0%	6.7%	1.0%	3.4%	3.3%	5.0%	3.8%
–	–	–	–	11(117)	5(249)	14(225)
				3.6%	4.7%	4.2%
–	–	–	–	–	–	–

Table 1.1 (*Contd.*)

Table 1.1 (*Contd.*)

	1952	*1957*	*1962*	*1967*	*1971*	*1977*
Others	47	31	34	45	53	52
	16.5%	7.6%	10.5%	10.0%	13.8%	9.9%
Independents (IND)	38	42	20	35	14	9
	15.9%	19.4%	11.1%	13.7%	8.4%	5.5%

Table 1.1 (*Contd.*)

Table 1.1 (*Contd.*)

1980	*1984*	*1989*	*1991*	*1996*	*1998*	*1999*
35	44	44	41	115	141	143
8.5%	10.0%	12.2%	12.1%	21.5%	26.3%	27.1%
9	5	12	1	9	6	6
6.4%	8.1%	5.2%	3.9%	6.3%	2.4%	2.8%

Source: David Butler, Ashok Lahiri and Prannoy Roy, *India Decides: Elections 1952–1995*, New Delhi: Books and Things, 1995; Election Commission of India, Statistical Report on General Elections, vol. I (ver. 1) – National and State Abstracts, for 1996, 1998 and 1999.

Notes: a. Elections were not held in 13 constituencies: 12 in Assam and 1 in Meghalaya.

b. Elections were not held in Assam (14 seats). Includes results for 4 seats which were countermanded.

c. Elections were not held in Jammu & Kashmir (6 seats) and Punjab (13 seats). Includes results for 10 seats which were countermanded out of a total of 13 countermanded seats.

BLD – Bharatiya Lok Dal
BJS – Bharatiya Jana Sangh
SW – Swatantra Party
INCU – Indian National Congress (Urs)
JPS – Janata Party Secular
INCO – Indian National Congress (Organized)
JP – Janata Party
KMPP – Kisan Mozdoor Praja Party
SOC – Socialist Party
SJP – Samajwadi Janata Party

coalitions. *This bipolar consolidation was the key feature and driving force of the fragmentation of the national party system.* In the 1990s, the relevant IOU is that of the alternative coalition versus the leading coalition in many states characterised by electoral alliances. A consolidation of the non-Congress opposition, and in the 1990s bipolar consolidation, whether Congress was a player or not, took place at the state level for Lok Sabha elections and for state assembly elections in parallel.

The following pattern of bipolarisation is discernible state-wise over 1967–89 for the general elections. In Madhya Pradesh, Rajasthan, and Himachal Pradesh, and the Union Territory of Delhi, the movement towards a two-party system began as early as 1967 with the consolidation of the non-Congress vote behind the Jana Sangh, the ancestor of the Bharatiya Janata Party (BJP). This system has remained stable to date. In three other states, Kerala, West Bengal, and Tripura, a bipolar, Congress-versus-Left, two-alliance system in which the Congress (West Bengal) or Congress-led alliance of state-based minor parties (Kerala, Tripura) on the one hand, contested against a Left Front coalition of the Communist Party of India (Marxist) (CPI-M), CPI (since the late 1970s in Kerala), and smaller Left parties, the two coalitions alternating in power.

In five other states, Punjab, Jammu and Kashmir (J&K), Andhra Pradesh, Assam, and Goa, a Congress-Regional Party two-party system came into being over 1967–89, disintegrating or changing in the 1990s with the rise of the BJP in all of these states.

In one major state, Tamil Nadu, the process began in 1967, and led to the elimination of the Congress from the top two positions, becoming an essentially bipolar contest between one of the two leading parties, the Dravida Munnetra Kazhagam (DMK) and the All India Anna Dravida Munnetra Kazhagam (AIADMK), and the other, with one of the two being allied to the Congress for parliamentary and state assembly elections. In this arrangement, which was stable from 1977 to 1996, the Congress was given the lion's share of the seats in the parliamentary elections in exchange for the regional ally being given the lion's share of state assembly seats.

In the North-Eastern Rim states of Mizoram, Meghalaya, Nagaland, and Manipur, and in Sikkim, an unstable two-party or two-alliance contest prevailed between the Congress and a variety of regional parties.

Finally, the Congress retained preponderance until 1989 in seven major states – UP, Bihar, Haryana, Gujarat, Maharashtra, Karnataka, and Orissa – where no alternative party or alliance consolidated itself as a successful challenger for parliamentary elections, although a broad-front anti-Congress alliance, if put together, could have challenged the Congress, as happened in 1967 and 1977.

Likewise, the following pattern of bipolarisation is discernible for party systems for state assembly elections. The Congress party's position eroded even more than for parliamentary elections, and the consolidation of principal challenger parties or alliances at the state level is even more marked.

In three states, Madhya Pradesh (MP), Rajasthan, and Himachal Pradesh (HP), and in the Union Territory of Delhi, there was a consolidation of non-Congress votes behind the BJP as second party over 1967–89.

In three states, Kerala, West Bengal, and Tripura, there was a bipolar Congress-versus-Left, two-alliance consolidation of the party system, with the Congress leading alliances of small, state-specific parties in Kerala (from 1952) and Tripura, and going it alone in West Bengal, while the Left Front was led by the CPI-M with the CPI (from the early 1980 in Kerala) and smaller Left parties.

In Tamil Nadu, there was a bipolarisation of the party system for the assembly elections between the DMK and the AIADMK since 1977 (following the split and emergence of the AIADMK in 1972) with the Congress allied (or with imperfect "seat adjustments", as in 1980) to the AIADMK from 1980 to 1996.

In Punjab, J&K, Goa, Andhra Pradesh, and Assam, a Congress–Regional Party bipolarisation came into existence over the 1967–89 period. While in the first three states, the Akali Dal, National Conference (NC), and Maharashtrawadi Gomantak Party (MGP) had a long history dating back to the first general elections and the liberation of Goa, in Andhra Pradesh and Assam the Telugu Desam Party (TDP) and Asom Gana Parishad (AGP) were born and emerged as significant parties in the 1980s.

In six small states, mainly in the North-Eastern Rim, viz. Sikkim, Arunachal Pradesh, Meghalaya, Mizoram, Manipur, and Nagaland, party systems took on a roughly Congress versus Regional Party configuration, but regional parties remained unstable and party systems still evolving. The normal process of party system evolution in the last three states mentioned, has experienced major interruptions due to insurgencies.

Finally, in the seven major states of UP, Bihar, Haryana, Gujarat, Maharashtra, Karnataka, and Orissa, the Congress remained in the "traditional" mould up to but not including the state assembly elections of 1989–90, with no consolidation of the opposition behind a well-defined party or alliance, although such an anti-Congress front could have seriously challenged the Congress as in 1967 and 1977. This happened in the 1989–90 assembly elections with either the Janata Dal or the Janata Dal–BJP alliance displacing the Congress from the government in all these states except Karnataka.

However, just after the 1989 elections and the state assembly elections in early 1990, the Congress remained the leading party in more states (12) in terms of Lok Sabha seats and in terms of vote share (17) than any other, and remained one of the two leading parties in more states (20) in terms of Lok Sabha seats and vote share (24) than any other. In the state assemblies it remained the leading party in more states (9) and also in terms of vote share (11) than any other, and one of the two leading parties in terms of vote share in more states (24, or all except Tamil Nadu) than any other. However, many of these were very small states, the Congress having lost UP, Bihar, Orissa, and Haryana to the Janata Dal, Madhya Pradesh and Himachal Pradesh to the BJP, and Rajasthan and Gujarat to a Janata Dal–BJP coalition in both Lok Sabha and state assembly elections (except Haryana, which did not have assembly elections in 1989–90).

The Evolution of the Pattern of Fragmentation of the Party System 1989–1999

The 1989 election results were not just another repeat of the broad-front anti-Congressism of the Janata Party kind, but signified a more far-reaching shift in the party system rooted in the shifts in party organisational strength and support bases at the state level in an increasing number of states, and in India's political economy and changing patterns of social mobilisation. The big story of 1989–99 is the relative decline of the Congress and the rise of the BJP and regional or state-based parties. While the Congress retained a vote plurality in all five elections over 1989–99, it failed each time to translate that into a seat majority, falling behind the BJP in seats in 1996, 1998, and 1999.

Prior to 1989, the BJP and its predecessor the Bharatiya Jana Sangh (BJS), the political arm of the Rashtriya Swayamsevak Sangh (RSS), had never exceeded 10 per cent of the vote or 35 seats nationally, except for 1977 when as a component of the Janata Party it won 99 of 295 seats won by the Janata Party (more than the 86 seats it won in 1989). Its rise since then has been steady in terms of both vote and seat shares. It experienced a meteoric rise in seats from a derisory two in 1984 (despite 7.4 per cent votes) to 86 (out of 226 contested, mostly in *de facto* alliance with the Janata Dal) in 1989 owing to the combination of three effects-seat adjustments with the Janata Dal resulting in one-on-one contests against the Congress in most of the seats it contested in UP, Delhi, Rajasthan, Gujarat, Himachal Pradesh, and Madhya Pradesh, a sizeable swing in its favour, and the regional concentration of this increase in votes.

In 1989–91, the BJP contested alone with a communally polarising platform against the backdrop of the Babri Masjid agitation of the late 1980s, the upper-caste backlash against the National Front government's decision to implement the Mandal Commission recommendations for reservation of government jobs for backward classes defined in caste terms, and the Rath Yatra launched by L.K. Advani to "liberate" the claimed "Ram Janmabhoomi" inside the Babri Masjid and the communal tension and violence in its wake. Its vote share zoomed to 20.1 per cent, and it won 120 seats (of an unprecedented 468 contested), becoming the second largest party in terms of seats and votes. It swept the key state of UP in both the Lok Sabha and the simultaneous assembly elections, marking a major leap forward in its positioning in the party system. It swept Gujarat, decimating the Janata Dal there, and turned in strong performances in its traditional strongholds of MP, HP, and Rajasthan, winning over 40 per cent votes in each. More significantly, and portending developments to come, it significantly increased its vote share, in several states of the south and east, and in Bihar, contesting alone, and took 20.2 per cent of the vote and five seats in Maharashtra in alliance with the Shiv Sena.

The BJP came to form state governments on its own for the first time ever in 1990. It formed the government on its own in MP and HP, and formed coalition governments with the Janata Dal in Rajasthan and Gujarat, dominating the former with the state BJP leader becoming the chief minister. The only time that it had dominated state governments earlier was when it was part of the Janata Party in 1977–9, during which period the Jana Sangh component of the Janata Party dominated the government and occupied the chief minister's post in MP, HP, and Rajasthan. Thus the BJP arrived as a *regional* political force, whereas earlier it had essentially been sub-regional, thereby contributing to national party system fragmentation.

In 1991, with the support of the 11-member AIADMK and some smaller allies, the Congress was able to form a minority government dependent on abstention in confidence votes by a section of the opposition. It began adding to its numbers by splitting small parties such as the TDP and Ajit Singh's faction of the Lok Dal, itself a breakaway from the Janata Dal after its defeat in 1991, in fractions of one-third or more (legal under the Anti-Defection law), and attained a majority on its own exactly halfway through its term (end-1993). However, these manoeuvres did not help it rebuild a party that could come back to power on its own. In 1996, its vote share declined still further to a then-historic low of 28.7 per cent, having been hit badly by the breaking away of the bulk of its Tamil Nadu unit to form the Tamil Maanila Congress (TMC) which won 20 seats, and marginally by the breaking away of factions called the Congress (Tiwari) and the Madhya Pradesh Vikas Congress. For the first time, the Congress was overtaken as the single largest party by the BJP, winning only 141 seats compared to the BJP's 161, although it remained the single largest party by vote share with 28.8 per cent compared to the BJP's 20.3 per cent.

In 1996, the BJP ran into the limits of contesting alone with a communally polarising agenda. Despite being catapulted to its higher-ever seat tally of 161 seats, due to its more regionally concentrated vote, making it the largest party in the Lok Sabha and able to form the government for 13 days, its vote share remained stagnant at 20.3 per cent and it failed to win parliamentary support from enough other parties to form a minority or coalition government. Six states – UP (52), MP (27), Gujarat (16), Rajasthan (12), Bihar (18) in alliance with the Samata Party, and Maharashtra (18), in alliance with the Shiv Sena – accounted for 143 of its 161 seats, with UP and MP alone accounting for almost half.

These results can be seen as a delayed reflection of the realignment of political forces that was represented by the results of the elections to the assemblies of fifteen states between November 1993 and March 1995, which, by and large, represented major gains for the BJP, some regional parties like the TDP and Shiv Sena, and state-based parties such as the Samajwadi Party, the Samata Party, and the BSP, while at best a holding operation for the Congress in some stronghold states such as HP and MP.[5] A United Front

[5] Yogendra Yadav, "Reconfiguration in Indian Politics: State Assembly Elections 1993–1995", *Economic and Political Weekly*, vol. 31, nos 2–3, January 1996.

government consisting of nine parties participating in government, four parties formally part of the United Front (UF) coalition but not participating in government, and supported from outside by the Congress was formed in June 1996. The Congress withdrew support to Prime Minister Deve Gowda in April 1997, but continued to support the UF government after his replacement as prime minister by I.K. Gujral, eventually withdrawing support to the UP in November 1997, precipitating fresh elections in February–March 1998.

The basic lesson of 1996 was clear. If the BJP had to come within striking distance of power, it had to be able to expand to non-traditional states, by alliances or otherwise, as well as expand its social base in its stronghold states. This was what it attempted to do in 1998 and 1999 by a significant shift in strategy consisting of seeking a wide range of alliances in its non-stronghold states, in the process shelving temporarily the main communally divisive points on its agenda, viz. construction of a Ram temple on the site of the demolished Babri Masjid, repeal of Article 370 (special autonomous status for Kashmir), and promulgation of a common civil code.

The 1998 election was different because of the BJP shelving its overt Hindutva agenda to strike explicit or tacit alliances with a range of state-based parties, both regional and other, many of them earlier with the UF, a strategy that it consolidated after its victory. The BJP strategy was certainly helped by the fact that the Congress had toppled the UF government and was the principal opponent of the constituents of the UF in several major states including West Bengal, Kerala, Tripura, Assam, Orissa, Andhra Pradesh, and Karnataka. Thus, in 1998, the BJP contested the elections with as many as 13 pre-election allies, including two Independents, with seat-sharing arrangements spread over nine states. These were the Akali Dal and Independent S.S. Kainth (Punjab), Samata Party (Bihar and UP), Independent Maneka Gandhi (UP), Haryana Vikas Party (HVP-Haryana), Biju Janata Dal (BJP-Orissa), Trinamool Congress (West Bengal), Lok Shakti (Karnataka), and AIADMK, Pattali Makkal

Katchi (PMK), Marumalarchi Dravida Munnetra Kazhagam (MDMK), Tamizhaga Rajiv Congress and Janata Party (all Tamil Nadu). The BJP won 25.5 per cent votes and its allies 11.6 per cent, votes, totalling 37.1 per cent for the alliance, and won a total of 258 seats. The BJP got 182 seats and its allies 76 seats, which were distributed as Samata Party 12, BJD 9, AIADMK 18, PMK 4, MDMK 3, Tanizhaga Rajiv Congress (TRC) 1, Janata Party 1, Akali Dal 8, Shiv Sena 6, Lok Shakti 3, Trinamool Congress 7, HVP 1, BJP-allied Independents 3. This catapulted the BJP to power as it emerged once again as the single largest party (the Congress got only 141 seats) and led the single largest pre-election alliance. With the help of 24 post-election adherents from seven parties and two nominated members it grew to 282, but this included the 12-member TDP and 2-member NC which supported it from outside only.[6]

State-wise, the BJP fared better in 1998 compared to 1996 due to the crucial support of its allies. It won more seats in all states except Haryana, Maharashtra, and Rajasthan, and enjoyed a positive vote swing in all states except Gujarat, Haryana, Rajasthan, and Meghalaya. In some states, notably Tamil Nadu, Andhra Pradesh, Orissa, Karnataka, and Punjab, it turned in its best-ever performance in seats, and except for the last two, in votes too, marking a major penetration of the south and Orissa, and winning its first ever seat in West Bengal.

Geographically and socially, the BJP spread its influence and consolidated itself in new areas and new social groups in the 1990s, in the south and east, among lower castes and classes.[7] Viewed

[6] For details of the alliances, pre- and post-election, in 1998, see Balveer Arora, "Negotiating Differences: Federal Coalitions and National Cohesion", in Francine Frankel, Zoya Hasan, Rajeev Bhargava, and Balveer Arora, eds, *Transforming India: Social and Political Dynamics of Democracy* (New Delhi: Oxford University Press, 2000), pp. 184–5, 190, 194.

[7] See Oliver Heath, "Anatomy of BJP's Rise to Power", *Economic and Political Weekly*, vol. 34, nos 34–5, August 21–8, 1999.

over 1989–1999, this expansion has been at the expense, primarily, of the Janata Dal, which appears to have been the loser in seat adjustments or alliances it had with the BJP in 1989, the BJP displacing the Janata Dal almost completely in Gujarat and Rajasthan, and marginalising it in UP, and secondarily of the Congress, principally in UP and Bihar.

A BJP-led, ideologically diverse, minority coalition government consisting of thirteen pre-election (including two Independents) and nine post-election allies (including five one-MP parties), and dependent on the support or abstention in confidence votes of at least the TDP and the NC, assumed power in March 1998.

In 1999, essentially the same BJP-led pre-election coalition fought the Congress-led coalition, the latter being a more tentative coalition with state-by-state agreements but no common national platform. The United Front disintegrated, being reduced to the Left Front and the rump Janata Dal (Secular) of Deve Gowda. The 24-party BJP-led alliance, formally christened the National Democratic Alliance (NDA), consisted of the BJP, Shiv Sena, Akali Dal, Samata Party, Lok Shakti, Janata Dal (Sharad Yadav group) – the latter three agreeing to formally merge to from the Janata Dal-United – TDP, DMK, MDMK, PMK, TRC, MGRADMK, MGR-Kazhagami BJD, Trinamool Congress, Sikkim Democratic Front, Arunachal Congress, Manipur State Congress Party, Loktantrik Congress, Janatantrik BSP, Himachal Vikas Congress, Indian National Lok Dal, Democratic Bahujan Samaj Morcha, Independent (Maneka Gandhi). The Congress and allies consisted of Congress, Rashtriya Janata Dal (RJD), AIADMK, Kerala Congress (Mani), Muslim League, and Rashtriya Lok Dal. The main differences were that the BJP was now allied to Chautala's Indian National Lok Dal (INLD) in Haryana and the DMK in Tamil Nadu while the Congress was allied to the AIADMK.

The NDA won a more decisive victory, getting 299 of the 537 seats (six seats were deferred), with the BJP alone getting 182 as in 1998. With post-election adherents like the NC the number went up to 305. The Congress got a lowest-ever 111 seats, and only 134 with its allies. The Left got 42 seats, the BSP 14, and Others 48. However, in terms of vote share, the BJP declined to 23.8 per cent while the Congress rose to 28.4 per cent, remaining the single largest party. The NDA formed the government with the 29-member TDP opting to support it from outside. However, it will take at least two allies together to reduce the government to a minority. So although the BJP's share of the NDA is less than in 1998, the NDA is less vulnerable to toppling.

The state-wise pattern testifies to the importance of alliances for the BJP's and NDA's performance. Alliances critically helped the BJP and its allies in Tamil Nadu, Bihar, Orissa, West Bengal, Andhra Pradesh, Maharashtra (aided by the Congress split), Haryana, HP, and even in UP. The Congress improved its vote share in most major states except Orissa, most notably in UP from 6 per cent to 14.8 per cent, but could not translate this increase into seats, except in UP, from none to 10, and in Punjab and Karnataka. It remains one of the two leading parties, or leading party in one of the two leading alliances, in eighteen states.

Four types of states, by party system polarity, emerged during the 1990s. First, most states remained bipolar, if not two-party, systems, by seat and vote share. The established two-party states that continued in the same pattern were HP, MP, Rajasthan, and Gujarat. Established bipolar states were those in which either two alliances or one party opposed by an alliance of two or more smaller parties, dominated the political space. These states were West Bengal, Kerala, and Tripura (Congress or Congress-led coalition versus Left Front), Maharashtra, and Punjab (Congress versus BJP-Regional Party coalition).

Second, there were states with three or more poles which seemed to be collapsing into bipolarity due to newly forged alliances, sometimes as a result of splits in existing parties, such as Karnataka, Bihar, and Orissa.

Third, a state like UP where a four-cornered contest continued, with the BJP as the dominant pole, having achieved that position in 1991.

Fourth, in a number of apparently bipolar or two-party states, *if we look at the vote shares, we find the presence of a significant, often growing, third party* which has a vote share in double digits but not yet large enough to win significant number of seats. *It is obviously cutting into the potential vote share of one or both of the two main parties or alliances in a way that makes it both a threat to either/both of the former as well as attractive as an ally of one to defeat the other.* This is the case in states like Assam, Orissa, Goa, West Bengal, Manipur, and Arunachal Pradesh. This rising third party was the BJP in all of these states, and the Bahujan Samaj Party (BSP) in Punjab, UP, and in a small way MP. The BJP, as a rising third party since its 1989 seat adjustments with the then much larger Janata Dal, has emerged as a significant state party in several states in three ways.

First, by displacing and decimating the Janata Dal as the major non-Congress force and occupying the place of one of the two dominant parties in a two-party system, like in Rajasthan and Gujarat since 1991, or even becoming the dominant pole displacing both the Janata Dal and its offshoots and the Congress, such as in UP since 1991.

Second, by emerging as a significant third party in vote share at the state level and, hence, both threatening to cut into the votes and seat prospects of either or both of the dominant parties, and hence *creating incentives for the weaker of the two leading parties to ally with it, typically the regional party*, since both the BJP, nationally, and the regional party in the state, face the Congress as their principal opponent. This is the pattern in Maharashtra, Punjab, Orissa, Goa, Bihar (its alliance with the Samata works both ways for it and the Samata), West Bengal (following the Congress split in which the Trinamool Congress emerged as the major Congress faction), Haryana, Karnataka (following the emergence of Lok Shakti after the Janata Dal split, though this works both ways as in Bihar), and in 1999, Andhra Pradesh and Tripura. In some of these states, possibly Maharashtra and Orissa, the BJP can potentially go on to eat up the share of its regional alliance partner and transform the state into a Congress-BJP two-party state, as happened in Rajasthan and Gujarat over 1989–91.

Third, there are states where the BJP still is a minor force, but where it can potentially repeat the story of the above states.

Thus a process of bipolar consolidation has been taking place in many states, but of *multiple bipolarities* (for example, Congress–BJP, Congress–Left, Congress–Regional Party), contributing to fragmentation at the national level, on the one hand, and fragmentation and transformation of two-party (for example, Orissa, Andhra Pradesh) and two-alliance systems (Tamil Nadu, West Bengal) at the state level in other states, contributing directly or indirectly to potential bipolar consolidation of a Congress-led alliance versus BJP-led alliance type at the national level on the other hand.

The Evolution of Electoral Alliances and Competing Explanations for Fragmentation (and Reconsolidation?) of the Party System

There are, broadly, seven explanations for the fragmentation of the Congress-dominated national party system over the decades, none of which excludes the other. *One of these can also potentially explain the process of reconsolidation of the party system into one with larger alliances and fewer poles.* We shall outline the competing explanations, in roughly chronological order of their beginning to be applicable to the decline of the Congress-dominated party system. We shall then outline the evolution of alliances drawing on the patterns of fragmentation and possible reconsolidation in the earlier sections, and finally make an argument for the best explanation for the process that has been unfolding.

The first (set of) explanation(s) is centred on the growing politicisation of social cleavages along regional lines since the late 1960s due to the increasing centralisation of the Congress party and Congress governments, and the insensitivity to regional concerns about language, cultural identity, political autonomy, and economic development, leading to the rise and/or further consolidation of regional parties such as the DMK and its offshoots, Akali Dal, National Conference, Asom Gana Parishad (AGP), and small parties in the North-Eastern Rim.[8]

The second explanation is that of the electoral-systemic feature of delinking between parliamentary and state assembly elections since 1971. This probably facilitated pre-electoral alliances and post-electoral coalitions of the non-Congress forces for national elections such as in 1977 and 1989, and of the non-BJP forces in 1996, since doing so became easier without compromising their fundamental interests at the state level where their basic social constituencies and power base lay. Delinking also meant smaller agendas and less crowded bargaining tables, and hence less insurmountable collective action problems, or to put it simply, one-at-a-time battles with the Congress.[9]

The third explanation emphasises the growth in political consciousness and assertion of newly prosperous or newly mobilised sections of the electorate, primarily intermediate and backward caste peasants in the Green Revolution areas of North India, both as a farmer's and intermediate castes' lobby from the late sixties to the early nineties.[10] These castes had not been part of the core base

[8] For a concise overview of regional parties in the party system up to the mid-1990s, see James Manor, "Regional Parties in Federal Systems", in Douglas Verney and Balveer Arora, eds, *Multiple Identities in a Single State: Indian Federalism in a Comparative Perspective* (Delhi: Konark, 1995).

[9] See Pradeep Chibber, *Democracy Without Associations* (New Delhi: Vistaar Publications, 1999), p. 105.

[10] See Paul Brass, "The Politicization of the Peasantry in a North Indian State: I and II", *Journal of Peasant Studies*, vols 7 and 8, nos 4 and 1, July 1980 and October 1980, for Uttar Pradesh; Ranbir Singh, "Changing Social Bases of Congress Political Support in Haryana", in Richard Sisson and Ramashray Roy, eds, *Diversity and Dominance in Indian Politics*, vol. 1 (Delhi: Sage, 1990); Francine R. Frankel, "Middle Classes and Castes in India's Politics: Prospects for Political Accommodation", in Atul Kohli, ed., *India's Democracy* (Delhi:

of the Congress in the northern belt and had not been granted a position of commensurate influence in the party power structure. Fragmentation, whereby these castes or interest groups tended to vote or form new parties of the erstwhile socialist (Praja Socialist Party-PSP / Samyukta Socialist Party-SSP)/agrarian Lok Dal/ Janata Dal kind, was rooted in the inability or unwillingness of the groups that controlled the Congress to accommodate them.

The fourth explanation, dovetailing with the first and third, and complementary to them, is that of the growing centralisation of, and suspension of democracy within, the Congress party since 1972, leading to the exit of those traditional voters and politicians whose voices were not being heard, particularly certain regional groups and intermediate and backward caste farmers in the northern belt, to new or other parties. This is in line with the logic of "disillusioned" voting whereby voters of a party from whom they fail to get their desired policy dividends, or have their voices heard, turn away to rival or new parties. This explanation stresses the importance of the *organisation and functioning of parties as machines* to retain and expand their voter base.[11]

The fifth explanation is that of the influence on incentives of a systemic feature of the polity, the division of powers in the Constitution between the Centre and the states. With the powers that are more relevant to the daily lives of the people in a largely rural

---

Orient Longman, 1991), and "Caste, Land and Dominmce in Bihar: Breakdown of the Brahmanical Social Order", in Francine R. Frankel and M.S.A. Rao, eds, *Dominance and State Power in Modern India,* vol. I (New Delhi: Oxford University Press, 1989).

[11] See Atul Kohli, *Democracy and Discontent* (New York: Cambridge University Press, 1991), for an analysis of the "crisis of governability" centred on the centralisation of the Congress party. This argument gells with Riker's ideal type of disillusioned voting, in William A. Riker, "The Number of Political Parties: A Re-examination of Duverger's Law", *Comparative Politics,* vol. 9, no. 1, 1976. See Pradeep Chibber, *Democracy Without Associations,* op. cit., ch. 5, for an argument emphasising exit of traditional supporters of the Congress rather than the entry of the new groups into politics.

society, such as agriculture and land, irrigation and water supply, electricity, policy, education, health, and other social expenditures, being vested in the states, there are incentives to organise for capture of power at the state level.[12]

The sixth explanation is that of the growing politicisation of communal and caste cleavages in the 1990s, leading to the collapse of a catch-all party like the Congress in states like UP, and Bihar where such politicisation led to a collapse of the middle ground, and the gravitation of the vote, particularty Scheduled Castes, Muslims, OBCs, and upper castes, to communal and caste-based parties such as the BJP, Shiv Sena, BSP, Samajwadi Party, and RJD (in Bihar).[13]

The seventh explanation, which we consider the most comprehensive and powerful, is one which attaches greatest significance not to social cleavages or to the dominant Congress party's structure and functioning, but to the *systemic properties of the first-past-the-post electoral system working themselves out in a federal polity.*[14] This is reinforced by the second (the delinking of national and state elections since 1971) and fifth (the division of powers making state-level power politically attractive). This explanation is based on the

[12] See Pradeep Chibber, *Democracy Without Associations,* op. cit., chs 2 and 5.

[13] For a general analysis of the decline of the Congress and the emergence of a post-Congress polity, see Yogendra Yadav, '"Electoral Politics in the Time of Change: India's Third Electoral System, 1989–99", *Economic and Political Weekly,* vol. 34, nos 34–5, August 21–28, 1999. For specifics that show the polarisation of the vote by community and caste, see Oliver Heath, "Anatomy of BJP's Rise to Power", op. cit., for the BJP vote, and Anthony Heath and Yogendra Yadav, "The United Colours of Congress: Social Profile of Congress Voters, 1996 and 1998", *Economic and Political Weekly,* vol. 34, nos 34–5, August 21–28, 1999. See Kanchan Chandra, "Mobilizing the Excluded", *Seminar,* August 1999, for an analysis of the rise of the BSP.

[14] See E. Sridharan, "Duverger's Law, Its Reformulations and the Evolution of the Indian Party System", Centre for Policy Research, May 1997, and IRIS India Working Paper No. 35, February 1997, IRIS Center, University of Maryland, for a detailed version of the argument presented here in capsule form.

proposition known as Duverger's law, viz. that the first-past-the-post system (single member-district, simple plurality system) tends towards a two-party system because of the tendency over time for third and more parties to get eliminated due to the combination of two effects – a "mechanical effect" of over-representation or under-representation of parties, depending on whether they get more or less than a certain (varying) threshold of votes; and a "psychological effect" whereby voters tend to not "waste" their votes on parties which have no realistic chance but vote "sophisticatedly" (or strategically/tactically) for the party which they feel has the best chance of defeating their least-liked party. These two effects taken in combination will tend to aggregate votes around the leading party and its principal rival. Duverger's law argues that the *first-post-the-post system produces an imperative of consolidation* of voters (and politicians) around a principal rival party to have a realistic chance of winning against a dominant party, thus leading to the elimination of third parties or at least an alliance of other parties against a leading party.

Duverger's law applies essentially at the constituency level. It need not translate to the national level and produce a national two-party system where strong state parties exist as in a federal polity, particularly one like India's where the states are linguistic and cultural entities reflecting such social cleavages. In such a system, where parties compete for forming the government at both national and state levels, Duverger's law can apply at the state level, leading to two-party or bipolar systems at the state level due to the consolidation of the opposition to the principal party in the state level, whether a national or regional party, in a principal rival, while at the same time leading to a multi-party system nationally because the state-level two-party systems do not consist of the same two parties. Indeed, they can consist of a variety of parties, some national, some purely state-level. The consolidation of two-party or two-alliance systems at the state level which we have described in the foregoing sections is the playing out of Duverger's law in practice.

The first, third, and sixth explanations are all variants of the social cleavage theory of party systems which postulates that parties will be formed around social cleavages and the party system will reflect this in its axes of polarisation.

The second, fifth, and seventh explanations relate to the behavioural incentives set up by the systemic features of the political system, the second and seventh relating to the electoral system specifically, with the seventh specifying a mechanism whereby behaviour of politicians, voters, and parties determine the change in the party system over time.

The fourth explanation focuses on political parties as machines and is intermediate between social cleavage theories and political-systemic theories.

Let us take an overview of the evolution of alliances before coming back to the competing explanations. The evolution of alliances began with broad-front anti-Congressism in the immediate pre-1967 period, promoted by the socialist ideologue Ram Manohar Lohia. As long as the Congress got around 40 per cent of the vote nationally and a similar share in most states, and as long as other parties received only a fraction of that nationally and much less than the Congress at the state level, the only way to dislodge the Congress was a broad anti-Congress front, howsoever disparate in ideological and social terms. In 1967, the Congress received a bare majority in Parliament and lost power in eight major states. In most of these, anti-Congress coalitions called Samyukta Vidhayak Dals (SVD) formed the government for at least some of the period between 1967 and 1974 (there were mid-term elections in four states in 1969).

These were the first wave of anti-Congress coalitions (barring a few earlier ones such as in Kerala). However, they were highly disparate in ideological terms, some being *coalitions of the ideological extremes* as in the case of the Akali Dal–Jana Sangh–CPI coalition in Punjab in 1967–9, and were extremely vulnerable to splits and defections. Most of the components of these coalitions were either parties based on the emerging rich peasantry of the intermediate castes such as the socialist parties and Charan Singh's Bharatiya Kranti Dal (BKD) in UP and Bihar, which were at odds with the traditional upper- and landowning caste-dominated Congress, or the Hindu chauvinist Jana Sangh, or the CPI, or breakaway factions of disgruntled Congressmen. There was no ideological policy or social glue which held together these alliances, only the necessity to hang together for power; hence, their instability. These were essentially post-election alliances. It was only in some states in 1967 and 1969 that such broad-front anti-Congress pre-election alliances were put together.

The next stage in the evolution of alliances was the unification of some political parties which had been partners in the SVD coalitions in the states in the 1967–74 period, in the context of the extra-parliamentary protest movement led by Jayaprakash Narayan in 1974–5. In 1974, the Charan Singh-led BKD, based primarily on intermediate caste peasant proprietors in UP, merged with the SSP (Raj Narain), Swatantra Party, Utkal Congress, and three minor parties to form the Bharatiya Lok Dal (BLD).

The next stage came in the post-Emergency 1977 elections with the formation of the Janata Party which came into being with the merger of the BLD, the Congress (O), the Socialist Party, the Jagjivan Ram-led Congress for Democracy, and the Jana Sangh.

The collapse and splintering of the Janata Party and the resurgence of the Congress in 1980 to form a majority government for the entire 1980s set back the process of broad-front anti-Congressism. However, it continued in certain states like Haryana, where the Lok Dal and the BJP formed an electoral allianee to defeat the Congress in 1987.

Alliance formation resumed in the late 1980s with the formation of the Janata Dal in 1988 by expelled Congressman V.P. Singh merging his supporters with the Lok Dals of both Ajit Singh and Devi Lal in North India, and with the Janata Party of R.K. Hegde in Karnataka. A broad anti-Congress informal coalition for seat adjustment for the 1989 elections so as to give the Congress one-on one opposition at the constituency level, state by state, was put together.

This was a two-level alliance. The first level was a formal coalition, the National Front, consisting of the Janata Dal and four others parties, the three regional parties, TDP, DMK, and AGP, and the Congress (Socialist). The second level was a more informal seat adjustment between the National Front and BJP on the one hand (Rajasthan, Gujarat, UP, Haryana) and the Left parties on the other, even though the Left and the BJP were poles apart. However, even the National Front stopped short of a 1977-style merger. Nor was it a purely power-seeking opportunistic coalition of the post-1967 SVD type, ignoring ideological differences. In fact, it remained a coalition of independent parties with a joint manifesto, limiting itself to seat adjustments state by state with the second level of the alliance, the BJP and Left, but agreeing to disagree on key ideological issues. The government formed in 1989–90 was also of this type, with the BJP and the Left supporting it from the outside. This set the stage for the alliances of the 1990s.

The 1991 election saw a three-cornered contest with roughly the same electoral alliances contesting, viz. the National Front comprising the Janata Dal, regional and Left parties, versus the BJP and the Congress, with the rump Samajwadi Janata Party (of Prime Minister Chandra Shekhar) as a minor fourth side, the main difference from 1989 being that the BJP contested alone and not in adjustment with the Janata Dal.

In 1996 again, the same three-cornered battle resulted in a broad front, post-election coalition government of UF, again constituted by the Janata family parties, regional and Left parties, dependent on support from their political rival, the Congress, in order to offer an alternative to the perceivedly extremist, "anti-system" BJP. This coalition's dependence on the Congress for support made it inherently unstable given that the Congress was the principal political opponent of many of the UF's constituent parties in their home states, particularly in Andhra Pradesh, Assam, and the three Left stronghold states. However, it should be noted that the BJP was not totally isolated, having an ideologically compatible ally in Maharashtra (Shiv Sena) and managing to forge alliances with splinter parties from the Janata family in Bihar (Samata) and Haryana (Haryana Vikas Party) and with the Akali Dal in Punjab; earlier, in 1995, it had formed a short-lived alliance with the BSP, which formed the government for four months, exploiting the SP–BSP breakup.

In 1998, the BJP realised the limits of Hindutva and the need to expand geographically to the south and east and socially downwards to the backward and Scheduled Castes, Scheduled Tribes, and poor. It successfully overcame its isolation by managing to exploit splits in the Congress (in West Bengal where it made seat adjustments with the breakaway Trinamool Congress) and Janata Dal (in Karnataka with Hegde's Lok Shakti, and in Orissa with the Biju Janata Dal), growing beyond its alliances in Punjab (Akali Dal), Maharashtra (Shiv Sena), and Bihar (Samata). Most importantly, it made inroads into Tamil Nadu with an alliance with the AIADMK-led group of regional parties, exploiting state-level rivalries in all cases. At the state level, which was the significant level for these alliances, the newly "moderate" BJP became an attractive partner for a regional or state-based party opposed to the Congress or Congress-allied regional rival (Punjab, Maharashtra, Tamil Nadu, Karnataka, Haryana, Orissa) or to a Congress faction (Trinamool Congress) versus the major regional party (West Bengal). *The logic of the enemy's enemy being one's friend overpowered the ideological incompatibility between these centrist, secular parties, and the BJP's ideology.* However, when it came to government formation the BJP-led coalition government adopted a National Agenda for Governance in which the BJP's Hindutva agenda items were dropped. Thus the BJP had to pay the price of at least tactical and temporary moderation to sustain the alliance. With this modified stand, it managed to win post-election allies (Chautala's Haryana Lok Dal) and external supporters (TDP, NC) for its coalition government.

In 1999, the BJP managed to sustain and expand the same coalition, now formally called the National Democratic Alliance (NDA) (adding the TDP, Goa's MGP, and the Patel faction of the Karnataka Janata Dal), in some cases switching partners, most dramatically in Tamil Nadu (to the DMK) and Haryana (to Chautala's INLD against erstwhile ally Bansi Lal's HVP). Again, the logic of the enemy's enemy being a friend worked against the Congress in most of the south and east where the Congress was one of the two principal parties facing a regional or state-based third party, the latter finding it expedient to ally with the BJP to add the latter's vote share to its kitty. However, again the BJP had to formally moderate its stand in the common NDA manifesto, shelving Hindutva issues in order to forge and sustain such alliances.

The evolution of alliances in the Indian party system can be summarised as follows. The first phase of broad-front anti-Congressism in the 1960s and early 1970s was characterised by *intra-state alliances* of the SVD type or the Janata Party, where within each state the component parties of the alliance or the Janata Party, for example, the Jana Sangh, BKD/BLD, Socialists, Swatantra, Congress (O), had their state units, strongholds, and interests while having no ideological glue.

The second phase, again of broad-front anti-Congressism, was that of the Janata Party, which unified ideologically disparate non-Congress parties so as to have one-on-one contests aggregating votes at the constituency level so as to win, reflecting the imperative of aggregation to win regardless of ideology. This also consisted of intra-state alliances of disparate parties within the overall umbrella of unification of those parties at the national level. Intra-state alliances cannot be stable unless there is *both an ideological and programmatic compatibility and an intra-state spatial compatibility* in that some of the parties have pockets of strength within the state which are not contested by their allies in the state; this applies in both the classic case of Kerala (for both the Left and the Congress) and in West Bengal. This spatial alliance was also fundamentally different from that of the Congress and AIADMK from 1977 to 1996 in that this was not based on a trade-off of state assembly seats for Lok Sabha seats between the national and regional parties.

The National Front coalition was a new departure in three senses. First, learning from the Janata experience, it did not try to unify very different parties but put together a coalition of distinct parties based on a common manifesto. Second, it brought in the explicitly regional parties like the DMK, TDP, and AGP, and the Left parties, unlike the SVD or Janata phase experiments. Third, it also marked the beginning of *inter-state alliances* of parties or *spatially compatible alliances* where parties do not compete on each other's turf. However, the spatially compatible loose alliance put together by the National Front–BJP–Left in 1989–90 foundered on the rock of ideological incompatibility. This indicated once again *the unsustainability* of *a broad anti-Congress coalition unless its ideological extremes moderated or set aside their position* (as the Jana Sangh did in the post-1967 SVD coalitions and in the post-1977 Janata phase). Another clear case of a *spatially compatible alliance* was the post-election coalition of the UF during 1996–8; however, it had a certain secular ideological mooring, ranged as it was against a hardline, perceivedly "anti-system" BJP.

The period since 1991 has also seen the growth and sustenance of *intra-state alliances based on ideology* (like the BJP–Shiv Sena) and based on spatial compatibility of two kinds, different from both the Left Front kind and the Congress–AIADMK trade-off kind of 1977–96. This consists of *intra-state alliances which are a reverse of the historical Congress–AIADMK kind* in which there is no trade-off of Lok Sabha for state assembly seats between the regional and national parties. On the contrary, the regional party allies with the state unit of the national party with the *regional party getting the lion's share* of *both Lok Sabha and assembly seats.* The examples are the BJP–AIADMK–smaller parties in 1998, the BJP–DMK–smaller parties in 1999, the BJP–TDP in 1999, the BJP–Trinamool Congress in 1999, BJP–BJD in Orissa in 1998 and 1999, the BJP–HVP in 1996 and 1998, and the BJP–INLD (Chautala) in 1999, and also the BJP–Shiv Sena since 1991.

There is also the reverse of this pattern, viz. *an alliance between a minor state party and a national party in which the latter gets the lion's share of both Lok Sabha and assembly seats,* the key being spatial compatibility in which the national party does not contest in the smaller regional party's intra-state strongholds. Examples are the BJP–Lok Shakti in Karnataka in 1998 and 1999, the BJP–Samata in Bihar over 1996–9, the BJP–Himachal Vikas Congress (HVC) in HP. It is anybody's guess how long these non-ideological alliances will last. In some of these cases, the base of the smaller party, or even the regional party which is a senior partner, may be eaten up by a larger, better-organised party like the BJP, as in fact happened to the Janata Dal in Rajasthan and Gujarat from 1989 to 1991. *The clear emphasis of alliances in the nineties has been on spatial compatibility at the expense of ideological compatibility*, particularly the BJP's alliances of 1998 and 1999, but even the UF coalition. This is an improvement on the SVD and Janata Party alliances which were neither programmatic nor spatially compatible. However, *the most important point to be noted is that in the whole history of alliances since the 1960s, with the exception of the Left Front limited to three states, alliances have been driven by the imperative to aggregate votes to win and not by ideology, programme or social cleavages.*[15]

With this observation we return to the competing explanations for fragmentation and reconsolidation of the party system. It is clear that the explanations deriving from the social cleavage theory of party systems, that is the first, third, and sixth explanations, can explain fragmentation of certain kinds. The first can explain the shift away from the Congress to regional parties in certain states like Tamil Nadu, Andhra Pradesh, Assam, Punjab, and J&K and the North-Eastern Rim states, including the formation of such parties as in the case of Assam. The third can explain the shift of votes away from or consolidation behind the agrarian parties of the Janata family

[15] For a detailed overview of state-level coalition politics in India, see E. Sridharan, "Principles, Power and Coalition Politics in India: Lessons from Theory, Comparison and Recent History", in D.D. Khanna and Gert W. Kueck, eds, *Principles, Power and Politics* (Delhi: Macmillan, 1999).

from the BKD, Socialists, BLD, Lok Dals, Janata Dal, and so forth, again including the formation of new parties. The sixth explanation can account for the rise of communal and caste-based parties like the BJP, Shiv Sena, BSP, and Samajwadi Party, including the formation of new parties. The fourth explanation can explain the exit of former Congress voters to rival or new parties. The fifth explanation reinforces these in that it explains the incentives for regional or single state-based party formation. The second further reinforces these by explaining how delinked state assembly elections facilitate collective action for alliances.

However, while these explanations can account for various types of fragmentation, they cannot explain the periodic counter-tendencies towards alliances that tend to reconsolidate the party system. It is here that we find the seventh explanation, based on Duverger's analysis of the systemic properties and imperatives of the first-past-the-post electoral system useful. This seventh explanation can account for *both fragmentation at the national level and tendencies towards alliances.* The key point here is to remember from the account of the first two sections that *fragmentation of the party system at the national level is a product of its opposite at the state level,* that is, the concentration of vote share between two parties or alliances, but *different* pairs of parties or alliances in most states, leading to a multitude of parties at the national level, each with a limited base in one or a few states. The latter phenomenon is explained by the systemic tendencies of the first-past-the-post system captured by Duverger's law, working themselves out at the state level since 1967.

The seventh explanation also fits well with the tendencies towards broad alliances driven, as we have seen, overwhelmingly by the imperative to consolidate votes, rather than by ideology, programme, or social cleavages.

We can conclude that the Indian party system is evolving over successive elections and the various trends and counter-trends will play themselves out over the coming years. It is too early to say whether the inexorable imperative to aggregate votes regardless of ideology will push the national party system to evolve towards loose bipolarity at the national level between two broad spatially compatible alliances, one broadly left and the other broadly right of centre, or whether India's multiple social cleavages intertwined with geographical diversity will prevail to create so diversified an ideological space that bipolar consolidation is impossible at the national level.[16]

[16] Ordeshook and Shvetsova, "Ethnic Heterogeneity District Magnitude and the Number of Parties", in *American Journal of Political Science*, 38, 4 (February) 1994, argue that Duverger's law will work even under conditions of social (ethnic, religious, linguistic, etc.) heterogeneity, while Taagepera and Shugart, in *Seats and Votes*, op. cit., tend to argue that the effective number of parties will increase with the increase in social heterogeneity.

2

Democracy Within Parties and the Accommodation of Diversity

Comparing India and the United States

INDIA SINCE 1989, and especially since 1996, has had a party system that is more competitive than most other established democracies, with more parties represented in parliament, and still more represented in state assemblies, and still again more contesting elections at national and state levels. It has also had the largest coalition governments in the world since 1996, when the coalition of governing and supporting parties has ranged from thirteen to twenty-four parties. This poses obvious problems of governmental stability and policy coherence. India has had six general elections between 1989 and 2004 in what would normally have been three parliamentary terms. There is vigorous political competition between a large number of parties, especially between the historically dominant Congress party and the BJP, which leads the National Democratic Alliance (NDA) coalition. Yet no party today can hope to dominate the scene or be sure of its prospects. Nor is there any real democracy within political parties – they function in a top-down style with the key decisions about political strategy, election nominations, and the raising and distribution of money excessively controlled by the party leadership.

This is in contrast to most parties in Western democracies, where the trend over the past four decades has been towards decentralisation and greater internal democracy. The two American parties have been the polar opposite to those in India in terms of decentralisation and internal democracy, particularly with respect to nominations and finance, to the point where the American parties as coherent organisations are threatened, and increasingly tend to become collections of candidate-centric structures. In the Indian case, the lack of internal democracy has been accompanied since the late 1960s at least, by repeated splits in major parties or their state units, the emergence of new and minor parties, and the frequent merger of small and new parties with other parties. This has continued to happen despite the anti-defection law (the 52nd Constitutional amendment) of 1985. It is tempting to conclude that the absence of internal democracy has caused many of these splits.

The issue of internal democracy in parties is vital for India for several reasons. Are party splits, endemic in Indian parties, due to the Hirschmanian logic of exit, voice, and loyalty?[1] That is, do factions, leaders, and voters exit a party after a period of declining loyalty when they find that they lack a voice within the party? Or do they exit because of the lack of democracy within parties and the instability of coalitions? Is there a link between the lack of democracy within parties and the capacity of governments to take a long-term view on policy issues, particularly policies which may be unpopular in the short run but may yield dividends only in the long run? And, central for this paper (but related to all of the above), is the accommodation of cultural, religious, and ethnic diversity. Can political accommodation of diversity take place by the formation of a multitude of small parties, each based principally on particular social groups and forming coalition governments, despite the lack of internal democracy within parties? And/or can single state-based parties merge across state boundaries to form federal par-

[1] Albert O. Hirschman, *Exit, Voice and Loyalty* (Princeton, NJ: Princeton University Press, 1970).

ties,[2] to achieve the same political accommodation unless there is greater democracy within the existing parties? The evolution of the party system to two or three broad-based federal parties would appear to require intra-party democracy. This is important in the context of the almost universally accepted opinion that there is no possibility of a single-party majority government in the foreseeable future.

Given the polar contrast between the functioning of the two major American parties along the dimension of internal decentralisation and democracy, and their absence in Indian parties, this paper seeks to explore the reasons why this is so. Also explored is the link between intra-party democracy and the capacity to accommodate religious, racial, ethnic, caste, linguistic, and regional diversity. Is it the weight of history? Political culture? Particular institutional arrangements? Or is it a combination of these factors? Is it in a particular historical sequence? The paper also brings in comparisons from trends in intra-party democracy in European parties, mostly intermediate on the spectrum between top-down and polyarchal/decentralised/democratic styles of functioning.

In the following sections, we outline:

(1) A typology of parties and party evolution from the point of view of party democracy.
(2) The main features of the evolution of the two major American parties, including the question of whether/how the internal processes of the parties conduces to intra-party democracy and the accommodation of diversity, and why newly mobilised interests have not opted for or successfully formed third parties.
(3) The evolution of the Indian party system and the major Indian political parties since Independence, focusing on

[2] Douglas V. Verney, "How has the Proliferation of Parties Affected the Indian Federation: A Comparative Approach", in Zoya Hasan, E. Sridharan, and R. Sudarshan, eds, *India's Living Constitution: Ideas, Practices, Controversies* (New Delhi: Permanent Black, 2002).

their internal democratic processes. We attempt to link this to whether there is accommodation of social diversity, repeated splits in parties, and the rise of new parties. Lastly, we draw some tentative conclusions for Indian parties, reflecting on the experience of American and European parties.

A Typology of Parties and the Evolution of Their Internal Functioning

Parties historically emerged as an organisational form most suited for the performance of certain functions. The key functions performed by parties are candidate nomination, electoral mobilisation, both constituting elite recruitment, and other related functions like issue structuration, societal representation, interest aggregation, forming and sustaining governments, and societal integration.[3] There are a vast variety of party typologies but a state-of-the-art, rich but parsimonious typology would be the following, based on Diamond and Gunther.[4] Their typology and the sequence of party evolution outlined further below does not necessarily fit every country but is the best for our purpose. They divide political parties into fifteen types or species clustered into five broader geniuses: elite, mass-based, ethnicity-based, electoralist, and movement parties.

The first genus of (traditional) elite parties consists of either parties of local notables or clientelistic parties based on local notables. These are weakly organised, mobilising support through the personal resources of notables or vertical patron–client networks, and making election nominations based on loyalty. Typically, they exist in premodern or early modernising rural polities.

[3] Larry Diamond and Richard Gunther, eds, *Political Parties and Democracy* (Baltimore: Johns Hopkins University Press, 2001), pp. 7–9.

[4] Ibid., pp. 3–39.

The second genus of mass-based parties, or the mass party,[5] is a party created outside the legislature, typically an industrial working-class party but could also be a peasant or religious or nationalist party in some circumstances, well organised, and with a mass membership. There are six species here – three pairs of socialist ideological parties, nationalist ideological parties, and religious ideological parties. Each of these pairs has an organisationally thin, pluralist type and an organisationally thick, proto-hegemonic type. Thus there are "class-mass" socialist, social-democratic, and labour parties, and there are Leninist revolutionary communist parties, both mass parties of the working class. There are broad-based nationalist mass parties, and ultranationalist or fascist parties, Christian Democrat-type religious mass parties, and religious fundamentalist parties. This genus of a party is controlled by its professional bureaucracy, has a variety of mass organisations, which it uses for mobilisation, and its nominations for elections are controlled by the top of the party bureaucracy.

The third genus of ethnicity-based parties can be either mono-ethnic parties that follow an ethnically exclusivist or even polarising strategy, or broad, multi-ethnic coalitional or congress parties. The first type may be well or weakly organised but they are typically not internally democratic. They tend to be controlled either by organised religious hierarchies or charismatic leaders, and nominations for elections are made by the top. Examples of the second type are the Indian National Congress up to the mid-1960s, the Malaysian Barisan National, and the Tanzania African National Union, all of which are multi-ethnic parties characterised by national integration ideologies combined with particularistic benefits. Nominations tend to be decentralised and part of a pattern of power-sharing in multi-ethnic societies.

The fourth genus are the electoralist parties. These may be personalistic, programmatic, or catch-all parties. Personalistic parties

[5] Maurice Duverger, *Political Parties: Their Organisation and Activity in the Modern State* (New York: Wiley, 1963).

are merely vehicles for the ambitions of leaders and are purely election-oriented, for example, Silvio Berlusconi's Forza Italia or Benazir Bhutto's Pakistan People's Party. Programmatic parties are also election-oriented and thinly organised but are more ideologically or programmatically coherent, for example, Thatcher's Conservative party or the post-1980 Republican party. The catch-all party is not a class party but essentially a machine oriented to winning elections.[6] It tends to cut across class and other cleavages and make direct appeals to voters through the mass media.

Lastly, the fifth genus of the movement party consists of parties that have evolved from contemporary social movements such as the Green Party in Germany or the various anti-immigrant extreme Right parties in Europe such as the Austrian Freedom Movement, which straddle parties and movements. They tend to be catch-all in character but with a distinct, often single-issue, programme.

Katz and Mair,[7] using many of the above party types, argue for an evolutionary sequence of party types, based on their relationship to civil societies and states in different stages of development in the context of European history, but their typology and staging can have useful insights for developing-world democracies too. They argue that the mass party,[8] which is often taken as the benchmark, is a product of industrial working-class societies and is only a stage in the continuing process of political evolution.

The mass party, typically working-class based, led to the development of Kirchheimer's catch-all party,[9] in what was essentially a reaction of older, less organised, conservative or liberal parties,

[6] Otto Kirchheimer, "The Transformation of the Western European Party Systems", in Joseph La Palombara and Myron Weiner, eds, *Political Parties and Political Development* (Princeton: Princeton University Press, 1996), pp. 177–200.

[7] Richard S. Katz and Peter Mair, "Changing Models of Party Organization and Party Democracy", *Party Politics*, 1995, vol. 1, no. 1, pp. 5–58.

[8] Maurice Duverger, *Political Parties*, op. cit.

[9] Otto Kirchheimer, "The Transformation of the Western European Party Systems", op. cit.

or even clientelistic parties of notables, focusing on broad appeals cutting across class barriers to counter traditional class-based mass parties. The catch-all party, as a type, made its appearance and grew in the post-war boom era with the growth of the middle class and the relative decline of the old industrial working class. The catch-all party or the electoral-professional party,[10] tended to pitch its appeal wide, concentrating on electoral mobilisation through the media rather than by grassroots organisations in an era of the spread of television and the rise of a professional political class. In the electoral-professional party,[11] the party in government has also tended to become stronger than the extra-parliamentary organisation, unlike in the older mass party.

Katz and Mair posit the rise of cartel parties in the post-1970s period,[12] when established parties, both of the moderate left and the right, which are closely integrated with the bureaucracies of a managerial state deeply involved in the economy, collude to limit competition. Some cartel parties, in their view, are part of the adaptation of the old mass parties to the rise of catch-all parties.

There has been a general trend over 1960–90 towards greater decentralisation and transparency within parties.[13] In several major parties in the democratic world, including both major British parties, particularly Labour, in the Spanish Socialist Party, and the

[10] Angelo Panebianco, *Political Parties: Organization and Power* (Cambridge, UK: Cambridge University Press, 1988).

[11] Ibid.

[12] Katz, "Changing Models", op. cit. Also, Richard S. Katz, "The Problem of Candidate Selection and Models of Party Democracy", *Party Politics*, 2001, vol. 7, no. 3, pp. 277–96.

[13] Lars Bille, "Democratizing a Democratic Procedure: Myth or Reality?", *Party Politics*, 2001, vol. 7, no. 3, pp. 363–80; Lawrence LeDuc, "Democratizing Party Leadership Selection", *Party Politics*, 2001, vol. 7, no. 3, pp. 323–41; Jonathan Hopkin, "Bringing the Members Back In? Democratising Candidate Selection in Britain and Spain", *Party Politics*, 2001, vol. 7, no. 3, pp. 343–61; Gideon Rahat and Reuven Y. Hazan, "Candidate Selection Methods: An Analytical Framework", *Party Politics*, 2001, vol. 7, no. 3, pp. 297–322.

Progressive Conservative Party in Canada, there have been movements by local and middle-level party activists and by the rank-and-file to reduce the power of entrenched party elites, whether legislative or party-bureaucratic. There have been strong movements within parties to democratise nomination and leadership selection processes and make them open to broader and more inclusive electorates.

Four caveats about the importance of intra-party democracy need to be recorded here.

(1) There may be a danger of overemphasising the importance of intra-party democracy for accommodativeness and representation. It may well be possible for accommodation and representation of all group interests to take place under an oligarchical leadership that is so inclined, while on the other hand, an emphasis on intra-party democracyin a context of majoritarianism in both the rules of intra-party democracy and the prevailing social ideology may marginalise minority interests in intra-party dynamics. This can result in internal democracy without the accommodation of social diversity.

(2) Intra-party democracy may not be entirely benign. It may help better representation but under certain circumstances, particularly in ideologically extreme parties, it may help extremists control parties since these will be the most active in getting themselves and their followers voted to party office and can up the ideological ante in intra-party debate.

(3) In any comparison of India and the US, it needs to be taken into account that in a parliamentary system, the major function of parties is to provide government, unlike in the US presidential system. Parties would need a degree of coherence. Therefore, in the US, a highly decentralised candidate-centred party may not matter as much to governance as it would in a parliamentary system. Thus, intra-party de-

mocracy may pose the problem of responsiveness versus responsibility.

(4) The argument can be made,[14] that in a very heterogeneous society and federal state, a multiparty system would quite likely evolve anyway despite Duverger's law and even if there was intra-party democracy in the major parties.

The American Parties

In this section, we view the American parties in the light of this background. The two major American parties, the Republican party and the Democratic party, are the world's most decentralised and least top-down in their internal functioning. This is so even in comparison to European political parties at the beginning of the twenty-first century, despite their recent democratising reforms and certainly in comparison to all Indian political parties. How did they become so? And is this characteristic at the expense of party coherence? Is the decentralised structure and functioning of the American parties due to a particular sequence of historical accidents? Or is it due to political culture, the relationship of parties with civil society, institutional features such as federalism, the system of primaries, or state regulation of party processes?

My understanding is that the decentralised and internally democratic nature of the two major American parties is due to a combination of the above features in a particular historical sequence, that is, a path-dependent evolution resulting in the outcome described. This internally democratic character, in turn, facilitates the accommodation of newly mobilised social, including racial, ethnic, and cultural, constituencies. Also, the structure of the parties and the party system as well as the single-member district, simple-plurality electoral system in combination with the presidential system, inhibits the formation and electoral success of third par-

[14] Rein Taagepera and Matthew Soberg Shugart, *Seats and Votes: The Effects and Determinants of Electoral Systems* (New Haven: Yale University Press, 1989).

ties, thereby encouraging newly mobilised groups to try to carve out space within the existing parties.

The historical origins of the party system in the 1790–1800 period are crucial. Parties emerged, like in England, from legislative factions. They were loose, factional coalitions of legislative notables without elaborate organisation, ideology, or discipline. In fact, the elites were highly pluralised. They functioned in a political regime of generally accepted norms about political freedom, and the state was a federal state with separation of legislative, executive, and judicial powers and a system of checks and balances. The political culture that evolved was one that tolerated party factionalism and dissent, and both the more elitist Federalists and more grassroots Anti-Federalists were ideologically flexible and encompassed a breadth of societal interests.

The period from 1824 to 1860, when the suffrage was expanded and mass participation grew, was also one in which embryonic party structures were established. The power to control and direct the party organisation was increasingly transferred to state and local party leaders upon whom national leaders depended for electoral mobilisation, with the powers over the party organisation increasingly transferred from parties' legislative leaders to state and local leaders who were not members of Congress or the state legislatures.

This was also the period when the earliest versions of the now well-established party structures, beginning with the Democratic party, emerged. The first national convention, based on delegates from state units, appeared in 1831–2 to co-ordinate party activities and the first national committee (of the Democrats) appeared in 1844. These structures transferred power from Congressional and state legislative party caucuses to non-legislative national, and crucially, state and local party leaders. Thus, decentralised state-level party structures, which were embryonic in the 1800–24 period, evolved and took root alongside the massification of parties during the period of 1824 to 1854, beginning with the Democratic party due to the efforts of Andrew Jackson and Martin Van Buren.[15] The Democratic party became the first national mass party in history. By 1840, the US had two national mass parties in place, the Democrats and the Whigs, with a turnout of 78 per cent of the eligible electorate.[16] The development of national party organisations was substantially due to the imperatives of competing for the presidency, As Epstein puts it, "the very office meant to be non-partisan is primarily responsible for the existence of national parties as well as for their special nature."[17] This is in addition to Duverger's law.

The post-Civil War period up to 1896 saw a consolidation of the Republican–Democrat two-party system (the Republicans emerging as a contender for the presidency in 1852 and rapidly replacing the Whigs). The significant developments were the development of urban political machines in the big cities, the adoption of legislation to protect the integrity of elections and, with that, the regulation of party organizations.

The next major period, 1896–1932, saw the emergence of primaries, which ultimately took the leadership-nomination function out of the hands of the party organisational leaders and put it in the hands of registered party voters. However, formal nomination for presidential elections remained in the hands of the national convention, though increasingly influenced by primaries. The first state direct primary was held in 1903: by 1912 a majority of states had adopted mandatory primary laws and by 1917 all but four states had direct primary laws for at least some state offices.[18] By 1955 all states had such primaries, though they were far from homogenous, being characterised by a bewildering variety of rules and practices from state to state. The first presidential primary was

[15] John W. Aldrich, *Why Parties? The Origin and Transformation of Political Parties in America* (Chicago: University of Chicago Press, 1995).

[16] Ibid.

[17] Leon D. Epstein, *Political Parties in the American Mold* (Madison: University of Wisconsin Press, 1986), p. 83.

[18] Ibid.

held in Florida in 1904 and today the great majority of states have presidential primaries. The 1896–1932 period also saw a movement towards non-partisan elections for municipal offices and moves to regulate campaign finance activities.

To elaborate on the growth of primaries and their effects on the nomination function in political parties – if we consider the whole period of 1832–1968, the era of presidential nomination by the party national convention – it is useful to distinguish two periods, one until 1912 and the other from 1912 to 1968. In the first period virtually all convention delegates were chosen within each state by party caucus, district convention, state convention, executive committeee or some combination of party organs. From 1912 to 1968, the system can be called mixed, following the spread of presidential primaries. However, from 1912 to 1968, in twenty-one seriously contested Republican and Democratic nominating contests (when incumbent presidents were not automatically renominated) on twelve occasions the winners of the largest number of primaties failed to secure the nomination. After 1968, the primaries determined the results. The important point, in comparative perspective, is that primaries in the US are subject to state law and operated by state and local officials and financed by public funds, in contrast to party primaries in the 1980s and 1990s in Europe, which were regulated by party rules and operated by party officials and funds.

The period 1936 to the present began with the New Deal coalition effecting a basic party realignment (though some scholars argue that a new party system came into effect from 1968). The major characteristics of this period are the much debated "decline" of parties, affecting both major parties, or, in other words, the decline of traditional mass parties. This has been constituted by, and complexly caused by, a range of interrelated developments, among which we can list the following: the decline of urban political machines, the increase in the proportion of convention delegates selected by direct primary elections from one-third to four-fifths over 1968–98 – along with the spread of presidential primaries –

the increase in ticket-splitting by voters, growing non-partisan voting in Congress up to 1980 at least (see Rohde for the re-emergence of partisanship in the 1980s),[19] the growing dependence on television, the greater regulation of campaign finance, and the rise of candidate-centred elections.[20]

To sum up, the principal factors, in our understanding, that have created and sustained highly decentralised and (by the standards of most other countries, certainly India) internally democratic parties, to the point of a decline of party coherence, are: first, the creation of pluralistic parties in a federal state with separation of powers from the outset, even before the growth of mass parties and the evolution of the two-party system consisting of the Republican and Democratic parties after the 1860s; second, the institution and spread of direct primaries and presidential primaries through the twentieth century; third, the decentralised wealth of a wealthy country; fourth, the spread of new media-dependent campaigning since the 1950s.

How have the two parties responded to and accommodated social diversity, especially race, the most significant ascriptive sociopolitical cleavage, particularly since the Civil Rights Movement? The Voting Rights Act of 1965 began a new era of substantial empowerment for African-Americans. The ending of formal constraints on political participation resulted in large increases in voter registration and voting in the states of the deep South. It also brought about large proportionate increases in the number of black elected officials, particularly to state and local political office such as state legislators and mayors.[21] It also led to the inclusion of black political agendas in national, state, and local politics.

However, all this took place within the existing political parties,

[19] David W. Rohde, *Parties and Leaders in the Post-reform House* (Chicago: University of Chicago Press, 1991).

[20] Martin P. Wattenberg, *The Decline of American Political Parties, 1952–1996* (Cambridge: Harvard University Press, 1998).

[21] Robert B. Albritton, George Amedee, Keenan Grenell, and Don-Terry, Veal, "Deracialization and the New Black Politics", in Huey L. Perry, ed., *Race,*

principally the Democratic party, in the same two-party system, indicating successful accommodation *by the parties* of a hitherto excluded group. A similar pattern characterises the increasing political participation of Hispanic groups from the 1980s onwards. So much so that some scholars have pointed to the rise of "deracialization" or a dropping or toning down of black political agendas as a political phenomenon associated with the campaigns of many successful black politicians, the best recent example being L. Douglas Wilder, the first black governor of any state (Virginia).[22] Why have politically emergent and assertive social groups either not opted to form third parties or been unsuccessful in doing so? And why has there been no phenomenon like the BJP in India, that is, a calculated attempt to create a majority–minority polarisation over race as the BJP has attempted over religion and culture?

To elaborate on the parties and race since the Civil Rights movement, it is not that race has disappeared as a determinant of party strategies. Indeed, since 1968 there has been a steady shift of white voters throughout the eleven southern states from the Democrats towards the Republicans as lower-middle-class and working-class whites threatened by desegregation and affirmative action, particularly in the issue areas of jobs, housing, crime, and schooling, have gravitated towards the Republican party.[23] The Republicans have been largely successful in effecting a shift of white votes in the South to themselves, reducing the Democrats to the votes of blacks plus liberal whites, who are not a majority in most of the South.

Politics and Governance in the United States (Gainesville: University of Florida Press, 1996), ch. 11, pp. 179–206.

[22] Huey L. Perry, ed., *Race, Politics and Governance in the United States*, op. cit.

[23] E.I. Dionne, *Why Americans Hate Politics* (New York: Simon and Schuster, 1991); Alan I. Abramowitz and Kyle L. Saunders, "Party Polarization and Ideological Realignment in the US Electorate, 1976–1994", in L. Sandy Maisel, ed., *The Parties Respond: Changes in American Parties and Campaigns*, 3rd edn (Boulder, CO: Westview Press, 1998).

However, the Republicans did not raise these issues in terms of race but in terms of opposition, on liberal-individualist and free-market grounds, to quotas, busing, and law and order, maintaining that they were actually talking about these issues when they raise them and not about race,[24] although the coded message was about race. In the southern states in 2002, electoral calculations of candidates of both parties were crucially about percentages of the white and black vote needed to win or deny victory.[25] However, in the US, both parties are basically catch-all parties that do not seek to *polarise* even when they may be indifferent or lukewarm to the empowerment aspirations of the principal racial minority. There have been episodic exceptions, but even here such polarisation is attempted only in coded language, as in the Bush campaign's use of the Willie Horton case in 1988.[26]

The striking fact remains that despite the presence of both ethnic diversity and federalism, third parties have been resoundingly unsuccessful in the US. This is so even at state level (unlike in Canada and India) and even in district-level minority pockets. In fact, third parties have disappeared even more noticeably in state and congressional elections than in presidential elections.[27] The reason for this is probably that "for state as for national third-party leaders, the direct primary no doubt made it easier to re-enter Republican or Democratic ranks than would an older organisational control of nominations. Thus early abandonment of evidently failing third parties may be encouraged by the same intra-party electoral opportunity that appears to make third parties less useful in the first place."[28]

[24] See E.I. Dionne, *Why Americans Hate Politics*, op. cit.

[25] David Broder, "50–50 America: The Southern Battleground", *Washington Post*, 13 October 2002.

[26] See E.I. Dionne, *Why Americans Hate Politics*, op. cit.; Mark Clapson, "Suburbia and Party Politics", *History Today*, September 2000.

[27] Leon D. Epstein, *Political Parties*, op. cit., pp. 124–5.

[28] Ibid., p. 132.

In presidential elections, the twenty-six presidential elections in the hundred years from 1864 to 1964 saw only four minor party candidates (and no independents) win over 5 per cent of the vote. But in the ten presidential elections from 1968 and 2004, the 5 per cent margin was exceeded four times (Wallace in 1968; Anderson in 1980; Perot in 1992 and 1996). However, third parties can arise in circumstances in which the electoral relevance of major parties declines. This can happen when they do not address issues perceived to be salient,[29] or if there is strong dissatisfaction with major party candidates, both of which appear to be the case in 1968 due to deep divisions in the Democratic party as a result of the Civil Rights movement and the Vietnam war.

However, blacks and other minorities are distributed as minorities in all states (except Asians in Hawaii), are not united, and are mostly in a minority even at the level of congressional districts. Therefore, third parties with a strong minority agenda would tend to lose, and there would be a strong incentive to work within major parties. The latter too would have incentives to accommodate minorities since there are no formal barriers to voting although blacks vote overwhelmingly for the Democrats. However, this outcome is a combination of class, race, and geographical effects – not race alone. Even at levels below the presidency, or perhaps particularly at these levels, serious candidates for Congress and state legislatures might prefer to attract resources from the major parties, rather than trying to build support without those valuable resources. The power of Congress and state legislatures leads to a built-in preference for working with established parties. Critics, however, have pointed out that a major reason behind these outcomes is that since the late nineteenth century both major parties have acted in concert to tighten ballot access rules and voter registration rules in most states, making the system, in effect, anti-

[29] James L. Sundquist, *Dynamics of the Party System: Alignment and Realignment of Political Parties in the United States*, 2nd edn (Washington DC: Brookings Institution, 1983).

working class and anti-poor, indirectly anti-immigrant and anti-minority.[30]

Lastly, it can be argued that the remarkable stability of the Republican–Democrat duopoly since the Civil War, masks diversity expressed in the intense electoral competition within parties as well as shifting alignments and realignments within and between parties over the course of nearly a century and a half. What it also reflects is the absence in American society of social blocs irreconcilably attached to particular ideologies and the prevalence of more pragmatic interest group politics.

The Evolution of the Indian Party System and Intra-Party Democracy in the Major Parties

The Indian electoral system follows the Anglo-American pattern of single-member districts and a simple-plurality system. There are 543 constituencies that send a single member each to the Lok Sabha (two members are nominated). This FPTP system, in common parlance, was adopted shortly after Independence, following debates in the Constituent Assembly (1946—9) and parliament (1950–1) just before the adoption of the Representation of the People Act, 1950 and 1951, and the first general elections of 1952. Two and three-member constituencies which accounted in aggregate for a third of the seats in 1952 and 1957, were abolished in 1961

This electoral system produced a party system in the ele[ctio]ns from 1952 to 1984, in which the single largest party won [a m]ajor- ity of the seats, and formed a single-party majority [gover]nment, despite only a plurality of votes. In all elections from 19[52 to 1]984, the single largest party (which formed a majority g[overnm]ent) was

[30] Micah L. Sifry, *Spoiling for a Fight: Third Party [Politics in] America* (New York: Routledge, 2002), pp. 9, 14, 52, 227–8.

[31] E. Sridharan, "The Fragmentation of the [Indian Part]y System, 1952–1999: Seven Competing Explanations", in Z[oya Hasan (e]d.), *Parties and Party Politics in India* (New Delhi: Oxford Univ[ersity Press, 2]002).

the Congress party, except for 1977 when it was the Janata Party – formed by uniting almost the entire non-Communist opposition. No Indian party has ever won a simple majority of votes, the maximum percentage of votes received being 48 per cent by the Congress in 1984. However, it always got a majority of seats, several times a two-thirds and (in 1984) even a three-fourths majority.

Since 1989, the party system has changed. The past six general elections in India – 1989, 1991, 1996, 1998, 1999, and 2004 – have resulted in hung parliaments and, as a consequence, minority and/or coalition governments. Even the Congress government of 1991–6 was a minority government for the first two and a half years of its term.

In the rest of this section, we outline the trajectory of intra-party democracy in the major Indian parties, focusing on the Congress party. Is the reconstruction of an umbrella party, like the Congress party was in its heyday, with coalition politics being played out within the party, and electoral politics not being played out along lines of social cleavage, possible at all? And can the present national party system evolve towards the development of what Verney has called federal parties,[32] that is, parties formed by the merger of single-state parties so as to form, first, a cross-state spatial coalition, followed eventually by unification into a federal party. For either o these developments to happen, a minimum condition would be that parties must be internally democratic and run their affairs ac-ding to transparent, rule-based democratic procedures so that th are incentives to work within the party and for newly mo-bili nterests to seek to work within existing parties rather than float parties.

The Congress Party[33]

The India nal Congress, or Congress party, was founded in 1885 by a English-educated Indian lawyers, journalists,

32 Douglas v Has the Proliferation of Parties . . .", op. cit.

33 The accoun ess in this section draws on E. Sridharan and Ashu-

businessmen, and other members of the emerging intelligentsia. It gradually grew from a collection of urban-based notables pressing for an improvement of the position of Indians under the colonial regime into both an umbrella party and a mass movement for independence. It also sought to include all religious communities, castes, linguistic and regional groups, and classes, as well as a variety of ideological strands.

The Congress was a broad, multi-ethnic coalitional or Congress party, in our typology, with an elaborate organisational machinery at the provincial, district, and lower levels. The organisation went all the way down to the village in large parts of the country. It faced parties with a much narrower social and geographical base who were hence unable to compete with it electorally. These parties at best offered localised challenges.

Internally, the Congress was a grand coalition of the major political and social forces. What held it together was a set of significant factors: its image of being the party which won India its independence; the name recognition and genuine popularity of its leaders, especially Gandhi and Nehru; a host of competent provincial stalwarts, who had participated in the national movement and managed the party organisation at the state level; intra-party democracy which, however imperfect, allowed all significant voices to be heard, facilitated internal bargaining and conflict resolution,

---

tosh Varshney, "Toward Moderate Pluralism: Political Parties in India", in Larry Diamond and Richard Gunther, eds, *Political Parties and Democracy* (Baltimore: Johns Hopkins University Press, 2001); Atul Kohli, *Democracy and Discontent: India's Growing Crisis of Governability* (New York: Cambridge University Press 1991); Richard Sisson and Ramashray Roy, eds, *Diversity and Dominance in Indian Politics: Changing Bases of Congress Support*, vol. 1 (New Delhi: Sage, 1990); James Manor, "Parties and the Party System", in Atul Kohli, ed., *India's Democracy* (Princeton: Princeton University Press, 1988); Rajni Kothari, *Politics in India* (New Delhi: Orient Longman, 1970); Stanley Kochanek, *The Congress Party of India* (Princeton, NJ: Princeton University Press, 1968); and Myron Weiner, *Party Building in a New Nation* (Chicago: University of Chicago Press, 1967).

and accommodated demands of various groups. Ideologically, the party was centrist, committed to democracy, secularism, federalism, and a mixed economy. The Congress as an internal grand coalition faced by a motley collection of smaller, narrower-based parties, was described in its ideal-typical phase – roughly the first two decades after Independence – by Kothari,[34] as a "party of consensus" surrounded by "parties of pressure".[35]

At the grassroots, membership was open to all who paid nominal dues and were not members of any other political party. This rule, therefore, opened the party to the masses as primary and active members. The latter category referred to those primary members who qualified by certain criteria of party activism. Above them was a hierarchy of local (sub-district, that is, panchayat or block), district, state, and all-India Congress committees. The last three were called the District Congress Committees (DCCs), Pradesh Congress Committees (PCCs), and the All India Congress Committee (AICC). At the annual Congress session, held in a different parts, of the country every year, the delegates were the members of the PCCs. They elected one-eighth of their members to the AICC for a two-year term and the AICC delegates elected the president of the party and a certain number of their members to the Congress Working Committee (CWC).

Thus, at the apex were the party president and the CWC, collectively described as the "high command", which ran the party at the national level on a day-to-day basis. The structures described above and the periodic internal elections at all levels facilitated a two-way communication between the leadership and the grassroots, and resolution of the factional conflict on personality, caste, regional, ideological, and other lines of cleavage.

The organisation gradually disintegrated during the 1960s over the issue of bogus memberships, as party leaders at all levels, especially the local, District Congress Committee (DCC), and PCC levels,

[34] See Rajni Kothari, *Politics in India*, op. cit.

[35] Ibid., p. 179.

recruited large numbers of unverifiable members to swell their "vote banks" for party elections. This was entirely possible in a poor, illiterate population, without registration of births and deaths in the villages, and without reliable forms of identification. These bogus members' votes would swell the vote of local bosses in intra-party factional competition. In 1969, there was a major split in the Congress party – between the faction led by the then prime minister Indira Gandhi, and the leaders in control of the party organisation. It led to an organisational crippling of the Congress from which it has still not recovered. Indira Gandhi used her personal popularity to win national elections, and defeat the organisational wing of the party. By the early 1970s, the organisational Congress was decimated in electoral politics, and Indira Gandhi's party gradually became recognised as the real Congress.

Confident of her charismatic ability to keep winning elections Mrs Gandhi decided to suspend the decades-old organisational principles of the Congress party, especially the norm of intra-organisational elections. Between 1972 until 1992, the Congress party was progressively turned into what Diamond and Gunther,[36] basing themselves on Kirchheimer,[37] call a catch-all party. This was election-oriented rather than oriented to social integration and transformation. Office-bearers at all crucial levels were no longer elected but appointed by the prime minister and Congress president, both the same person. Party nominations for elections, and increasingly even for state assembly elections, had to be approved, if not decided, by the party high command, especially Mrs Gandhi (until her assassination in 1984). The criterion increasingly became one of personal loyalty to the leader over all other considerations. Earlier, party nominations for elections were decided by the state party leadership with the CWC sending observers to act as arbitrators

[36] Diamond and Gunther, *Political Parties and Democracy*, op. cit., pp. xv and 25.

[37] Otto Kirchheimer, "The Transformation of the Western European Party Systems", op. cit.

between major state-level faction leaders in the event of factional clashes. These centralising tendencies weakened the party's leadership at the state and local levels.

In 1992, after a gap of twenty years, attempts were made to repair the organisation and intra-party organisational elections were finally held. In 1997, they were repeated again, but after that the CWC has been nominated by the party president. The latest development in the Congress party is the rise of Sonia Gandhi, Rajiv Gandhi's Italian-born widow, now a naturalised Indian. In the 1998 campaign, she sidelined the formally elected party president, who simply could not lead the party organisation and had to give in to her rising popularity. In retrospect, it is clear that Sonia Gandhi's election campaign energised the party organisation and prevented a further drift of Congress voters to other parties. After the elections, she was installed by the CWC as both party president and leader of the Congress parliamentary party, leading to the ouster of the existing party president. In November 1998, her stature rose even further, as the Congress under her leadership and campaign did extremely well, defeating the incumbent BJP state government in two states and winning the election for the incumbent Congress government in a third state. However, in 1999, despite a rise in its vote share to 28.3 per cent from an all-time low of 25.8 per cent in 1998, it fell to an all-time low of 114 seats, recovering to 26.2 per cent and 145 seats in 2004.

Sonia Gandhi's role in Congress politics is paradoxical. She became party president and leader of the Congress parliamentary party in 1998 despite never having won an election as a MP – this was in line with the long-term de-institutionalisation of the party. However, her declared goal and her first acts as party president were to rebuild the party organisation, state by state, and increasingly at the district levels. At this she has been only partly successful but, the reversion to nomination of the CWC indicates that the attempt to restore intra-party democracy is over for the time being, as of 2006.

The long-term trend towards organisational decay has been accompanied by a change in party finance and election campaigning styles.[38] Private donations by companies and wealthy supporters were the mainstay of party finances since party dues by individual members were never an adequate source of funds in a poor country. Indian laws after 1969 banned company donations to political parties and since then there has been an increasing resort to illegal means of raising election funds. In the absence of state funding, the ban on company donations, mandated by Indira Gandhi, left no legal source of large-scale finance for elections. With the increasing cost of elections, this has led to an increasing reliance on kickbacks on licences and state contracts in a highly regulated economy. The increasingly regulatory policy regime of the 1970s strengthened the political leadership's hands vis-à-vis the private sector. Indira Gandhi's plebiscitary style of campaigning increased the need for money, devaluing the tradition of door-to-door campaigning. It also led to centralisation of party finance, party office appointments, and election nominations.[39] The increasing "Americanisation" of campaigning, beginning under Rajiv Gandhi in 1989, that is, reliance on television and radio, advertising, and criss-crossing of the country by national leaders by air to address mass rallies, accentuated the neglect of the party organisation and its year-round grassroots political activity by a multitude of party workers.

The re-legalisation of company donations in 1985 made no difference to these trends because the system had by then become too deeply entrenched. Election finance remains essentially unreformed, despite a reduction in the campaign period to fourteen days

[38] Based on extensive interviews conducted by the author. For details, see E. Sridharan, "Toward State Funding of Elections in India: A Comparative Perspective on Policy Options", *Journal of Policy Reform*, 1999, vol. 3, issue 3.

[39] Further, the amendment of the law governing election expenditure limits in 1975, effectively making party and supporter expenditure on behalf of a candidate not count towards the candidate's election spending ceiling, removed all effective checks on election expenditure.

since the 1996 elections, an increase in the expenditure ceiling for candidates, and the availability of some free television and radio time in the 1998, 1999, and 2004 campaigns. The existing system strengthens the hands of the national party leadership, and reinforces the centralisation of nominations.

The lack of internal democracy in both factions of the Congress since the split of 1969 and the suspension of organisational elections for two decades from 1972 was a major contributory factor to a series of splits in the party. Earlier, there were minor state-level splits. The first major Congress split was that of 1969 which took place at the national level in what was essentially an intra-leadership struggle, which was cast in ideological and policy colours, as well as in parliamentary versus organisational wing colours. The victorious Indira Gandhi-led Congress (I) that emerged as the main faction took most of the Congress vote with it to emerge with a two-thirds majority in the 1971 elections (43.7 per cent and 352 seats versus 10.4 per cent and 16 seats for the losing Congress organisation). On the eve of the post-Emergency 1977 elections, the Congress split again, with veteran SC leader Jagjivan Ram leading a faction called Congress for Democracy into a merger with the newly-formed Janata party. The next major split took place in February 1978 when the Congress was in the opposition with only 154 MPs after its defeat in 1977; the Congress (I) that emerged had only 78 MPs. The breakaway faction led by K. Brahmananda Reddi and Karnataka chief minister Devaraj Urs called itself the Congress (U), split again to merge with the Congress, leaving a rump that became the Congress (Socialist) in 1981, confined to a pocket in Kerala.

The next significant splits in the Congress took place during the Narasimha Rao government as the 1996 elections neared. Former UP chief minister Narain Dutt Tiwari left the Congress to float a party called the All India Indira Congress (Tiwari) which cut into the Congress vote in a small way (3-4 per cent) in Madhya Pradesh, Uttar Pradesh, Assam, and Rajasthan, winning four seats in 1996 and one in Rajasthan in 1998. Former cabinet minister Madhavrao Scindia floated a faction called the Madhya Pradesh Vikas Congress which won one seat in MP in 1996. However, these factions soon rejoined the Congress, on the latter's terms. In Haryana, former Congress leader Bansi Lal broke away before the 1996 elections to form the Haryana Vikas Party (HVP), but returned to the Congress in 2005.

However, the most significant and damaging split was in the Tamil Nadu unit of the Congress just before the 1996 elections, in revolt against the decision to ally with the All India Anna Dravida Munnetra Kazhagam (AIADMK). The major faction that emerged from this split formed a new party, the Tamil Maanila Congress (TMC). This split cost the Congress dearly, as the TMC won 27 per cent votes (against the official Congress' 18.3 per cent) and twenty seats in alliance with the DMK (25.6 per cent and 17 seats) while the official Congress' AIADMK ally got none and 7.8 per cent votes. With the TMC's twenty seats, and those of the Tiwari Congress (four) and the Madhya Pradesh Vikas Congress (one), the Congress could have emerged as the single largest party in 1996, ahead of the BJP. Splits were now a serious concern for the Congress.

Another important state-level split took place in the UP unit of the Congress when nineteen out of thirty-seven MLAs broke away to form the Loktantrik Congress Party (LCP) in October 1997 and allied with the BJP to form a coalition government. Two other significant splits took place just before the 1998 elections as the Congress appeared to be disintegrating under the presidency of Sitaram Kesri between the fall of the United Front (Gujral) government in November 1997 and the February 1998 elections. The major one was the breakaway in West Bengal of the faction led by Mamata Banerjee to form the Trinamool Congress, which then proceeded to ally itself with the BJP in the state and won seven seats and 24.4 per cent votes in 1998 while the official Congress won only one and 15.2 per cent votes. Clearly, the bulk of the state Congress went over to the Trinamool Congress. The provocation for the split was an intense conflict in the state unit of the Congress in which the central leadership of the Congress backed the less popular formal leadership of the state unit against Mamata Banerjee. This could never have happened if the party practised the basic internal democracy that would leave such decisions on state leadership to democratic processes within the state unit. In Arunachal Pradesh, again just prior to the 1998 elections, the chief minister Gegong Apang broke away to form a new party, the Arunachal Congress, which won both seats in the state and 52.5 per cent votes against 23.9 per cent for the Congress. The Arunachal Congress split again in 1999, the bulk of it merging with the Congress again.

The most damaging recent split in Congress was the May 1999 split led by the Maharashtra political heavyweight Sharad Pawar, former Lok Sabha Speaker P.A. Sangma, and Bihar leader Tariq Anwar. Ostensibly against Sonia Gandhi's fitness to be projected as the Congress prime minister in the event of victory in the 1999 elections on account of her foreign birth, the trio called for a constitutional amendment to bar foreign-born citizens from high political office. The move was triggered off by Congress president Sonia Gandhi's implied claim to prime ministership in the event of the Congress forming a government in the aftermath of the BJP-led government's resignation in April 1999, without due consultations within the CWC. The trio were expelled and went on to form the Nationalist Congress Party (NCP).

These splits are not only about personality clashes or power struggles at the top but also, crucially, about defection of erstwhile segments of the party's social base to other or new parties, and the inducements offered for such defection by new parties formed by newly mobilised and assertive groups. The decline of the Congress has also been due to social reasons. Key segments of the traditional Congress voter base have been moving to other parties in the 1990s.[40]

[40] Subrata Mitra and V.B. Singh, *Democracy and Social Change in India* (New Delhi: Sage, 1999); Oliver Heath, "Anatomy of BJP's Rise to Power: Social, Regional and Political Expansion in 1990s", *Economic and Political Weekly*,

The first major social constituency to go over to the non-Congress opposition was the emerging rich-farmer constituency, largely belonging to "lower castes", or the so-called "middle castes", in the Green Revolution belt of north-western India. The rising "lower" or "middle"-caste peasantry resented the domination of the Congress organisation by the "upper" castes, principally Brahmins and Rajputs, especially in the very large state of UP.[41]

The second major challenge to Congress dominance came from the regional parties, beginning with the victory of the DMK in the state of Tamil Nadu in 1967. Regional parties have focused on regional or linguistic identity and on demands for greater state autonomy in India's federal system. As the Congress party centralised decision-making under Mrs Gandhi, regional parties gained strength.

The SCs (ex-untouchables), constituting 16.5 per cent of India's population, are the third major constituency to move away from the Congress in several parts of India, particularly in the crucial states of UP and Bihar, and to a lesser extent Punjab, Haryana, and Madhya Pradesh. Their growing assertiveness and organised political activity in North India is identified with a new party, the BSP.[42] Finally, the Muslims, comprising over 13 per cent of the total population, are the fourth major social constituency to part ways with the Congress in several states, crucially in the two largest states of UP and Bihar. The alienation of the Muslims began in the late 1980s,

---

21–28 August 1999; Anthony Heath and Yogendra Yadav, "The United Colours of Congress: Social Profile of Congress Voters, 1996 and 1998", *Economic and Political Weekly*, 21–28 August 1999.

[41] Paul Brass, "The Politicisation of the Peasantry in a North Indian State", in Sudipta Kaviraj, ed., *Politics in India* (New Delhi: Oxford University Press, 1997).

[42] Kanchan Chandra, "Mobilising the Excluded", *Seminar 480*, August 1999; Kanchan Chandra, "The Transformation of Ethnic Politics in India: The Decline of Congress and the Rise of the Bahujan Samaj Party in Hoshiarpur", *Journal of Asian Studies*, 59:1, February 2000, pp. 26–61.

when the Congress did not resolutely challenge the rising Hindu nationalist movement, culminating when the Congress government failed to prevent the demolition of the Babri Mosque in 1992 by the Hindu nationalists. The Muslim vote has gravitated to viable anti-BJP parties where they exist, like the Samajwadi Party and BSP in UP, or the Rashtriya Janata Dal in Bihar, but has tended to remain with the Congress in states where it is the only viable anti-BJP formation.

In addition to this, the post-1990, post-Mandal (reservation) policy led to a partial consolidation of the new, policy-created OBCs (in effect, "backward" castes, below the traditional upper castes but above the SCs in the traditional caste hierarchy, comprising small farmers and artisans) around parties other than the Congress, which had for them the unattractive track record of ignoring their aspirations.

The gradual erosion of the party's base due to the desertion by erstwhile support groups, the failure to incorporate newly mobilised groups, and the substantially related phenomenon of repeated splits in the party or its state units, due to factional fights in the absence of clear rules, pose the central question of whether democracy within the party could have produced compromises that may have averted such developments.

The Bharatiya Janata Party[43]

The BJP overtook the Congress to become the largest party in the lower house of parliament in the 1996, 1998, and 1999 elections. It came to power in March 1998, leading a large coalition of pre- and post-election allies, and yet again in October 1999, leading much the same coalition in an early election, and governed until May 2004. The BJP began as the Bharatiya Jana Sangh (BJS), founded in 1951 as the political arm of the RSS, a tightly centralised secretive organisation formed in 1925 dedicated to the creation of a Hindu

[43] For this and the next two sections I draw heavily on Sridharan and Varshney, "Toward Moderate Pluralism", op. cit.

nation. It conceived of India as a Hindu nation in which Muslim and Christian minorities were essentially aliens and towards whom it was explicitly hostile, particularly to the former, regarding Muslims as descendants of invaders and Christians as converts, whose holy places lay outside India in distant Arabia and Palestine. The RSS did not take part in the independence movement, choosing to target the Muslim community rather than resist British rule. It also took no part in electoral politics until 1951 when the BJS was formed. The BJP is the new name adopted by the party in 1980 after its demerger from the Janata Party into which the BJS had merged in 1977. The BJP is the political party of the family *(parivar)* of civil society organisations spawned by the RSS (called the Sangh Parivar). It can be described as a Hindu nationalist party, its ideology of "Hindutva" (Hinduness) being close to both classical fascism in many respects, minus the leader cult, and to the ethnic party type with ethnicity being defined by Hindu religious and cultural markers in this case. It mobilises people and conducts propaganda against Muslims and Christians, ranging from criticism to hatred and even periodic violence, and characteristically employs Hindu–Muslim, and less frequently Hindu–Christian polarising electoral strategies.

The BJP organisation has a layered, multi-level organisational structure from the village and district levels to the state and national levels. The core urban unit is the *mandal* (ward). Intra-party elections take place regularly, though these are rarely contested and leadership succession is usually settled by consensus at all levels. The party has remained one of the most cohesive of Indian parties.[44] Intra-party conflicts lay dormant for decades until recent years when the party enjoyed power for six years and has since been out of power for two years at the time of writing. This is quite in contrast to the Congress as well as the Janata parties.

[44] Walter Andersen and Shridhar D. Damle, *The Brotherhood in Saffron* (New Delhi: Sage Vistaar, 1987); Thomas Blom Hansen, *The Saffron Wave* (New Delhi: Oxford University Press, 1999).

With its growth as a mass party in the 1990s, internal factionalism has increasingly come out into the open. The first major split was that of its Gujarat unit in 1995 in which a major state-level leader and former chief minister, Shankarsinh Vaghela, split the party, taking a large chunk of it with him, and eventually joined the Congress. Differences have been both over ideology between extremists and moderates and over the fruits of office, especially in its stronghold states in northern, central, and western India. During the years in power, the BJP, as the party in power, gained ascendancy over the RSS and the rest of the Sangh Parivar, a trend that was resented by the latter as signifying, among other things, ideological dilution in the interest of managing a diverse coalition and staying in power. This is not surprising and parallels the gap between the governmental and organisational wings of the party and its front organisations that has been seen in a variety of mass parties in democracies.

The Janata Family of Parties[45]

The Janata family of parties can be traced back to the Congress Socialist Party of the 1930s, a faction within the larger Congress-led national movement. It was pro-land reform, rural-based, and wanted to steer the centrist Congress party towards its own more pro-poor peasant, socialist-ideological ends. After 1947, some of the socialists left the Congress to form socialist parties, which

[45] This account of the Janata family of parties relies heavily on Sridharan and Varshney, "Toward Political Pluralism", in Larry Diamond and Richard Gunther, eds, *Political Parties and Democracy* (Baltimore and London: Johns Hopkins University Press, 2001), and on state-wise accounts of Congress dominance and decline in Richard Sisson and Ramashray Roy, eds, *Diversity and Dominance in Indian Politics*, vols I and II (New Delhi: Sage, 1990); Francine R. Frankel, "Middle Castes and Classes", in Atul Kohli, ed., *India's Democracy* (Princeton: Princeton University Press, 1988); Francine R. Frankel and M.S.A. Rao, eds, *Dominance and State Power in Modem India*, vols I and II (New Delhi: Oxford University Press, 1989).

became the single largest group of non-Congress parties by vote share during in the 1950s. They disliked the landlord- and upper-caste dominated organisational machinery of the Congress party at the district and state levels, as well as its promotion of big industry instead of agriculture. Ram Manohar Lohia, a socialist MP advocated the coming together of all non-Congress parties in a broad-front anti-Congress alliance to avoid splitting the non-Congress majority vote which repeatedly converted the plurality vote of the Congress into a seat majority. These developments led to the formation of non-Congress coalition governments in several major Indian states in the period 1967–71, when the Congress lost eight major states to such alliances in the state assembly elections. In the general elections held after the lifting of the Emergency (1975–7), in which democratic freedoms and civil liberties were suspended, four non-Congress parties came together to form the Janata party, also a broad, multi-ethnic coalitional or congress party, and won a thumping victory.

The Janata party of 1977–9 has by now split into so many parties that it is best to describe the entire set as the Janata family, although its offshoots are in different coalitions and they do not constitute a political cluster or front with a common programme. In terms of vote share for the period 1977–89, the Janata family of parties was collectively the next largest to the Congress, losing that position to the BJP from 1991. All the various splinter groups are essentially based on particular state-specific caste blocs, mobilised through primordial ties and the promise of a share in power, and are somewhere between multi-ethnic coalitional parties and ethnic parties.

However, the original Janata party was a fractious party composed of incompatible elements ranging from the Hindu nationalist right to the socialist left. It failed to develop an organisation, let alone conduct party elections, and in July 1979 it split into two factions. In the 1980 elections, the two factions of the Janata party won 19.0 per cent votes (31 seats) and 9.4 per cent votes (41 seats) respectively, as against the Congress' 42.7 per cent and 353 seats. After this defeat, the Janata party disintegrated. In 1989, after a gap of eight years, the party was reborn as Janata Dal, led by V.P. Singh, former finance minister (and prime minister later in 1989–90), and was given a lower-caste-based peasant orientation once again with the August 1990 decision to reserve 27 per cent of government jobs for OBCs based on caste criteria, in addition to reservation for the SCs and STs. In the 1989 elections the Janata Dal had won 17.7 per cent of the vote and 142 out of a total of 543 seats.

However, personality clashes between ambitious leaders tore the party apart. In 1991, reduced by a split, the rump of the party that retained the name Janata Dal received 11.8 per cent of the vote and 59 seats. In the 1996 elections, after another split, the rump that again retained the name Janata Dal got 8.1 per cent of the vote and 46 seats. Before the 1998 elections, it underwent two splits, and was more or less was decimated. The rump that yet again retained the name Janata Dal won only six seats and 3.25 per cent of the vote. In the 1998 and 1999 elections, an apparent disintegration of the Janata family of parties took place, with the virtual collapse of the United Front. Several Janata family splinters, less ideological and more power-oriented, aligned with the BJP-led coalition of parties. A year after the BJP's exit from power, the various offshoots of the Janata family of parties remain in different coalitions led by the BJP and the Congress with some major offshoots like the Samajwadi Party in the key northern state of UP remaining independent.

The support base of the Janata family of parties has consisted of small peasant proprietors of the lower castes, whose interests were not adequately represented in the caste coalitions that underpinned the Congress, and whose special demands for social justice, subsequently, were not recognised by Hindu nationalists. This peasant proprietor base went in different directions in different states during the successive splits suffered by the party to the Samajwadi Party in UP, to the Rashtriya Janata Dal and Samata

Party in Bihar, and to the splinter Biju Janata Dal in Orissa, as the BJP successfully attempted to co-opt intermediate caste peasant proprietors, playing on their fears of job quotas for some castes and the mobililisation of SC landless labour.

However, the main weakness of the Janata family of parties is and has always been organisational. They have been the most weakly organised of the major political parties in India, and have never had credible organisational elections. Why has the Janata family of parties not been able to put together a cohesive front? Their potential unity has problems of both a vertical and a horizontal nature and the lower castes have their own internal hierarchy, varying state by state, for they include the OBCs as well as the SCs. As a result, an internal differentiation within the presumed "lower-caste" unity has emerged. In some states like UP, the SCs have openly rebelled against the lower castes, calling them the new oppressors.

There are also problems of horizontal aggregation across states since the "lower castes" in one state may have little to do with the "lower castes" elsewhere because the specifics of the caste hierarchy as well as particular castes themselves are unique to particular states, as are their "oppressor" castes. And as part of being less institutionalised, the Janata family parties are even less allied to formal civil society organisations.

The Left Parties, Regional Parties, and the Bahujan Samaj Party

As far as organisation, nomination of candidates, fund-raising and distribution, and other key political decisions, the Left parties, the various regional parties, and the SC-based BSP, one of the fastest rising parties in India in terms of votes, are as top-down in their functioning as the major parties described. This does not mean that they are as weakly organised as the Janata family parties. Some of them, such as the Left parties, the DMK in Tamil Nadu, the fascistic Shiv

Sena in Maharashtra, and some others may be relatively tightly organised, but they remain essentially top-down, not decentralised or internally democratic. Key decisions like nominations, finance, and electoral strategies are decided by party leaders or oligarchies. All of these parties, beginning with the CPI in 1964, have undergone at least minor splits, most them quite a few times, and in many major cases over clashes between rival leaders.

Conclusion: Democracy, the Accommodation of Diversity in Indian Parties and the American and Other International Experience

In this section we try to put forward some tentative conclusions from the American and European experience for the prospects of democracy within the major Indian parties, principally for the Congress party and other middle-of-the-road national parties and its implications for the political management of diversity. As far as the BJP is concerned, it is essentially controlled by an extraparliamentary, secretively run, highly ideological and hierarchical organisation, the RSS,[46] upon which it is crucially dependent for electoral mobilisation.[47] It is unlikely to be amenable to the kinds of internal democracy discussed in this paper. Due to its ideology, it cannot

[46] See Andersen and Damle, *The Brotherhood in Saffron;* Christophe Jaffrelot, *The Hindu Nationalist Movement in India* (New Delhi: Viking Penguin, 1996); Thomas Blom Hansen, *The Saffron Wave*, op. cit.; Thomas Blom Hansen and Christophe Jaffrelot, *The BJP and the Compulsions of Politics in India* (New Delhi: Oxford University Press, 2001); Partha S. Ghosh, *The BJP and the Evolution of Hindu Nationalism: From Periphery to Centre* (New Delhi: Manohar, 2000).

[47] This is clear from the literature on the BJP and RSS and was clear to me in an election survey in the 1999 elections that there is no BJP cadre distinct from the RSS cadre; the BJP is totally dependent on the RSS and its affiliates, not only for election campaigning but also for inter-election political work. The relative autonomy of the parliamentary party leadership is only relative and is under continuous pressure.

be expected to be accommodative of Muslim and Christian minorities beyond purely token and tactical gestures. However, it has tried to accommodate the OBCs and Dalits, as well as persons from regions like the South and East which are not its traditional sphere of influence, through a process of "social engineering" and stage-managed intra-party democracy, which has been electorally fairly successful.

Our principal conclusion is that, since the late 1960s, the umbrella Congress party has both failed to retain its traditional voter base and failed to accommodate newly mobilised regional and caste groups, and this is crucially related to the erosion of the mechanisms of intra-party democracy. The lack of intra-party democracy has led to splits in the party, and likewise, splitting of other parties and the emergence of new parties based explicitly on region, language, and caste, state-wise, to give expression to the aspirations for empowerment of state-specific ethnic groups. However, splits are also due to clashes, factional, personality, or interest groups, in addition to the lack of accommodation of social diversity. Conversely, lack of internal democracy alone need not lead to splits. The most tightly organised but top-down parties of the ideological extremes have also been the least split-prone – the BJP, Shiv Sena, and the Left parties.

Thus, the pattern of accommodation of diversity has shifted from the classic umbrella party mechanism – Kothari's party of consensus[48] – to a politics of presence in which parties are based on specific ethnic groups. In other words, there is a shift to the representation of diversity by a host of parties rather than the negotiated accommodation of diversity within a few major parties. Electoral and governing coalitions of such parties are now the much less stable and more confrontational mechanism for the accommodation of diversity. This is in sharp contrast to the American pattern of two internally democratic and decentralised catch-all parties.

[48] See Rajni Kothari, *Politics in India*, op. cit.

We also conclude that the most important feature of internal democracy in the American parties – American-style primaries – are not feasible in the Indian parties because they presuppose state regulation of party processes; registration of voters with a declaration of party identification, a declaration most Indian voters will not be ready to make; a fairly stable two-party system, unlike the current flux in the Indian party system since 1989; and fairly high and stable party identification. None of these obtain in the Indian situation and are likely to in the foreseeable future, quite apart from the fact that primaries may lead to the further disintegration of already highly unstable and split-prone parties.

Even European-style primaries, managed by party managers under party rules, as was supposed to have existed, in theory, in the Congress party before the suspension of internal elections since 1972, are open to a great deal of abuse. In fact, the system began to break down in the 1960s precisely over the bogus membership issue, party membership being something that can be manipulated in what is still a largely rural and poor country.

However, even a return to such a system of internal democracy in what is a less poor, less illiterate, more politically aware selectorate than in the 1960s, one in which it is easier to maintain verifiable membership records, given current information technology, and one in which elections to the third tier of local government give the public experience that can translate into party elections, can go a long way in democratising parties. At the very least, it can help federalise, if not democratise from bottom-up, the structure of political parties. That is, decentralising power within the leadership of parties so that power is not excessively concentrated at the national leadership level. This would be a very important first step. Some such institutionalisation of internal democracy and accountability within political parties would also be necessary if any sort of state funding of elections is to be instituted. The latter is a step that can potentially push internal democracy much further.[49]

[49] E. Sridharan, "Toward State Funding of Elections in India", op. cit.

In the present situation of a near-total lack of democracy within parties, a return to internal party elections, by party rules, and under party management, where the selectorate are "active members" by some organisational criteria, beginning from the district and state levels, would be a very important first step. This would also provide incentives to newly mobilised social groups and would-be party formateurs to work within the rules of existing parties to try to capture a greater share of power in such parties, whether in terms of party offices or election nominations or influence in the shaping of party policy on issues of concern to them. Democratising of parties could help to shift the process of accommodation of social diversity away from the formation of new parties, which try to win as many seats as possible and then bargain for power in (inevitably fractious) electoral and government coalitions, to one in which emergent groups try to work within, and are accommodated within, existing parties. This would also bolster the governance capacities of the party/parties in government and that of the state by making parties more inclusive.

Acknowledgements

I would like to acknowledge the financial support of the Ford Foundation for this study and the project it is a part of. I would like to thank Pradeep Chhibber, Larry Diamond, Samuel Eldersveld, Scott Mainwaring, Jack Nagel, Marc Plattner, Austin Ranney, Ashutosh Varshney, and Ray Wolfinger who made time for me during a visit to the United States on this project for a month in October–November 2000, and particularly Douglas Verney who gave me detailed comments on a first draft. Neera Chandhoke, Peter de Souza, Nathan Glazer, Arend Lijphart, Juan Linz, Alfred Stepan, and Zoya Hasan gave me useful feedback and suggestions for follow-up after the mid-term and final workshops of the project. K.P. Vijayalakshmi suggested and gave me useful readings. I alone am responsible for the views expressed here.

3

Does India Need to Switch to Proportional Representation? The Pros and Cons

A SIGNIFICANT TREND IN Indian politics since the decline of the encompassing, umbrella Congress party since 1989, compared to the Congress heyday of 1947–89 particularly 1947–67, is the rise of identity politics and parties based on ascriptive identities at the national and state levels.[1] This includes, most importantly, Hindu majoritarianism manifested in the rise of the Bharatiya Janata Party (BJP) and the like-minded Shiv Sena in Maharashtra, Kashmiri Muslim secessionist insurgency since 1989, and the rise to prominence and consolidation of one-state regional political parties including the Dravidian parties in Tamil Nadu, the Akali Dal in Punjab, the Asom Gana Parishad in Assam and the Telugu Desam Party in Andhra Pradesh. Identity politics also encompasses continuing secessionist insurgencies in Assam, Nagaland, and Manipur, and movements within some states to secede and form new states in parts of existing states. Of the latter movements, the Uttarakhand movement in Uttar Pradesh, the Jharkhand movement in Bihar, and the Chhattisgarh movement in Madhya Pradesh have been successful, with these three new states having been created since 2000, while Telangana was created in 2014. Lastly, the

[1] I thank Arend Lijphart and Douglas Verney for detailed comments on a much earlier draft, and Jack Nagel for useful suggestions.

rise of the Bahujan Samaj Party (BSP) is a manifestation of a sharpened pan-Indian Dalit identity. The Samajwadi Party of Uttar Pradesh and the Rashtriya Janata Dal of Bihar also have distinct caste bases. Communal extremism and secessionism on the part of some religious and/or ethnic minority-dominated states (most notably Kashmir) and the Hindu majoritarianism of the BJP have at times fed on each other in a downward spiral of social tensions and the spread of communal fears and prejudices.

The question that arises is: is the rise of such forces over time and the social cost in terms of the fears of majority domination, political marginalisation, and cultural submergence, and the furies they unleash, ultimately rooted, at least in part, in the majoritarian bias of the single-member, simple plurality system, also known in common parlance as the first-past-the-post (FPTP) electoral system?

If so, is there a possible rationale for considering a switch to a proportional representation (PR) system? A PR system, because of its rough vote-seat proportionality, unlike the vote-seat disproportionality of the FPTP system, could arguably tend to represent parties roughly proportional to their votes and indirectly allow minorities to be better represented. It would also tend to throw up coalition governments, since the likely vote pluralities which have characterised Indian parliamentary elections throughout would not convert to seat majorities. The imperatives of coalition politics would lead to a more accommodative politics based on bargaining and compromise, which could help build consensus on major national policy issues. It could thus prevent the emergence of steamroller majorities at the centre, at least, if not in the states, relatively empower numerically small minorities, by every criterion, and reduce the magnification of pluralities into steamroller majorities.

This paper explores the possible options in switching to a PR system and then discusses the possible consequences in terms of greater representativeness and party system changes.[2] However, I

[2] The debate on this issue in India began with a working paper, "Reform of

reiterate at the outset that I am *not* advocating the PR system or any variant of it. Rather, what I am attempting is to explore the consequences of the adoption of PR for the solution of potential problems that would arguably favour such an adoption.

The FPTP System, Magnified Majoritarianism, and the Intensification of Minority Fears and "Ethnic" Tensions

How is the FPTP system negatively linked to communal, regional, and caste tensions? The FPTP system tends to magnify the legislative and hence, indirectly, the executive strength of the single largest party and, in "ethnicised" party systems, the power of the social groups dominant in, and the ideology of, the single largest party. Parties with only a plurality can win a majority, even a two-thirds or three-quarters (as in 1984) majority. In 2014, the BJP won a simple majority of 52 per cent seats on the basis of a 31 per cent vote share, a conversion ratio of 1.67, the highest in parliamentary elections so far. In FPTP systems, the collective majority of voters can remain unrepresented in the government formed. This has always been the case in India as all governments at the centre have been formed only on the basis of a plurality, not a simple majority of votes. If this pattern of votes had been cast in a PR system, then all governments in India would have been minority governments or would have had to form coalitions with additional parties to form

---

Electoral Laws", by the Law Commission of India, discussed at a public symposium in New Delhi on 23–24 January 1999 (Law Commission of India 1999). The paper recommended increasing the number of seats in the Lok Sabha by 25 per cent (of the maximum of 550) to 138, these seats to be allotted to candidates of political parties on the basis of their pre-declared list (the list system) according to the parties' vote share in states, some smaller states being lumped together in territorial constituencies. For example, Andhra Pradesh with 42 Lok Sabha seats would have 11 extra seats to be filled on a party vote share basis going down the party list.

majority governments. The lack of representation in the executive for the majority of voters under such FPTP outcomes can, over time, lead to feelings of frustration, even political powerlessness. If, as in the England of the nineteenth and early twentieth centuries, where the FPTP system based on progressively universal franchise evolved, the society in which the electoral system is adopted is relatively homogeneous in ethnic, linguistic, and religious terms, the pluralities and majorities that one considers are not only numerical but also felt to be only numerical.

However, in societies with "ethnic" (I use the term "ethnic" to include ethnic, racial, religious, linguistic, caste, tribal, and other ascriptive) differences, some of these being territorially demarcated, the numerical pluralities or majorities in votes and majorities in seats also tend to coincide with such ethnic boundaries, creating a perception of these boundaries as cleavages. The sense of powerlessness of those who are unrepresented in government and/or under-represented in national and state legislatures because they belong to minority groups by one or the other criteria, that is, those who are structurally in a permanent minority, can actually reinforce ethnic identities and identity politics. This process can be of an extreme kind, and it can lead to a majoritarian backlash and identity reinforcement among majority or dominant groups.

Why was the long period of Congress rule, enabled by the FPTP system, especially in the 1950s and 1960s, characterised by less regional, communal, and caste tensions than the period since 1989? One can argue that the rise in identity politics was relatively constrained during the heyday of Congress dominance in the 1950s and 1960s due to the Congress being an internally (relatively) democratic and coalitional party that sought to accommodate all interests. Second, parties of religious and caste identities and separatist regional parties were relatively weak in the first three decades of independence partly due to the delegitimisation of the Rashtriya Swayamsevak Sangh (RSS) following the assassination of Gandhi and the ascendancy of Nehru, and the fact that the consolidation of a pan-Indian Hindu identity was inevitably a slow process. Third, brute majoritarianism was constrained by two institutional (and constitutional) features of Indian democracy. One was the presence of fundamental rights and judicial review as essential features of the Constitution and therefore a part of its basic structure. These included cultural and educational rights of religious and linguistic minorities and the right to constitutional remedies. The second was the key feature, as Lijphart (1996) has argued, of the reorganisation of states on linguistic lines from 1956. This accommodated regional ethno-linguistic identities and prevented conflict on those lines, except for the outbreak of anti-Hindi riots in Tamil Nadu in the mid-1960s, a situation which was accommodatively handled by the central government. Taken together, these features checked or qualified majoritarianism at the national level and, to a lesser extent, at the state level, helping to contain possible polarisation on Hindu versus religious minorities/Muslim lines or Hindi versus non-Hindi lines.

However, with the suspension of internal democracy within the Congress, and the centralisation of its functioning since the early 1970s, the party's capacity to accommodate the demands of emerging, politically assertive interests such as intermediate-caste farmers, regional movements, and later Muslims and Scheduled Castes, was greatly weakened. This led to the gradual drift away from what was seen as an unresponsive party and to the more particularistic assertion of their interests by such groups in the form of regional and other parties such as the Janata Dal, the Samajwadi Party and the BSP.

With the rise of assertive identity politics since the 1990s, the polarisation of Indian politics on religious and caste lines, and the spread of feelings of powerlessness and alienation among important sections of the population – both religious minorities and regional or caste-defined sections – have been potential dangers to India's unity. It also exposes the limits of the checks on steamroller majoritarianism that fundamental rights and linguistic federalism embody, especially in the politically and culturally crucial areas of educational and linguistic rights at the national and state levels, the contest for symbolic space in the public sphere and the mass media, and even in protection for minorities from physical violence against their lives, property, and religious and cultural heritage.

Structural majorities, of course, exist and will continue to do so because the ethnic composition of the population is stable. The point here is that structural majorities become dangerous for national integration and political stability when structural ethno-political majorities emerge at the national and/or state level. Here religious, linguistic and other ethnic divisions begin to wholly or largely coincide with political or party identification, thus leading to clear ethno-political fault lines. Such ethno-political majorities have destroyed or riven polities such as Sri Lanka, Cyprus, Northern Ireland, and other ethno-politically polarised societies, in which a vicious circle of mutual reinforcement through action and reaction between politically dominant majority ethnic groups and politically subordinated minority groups reinforces identity politics of extreme and uncompromising kinds.

The point here is that the FPTP system not only conduces to such growth over time by the mechanisms of domination and powerlessness, action and reaction, under certain circumstances, but also offers only very weak mechanisms for accommodation and stable coalition building once identities harden and are reinforced by political mobilisation strategies that deliberately seek to divide people on ethnic lines along with their inevitable ideological package of political mythologies and mythologised histories. One is not arguing that this is necessarily so under the FPTP system. On the contrary, the *aggregative imperative* of the system to achieve the pluralities necessary for winning seats conduces to bargaining and compromise among groups. However, it can also be extremely exclusionary – for example, a possible pan-Indian Hindu consolidation (a declared goal of the BJP and its RSS-spawned sister organisations) that marginalises religious minorities, particularly Muslims. What is crucial is whether political and ethnic identities get consolidated along the same lines of cleavage.

The FPTP system is particularly exclusionary for minorities that are distributed so as to be in a minority almost everywhere lacking majorities at either state or constituency levels. This applies especially to Muslims who are in a majority only in Jammu and Kashmir state and in four constituencies in Bihar, Telangana, and Lakshadweep, the population so covered being under 14 per cent of the Muslim population.[3] Elsewhere, Muslims are 40–50 per cent of the population only in 9 constituencies, 20–40 per cent in 64 constituencies, 10–20 per cent in 168 constituencies, and below 10 per cent in 287 constituencies. This applies to a lesser extent to Christians, in a majority only in Meghalaya, Nagaland, and Mizoram, and perhaps a couple of constituencies in Kerala, covering only a small minority of the Christian population. The Scheduled Castes are distributed as a minority almost everywhere including in reserved constituencies, making the non-Scheduled Caste vote decisive even in such constituencies. The Scheduled Tribes are geographically much more concentrated, enjoying majorities or near-majorities in many of their reserved constituencies. However, they are not the majority in any state except Arunachal Pradesh, Meghalaya, Mizoram, and Nagaland, the population in these states totalling under 5 per cent of the Scheduled Tribe population.[4]

This perceived minority character can potentially also apply to upper-caste Hindus if a consolidation of Other Backward Classes, Scheduled Castes, and Scheduled Tribes takes place on the lines of the BSP's ideally desired original Bahujan concept, for example, and is arguably the case de facto for the Brahmins in Tamil Nadu. It can also be the case in most states for the inevitably growing ethno-linguistic minorities at the state level who are economic migrants from other states. And if the differential rates of population growth at the state level are projected a few decades into the future,

[3] See Rudolph and Rudolph (1987), p. 196, Table 16, for constituency estimates.

[4] See Bose (1996) for the state (not constituency) percentages of Muslims, Christians and Scheduled Tribes.

with the Hindi-speaking states' populations growing faster than those of the South, Hindi speakers may well become a simple majority who could, hypothetically, possibly seek to impose Hindi as the sole official language at the central level on the rest of the country.[5]

All of the possible minorities are vulnerable to steamroller majoritarianism at the national and/or state levels, with all the consequences that such developments can unleash – suspicion, fear, perceived powerlessness, fury, violence, backlash, instability, chaos, and even national disintegration. This points to the need to qualify the political system's majoritarian tendencies in the interest of long-term social and political stability. One way, without changing the electoral system, is to define the fundamental rights more precisely, especially as regards the extension of individual rights to derivative group rights, with special attention to religion, places of worship, and cultural heritage sites and structures, place names, language, script, educational rights, second official language status in the states, and the like. Such an extension of individual fundamental rights to derivative group rights and freedoms can be intellectually justified.[6] This would qualify majoritarianism by limiting the range and extent of basic policies and institutions which can be altered by legislative majorities or by executive order.

A second way, and one which is not a policy option but a development that has to come about in the natural course of political evolution if it is to happen at all, is the reconstruction of an internally grand-coalitional umbrella party, like the Congress party was in its heyday, in which coalition politics was played out within the

[5] See McMillan (2000) for projections of seats lost or gained by states in the event of inter-state reallocation of seats on the basis of the 1991 and projected 2001 censuses. The latter projection shows that Tamil Nadu (6) and Kerala (3) would lose 9 seats, the southern states 11 seats, while the Hindi-speaking states would gain 15 seats, Uttar Pradesh alone gaining 7.

[6] See Chandhoke (1999) for an argument justifying group rights for minorities derivable from and compatible with liberal-democratic individual rights; see also Rajan (1998).

party and electoral politics was not being played out along lines of social cleavage.

A third way, not in contradiction to at least the first, is to change the electoral system to some variant of PR to ensure better representation of minorities, especially the thinly spread minorities most vulnerable to underrepresentation, and simultaneously ensure that coalition and/or minority governments are more faithfully representative of the popular vote as well as more stable, and hence coherent in terms of policy and governance. However, it would be necessary to simultaneously ensure that PR's tendency towards extreme fragmentation of the party system by undermining the FPTP system's incentive to aggregate votes, and hence to build social coalitions, is checked.

The Implications of Various PR and Mixed Systems for India

Coming to the main types of PR and mixed PR systems, the focus of interest here is the way in which the various PR variants affect: (a) the proportionality or otherwise of both party and ethnic minority representation, and voters' control of party lists which impinge on the following two characteristics; (b) legislative fragmentation and hence the number of partners in potential coalition governments; and (c) the incentives for ethnic party formation as against politically programmatic inclusive parties.

There are two major variants of PR electoral formulae, namely, divisor or highest "average" formulae and largest remainder (LR) or quota formulae, and a third minor variant, the single transferable vote (STV).[7] The first two types of systems are also called list-PR systems, since voters cast their votes for a party list, not for individual candidates, although they may be able to express preferences

[7] For details of the various types of PR and mixed systems, see Lijphart (1994) and Taagepera and Shugart (1989). I do not describe the various electoral formulae in detail as this would take us beyond the scope of this paper.

for individual candidates within a party list. The variants in which preferences for individuals in a list can be expressed are called open-list systems as against closed-list systems. In open-list systems, the order in which seats are allocated to individual candidates on a party list is determined not only by the party's internal processes but by voters. The most common class of electoral formulae used are the highest "average" or divisor systems such as the d'Hondt or modified Sainte Lague, followed by largest remainders (LR) or quota systems such as the LR-Hare, LR-Droop, two LR-Imperiali systems. The STY system used in Ireland and Malta is a preferential system in which voters express a preference for individual candidates rather than a list system. However, STY is also a quota system since it needs to select a quota to elect a candidate. In practice, the Droop quota is always used. If most voters vote on party lines, it becomes, in effect, like an open-list PR system.

There are also a variety of semi-proportional systems such as the single non-transferable vote (SNTV) used in Japan during 1947–93. This system is important for it is very favourable for minority representation. This is a multi-member district (constituency) system that employs the simple plurality formula where the voter has a single vote. Candidates in a district get seats in order of the number of votes. Thus, parties can run several candidates, hoping to get all or several of the seats in a district, and these candidates will effectively be competing against not only other party candidates but also against each other, introducing party and candidate-centred and, implicitly, ascriptive characteristics-centred competition. In Japan, SNTV with an average district magnitude of four seats had an upper threshold, above which a candidate is guaranteed a seat, of the Droop quota of 20 per cent (that is, 100%/M + 1), much lower than FPTP though it is also a plurality system amounting to a semi-PR but not true PR system (Lijphart 1994: 39–42).

The key variables that influence proportionality of representation are the electoral formula, district magnitude or the number of legislators returned by each district, and effective thresholds of representation and exclusion. The general findings about the proportionality of different PR variants are as follows. The single most important variable affecting proportionality is district magnitude. The larger the district magnitude, the more proportional the representation of parties at the district level and, by extension, at the national level. However, this is subject to the assembly size being large enough; the larger the assembly size, the more proportional the representation. In most PR systems, average district magnitudes vary from at least 5 seats per district upwards to 120 or 150, or the whole country as a single district, as in Israel and the Netherlands, in sharp contrast to the Anglo-American and Indian single-member districts. Some countries also have two-tier districting, with smaller-magnitude districts in the lower tier, the upper tier often being a national district in which seat allocations compensate for the disproportionality at the lower tier. In the German system, now adopted in New Zealand with modifications, this is carried to its extreme with the lower-tier districts being single-member districts using the plurality rule (FPTP). The German system can be regarded as a mixture of plurality rule and PR, but it is in effect a PR system since the upper-tier compensation formula works to produce proportionality in the Parliament as a whole, not in the upper tier alone. Italy, which shifted from pure PR to a mixed system in the 1990s, is a better example of a mixed system in that proportionality in the upper tier is limited to allocation of seats in that tier alone. The Japanese system, post-1994, is a mixed system in which three-fifths of the seats are contested on the basis of FPTP and two-fifths on the basis of PR, and the two are not connected to each other; it is in effect a parallel, and not a mixed, system.

Second, as far as the effect of electoral formula on proportionality is concerned, the d'Hondt and LR-Imperiali quota systems are the least proportional, discriminating against small parties and relatively advantaging the largest parties. The modified Sainte Lague, LR-Droop quota, and STY form an intermediate category, while the LR-Hare quota system is the most proportional. It should be remembered, however, that even the least proportional PR systems are more proportional than FPTP, even for the largest parties.

Third, proportionality is also affected by the use of legal thresholds, usually a minimum percentage of the vote, to be eligible for representation in the assembly. However, even in the absence of legal thresholds, as is in fact the case in the majority of PR systems, effective thresholds are determined by the combination of electoral formula and district magnitude, especially the latter, which is a barrier to small-party representation. The issue of effective thresholds and proportionality is complicated by the fact that the effective threshold is a range rather than a fixed percentage, and can be conceived of as having an upper and a lower bound. The upper bound is the threshold of exclusion or the maximum percentage of the vote under the most unfavourable conditions that may be insufficient for a party to win a seat. Anything over this guarantees a seat. The lower bound or threshold of representation (or inclusion) is the minimum percentage of the vote, under the most favourable conditions, that can win a party a seat. The exact effective threshold in any particular system would lie somewhere between these upper and lower bounds and would be determined by district magnitude, the electoral formula, and the number of competing parties.

Lijphart (1994: 26) arrives at an average upper threshold of 100%/M+1 vote percentage, where M is the district magnitude. For instance, in a 10-seat district, for a party to win a seat it would have to win at least 9 per cent of the vote; in a 5-seat district, at least 17 per cent of the vote. These are much lower percentages than anything conceivable under FPTP. For example, in a small (for PR systems) district of 5 seats, one-sixth of the votes would be sufficient for winning a seat but not one-tenth, whereas in a 10-member district, one-eleventh would be sufficient. Compare these cases with an average effective threshold of 35 per cent of the vote under FPTP in an Indian single-member constituency for general elections during 1952–84, and likewise for post-war elections in the UK, Canada, Australia, New Zealand, and USA (Congressional) (Lijphart 1994: 17, Table 2.1). Lijphart has, with Taagepera, modified his formula for effective threshold to 75%/(M+1) which yields even lower effective thresholds for every district magnitude. By this formula, the effective threshold under FPTP is 37.5 per cent, while for a 5-seat district it falls from one-sixth to 12.5 per cent or one-eighth (ibid.: 182–3, n. 29).

Without getting into the extremely complex details of the great variety of PR systems possible, let us try to apply these findings to India and see what they would imply. At the outset, one would have to take into account the fact that there are several important differences between India and almost any other democratic society. These include India's extreme heterogeneity: its federal system which creates and sustains a national party system (in flux) that is really an aggregation of distinct state-level party systems; its political parties which are relatively uninstitutionalised, not internally democratic, and highly prone to splits and mergers; and the large number of small parties, usually based in single states. What this implies for proportionality is that a very proportional party system, that is, one with large district magnitudes and/or a highly proportional formula leading to low thresholds of exclusion and representation, would lead to a great number of small parties winning seats and a highly fragmented legislature, and, hence, unstable coalitions with a large number of parties.

Such a system may be good from the point of view of representation of small parties and minorities, especially territorially thinly spread minorities, but it may be bad from the point of view of coalition stability and effective governance. However, the representation of minorities would also critically depend, in list PR systems, on whether open-list or closed-list systems are followed. The former allow strategic voting, and facilitate minorities getting representation for their candidates within their preferred parties. In closed-list systems, minority representation depends on internal democracy and accommodative politics being practised within parties. If lists are the prerogative of party leaders, which would most likely be the case given that all of India's parties are top-down in their internal functioning, such effects may be diluted.

Conversely, a highly proportional combination of electoral formula and district magnitude would also tend to reduce incentives for party aggregation and its basis, the building of coalitions of interest at the societal level, by making it easier for very small groups to gain representation. It may also tend to destabilise existing large parties and the party system by raising incentives for very small groups to bargain with several parties or to float their own parties.[8] If this happens along ethnic lines, it could create new politico-ethnic cleavages that could be socially and politically destabilising. Certain systems like STV and SNTY, while favouring minority representation, and indeed tactical voting by minorities to aid this, also tend to undermine programmatic politics and raise incentives for ethnic parties in part due to their relatively candidate-centric rather than party-centric competition.

The key issue then is one of legal and/or effective thresholds. Legal thresholds that deny representation to very small parties are a possible solution. However, in the Indian context of a federal party system, there are several parties that are significant parties in their states but may fall well below a, say, 5 per cent national threshold. One would then need to have not national legal thresholds but perhaps state-level legal thresholds in addition to district-level legal thresholds. However, legal thresholds are more relevant in the second tier of mixed-member systems like Germany where FPTP is used to fill in the first tier of single-member districts and PR the second tier of adjustment seats. Like in most PR systems, it would be possible to dispense with legal thresholds by adopting a combination of electoral formula and district magnitude that raises the effective threshold to, say, 15–20 per cent at the district level, a

[8] Ordeshook and Shvetsova (1994) have shown that multiple parties are correlated with ethnic heterogeneity, especially in PR systems.

level consistent with giving much greater representation to locally significant but considerably underrepresented parties, for example, the BSP, or to similarly placed minorities like the Scheduled Castes, Muslims, and smaller religious, linguistic, and other-state migrant minorities in their areas of relative concentration, not to speak of most of the principal castes in most states, than possible under FPTP. In fact, this would enable the abolition of the present system of reserved constituencies for Scheduled Castes and Tribes, if this is considered desirable, to achieve the same goal of ensuring adequate representation.

A combination of formula and magnitude ensuring an effective threshold of about 15–20 per cent of the district-level vote would, in combination with open-list PR, ensure adequate representation of locally significant but not miniscule parties, as well as minorities, to a far greater degree than PR, but at the same time, since it does not go down to the 0–15 per cent threshold range, preserve incentives for social coalition building and political interest aggregation into fairly substantial parties stretching to state-wide, multi-state and national levels.

However, despite these potential advantages, there are also potential difficulties due to the Indian system being a federal system. If such a system is used at the national level, a consistent, that is, appropriately scaled down, system would have to be used for state assembly elections. Such a PR system at the state level would throw up far more parties and would lead to a party system with more significant competing parties at the state level than is the case today under FPTP; most states in the 1990s had two-party or two-alliance systems. Furthermore, if a larger number of competing parties are significant at the state level, there will inevitably be more significant competing parties for parliamentary seats in each state than is now the case.

This would necessitate a far more complex process of social coalition building and pre-election alliances for parliamentary elections than is the case now, and there would be a real danger of the splintering of state-level party systems into caste- and religion-based parties, with its reflection on the national party system since the latter is an aggregation of the former. This is because with an effective threshold of 15–20 per cent for state-level assembly constituencies, or even for the much larger parliamentary assembly constituencies in states (six–seven assembly constituencies per parliamentary constituency), most significant castes or religious communities in each state, in their areas of concentration, would be assured of representation even if they ran purely caste or communal parties, since most significant castes and communities would be 5 per cent plus in the state-wide population share and much higher in areas of concentration. There is thus a real danger of PR of any type giving rise to caste and communal splintering of the party system in India, precisely because of the national party system being an aggregation of state-level systems. With the splintering of state-level party systems, quite likely on a caste and/or communal basis, one can expect coalition governments at the state level, most likely of a multi-party type, unlike the present situation in which most states have single-party majority governments. This will make for more instability at the state level, which will inevitably be reflected in pre-election alliances at the state level for parliamentary elections, and hence make for more complicated coalitions at the national level.

A possible alternative is the introduction at state and national levels of a German-type two-tier system in which the lower tier of single-member constituencies is filled by the FPTP system and an upper tier of national constituencies is filled by PR employing a closed-list system (since the voter has only one ballot). The electoral formula applied (to the votes cast in the lower tier for filling up the upper tier) can be the relatively most proportional LR-Hare formula, to compensate for FPTP's disproportionality in the lower tier. This disproportionality will be more marked if the present 543 elected seats (in India's lower house) are apportioned 50–50 to the two tiers, since the lower tier subject to FPTP will have twice as many voters per constituency as in the present system.

A vote percentage legal threshold for representation by allocation of adjustment seats for proportionality in the upper tier can be incorporated to eliminate very small parties and preserve incentives for party aggregation. This threshold can be applied not nationally but state-wise, if the upper-tier seats are to be filled by filling state quotas rather than nationally, as would be appropriate in the Indian context. An alternative state-wise seat threshold of a certain minimum number of seats in the lower-tier FPTP contest can be incorporated. The state-wise threshold could be, say, 15 per cent of the vote or 1 seat, with special arrangements for small states with under 10 seats. When we talk of state-wise thresholds, whether of votes or seats, we mean here votes or seats in the parliamentary elections from the state, for example, vote share or seats in the elections for the 48 seats (or 24 given that only half the seats will be in the FPTP lower tier) from Maharashtra, and not the 288 seats in the assembly. It should also clearly be understood that all the members of Parliament (MPs) elected, whether in the lower or upper tier, will have the same rights and obligations; there will not be two classes of MPs.

This system would tend to institutionalise disincentives against fragmentation and produce relatively less proportional results overall, and fewer small parties represented in the Parliament, hence smaller coalitions and more stable governments, all due to the effect of FPTP in the lower-tier seats. Incentives for ethnic party formation by territorial minorities will also be diluted since the effective thresholds will be higher in a semi-FPTP system despite partial compensation in the upper tier.

The drawback, however, is that only half the MPs will be directly responsible to the electorate, while the other half will be allotted seats by a necessarily closed-list system (since the voter has only one ballot), which means that who gets a seat in the upper tier, and hence the representation of various interests and minorities, depends on the internal democratic processes of political parties.

A more important drawback is that no matter what sort of PR or mixed system India might choose to adopt for a more proportional representation ofthe preferences of the electorate, the problem of steamroller legislative majoritarianism and the fear of cultural submergence for minorities by any criterion remain, since structural ethnic majorities are stable, nationally and state-wise. It would only be alleviated by the institutionalisation of better-defined fundamental rights, especially better-defined group rights directly derivable from individual rights relevant and conducive to the preservation of cultural identities, including rights to the option of education in one's language and script, use of second official languages at the state level, and sanctity of places of religious and cultural heritage and the like. A switch to PR in the absence of such extended definitions of rights and safeguards against steamroller majoritarianism would not be effective, even while contributing to more fragmented party systems, legislatures, and less stable multiparty coalition governments at both the centre and in the states. A change of electoral system to a more complicated one in a country of low educational levels in which the public would have difficulty in understanding the electoral formula would be difficult.

In conclusion, while India needs to address the problem of magnified majoritarianism and minority representation and possible alienation, changing the electoral system to some PR variant is only a second-best solution. This is because its effects have to be weighed against the removal of the FPTP system's imperative to aggregate votes and hence politicians' incentives to cast their net wide with non-polarising platforms. This is so also because PR will better protect minorities by enabling better representation only if the power of legislative majorities is qualified by more precisely defined and extended fundamental rights, including group rights affecting cultural identities that are derivable from individual rights. However, if this is effected, then PR may become redundant as a means to ensure such better protection.

References

Bose, Ashish 1996. *India's Basic Demographic Statistics* (New Delhi: BR Publishing Corporation).

Chandhoke, Neera 1999. *Beyond Secularism: The Rights of Religious Minorities* (New Delhi: Oxford University Press).

Law Commission of India 1999. *Law Commission Report No. 170: Reform of the Electoral Laws*, https://www.latestlaws.comllibrary/law-commission-of-india -reports/law -commission-report -no-170 reform-of-the-electoral-laws-1999/, accessed 15 July 2019.

Lijphart, Arend 1994. *Electoral Systems and Party Systems: A Study of Twenty-Seven Democracies, 1945–1990* (New York: Oxford University Press).

—— 1996. "The Puzzle of Indian Democracy: A Consociational Interpretation", *American Political Science Review*, 90 (2), pp. 258–68.

McMillan, Alistair 2000. "Delimitation, Democracy and End of Constitutional Freeze", *Economic and Political Weekly*, 35 (15), pp. 1271–76.

Ordeshook, Peter C. and Olga Shvetsova 1994. "Ethnic Heterogeneity, District Magnitude and the Number of Parties", *American Journal of Political Science*, 38 (4), pp. 100–23.

Rajan, Nalini 1998. "Multiculturalism, Group Rights and Identity Politics", *Economic and Political Weekly*, 33 (27), pp. 1699–1701.

Rudolph, Lloyd, and Susanne Rudolph 1987. *In Pursuit of Lakshmi: The Political Economy of the Indian State* (Chicago: University of Chicago Press).

Taagepera, Rein, and Matthew Soberg Shugart 1989. *Seats and Votes: The Effects and Determinants of Electoral Systems* (New Haven: Yale University Press).

4

Is the Coalition Era Over in Indian Politics?

Introduction

India has had seven consecutive elections (1989–2009) in which no single party won a majority of seats in the Lok Sabha (lower house), resulting in minority situations (hung parliaments) whose solutions were in all cases minority governments dependent on external support. In 1991, the Congress formed a single-party minority government (which achieved a majority halfway through its term), but in all other cases minority coalitions dependent on external support were formed, these being large multiparty coalitions with the participation of several regional parties since 1996.[1] With the Bharatiya Janata Party (BJP) winning a majority in the 2014 election, the question arises as to whether the coalition era in Indian politics is over and a new era of majority governments, led this time by the BJP, replacing the Congress, has begun. In this article, we analyse the nature of the BJP majority and the state of the opposition and conclude that coalition politics – particularly the importance of pre-electoral coalitions for victory, coalition government for effective governance, and for the BJP's future expansion – remains very much alive, and that the coalition era is not over.

[1] See Sridharan 2012 for details of governments formed during the coalition era elections, 1989–2009.

Importance of Pre-Electoral Coalitions

We begin by looking at pre-electoral coalitions in the coalition era that began in 1989. In the run-up to all elections since 1989, particularly since 1998, one of the keys to victory for both the leading national parties, the Congress and the BJP, is the number of state-level pre-electoral coalitions formed, for pooling votes based on seat-sharing agreements.

Why pre-electoral coalitions? What are the incentives for national parties to form such coalitions, and under what circumstances? Given the first-past-the-post system, aggregation of votes at the constituency level is vital for winning seats. By implication, given the breakdown of the national party system into distinct state party systems, the formation of alliances with parties commanding a significant state-level vote share helps aggregate constituency-level votes shares in states where one's own party is not strong enough to go it alone. Pre-electoral coalitions have the potential to increase the number of seats won, although at the expense of conceding a certain number of seats to allies, and also including such allies in a post-election government.

The underlying principle is that a third party could leverage expected vote share in states where it is perceived to be a significant third party with a potentially "bridging vote share", i.e. perceived pivotality for electoral victory, helps it to form electoral coalitions with the first or second parties in the states in which it is allocated more seats to contest than in the previous elections.[2]

The BJP, since 1989, has grown partly on the basis of its own ideological appeal and mobilisation and partly by leveraging coalitions,[3] while the Congress turned to coalitions with success in 2004.[4]

[2] Sridharan 2005, p. 197.
[3] Sridharan 2005.
[4] Sridharan 2004.

What were the impacts of pre-electoral coalitions – or their absence – in 2004 and 2009 on Congress victories and BJP defeats? In 2004, coalitions – or the absence of a coalition for the BJP – played a key role in the very narrow victory of the United Progressive Alliance (UPA).[5] Coalitions in Tamil Nadu, Andhra Pradesh, Bihar, Jharkhand, and Jammu and Kashmir, and the absence of a coalition for the BJP in Haryana, Assam, and Jharkhand were critical for the UPA, as were coalitions in Maharashtra and Goa – with the Nationalist Congress Party (NCP) compared with the absence of such in 1999 – to reduce defeat margins. Similarly, in Orissa and Punjab coalitions were critical to National Democratic Alliance (NDA) victories. In 2009, the Congress was critically dependent, despite a swing in its favour and a swing against the BJP, on pre-electoral coalitions in Maharashtra, West Bengal, and Tamil Nadu, besides its long-standing United Democratic Front (UDF) coalition in Kerala.

The general finding on pre-electoral coalitions is that the seat-sharing ratio between partners tends to get stuck in a narrow band, and not adjust smoothly upward or downward according to the demands of a partner perceiving its popularity to be on the upswing demanding more seats. For example, both the Congress–NCP and BJP–Shiv Sena coalitions in Maharashtra, the BJP–Janata Dal (United) (JD[U]) coalition in Bihar and the BJP–Akali Dal coalition in Punjab, as well as the Left Front coalitions in West Bengal and Kerala, and the Congress-led UDF coalition in Kerala, all tended to remain stable in their seat-sharing ratios over the past two or more elections, with adjustments happening within a very narrow band.[6] It is only when old coalitions are discarded and new coalitions are formed that new ratios can be established. In this we would expect parties that are perceived to be on the upswing to be able to attract more allies and on more favourable terms.

[5] See Sridharan 2004 for details.

[6] Sridharan 2014.

If one compares the pre-electoral coalitions for 2009 with 2014 for both alliances, NDA and UPA, this is precisely what we can see. The BJP struck a range of new alliances, most of them on more favourable terms than in the past, while retaining its key old alliances (Shiv Sena, Akali Dal) on the same terms. Thus, in 2014 the BJP had pre-electoral alliances in 10 states (Tables 4.1 and 4.2) compared with six alliances in 2009 in which both it and its partner(s) contested seats, of which seven were new alliances – Bihar, former Andhra Pradesh, Tamil Nadu, Haryana, Kerala, Meghalaya and Uttar Pradesh (UP) – and on more favourable terms, contesting more seats than in earlier alliances in Bihar, former Andhra Pradesh, Tamil Nadu, and Haryana.

The BJP pursued a strategy whereby it could increase the geographical breadth and extent of its alliances. Accordingly, it made its electoral partnership with the Shiv Sena in Maharashtra but expanded the alliance to include parties such as Swabhimani Paksha, Republican Party of India (A) (RPI[A]), and Rashtriya Samaj Paksha (RSP). In Bihar, the BJP resumed its earlier pre-2002 partnership with the Lok Janshakti Party (LJP), and continued its alliance with Shiromani Akali Dal (SAD) in Punjab. In Haryana, the BJP forged an alliance with Haryana Janhit Congress (HJC), a breakaway faction of the Congress party. The party made a foray in Tamil Nadu and Kerala by proactively seeking out smaller parties. In Tamil Nadu, the BJP benefitted with its alliance by winning one of the seven seats contested. Though the BJP failed to open its account in Kerala, it secured a respectable vote share of 10.3 per cent. In UP, the BJP formed an alliance with minor party Apna Dal (AD). This alliance benefitted the BJP in eastern UP. In the east, the party made its foray by seeking new allies in West Bengal – Gorkha National Liberation Front (GNLF) and Kamtapur People's Party (KPP) – and in the states in the north-east, except Assam. The BJP's alliance in Meghalaya with P.A. Sangma's National People's Party (NPP) helped it to secure one seat. In Goa the party consolidated its base by seeking an alliance with Maharashtravadi Gomantak Party (MGP).

Table 4.1: Indian Election 2014 – Seats and Votes of Major Parties

Party/Coalition	*Seats Contested*	*Seats Won*	*Seat Share (%)*	*Vote Share (%)*
NDA				
BJP	426	282	51.93	31.00
SHS	58	18	3.31	1.85
TDP	30	16	2.55	2.95
SAD	10	3	0.74	0.30
LJP	7	6	1.10	0.04
AD	2	1	0.18	0.15
NPP	7	1	0.18	0.10
NPF	1	1	0.18	0.18
PMK	8	1	0.18	0.33
AINRC	1	1	0.18	0.05
SWP	2	1	0.18	0.20
Rashtriya Lok Samta Party	4	3	0.55	0.90
UPA				
INC	464	44	8.10	19.31
NCP	36	6	1.10	1.56
RJD	30	4	0.74	0.66
IUML	25	2	0.37	0.20
JMM	21	2	0.37	0.30
Left Front				
CPI(M)	93	9	1.66	3.25
CPI	67	1	0.18	0.78
RSP	6	1	0.18	0.30
AIFB	39	0	0.00	0.22
Major regional parties				
AIADMK	40	37	6.81	3.27
AITC	131	34	6.26	3.81
BJD	21	20	3.68	1.71
Others		57	12.39	24.97

Notes: BJP, Bharatiya Janata Party; SHS, Shiv Sena; TDP, Telugu Desam Party; SAD, Shiromani Akali Dal; LJP, Lok Janshakti Party; INC, Indian National Congress; NCP, Nationalist Congress Party; RJD, Rashtriya Janata Dal; IUML, Indian Union Muslim League; CPI(M), Communist Party of India (Marxist); CPI, Communist Party of India; RSP, Revolutionary Socialist Party; AIFB, All Indian Forward Bloc; AIADMK, All India Anna Dravida Munnetra Kazhagam; AITC, All India Trinamool Congress; BJD, Biju Janata Dal; other acronyms are of the minor parties.

Source: Election Commission of India http://eciresults.nic.in/PartyWiseResult.htm.

Table 4.2: National Democratic Alliance 2014

Party	*State*	*Seat Contesting*	*Seats Won*	*Vote Share (%)*
BJP	National Party	426	282	31.00
BJP	*Tamil Nadu*	7	1	5.50
Desiya Murpokku Dravida Kazhagam	Tamil Nadu	15	0	5.10
Pattali Makkal Katchi	Tamil Nadu	8	1	4.40
Marumalarchi Dravida Munnetra Kazhagam	Tamil Nadu	7	0	3.50
Kongunadu Makkal Desia Katchi	Tamil Nadu	1	0	
Indhiya Jananayaga Katchi	Tamil Nadu	1	0	
New Justice Party	Tamil Nadu	0	0	
BJP	*Andhra Pradesh*	13	3	8.50
TDP	Andhra Pradesh	30	16	29.10
Jana Sena Party	Andhra Pradesh	0		
BJP	*Maharashtra*	24	23	27.30
Shiv Sena	Maharashtra	20	18	20.60
Swabhimani Paksha	Maharashtra	2	1	2.30
Republican Party of India (A)	Maharashtra	1	0	0.10
Rashtriya Samaj Paksha	Maharashtra	1	0	0.90
BJP	*Bihar*	30	22	29.40
Lok Janshakti Party	Bihar	7	6	6.40
Rashtriya Lok Samta Party	Bihar	4	3	3.00
BJP	*Punjab*	3	1	8.70
Shiromani Akali Dal	Punjab	10	4	20.30
BJP	*Haryana*	8	7	34.70
Haryana Janhit Congress	Haryana	2	0	6.10
BJP	*Uttar Pradesh*	`78	71	42.30
Apna Dal	Uttar Pradesh	2	2	1.00
BJP	*Kerala*	18	0	10.30
Kerala Congress (Nationalist)	Kerala	1	0	0.25
Revolutionary Socialist Party (B)	Kerala	1	0	0.24
All India NR Congress	Puducherry	1	1	34.60
BJP	*Meghalaya*	1	1	8.90
National People's Party	Meghalaya	1	1	22.20
Naga Peoples's Front	Nagaland	1	1	68.67
United Democratic Front	Mizoram	1	0	47.17
Manipur Peiople's Party	Manipur	0		
North East Regional Political Front	North East	0		
BJP	*West Bengal*	42	2	16.80
Gorkha Janmukti Morcha	West Bengal	0		
Kamtapur People's Party		0		
BJP	*Goa*	2	2	53.40
Maharashtrawadi Gomantak Party	Goa	0		
Goa Vikas Party	Goa	0		

Note: *NPP, NPF contested one seat each and another nine members supported the NDA candidates.

Source: Election Commission of India, http://eciresults.nic.in/PartyWiseResult.htm.

In 2014, the BJP clearly benefitted in a major way from its alliance in states such as Maharashtra, Bihar, and Haryana, and in a less but still important way from alliances in Tamil Nadu, Meghalaya, West Bengal, Uttar Pradesh, and Goa. By contrast, the Congress in 2014 had alliances in eight states (Table 4.3), one more than its seven in 2009 on essentially the same terms as before, except that in UP and Bihar it contested in coalition, unlike in 2009, and with an improvement over the terms of 2004, the last time it allied with the Rashtriya Janata Dal (RJD) in Bihar, and with two minor allies in UP. In all other states the terms remained essentially the same.

Coalitionability at the state level also depends on various local factors. In bipolar state party systems (almost all major states except UP and currently Bihar), either of the two leading parties is an attractive coalition partner for significant third or fourth parties, provided there are no basic ideological contradictions or aversion of their voters. In some cases, there is an ideological or social-base compatibility, such as the BJP–Shiv Sena and BJP–Akali alliances in

Table 4.3: United Progressive Alliance 2014

Party	*State*	*Seat Contesting*	*Seat Won*
Indian National Congress	National Party	462	44
Bodo People's Front	Assam	1	
Rashtriya Janata Dal*	Bihar	28	4
Nationalist Congress Party*	Maharashtra+Bihar	22	6
Jammu- Kashmir National Conference	Jammu & Kashmir	3	
Jharkhand Mukti Morcha	Jharkhand	4	2
Indian Union Muslim* League	Kerala	2	2
Socialist Janata (Democratic)	Kerala	1	
Revolutionary Socialist Party	Kerala	1	
Kerala Congress	Kerala	1	
PPP	Punjab	1	
RLD	Uttar Pradesh	8	
Mahan Dal	Uttar Pradesh	3	

Note: *Number of seats contested in alliance with the INC. Otherwise the total number of seats contested by RJD, NCP and IUML was 30, 36 and 25, respectively.

Maharashtra and Punjab, respectively. Conversely, such significant third or fourth parties are attractive coalition partners, adding to the vote pool, for either of the two leading partners, subject to the same caveat. One can, therefore, expect coalitions between the BJP and third parties not dependent on Muslim/Christian minority votes when the former is a leading party in a state, or between a regional party, even if dependent on minority community votes, if the latter is the leading party and can check the BJP as a junior partner at the state level – e.g. JD (U), earlier Telugu Desam Party (TDP), All India Trinamool Congress (AITC), Biju Janata Dal (BJD). Likewise, one can expect coalitions between the Congress and a regional party if the Congress is a third/fourth party and the regional party's main opponent is another party or the BJP – e.g. Dravida Munnetra Kazhagam (DMK)/All India Anna Dravida Munnetra Kazhagam (AIADMK) in earlier years, or RJD in Bihar, and AITC in West Bengal currently.

Importance of Pre-electoral Allies

The BJP won 282 seats, a majority of the 543 elected, and 545 seats (including the two nominated Anglo-Indian members) in the Lok Sabha; it formed a surplus majority NDA government with its pre-electoral coalition partners, the principal ones being the Shiv Sena, LJP, TDP, and SAD, taking its majority in the Lok Sabha to 334, a seemingly unassailable position, given that the next largest party, the Congress with only 44 seats, would find it impossible to be the nucleus of any possible alternative coalition. However, the question arises as to how unassailable the BJP's majority is in future elections and with that the implications for the continuing importance of coalitions.

The importance of pre-electoral allies for the BJP's current majority needs to be noted because this is an NDA government with five non-BJP ministers in the 45-member council of ministers (four in the 23-member cabinet, of whom one each is from the Shiv Sena, TDP, SAD, and LJP, and one out of the 22 ministers of state is from a minor Bihar party). Of the 282 seats won by the BJP, as many as 57 seats are accounted for by states in which the BJP depended significantly on coalition partners (not counting UP, where the AD was a minor ally). These are Maharashtra (23 seats), Bihar (22 seats), Haryana (7 seats), Andhra Pradesh (2 seats), Punjab (2 seats) and Tamil Nadu (1 seat), the figures in parentheses indicating the number of BJP seats, and principal allies in these states being the Shiv Sena, LJP, HJC, TDP, Pattali Makkal Katchi (PMK), and several minor parties (in Tamil Nadu), respectively (Table 4.2). Now, even if we assume that two-thirds of these 57 seats would have been won by the BJP contesting alone, this would still leave it 19 seats short of its present total and short of a majority. Hence, the BJP's majority in 2014 was crucially dependent on vote transfer from its pre-electoral allies, a calculation that undoubtedly had weight in the formation of a surplus majority NDA coalition government.

The Rajya Sabha Factor

Coalition politics that goes beyond the NDA coalition to reach out to other parties formally in opposition, to be able to pass legislation in the Rajya Sabha (upper house) as ordinary bills, not to speak of constitutional amendments (which in effect need two- third majorities in both houses) that need to be passed by simple majorities in both houses, is necessitated by the fact that the NDA has only 57 seats in the 245-member Rajya Sabha while the Congress has 68 seats. The NDA tally of 57 falls far short of the halfway mark of 123. In the NDA, besides BJP's 43 members, TDP has 6 members, Shiv Sena 3, SAD 3, RPI(A) 1, and Nagaland People's Front (NPF) 1, or 14 in all for allies.

The Rajya Sabha is elected by the members of the legislative assembly of the state assemblies by proportional representation and the BJP controls only seven state assemblies as of September 2014, including two with its NDA partners (Punjab and Seemandhra). Tables 4.4 to 4.6 show the number of Rajya Sabha seats falling

Table 4.4: Number of Rajya Sabha Seats Falling Vacant Before the Next General Assembly Elections

State	*State Assembly Elections*	*Total Number of Rajya Sabha Seats*	*Seats Vacant 2014*	*Seats Vacant 2015*
Seemandhra	May 2019	11		
Arunachal Pradesh	December 2018	1		
Assam	April 2016	7		
Bihar	October 2015	16		
Chhattisgarh	December 2018	5		
Goa	March 2017	1		
Gujarat	December 2017	11		
Haryana	October 2014	5		
Himachal Pradesh	November 2017	3		
Jammu & Kashmir	November 2014	4		4(2-10/022-15/02)
Jharkhand	October 2014	6		
Karnataka	May 2018	12		
Kerala	April 2016	9		3(21/04)
Madhya Pradesh	December 2018	11		
Maharashtra	October 2014	19		
Meghalaya	February 2018	1		
Manipur	January 2017	1		
Mizoram	November 2018	1		
Nagaland	February 2018	1		
NCT of Delhi		3		
Nominated		12		2(17/11)
Odisha	May 2019	10		
Puducherry	April 2016	1		1(6/10)
Punjab	March 2017	7		
Rajasthan	December 2018	10		
Sikkim	May 2019	1		
Tamil Nadu	April 2016	18		
Telangana	May 2019	7		
Tripura	February 2018	1		
Uttar Pradesh	March 2017	31	10(25/11)	
Uttarakhand	January 2017	3		
West Bengal	May 2016	16		
Total		245	10	10

Seats Vacant 2016	*Seats Vacant 2017*	*Seats Vacant 2018*	*Seats Vacant 2019*
4(21/06)		3(2-04)	
2(2/04)			2(14/06)
5(7/07)		6(2/04)	
3(29/06)		1(2/04)	
		1(28/07)	
		3(18/08)	4(2/04)
1(1/08)		1(2/04)	
1(2/04)		1(2/04)	
1(7/07)		2(3/05)	
4(30/06)		4(20/04)	
3(2/04)		3(12/07)	
3(29/06)		4(2/04)	
4(4/07)		6(2/04)	
1(2/04)			
		3(27/01)	
5(21/03)		4(26/01)	
3(1/07)		2(3/04)	
7(5-9/042-4/07)			
4(4/07)		3(2/04)	
		1(23/02)	
6(29/06)			6(24/07)
2(21/06)		3(2/04)	
1(2/04)			
11(4/07)		10(2/04)	
1(4/07)		1(2/04)	
		6(18/08)	5(2/04)
72	10	67	8

Note: Figures in parentheses are the day and month of retirement.
Source: http://rajyasabha.nic.in/

Table 4.5: Number of BJP Rajya Sabha MPs Retiring Before the Next General Elections

State	*2014*	*2015*	*2016*	*2017*	*2018*	*2019*
Seemandhra			1			
Arunachal Pradesh						
Assam						
Bihar					2	
Chhatisgarh			1		1	
Goa						
Gujarat				2	3	
Haryana						
Himachal Pradesh			1		1	
Jammu & Kashmir						
Jharkhand						
Karnataka			2		2	
Kerala						
Madhya Pradesh			2		3	
Maharashtra			1		1	
Meghalaya						
Manipur						
Mizoram						
Nagaland						
NCT of Delhi						
Nominated						
Odisha						
Puducherry						
Punjab			1			
Rajasthan			1		1	
Sikkim						
Tamil Nadu						
Telangana						
Tripura						
Uttar Pradesh	1		1		1	
Uttarakhand			1			
West Bengal						
Total	1		12	2	15	

vacant, state-wise, including the number of BJP members retiring every year until the mid-2019 election, and the timing of state assembly elections until then.

Table 4.6: Number of National Democratic Allies Retiring Before the Next General Election

State	*Party*	*2014*	*2015*	*2016*	*2017*	*2018*	*2019*
Seemandhra	Telugu Desam Party			1		1	
Telangana	Telugu Desam Party			1		1	
Maharashtra	Shiv Sena			1		1	
Nagaland	Naga People's Front			1			
Punjab	Shiromani Akali Dal			3			
Total				7		3	

Source: http://rajyasabha.nic.in/.

The prospects for the BJP and NDA increasing their Rajya Sabha strength over the rest of the government's term, in effect, until the politically relevant date of late 2018 (elections will be held in April–May 2019), can be estimated as follows. Elections for the Rajya Sabha seats are due in November 2014. Elections will be held for the 10 seats from Uttar Pradesh that will fall vacant in November, and for a lone vacancy in Uttarakhand. In the recent Rajya Sabha Elections the BJP won a seat from Uttar Pradesh. In Uttarakhand thc lone seat was won by the Congress.

The next round will be in November 2015, for 3 seats from Kerala, 4 seats from Jammu and Kashmir, and 1 in Puducherry. There will be two openings in the nominated category as well with two members completing their term. While the BJP will not win a single seat in Kerala as it does not have a legislative presence in the state assembly, in the case of Jammu and Kashmir the BJP tally will depend upon the party's performance in the forthcoming assembly elections. The BJP ally All India NR Congress (AINRC) is likely to win the Puducherry seat in 2015. In 2016, Rajya Sabha elections will be held to fill the 72 seats falling vacant as a result of retirements. Of these, 12 are with the BJP and 6 belong to its alliance partners. In Assam, Kerala, Uttar Pradesh, and Uttarakhand, the BJP and its allies will find it difficult to improve upon their existing tally owing to their poor strength in the existing assemblies. Thus, the BJP in all likelihood will be able retain its sole vacant seat in UP.

In Uttarakhand, the lone vacancy is likely to be filled by the Congress. The BJP, on the basis of its strength in the current Karnataka assembly, will barely manage to retain one seat of the four vacancies arising in 2016. In Nagaland, the BJP ally NPF will be able to retain its existing seat.

It is in Seemandhra, Madhya Pradesh, Rajasthan, and Punjab that the NDA and the BJP will register an increase. This will be due to the remarkable performance of the BJP and its allies, barring Punjab where elections are due in 2017, in the last assembly elections. In Seemandhra, the TDP is likely to improve its tally from 1 to 3 and the SAD in Punjab from 3 to 4. The BJP will be able to retain its lone seat in Punjab. In its stronghold states of Chhattisgarh, Madhya Pradesh, and Rajasthan, the BJP will improve its tally from the existing 1, 2 and 1, to 2, 3, and 4, respectively. The BJP will also be able fill the five vacancies due to appear among the nominated members in March 2016.

In Assam, the two seats are falling vacant in February 2016 and the state assembly elections are due sometime in April. Therefore, the two seats are likely to be retained by the incumbent Congress party. The same is the case with Kerala, where the seats fall vacant in early April and the assembly elections might happen sometime in April or May. Thus, there is a likelihood of the existing assembly electing the members to fill the vacancies. The BJP and its allies will not be in a position to open their account in Kerala at least until 2016. In Tamil Nadu, elections to the state assembly are scheduled in April or May 2016. Hence, the six Rajya Sabha seats falling vacant from Tamil Nadu can be elected only by the new assembly. Unless the NDA were to perform remarkably in the assembly elections or reach some kind of understanding with the two major Dravidian parties – the AIADMK and the DMK – one could assume that at best the NDA could gain one seat in the Rajya Sabha from Tamil Nadu in 2016.

The state assembly elections are due in 2014 in Maharashtra, Jharkhand, Haryana, and Jammu and Kashmir, and in 2015 in Bihar. Even if we were to assume that the BJP-led NDA will win an absolute majority in these five states and capture all the 15 vacant Rajya Sabha seats – 5 in Bihar, 1 in Haryana, 4 each in Jammu and Kashmir and Maharashtra, and 1 in Jharkhand – the NDA tally would reach 59 by August 2016, still way short of the majority mark of 123 in the Rajya Sabha.

Therefore, it is reasonable to expect that even if the BJP and its allies were to perform remarkably in the state assembly elections of 2014–18, they are still likely to fall short of the halfway mark in the Rajya Sabha. This underlines the imperative for the BJP-led NDA to rework its strategy and seek new allies and forge fresh coalitions at the state level, such as perhaps with the AIADMK in Tamil Nadu, BSP in UP, and BJD in Odisha, in the next two years. The upshot is that even by late 2018 the NDA will not attain a Rajya Sabha majority even under favourable assumptions.

Limited Regional Presence

Coalition politics will also remain important because the BJP will need to expand its base outward from its current strongholds in the northern and central Hindi-belt states and the three western states and Karnataka towards other states in the south and east. For this it will need allies in the other southern states and possibly in Odisha, West Bengal, and Assam – in all of which it has had BJD, AITC and Asom Gana Parishad (AGP) as allies at various times in the past. This is because its narrow majority of 52 per cent of the seats is based on the lowest ever vote share (31 per cent nationally, 38 per cent with its NDA allies) to convert into a seat-majority in Indian elections, a conversion ratio of 1.67 (per cent seats for per cent votes), which is more than even the Congress victories of 1952 and 1984.

Disaggregated by region, this victory is very disproportionately based on an unprecedentedly sweeping victory in the Hindi-speaking northern and central states and Union Territories (Delhi, Chandigarh, Himachal Pradesh, Uttarakhand, Uttar Pradesh, Bihar, Jharkhand, Chhattisgarh, Madhya Pradesh, Rajasthan, and Haryana), and western states and Union Territories (Gujarat, Maharashtra, Goa, Dadra and Nagar Haveli, and Daman and Diu) (Table 4.7). Of the BJP's 282 seats, as many as 244, or 87 per cent, came from this Hindi-belt plus western India stronghold, or in other words, it won a whopping 81 per cent of the 304 seats in this region, or an even more whopping 92 per cent of the seats contested (244 out of 266 contested) in this region based on a 44 per cent vote share in this region. Replicating such a strike rate in this region would be extremely improbable. Expansion into the south and east will be necessary and would require either an improbable quantum jump or, more realistically, the formation of pre-electoral coalitions with regional party allies.

Opposition Space

Finally, coalitions will remain critical in the opposition space in Indian politics and can make a huge difference in some places. Most recently, for example, in the August 2014 by-elections to 10 assembly

Table 4.7: 2014 Results – BJP's Stronghold and Rest of India

Coalition/Party	*BJP's stronghold (304 seats)**				*Rest of India (239 seats)*			
NDA	*Seats contested*	*Seats won*	*Seats (%)*	*Vote (%)*	*Seats contested*	*Seats won*	*Seats (%)*	*Vote (%)*
BJP	266	244	81	44	161	38	16	19
BJP allies	39	29	10	5	75	18	8	11
UPA								
INC	233	10	3	19.8	229	34	14	21
INC allies	65	11	5	6	6	4	2	1
AIADMK					41	37	15	8
AITC					60	34	14	9
BJD					21	20	8	4
Left Front					78	11	5	10
Others						42	20	44

Note: For party acronyms, refer to Table 1. *Hindi Belt + Gujarat + Maharashtra + Goa+ Dadra - Nagar Haveli + Chandigarh + Daman and Diu (304 seats).

Source: Election Commission of India, http://eciresults.nic.in/PartyWiseResult.htm

seats in Bihar, barely three months after the BJP sweep in the Lok Sabha election, the newly formed JD(U)–RJD–Congress coalition won 6 out of 10 seats. For the Congress in particular, a viable recovery path will of necessity involve coalition formation either before or after elections in a number of states, particularly states such as Tamil Nadu, Seemandhra, Telangana, West Bengal, Jharkhand, and, perhaps, Assam, in addition to existing coalitions in Kerala and Maharashtra.

Not Yet a One-Party Hegemonic System

The party system, as indicated by the effective number of parties by votes and seats in 2014 (see Table 4.8), remains a multi-party system and is not like the party system that prevailed in the era of Congress hegemony from 1952 to 1984 (except 1977), not even during the low point of 1967. The party system as measured by a standard index, that of the Effective Number of Parties (*N*), by seats (*Ns*) and by votes (*Nv*), remains a multi-party system with *Nv* at 7.06, which is higher than that in all elections during the Congress hegemonic period up to 1989 (never above the high point of 5.2 in 1967), and *Ns* at 3.5 being higher than any *Ns* during the pre-1989 period (the highest was 3.2 in 1967 during that period). Hence, it is too early to say that the BJP has become hegemonic in the party system, like the Congress was before 1989.

Conclusion

For the multiple reinforcing reasons detailed in this paper, it is premature to conclude that the era of coalition politics is over in India or that a new one-party hegemonic system dominated by the BJP is now in place. Coalition politics, in government, at the centre, and in many states, and for party strategies in coming state assembly elections and the next general election, will remain central to Indian politics.

Table 4.8: Effective Number of Parties in Lower House Elections

S. N.	*Year*	*Nv. Effective Number of Parties (Votes)*	*Nv. Effective Number of Parties (Seats)*
1	1952	4.53	1.80
2	1957	3.98	1.76
3	1962	4.40	1.85
4	1967	5.19	3.16
5	1971	4.63	2.12
6	1977	3.40	2.63
7	1980	4.25	2.28
8	1984	3.99	1.69
9	1989	4.80	4.35
10	1991	5.10	3.70
11	1996	7.11	5.83
12	1998	6.91	5.28
13	1999	6.74	5.87
14	2004	7.60	6.50
15	2009	7.98	5.01
16	2014	7.06	3.50

Source: See *Journal of the Indian School of Political Economy*, XV/1–2 (January–June 2003), Statistical Supplement, Tables 1.1–1.13, 293–307. For 2004, the index was calculated by the Centre for the Study of Developing Societies, New Delhi; for 2009 and 2014 by the authors.

References

Sridharan, E. (2004). "Electoral Coalitions in the 2004 General Elections: Theory and Evidence", *Economic and Political Weekly*, XXXIX (51), pp. 5, 418–25.

Sridharan, E. (2005). "Coalition Strategies and the BJP's Expansion, 1989–2004", *Commonwealth and Comparative Politics*, 43(2), pp. 194–221.

Sridharan, E. (2012). "Why are Multi-party Minority Governments Viable in India? Theory and Comparison", *Commonwealth and Comparative Politics*, 50(3), pp. 314–43.

Sridharan, E., ed. (2014). *Coalition Politics in India: Selected Issues at the Centre and the States* (New Delhi: Academic Foundation).

5

Cross-state Learning in Service Delivery in India's Federal System

Economic Performance, Voting Behaviour and Incentives for Cross-State Learning and Borrowing in India's Federal Democracy

THERE IS A VAST literature, almost entirely based on developed-country experience, on the relationship between economics and voting behaviour.[1] The overall finding is not straightforward. While voters tend to reward incumbents for economic performance, the evidence is not overwhelming and elections are found to be multi-factoral in their outcomes (Anderson 2007). One problem is that voters face informational and cognitive barriers in assessing economic performance.[2] Pacek and Radcliff (1995) indicate that voters tend to punish incumbents when the economy worsens but do not necessarily reward good economic performance. This would indicate that what matters is not just performance on economy and related governance issues but, in the Indian context of a less educated and information-poor electorate, the formation of perceptions. Vaishnav and Swanson (2015) show

[1] For a somewhat dated survey article of this vast literature, see Lewis-Back and Stegmaier 2000.

[2] In the Indian case, voters might not be clear about what level of government, Centre or State, and hence which party, is responsible for what policies and programmes.

that, for India, there do seem to be increasing electoral returns at the state level since 2000 for governments that deliver increased economic growth rates, and argue that there has been a significant shift in voter behaviour. It would appear that there has been a gradual shift away from the politics of patronage and clientelism to the politics of performance and growth and that this has changed policy-maker incentives.

We could hypothesise that incumbents would have an incentive to improve performance most of all in programmes that have a broad citizen interface so as to impact perceptions and reap electoral rewards. Derivatively, we could hypothesise that cross-state (and cross-national) learning as well as actual borrowing of programmes/best practices to improve/innovate on government programmes and service delivery would be incentivised for incumbent state-level political leaderships. The fact of inter-state competition for private investment in an increasingly private investment-led economy, and the fact that better governance and infrastructural performance is a significant determinant of investment decisions would only add to such incentives for cross-state learning for best practices and adoption of innovative programmes.

The comparative literature on subnational policy diffusion across states/provinces in federal systems throws additional light on incentives for and drivers of such diffusion. Sugiyama (2008) argues that in the case of social sector policies in Brazil electoral competition does not explain diffusion so much as leftist ideological factors and public officials following professional norms. Segatto (2018) on the diffusion of education policies across states in Brazil finds that the movement of ideas and people were key. Wallner (2017) finds that horizontal diffusion of education policies in Canada was driven by the interaction of institutional and ideational conditions, although no single factor was necessary and sufficient. Niedzwiecki (2016), analysing social policy implementation in Argentina and Brazil, found that co-partisanship helps while opposition party-led state governments tend to hinder implementation of social policies if policies carry the clear attribution of responsibility. The literature in summary yields three important possible drivers of cross-state policy learning/borrowing in India – co-partisanship, professional networks of public officials, and ideological/ideational factors – besides electoral incentives. While taking these three factors from the comparative literature into account in the Indian context, our starting point is how electoral incentives are potentially reshaping policy behaviour in India from competitive patronage to better performance in service delivery.

Incumbency, Performance and Re-election in Indian States: Political Incentives for Improvements in Governance and Service Delivery

The historical backdrop to the issue of cross-state learning and borrowing in service delivery is the changing patterns of electoral politics in India, particularly at the state level and the incentives that it creates for state behaviour in governance and service delivery. I hypothesise that changing electoral patterns at the state level since 2004 have created incentives for better performance in governance and service delivery by state governments and ruling parties rather than resorting to populist patronage politics or identity politics around religion and caste. The evolution of electoral patterns at the state level is as follows.

Before the 2000s, there was a pronounced tendency towards anti-incumbency in state assembly elections in India. However, Yadav and Palshikar (2009) have shown that state governments are being increasingly frequently re-elected since the early 2000s. Gupta, *et al.* (2013) point out that the percentage of state assembly elections in various periods of India's electoral history won by incumbent parties declined from 85 per cent (1951–66), 54 per cent (1967–79), 51 per cent (1980–8) to a low of only 27 per cent (1989–98), recovering to 39 per cent (1999–2003). The last two periods characterised by a transition to multi-party competition nationally lead to a new conventional wisdom that Indian state elections are exemplified by the anti-incumbency sentiments of an impatient and demanding electorate faced with poorly performing state governments, or what Ravishankar (2009) calls the "costs of ruling". However, since 2004, there seems to have been a reversal with 54 per cent of incumbents re-elected over 2004–12 (Gupta, *et al.*, 2013). From 2013 to 2019, 41 per cent of incumbents got re-elected.

Is this reversal of anti-incumbency linked to electorate perceptions of performance and to actual economic performance? Gupta, *et al.* (2013) demonstrate that in 74 per cent of the cases (23 of the 31 cases of re-election in the period 2002–12) there was a correlation between people's satisfaction with government performance (measured by a net score defined as the percentage of responses saying "fully or somewhat satisfied" minus the percentage of responses saying "fully or somewhat dissatisfied") and its being voted back to power. There was also a correlation between actual development (measured by a composite of the real growth rate of Gross State Domestic Product of the state and the percentage improvement in the Human Development Index score) and net satisfaction score in 12 of 20 cases (Gupta, *et al.* 2013). Now, while elections are about many factors including identity politics, leadership and other intangibles, this does give us some basis for linking performance (on the development and governance), electorate satisfaction and re-election. Hence, it would appear that there are clear political incentives for improved delivery of public services, more so for those services that have the broadest citizen interface with the delivery programme.

There is also some evidence that good economic performance has begun weighing larger in the thinking of voters in recent years compared to identitarian (caste, religion, tribe, regional/linguistic identity) and patronage/clientelist politics that were said to dominate electoral mobilisation and political alliances at the state and national levels from the late 1980s to the 2000s by several scholars

(Chandra 2004 on caste, religion and patronage; Keefer and Khemani 2004 on clientelism and patronage). An earlier study (Khemani 2001) found that there was a positive relationship between state-level average growth over the term and re-election even before 2000 (for 1960–92). In this context, we could hypothesise that incumbent governments have an incentive to improve economic and governance performance, particularly in delivery of important public services, and move away from "patronage democracy" (Chandra 2004) or competitive populism in government patronage to getting re-elected through better performance in service delivery and its knock-on effects including attracting greater investment in the context of interstate competition for the same.

Cross-state Learning Incentives, Drivers and Facilitating Features at the Political and Bureaucratic Levels

The above logic could be expected to hold at the level of incumbent state-level political leaderships. This seems to have started under the Congress party while in opposition in the early 2000s with sharing of experiences on programme implementation across states (among political discussions) by Congress chief ministers in conferences held in November 2001, April 2002 (during which the decision to introduce rural employment guarantee if in power was made), November 2002, and November 2003. This sharing went on until Congress chief ministers' conferences in February and September 2006, after which it petered out.[3]

Subsequently, the Bharatiya Janata Party (BJP) while in opposition took cross-state sharing of experiences on programme implementation and service delivery further. Chief ministers of BJP-ruled states have been getting time slots to share experiences, innovations, and best practices at meetings of the BJP National Executive, usually

[3] Interview with Jairam Ramesh, former Union Minister of State for Rural Development, January 26, 2015, in which he also shared the fact about employment guarantee in the last sentence.

held three times a year, since 2006, showcasing successful programme innovations.[4] When Nitin Gadkari took over as party president in 2010, a Good Governance Cell was established in the party in April–May 2010 with former Goa chief minister Manohar Parrikar as the convenor. A National Convention on Good Governance (Suraj Sankalp Sammelan) was organised in June 2010 at the BJP's training centre, the Rambhau Mhalgi Prabodhini in Mumbai, with the participation of all BJP chief ministers and as many as fifty-five state-level ministers holding important portfolios. Subsequently, while this major convention was not institutionalised, periodic meetings were held from then on up to the 2014 general election, of the BJP's state-level ministers for finance, education, agriculture and food/civil supplies, water, and tribal welfare. They have met – in separate groups at various times – to compare notes and learn best practices. These are sure indications that the party considered improved governance and service delivery as important for electorate perceptions of good performance and key to increasing the party's future electoral strength, and implicitly, a recognition that performance and not identity politics alone is key to improved electoral strength. The driver has clearly been a political push from the party leaderships in response to the perceived electoral incentives outlined in the last section.

What of the bureaucratic level? Do civil servants have similar incentives and/or are such imperatives built into their training? One can hypothesise that civil servants will be sensitive to the requirements of their political masters.[5] As far as their training is concerned, the information available on cross-state learning and borrowing processes is as follows. Indian Administrative Service (IAS) officers go through three phases of mid-career training, last-

[4] This paragraph is based on an interview with the then BJP Vice-President Vinay Sahasrabuddhe, also head of the Rambhau Mhalgi Prabodhini, Mumbai, and of the party's Public Policy Research Centre, January 23, 2015, and materials provided by him. And on Mishra (2011).

[5] A point agreed to by a wide range of serving bureaucrats interviewed and in informal conversations.

ing five to eight weeks, held in recent years at the Lal Bahadur Shastri National Academy of Administration (LBSNAA) in Mussoorie. Phase III training is for officers of 7–9 years' service, Phase IV for officers of 14–16 years' service, and Phase V for officers of 26–28 years' service. A perusal of the topics of such training programmes shows that the sessions are either sectoral or on specific issues/topics, but there is nothing explicitly on cross-state learning/borrowing.[6] Only one out of sixty-one topics listed in the Phase V training programmes are explicitly on comparing state experiences and this was on a session on strengthening public health systems.[7] The same is the pattern revealed by the training programmes conducted by the Department of Personnel and Training.[8] Nevertheless, since all sessions are attended by officers belonging to a range of state cadres, there are examples and experiences from states that are widely shared, including exposure to innovations and best practices. However, this constitutes what can be called informal or tacit learning processes, and whether the lessons picked up are actually borrowed and implemented in another state depends entirely – and this is my key finding – on state-level incentives and the driver of a political push from the top.[9]

As far as cross-state learning and borrowing in Centrally Sponsored Schemes (CSS) are concerned, particularly in the major national missions like the Mahatma Gandhi National Rural Employment Guarantee Act (MGNREGA), National Rural Health Mission, Jawaharlal Nehru National Urban Renewal Mission, Sarva Shiksha Abhiyan, Prime Minister's Gram Sadak Yojana, etc., there

[6] Phase III, Phase IV and Phase V Course Handbooks, including timetables and listings of strategy topics, from LBSNAA website, for 2012 and 2013 training programmes. Earlier listings are not on the site. Discussions with officers at the LBSNAA, April 15–16, 2015, confirmed that while cross-state experiences are commonly shared as part of sectoral or issue-focused programmes, cross-state learning is not considered a topic in itself.

[7] Ibid.

[8] Listed on Department of Personnel and Training website.

[9] This is the general view of a wide range of serving bureaucrats.

is considerable cross-state learning and transfer of best practices.[10] National missions have among their stated objectives that of sharing of experiences in programme implementation among the states.[11] The National Informatics Centre (NIC) also promotes cross-state learning in national missions.[12] However, the Centre is only a facilitator and funder in CSS and national missions. A great deal depends on the initiatives of the minister concerned at the Centre, and on the initiatives of ministers and bureaucrats at the state level who are in charge of implementation of CSS.[13] The Centre acts as a clearing house and the extent to which the states pick up best practices and implement them depends on them. To this extent, cross-state learning and borrowing continues to be informal, tacit, and dependent on individual initiatives at the political and bureaucratic levels in the states, and hence on political and systemic incentives to do so.

Another important incentive-shaping issue in CSS is the fact that the Centre's and hence states' approach to CSS is input/disbursement oriented and not outcome-oriented.[14] There is a need to incentivise performance and this is not helped by a systemic distrust of states with untied funds; the latter would help to incentivise and promote innovation suited to local needs rather than carry out pre-fabricated programmes. Since the input-orientation of CSS

[10] The CSS are centrally funded welfare and development programmes with some degree of matching participation by state governments. Interview with K.P. Krishnan, Additional Secretary, Ministry of Rural Development, January 30, 2015, and Narendra Jadhav, former Member, Planning Commission, January 30, 2015.

[11] Interviews with Jairam Ramesh, former Union Minister of State for Rural Development, January 26, 2015, and Narendra Jadhav, former Member, Planning Commission, January 30, 2015.

[12] Interview with K.P. Krishnan, Additional Secretary, Ministry of Rural Development, January 30, 2015.

[13] Interviews with Jairam Ramesh, former Union Minister of State for Rural Development, January 26, 2015, and Narendra Jadhav, former Member, Planning Commission, January 30, 2015.

[14] A point made by a very senior serving bureaucrat in a state government.

does not make outcomes important let alone critical, the state-level which receives the funds has no incentive to innovate programmatically, technically, or organisationally. The challenge is how to transition CSS to outcome-orientation mode. In recent years, the Planning Commission has also tended to identify and publicise best practices (for example, the *Mid-term Appraisal of the Eleventh Five Year Plan, 2007–2012* has boxes showing best practices in CSS) but ultimately their adoption and cross-state borrowing depends on the initiatives at the state level or at least a push from the Central ministry concerned (Planning Commission 2012).

On features that facilitate cross-state borrowing, two important features that facilitate the ease of borrowing are: first, the presence of a generic law that can be adopted by another state with suitable modifications; second: an Information and Communications Technology (ICT) package that can be easily adopted and tweaked by the borrowing state.

Finally, coming to the difficulties in borrowing, these derive from state-specific conditions that need major changes in order to adopt a borrowed innovation, or cannot easily be changed, including the presence of entrenched vested interests.

A Framework and a Typology

Types of Learning/Borrowing, Drivers, Mechanisms and Types of Diffusion

I develop the following framework of cross-state learning, borrowing and adaptation in a federation, in which I situate my cases, as follows.

Learning, Borrowing, Adaptation, and Leapfrogging

Cross-state learning can be limited just to learning based on studying another state's experience through exploratory visits or inquiries or exposure to the key actors in another state's service delivery programmes. It can go from learning to borrowing another state's programmes and innovations by adopting and implementing such programmes/innovations in one's own state with or without minor adaptations. It can go beyond borrowing to (significant) adaptation to one's own state's circumstances by tweaking the borrowed programme appropriately. It can go still further beyond adaptation to leapfrogging, that is, to learning from another state but jumping altogether ahead by a further innovation that achieves more than the programme from which learning took place or inspiration was derived.

Drivers. When it comes to the drivers of learning, borrowing and adaptation, there can be three main ones, which are all processes, not discrete events: a CSS that promotes diffusion; networks within political parties, particularly, networking among state-level political leaders; networks within the bureaucracy across states including exposure to other-state experiences during formal training programmes. Such processes can also initiate learning/borrowing.

Facilitating Features. When it comes to features that, when present, facilitate borrowing and adaptation, there are two principal features: generic laws that can be borrowed, tweaked, and enacted by another state; ICT packages that can, likewise, be borrowed and tweaked to suit another state's circumstances.

Types of Diffusion. The types of diffusion of service delivery experiences across states in a federation can be classified as: (a) bilateral, when a state borrows from another state; (b) multi-state, when several states borrow and adapt from the original state (including, for example, in CSS, though multi-state diffusion can occur outside CSS too). Bilateral borrowing or diffusion can take place as a chain in which a state borrows and adapts from the original state and then other states borrow and adapt from the borrowing state one by one in a chain that might include adaptation/innovation including cases of leapfrogging the original innovator altogether. Such innovations/adaptations, including leapfrogging, can also punctuate multi-state diffusion when a state adapts/leapfrogs and then such innovations diffuse multi-state in a further round of diffusion in or without a CSS.

A Four-fold Typology of the Six Cases

Using this framework for classifying cross-state learning, borrowing, adaptation and diffusion of service delivery programmes, I situate the six cases in this paper in the following fourfold typology to bring out specific features when I discuss the cases in the following and concluding sections. This fourfold typology was derived by classifying the empirical material available, that is, the actual case studies and their characteristics.

Type I: These are cases of bilateral borrowing of programmes in which there are popularity incentives for the political leadership in case service delivery/governance improves, due to either a broad public interface or a significant mass signalling effect that the leadership is serious about good governance.

Type II : This is a case of large-scale and rapid (within three/four years), multi-state diffusion by borrowing from the originating state but without the driver of a Central programme, and is characterised by (i) a programme with a broad citizen interface and hence, popularity incentives; (ii) a generic law and/or ICT package that lends itself to borrowing and tweaking. This case also contains within it a case of (significant) adaptation by a state, followed by further multi-state diffusion of that state's adaptations.

Type III: This is also a case of large-scale and rapid (within three/four years), multi-state diffusion by borrowing from the originating state and includes two instances of leapfrogging over the original programme – and is characterised by (i) the origins as well as subsequent multi-state diffusion lying in Central programmes; (ii) a broad citizen interface hence, popularity incentives; (iii) a generic law and/or ICT package that lends itself to borrowing and tweaking. The two instances of leapfrogging further led to further rounds of rapid, multi-state diffusion, due to a Central programme.

Type IV: A case of cross-state learning and borrowing characterised by difficulties where (i) state-specific conditions including entrenched vested interests slow the process of adoption, and hence, mixed incentives; (ii) there is no generic law or ICT package.

Selected Cases of Cross-State Learning/Borrowing

In this section, I try to trace the process of six selected cases of cross-state learning/borrowing including one sub-case of significant adaptation and two sub-cases of leapfrogging in a chain of borrowing from a particular original programme, which I have classified as sub-cases rather than distinct cases in themselves because they were part of a chain of borrowing, adaptation, and subsequent diffusion. The selection of these cases was based on an information availability basis, given that there is no documented database of such cases since this is not a systematically explored area of investigation in the government or research community. The availability of information was gleaned from discussions with bureaucrats, journalists and some politicians. The methodology was one of focused interviews with persons who had been or were currently actively involved with each of the cases. There were twenty-two interviews, of which twelve people have been referred to in the footnotes and another ten, mostly serving bureaucrats, chose anonymity. I lead into each case from the typology above, and at the end of each case, I analyse the case in terms of the framework.

Type I, Case I: Bilateral Borrowing Driven by Popularity Incentives

Samadhan Online, A Public Grievances Redressal System in Madhya Pradesh Borrowed from Gujarat

This is a case of bilateral borrowing of a public grievance redressal system, which by its very nature has a broad public interface and hence major popularity incentives for the political leadership if grievance redressal is made quick and fair. Madhya Pradesh borrowed and modified an online public grievance redressal system pioneered by Gujarat called Swagat Online, calling it Samadhan Online.[15] Gujarat, on the initiative of its then Chief Minister Narendra Modi, started an online grievances redressal system called Swagat Online in 2003.[16] It was designed to enable direct communication between citizens and the CM on the fourth Thursday of every month, called Swagat (Welcome) day. It is meant to enable citizens to get pending grievances redressed once a month. Gujarat has a three-tier grievance redressal system at the Taluka, District and State levels respectively. The way the system works is that grievances are entered, transmitted, and made available to officers concerned online on that day, reviewed by the CM and senior officers and response formulated and sent out within four hours. The CM holds a video conference with all districts at 3 pm and examines each complaint and attempts are made to send out a reasonable and acceptable solution within the day, with no complainant left without a firm reply. District and sub-district officers attend the programme through video conferencing.

The Swagat Online system builds on the state's information and communications technology (ICT) infrastructure, particularly the Gujarat State Wide Area Network (SWAN), commissioned in 2001. This network connects the State Secretariat in Gandhinagar with all central ministries and departments and with all the district headquarters and hundreds of district-level offices (the state gov-

[15] Interview with Anurag Jain, Joint Secretary, Prime Minister's Office, former Secretary to Chief Minister and Secretary, Information Technology, in Madhya Pradesh, January 19, 2015.

[16] Swagat.gujarat.gov.in; also see http://www.narendramodi.in/swagat-online- grievances-redressal-program-provides-satisfactory-solutions-to-people%E2% 80%99s-problems/. For Samadhan Online, see http://www.mpsamadhan.org and http://www.nic.in/projects/samadhan-line-public-grievances-redressal.

ernment's second tier), and all 225 taluka headquarters (the state government's third tier). Clearly, the Swagat Online system was an innovation that quickly exploited the ICT network then set up for a broad-spectrum citizen interface programme of grievance redressal by an enterprising CM.

This system was borrowed by Madhya Pradesh and called Samadhan Online in February 2006.[17] The initiative had political origins in that the chief ministers of Gujarat (then Narendra Modi) and Madhya Pradesh used to interact regularly and Chief Minister Shivraj Singh Chauhan asked district officers to look at Gujarat's online grievance system after a presentation on the system was made to him. Like in Gujarat, all department and district level officials are asked to remain in office during the process of grievance redressal on that day, with the district officials participating through the video-conferencing facility maintained by the National Informatics Centre (NIC) while the departmental secretaries participate from the Secretariat's video-conferencing facility. An application fee for complaints for which a receipt is given incentivises operators of the system to be responsive to citizens. The system keeps the bureaucracy on its toes like in Gujarat, and has resulted in an increase in the disposal of grievance cases since the officers know that the CM is personally involved.

This case of learning and borrowing from another state's programme originated at and was driven by the political (CM) level due to interaction between the CMs of two states ruled by the same party. It involves adoption and minor adaptation of a programme with potential political rewards both for the party and the CM personally due to its broad citizen interface with government and the creation of an image of a responsive leadership. A facilitating feature for this case of bilateral diffusion was the presence of an adaptable ICT package.

[17] Interview with Anurag Jain, Joint Secretary, Prime Minister's Office, former Secretary to Chief Minister and Secretary, Information Technology, in Madhya Pradesh, January 19, 2015.

Type I, case II: Bilateral Borrowing Driven by Popularity Incentives

MPOnline – Madhya Pradesh's Online Public Services Provision System Borrowed from Andhra Pradesh

This is a case of bilateral borrowing, with some modification and expansion, of an online public services provision system, which by its very nature has a broad public interface and hence popularity incentives for the leadership. Madhya Pradesh borrowed the concept of an online public service provision portal, now called MPOnline, initially for provision of enrolment and examination forms, birth certificates, online counselling, and other such citizen services, from Andhra Pradesh's APOnline which also offered a limited range of services.[18] The initial push again came from Chief Minister Chauhan who was keen to improve public service delivery and the administrative follow-up was undertaken by the then IT Secretary Anurag Jain.[19] However, the borrowed concept underwent significant modifications right from the beginning, being set up as a joint venture company between the Madhya Pradesh government and the information technology company Tata Consultancy Services (TCS) in 2006. The second key decision, apart from adopting a joint venture format with TCS, was the integration of the existing 9232 Citizen Service Centres (CSCs) that offered government-to-citizen services in rural areas. MPOnline and the CSCs were integrated to make the latter extensions of the former, thus building on an existing service provision network but making it IT-enabled. Jain changed the concept of CSC to a one-time membership fee, for operators, of Rs 1000. Scaling up was easy as TCS had the neces-

[18] See MPOnline Limited website (http://www.mponline.gov.in/) for a full description and its functioning and services.

[19] Interview with Anurag Jain, Joint Secretary, Prime Minister's Office, former Secretary to Chief Minister and Secretary, Information Technology, in Madhya Pradesh, January 19, 2015.

sary human resources and implementation capabilities and sent software development personnel on deputation to MPOnline. In three years, revenues grew 300 times to Rs 400 million.

MPOnline is a case of borrowing and adaptation, in a bilateral type of diffusion, of a state-level innovation for service delivery with a broad citizen interface, and hence the associated popularity incentives, the process being facilitated by a push from the CM supported by innovative bureaucrats, the feature facilitating it being an easily modifiable and scalable ICT package, its spread being further facilitated by the participation of a leading private sector IT firm TCS as well as being able to leverage the existing service delivery network of CSCs.

Type I, case III: Bilateral Borrowing of an Institutional Innovation with a Mass Signalling Effect and Hence Popularity Incentives

Bihar Special Courts Act Borrowed from Orissa – With Further Borrowing by Madhya Pradesh

This is a case of two bilateral borrowings, in a simple three-state, two-step chain, of an institutional innovation that does not have a broad citizen interface but nevertheless has popularity incentives for political leaderships due to its mass signalling effect that the government is serious about tackling corruption. It had a domino effect in that Bihar's innovation was further borrowed by Madhya Pradesh due essentially to the same political incentives. Bihar took a legal initiative in attempting to swiftly bring corrupt officials to book in enacting the Bihar Special Courts Act 2009 under the Janata Dal (United)-BJP coalition government led by Chief Minister Nitish Kumar. The Bihar Special Courts Act of 2009 allows confiscation of the immoveable and moveable properties of corrupt public servants including ministers, MPs, MLAs, and bureaucrats who are charged with corruption even while they are being tried.[20] The Act sets up Special Courts to try cases of offences specified under Art. 13(1)(e) of the Prevention of Corruption Act, 1988, which is about possessing assets disproportionate to known sources of income. The Act also sets a one-year time limit for the trial to be completed in a corruption case in a Special Court. The Act came into effect from March 2010. The Bihar Act was modelled on the earlier Orissa Special Courts Act of 2006 but with the difference that the Bihar Act is more comprehensive in coverage and applies to all sections of government employees while the Orissa Act applies only to Class I officers. The Bihar Act follows the Orissa Act almost clause by clause.

In turn, the Bihar Act has been adopted almost exactly by Madhya Pradesh with the passing of the Madhya Pradesh Special Courts Act in 2011 coming into force in February 2012. Like in Bihar, disproportionate assets can be confiscated even while the trial is under way and again like in Bihar the government can use them as public assets as, for example, houses being converted to schools of dispensaries. Likewise, there is a one-year time limit for trials. The driver of borrowing was an initiative at the highest level by Chief Minister Chauhan and due to exchange of ideas with Bihar Chief Minister Nitish Kumar and Deputy Chief Minister Sushil Modi.[21]

Although Special Courts are not characterised by the incentives of a mass contact programme with a broad citizen interface, the motivation for such borrowing is probably the political need to demonstrate that the state government is serious about tackling corruption, particularly in the context of exposure of major corruption in the media at the national level from 2010 onwards. This case of bilateral borrowing and further borrowing was facilitated by the feature of a tweakable Act although no ICT package was involved.

[20] See Bihar Special Courts Act, 2009, http://vigilance.bih.nic.in/Acts/Vigilance- Special-Court-Act-2009.pdf.

[21] Anonymous bureaucrats.

Type II, case I: Multi-state Diffusion of a Service Delivery Innovation Due to Popularity Incentives

Madhya Pradesh Public Services Guarantee Act 2010, Borrowed by Bihar and Other States, and Modified by Karnataka With Further Multi-state Diffusion Downstream

This is a case of simultaneous multi-state diffusion, without a Central programme driving it, of a service delivery innovation with a broad public interface, due to popularity incentives. It led to a further innovation in one of the borrowing states, Karnataka, which led to further multi-state diffusion downstream of that adaptation.

Twenty states have so far emulated, with some modifications, the Madhya Pradesh Public Services Guarantee Act of 2010, the first of its kind in India, and others are in the process of adopting it.[22] This is a case of rapid and bunched – within four years – multi-state diffusion. Madhya Pradesh initially supplied copies of the software that underpins the system. This in itself makes the MP PSG Act 2010 an interesting case. The Act covers as many as 52 services that are the responsibility of 16 government departments. Applicants for services submit applications at any of the 336 Public Service Centres (PSCs, or Lok Seva Kendras) in the state, operated by a PSC operator who registers the application online after seeking details and documents, which are scanned and uploaded with the application. The PSC operator gets Rs 25 of the Rs 30 application fee, with Rs 5 going to the District E-Governance Society managed by the state government. Complete applications are forwarded to designated officers for processing and response within prescribed time limits, failing which the officer concerned will be fined. This is the "guarantee" part of the Act. When an applicant appeals, the

[22] See Public Services Delivery Guarantee Act 2010 in "Important Schemes – Govt. of MP India" (mp.gov.in/en/impschemes) for a description.

PSC operator brings the case to the notice of the First Appellate Authority, and if there is no response again within a time limit, to the Second Appellate Authority, and likewise to the Third Appellate Authority. The Second and Third Appellate Officers have been empowered to *suo motu* call for cases pending beyond the time limit and take action on them. Over 12.5 million applications were received in the first two years and 99 per cent of them serviced. However, the shortcoming is that a large part of the public is not aware of the Act and hence, their rights under it.

The Act had its origins again at the political leadership level, when, in October 2009, Chief Minister Chauhan asked his officers about putting *patwaris* (land records officers), who were recalcitrant in service delivery at the village level, in their place.[23] His then Secretary, Anurag Jain, and another bureaucrat, Manohar Dubey, who was later involved in drafting the Act, suggested enactment of a Citizen's Charter.[24] This was approved at a two-day brainstorming forum, called Manthan, of politicians and district officers. All ministers and departmental secretaries accepted it. The Act was put in place to enforce the Citizen's Charter, with the notification listing the services covered, which have now grown to 101 services covering nearly all departments. The Act focused on entitlement-based services, e.g. birth, death, caste, domicile certificates, khasra (land record) copies and mutation copies rather than allocation-based services, except tap water supply connection, at least initially. Bureaucrats commented that politicians accept good ideas that they feel will bring them popularity, a comment encountered across states and cases.

While the Act got favourable media publicity, the diffusion of the right to public services by borrowing to a range of other states

[23] Interview with Anurag Jain, Joint Secretary, Prime Minister's Office, former Secretary to Chief Minister and Secretary, Information Technology, in Madhya Pradesh, January 19, 2015.

[24] Detailed phone interview with Manohar Dubey, IAS, Madhya Pradesh, May 6, 2015.

ruled by a variety of parties, which enacted their own Acts, happened crucially because of political interest in adoption at the top in those states supplemented by able bureaucrats. Two prominent examples are Bihar and Karnataka.

The Bihar Act was passed in May 2011. It originated with the M.P. Chief Minister writing to all other chief ministers.[25] In the Bihar case, it was adopted for reasons of the perceived political popularity of improved governance by Chief Minister Nitish Kumar and what was done was that the services chosen to be guaranteed in the Act's notification listing the services were a selection of those that were being delivered anyway, the difference being that these were now to be delivered within a time limit, there was to be an appellate process, and responsibility for delivery could be fixed on an individual officer. We analyse the case in the light of our framework after the next sub-case.

In Karnataka, an innovation took place on the original borrowing, which attracted attention and further multi-state borrowing downstream. A similar Act was enacted in Karnataka in 2011 and it was the initiative of the BJP Chief Minister D.V. Sadananda Gowda after a meeting with other chief ministers to improve his government's image.[26] The Mysore Administrative Training Institute created a training module which was more service-oriented than technical, relying on the software created by NIC as well relying on an innovative portal for public interface for service delivery created by the programme, not the Institute. The basic challenge was to change the mind-set of bureaucrats in service delivery to one of responsiveness. An E-conclave or meeting of E-governance cells of the BJP units of different states towards the end of 2012, pushed the

[25] Detailed interviews on the Bihar case with B. Muralidharan, a former UN official who worked in Bihar on the public service guarantee, May 5, 2015, and with Deepak Kumar, IAS, Bihar, who handled the matter in 2011, June 26, 2015.

[26] Detailed phone interview on the Karnataka case with Shalini Rajneesh, IAS, Karnataka, May 6, 2015.

process of using information technology for public services guarantees. Karnataka's innovations of the training module and the portal, despite starting later than some other states, were in turn borrowed from states that had started earlier such as M.P., Bihar, and Punjab, and also by Kerala, Jharkhand, and Odisha. There has even been international interest from Afghanistan, Bangladesh, and Pakistan, particularly in the NIC-developed portal for Karnataka, which can be easily tweaked, and the Mysore Administrative Training Institute's training module.

Taking stock of the above case of Right to Public Service legislation adopted by Bihar and twenty other states from the original M.P. model, including the sub-case of Karnataka's adaptation of developing a training module and associated portal and its further multi-state diffusion downstream, the role of the state-level political leadership has been the key driver of the spread of the right to public services. This driver is rooted in perceived political popularity for the government, ruling party as well as the individual chief minister.[27] In the case of the Karnataka adaptation, the role of intra-party networking, that is, of the E-governance cells of BJP state units, as a driver was also important. As far as the facilitating features are concerned, the fact that the M.P. Act was generic and could be tweaked for each state, and that the NIC-developed software package could also be tweaked and translated fairly easily to suit the needs of different states, helped diffusion. A later political incentive as the process gathered momentum has been that imposing delivery time limits and an appellate process also helps the chief minister control his bureaucracy down the line, this being a result of the process after implementation rather than a political driver at the outset.[28] A lesser point that emerged is that competition for recognition like UN Public Services Awards also makes states look

[27] This is corroborated by key officials implementing public service guarantee in M.P., Bihar, and Karnataka.

[28] Detailed interview with B. Muralidharan, a former UN official who worked in Bihar on the public service guarantee, May 5, 2015.

at what other states are doing and helps cross-state learning/borrowing.[29] The spread of the right to public services has been a case of multi-state diffusion of the original M.P. model as well as further multi-state diffusion of a downstream adaptation by Karnataka.

Type III, case I: Multi-state Diffusion Driven by Central Programmes and Popularity Incentives at the State Level

Online Delivery of Land Records: Karnataka's Bhoomi Programme Borrowed by Other States – With Leapfrogging Innovations by Gujarat and Maharashtra

This case is one of both a central programme as well as popularity incentives from good governance driving innovations and multi-state diffusion in a broad public interface governance and service delivery programme. It is also one with two important sub-cases of leapfrogging innovations that were further diffused, multi-state, due to both another Central programme as well state-level popularity incentives.

Karnataka's Bhoomi (land) project of online delivery of land records has been a pioneer in land records computerisation and management, including continual updating. It has been replicated in almost all states by now, and with important modifications to suit local needs. It originated in a central programme, Computerisation of Land Records (CLR) in 1988–9. Land records digitisation and management is critical for farmers as the basis for ownership, sale, and inheritance claims, and for securing loans against collateral, as well as for social justice programmes and for the government getting its due returns, besides being critical for attracting investment.[30]

[29] Detailed interview with B. Muralidharan, a former UN official who worked in Bihar on the public service guarantee, May 5, 2015.

[30] A McKinsey study estimated that India loses a potential 1.3 per cent growth due to poorly maintained land records (cited in Chawla and Bhatnagar, 2004, p. 1).

The origins of the project lay in the 1985 conference of the revenue ministers of states which led to a centrally sponsored pilot scheme on Computerisation of Land Records (CLR) in eight districts across states in 1988–9, extended in 1991–2 to 24 districts, after which little progress was made till 1998 due to the lack of skilled manpower (Chawla & Bhatnagar 2004, pp. 16–17). A decision was made then that the district was not the appropriate level and that this was the subdistrict or taluka. Karnataka took the lead from then on with Bhoomi. By 1996, computerisation projects were sanctioned for all districts in the state, and the Bhoomi programme was launched by the state government which mandated the completion of computerisation of land records in all talukas by 2002. The system depended on the development of a comprehensive data entry software system called Bhoomi to record legacy data records from the manual registers of Village Accountants numbering about 20 million records. Bhoomi has revolutionised land records management, empowered farmers and the general public, enhanced revenue, enabled better planning and programme implementation and loan recovery by banks, and eased one hurdle in the investment climate. Currently, the system is searchable by as many as forty-seven information "fields" such as owners, tenants, crops, yield, mortgage details, bank loans, etc. The incidence of mutation has increased threefold and land-based litigation has been reduced. The Bhoomi system is being extended to urban land records management via the municipalities.

In Karnataka, while the chief minister and revenue minister fully backed the project, the initiative and driving forces were civil servants, a pattern common to other e-governance initiatives in the state in a bottom-up way deriving from the need to tackle problems at the ground level. As the key change agent at the bureaucratic level put it, "Perhaps a desire to project a pro-poor image of the Government led the politicians to lend full support to the project" (Chawla and Bhatnagar 2004, p. 18). However, there were also external change agents including the central government which provided critical funding and also the World Bank which provided a

Structural Adjustment Loan and was supportive of e-governance programmes.

Bhoomi was declared to be the national model for replication by the Ministry of Information Technology of the central government and initial funds provided for this, with almost all states taking up replication, with modifications and innovations. Two interesting developments that built ultimately on the borrowing from Bhoomi but leapfrogged well beyond it are what we classify as the sub-cases of digitisation of land records management and cadastral mapping in Gujarat, and e-Registration in Maharashtra. We discuss the Gujarat and Maharashtra sub-cases of leapfrogging before a case analysis.

Gujarat leapfrogged well beyond a Bhoomi-type programme by undertaking a comprehensive preservation and computerisation of land records by digitisation of village-level cadastral maps.[31] This was a massive preservation exercise of the vulnerable manual records. Manual Record of Rights stopped being issued from 2004–6 with a switch to fully electronic records including those related to mutations. Land records were integrated since 2010 under the Integrated Land Records (e-Jamin) programme run by the National Informatics Centre (NIC), converted to centralised format and put on central servers at the State Data Centre (SDC). New software was developed by which automatic mutation gets registered for agricultural land when property transactions take place. The access of banks and Land Acquiring Authorities to the Record of Rights data support market development including expediting bank loan processing.

[31] Interview with K.P. Krishnan, Additional Secretary, Ministry of Rural Development, January 30, 2015 on cross-state borrowings and innovations in land records management. For details of the National Land Records Management Programme, see http://nlrmp.nic.in. For the following description of the Gujarat case, see "Best Practices in Land Records: Gujarat State", Presentation by Manoj Aggarwal, Settlement Commissioner and Director of Land Records, Gujarat, National Workshop on NLRMP, Western and Northeastern Regional Meeting, September 2014. Also see the description of Integrated Land Records (e-Jamin) (http://www.nic.in/projects/integrated-land-records-e-jamin).

More importantly, with current and forward implications for land records management and the development of land and property markets, from 2005–6 a massive digitisation of all cadastral maps in the state was undertaken, the maps being digitised up to land parcels and geo-referenced on satellite images and scanned. This exercise covered all 18,352 villages and 24,500 map sheets, with the data being made available to all government departments on GSWAN (Gujarat State Wide Area Network), and copies of the digitised maps are available to all. A central programme, the National Land Records Modernisation Programme (NLRMP), launched in August 2008, was a based on ICTs of the much earlier Central programme for Computerisation of Land Records (CLR) from which Karnataka's Bhoomi originated; the major difference is what is possible with modern ICTs which have evolved generations since the pre-internet 1980s and early 1990s.

Gujarat has been considered a leader in implementation of the NLRMP and has attracted visits from officials of other states to study its experience as part of the cross-state learning and adoption of best practices that is promoted in central programmes. Teams from as many as nine states ruled by diverse political parties, sometimes repeat visits, have taken place.

Maharashtra, another sub-case of leapfrogging, leapfrogged from computerisation of land records to e-registration or online registration of land and property transactions and hence continual updating of the system, conducing to the emergence of a system without intermediaries, corruption, wastage of time and money, inaccuracies and non-transparency.[32] The process of registration of property documents was earlier manual, as were land records, and governed by the (Central) Registration Act, 1908, and the Maharashtra Stamp Act and administered by over 500 Sub-Registrar Offices (SROs), state-wide, coming under the Department of Registration and

[32] For a historical and internationally comparative overview of the evolution and debate on land titling, see Chockalingam, *et al.* (n.d.), and for the evolution of Maharashtra's system of e-Registration described in the following paragraphs, see Srinivas and Ghatge 2014.

Stamps. The idea was to set up an online system that allowed people to do the entire registration process online without having to go to an SRO and was initially inspired by an early experiment in Andhra Pradesh in 1996.[33]

The process of computerisation, and moving out of manual mode, began in 2002 with the launch of the i-SARITA (Stamp and Registration Information Technology Application) project. This transitioned from standalone computerisation to web-based centralised system from 2012, developed by NIC, and finally to a fully online e-Registration system from 2014. The application software was developed by the Centre for Development of Advanced Computing (CDAC), Pune, and the project was implemented on a PPP (private-public partnership) basis with private partners appointed by the Department on a BOT (build-operate-transfer) basis for hardware, software and consumables support.

This system also helps to develop property markets and hence conduces to supporting market-oriented reforms by protecting the property of citizens by helping prevent three widely prevalent types of fraudulent transactions from occurring. The three major types of property-related fraud are (1) multiple transactions of the same property; (2) impersonation of the owner in a fraudulent transaction; (3) property transfers by persons who have disputed titles.[34] The i-SARITA system's centralised database and most recently the advent of e-Registration help to pre-empt all three types of frauds.

To take stock of the above cases of cross-state borrowing and multi-state diffusion – Karnataka's Bhoomi and the Gujarat and Maharashtra leapfrogging innovations sub-cases – the digitalisation of land records management and its spread across states and innovations at the state level had several process drivers. Initially, while the computerisation of land records was a CSS (CLR), the success

[33] Detailed phone Interview, S. Chockalingam, IAS, former Inspector-General, Registration, Maharashtra, February 28, 2015.

[34] For the three main types of frauds that are possible, see Chockalingam 2013.

in Karnataka came from a political push, as did the innovations in cadastral mapping in Gujarat, and the adoption of i-SARITA and e-Registration in Maharashtra.[35] In Maharashtra there was full political backing for the introduction of i-SARITA in the assembly at the time of introduction as it was a high revenue-earning department, next only to sales tax. Here the political incentive can be traced not only to popularity in a broad citizen interface programme but also to revenue considerations.

It must be noted though, that borrowing from Bhoomi meant the borrowing of ideas not replication of the software module, whereas the spread of innovations like cadastral mapping and e-Registration to other states is facilitated by the replicability of the software module. Several states including Rajasthan, Jharkhand, Chhattisgarh, U.P., and Odisha, have followed Maharashtra's example, and have, with its permission, borrowed and built on its software module. However, apparently the NIC state units are not good at sharing best practices across states within sectors; another hurdle is that registration departments in many states are not manned by IAS officers and therefore are not part of the informal IAS networking. Yet reforms spread because while there was no formal co-ordination for state registration departments at the central level, exchange of ideas took place through the Finance Ministry's quarterly meeting of IGs of Registration. However, cross-state learning and adoption was promoted and took place as part of the process of spreading best practices at the level of the bureaucracy in CSSs, also due to cases being discussed in sectoral training programmes, and to individual bureaucrats' initiatives in the states. In addition, the technological push factor that operated over the past decade of rapid spread of web-based ICTs across India in general made it easier to develop public service delivery innovations.

Digitisation of land and property records management is a story of multi-state learning and diffusion due to the role played by a CSS both earlier in the form of the CLR and recently in

[35] Anonymous bureaucrats and detailed phone Interview, S. Chockalingam, IAS, former Inspector-General, Registration, Maharashtra, February 28, 2015.

the form of the NLRMP, in contrast to standalone bilateral cases of learning, as well as a certain central facilitation and technology push also linked to a central agency like NIC due to the replicability and modifiability of the requisite software. Repeated central meetings of state level officials in charge of these programmes helped the process of learning, borrowing and multi-state diffusion a part of the NLRMP, a process helped by highly motivated and dynamic bureaucrats in key positions. However, what is interesting and noteworthy is that a central push does not necessarily mean uniformity; it can help diffuse quite diverse innovations originating from the state level.

Type IV, Case I: Difficulties in Borrowing Due to Vested Interests Against Change

Bihar Borrowing from Chhattisgarh's Experience in Grain Procurement and Public Distribution System (PDS) Reform

This is a case of attempted borrowing, driven by potential popularity incentives in broad public interface institutional innovations, that ran into difficulties due mainly to vested interests against change and due to the state-specificity of the original programme sought to be borrowed and adapted.

As many as ten states had sent officials to Chhattisgarh to study its PDS reforms and their necessary precursor, grain procurement reforms, which are seen to be effective in checking waste and corruption.[36] At one time, Kerala and Tamil Nadu were generally held to be leaders in PDS operations but Chhattisgarh has over the past few years been considered a model. Before 2004, the PDS distribu-

[36] Detailed phone interview with Tripurari Sharan, IAS, former Food Secretary, Bihar, January 28, 2015. For a detailed account of Chhattisgarh's rice procurement and public food distribution system and its evolution and reforms, see Garg 2013.

tion outlets were in the hands of private traders.[37] In response to a mobilisation on Right to Food from 2003–6 de-privatisation started in early 2005 and shops were given to panchayats and cooperatives and the number of shops doubled. PDS reform took about four years of continuous work. Procurement reforms had started earlier in 2002 with decentralised procurement by farmers' co-operatives almost from farmers' doorsteps (within 10 kms), and direct transport to millers from procurement centres and quick milling, all saving on wastage of grain, time, and money, all information being put on the web for transparency.

In July and again October-November 2010, a team of bureaucrats led by Tripurari Sharan, then Principal Secretary, Food and Consumer Protection, went from Bihar to Chhattisgarh to study its procurement and PDS models and pick up lessons.[38] The main learning from the Chhattisgarh model was decentralised procurement by farmers' co-operatives which would save on wastage of grain, time, and money by enabling quick milling. Earlier, in Bihar there were two government agencies involved, the Food Corporation of India (FCI), with a limited number of centres in the state which would procure grain directly from farmers, and the Bihar State Food Corporation (BSFC) with more centres, working with block level officers, which would also procure grain from farmers. By contrast, in Chhattisgarh, the Primary Agricultural Credit Societies (PACSs), controlled by farmers, would do the procurement operations in a completely decentralised manner. There were a far larger number of PACSs in Chhattisgarh than there were centres of government agencies in Bihar where there were no PACS equivalents doing procurement.

This system was sought to be adopted in Bihar with modifications. In Bihar, after reform, the BSFC is the nodal agency for

[37] See Garg 2013 for the following description of the Chhattisgarh procurement and PDS reforms.

[38] Detailed phone interview with Tripurari Sharan, IAS, former Food Secretary, Bihar, January 28, 2015.

procurement through its purchase centres in each block in the state for purchase from farmers.[39] However, PACSs like in Chhattisgarh were also created in parallel to BSFC to procure from farmers directly, but these function through the BSFC. The BSFC will thus acquire grain directly from farmers as well as the grain procured by the PACSs and deliver this to the FCI. The new system is now said to be in full swing except for limitations which arise from the absence of other components of procurement and PDS reform that are prerequisites for the success of the Chhattisgarh system. These are the need for seamless integration between on-the-ground procurement and milling and storage infrastructure of the state food corporation, which means the required storage capacity has to be available. The Bihar State Food Corporation is the repository and has a shortage of storage capacity. Also, electronic tracking of grain movements has not been streamlined as in Chhattisgarh, making it harder to check the diversion of foodgrains at different stages of the delivery chain. However, procurement decentralising reform is only the necessary step for the crucial next step which is issue of foodgrains from the repository to PDS dealers. In Chhattisgarh, there has been investment in the delivery infrastructure and the very same PACSs that were the procurement agencies were the PDS dealers, whereas in Bihar the PDS dealers are private traders and they resist the equivalent of PACS becoming dealers as it is loss of legitimate and corrupt incomes for them. The popularity incentive for the reform lies in the reform of the PDS to reduce leakages and ensure that the poor get their rations, not so much the decentralisation of procurement which is only the precursor to PDS reform. The Bihar case of borrowing from the Chhattisgarh model of procurement and PDS reform can be said to be only a partial success due to the resistance of the vested interests of PDS shop owners. As a Chhattisgarh bureaucrat said, his state's model needs legal and process reforms that need two to three years preparation for

[39] See http://sfc.bihar.gov.in/login.htm for an account of the BSFC and its operations.

successful implementation given that there are entrenched vested interests like PDS dealers and state procurement agencies to be dealt with as part of the reform.[40]

This is a case of bilateral borrowing with political incentives as reform of PDS, dependent on upstream reform of procurement, which can be politically popular among poor voters. The initiative for this attempted borrowing was also initially political and at the chief minister level though the states were ruled by different leading parties (although the BJP was a coalition partner of the JD[U] in Bihar) but both parties were keen on performance on development after fifteen years of rule by the Rashtriya Janata Dal which prioritised caste identity politics at the expense of development and governance.[41] There were no facilitating features such as a generic law or ICT package involved, and the structure of agrarian and commercial interests is highly state-specific, not conducing to easy adoption of another state's reforms in this policy and institutional sphere, besides leading to mixed incentives because of the contradiction between potential future popularity if the reforms succeed versus the expenditure of political capital in confronting powerful vested interests.

Cross-State Learning/Borrowing: Incentives, Drivers, Facilitating Features, Diffusion, and Looking Ahead

Incentives, Drivers, Facilitating Features and Types of Diffusion

From the six selected cases – in our four Types – of cross-state learning/borrowing in public service delivery that have been outlined in capsule form in this paper, what can we conclude about the

[40] Detailed phone interview with N. Baijendra Kumar, Additional Chief Secretary, Chhattisgarh, January 15, 2015.

[41] Anonymous bureaucrats.

incentives, drivers, facilitating features, and types of diffusion of such learning/borrowing?

First, as regards incentives, in line with my hypothesis stated at the outset about the perceived electoral importance of better governance and service delivery, four of the five successful cases of cross-state borrowing are in service delivery programmes with a broad citizen interface such as online grievance systems, online service delivery for common services, right to public service delivery, and land and property records reform, etc., where the popularity impact of perceived improvement in service delivery would be maximum. An exception would be special courts which I have put in Type I, but such courts, though they do not deliver mass services, have a signalling impact on the electorate at large and hence a potential popularity dividend.

Second, as regards the driving forces that initiated, facilitated or propelled all the cases of borrowing across states – except partly the Type III case and sub-cases that originated in and were diffused partly by central programmes – the initiatives came from a political push from the state political leadership and by political support to key bureaucrats in charge of such programmes. Even in the Type III case and sub-cases, the innovations in Karnataka and by leapfrogging in Gujarat and Maharashtra were owing to state political leadership. While several of these have happened in BJP-ruled states, singly or in coalition as with the JD(U) in Bihar, with the BJP in recent years prioritising better governance and learning of cross-state lessons in formal political interaction of chief ministers and functional ministers, such learning/borrowing has also taken place across states ruled by different parties such as in Maharashtra or from Andhra Pradesh or Odisha. That is, while co-partisanship – and implicitly, the ideological and ideational factors – is an important facilitator as per the comparative literature's findings, it does not exclude borrowings from states ruled by different parties. An additional political incentive in public service guarantee programmes is tighter control of the bureaucracy by the political leadership as a result of implementation of the programme. However, a lot of cross-state learning is tacit and informal, aided by informal networking among IAS officers as well as formal mid-career training programmes albeit sector/issue-focused. These cases support the comparative literature's findings about the importance of professional networks of public officials.

Third, as regards features that facilitate borrowing, two are key – a generic law that is modifiable by other states and/or a modifiable ICT package. A lot of cross-state learning takes place in CSS, particularly in national missions, and is also promoted by the NIC as far as ICT applications go, and at the initiative of bureaucrats, particularly in implementation.

Fourth, as regards the types of diffusion, those that do not originate in Central programmes are typically bilateral, while those that originate in Central programmes tend to be multi-state, an exception being the multi-state diffusion of the right to public services, which did not have a central programme origin. Adaptation and leapfrogging in diffusion processes can be seen both in non-central programme-origin borrowing (Karnataka's training module and portal in right to public service) and in those originating in central programmes (cadastral mapping in Gujarat, E-registration in Maharashtra), such adaptation and leapfrogging being unpredictable events governed by specific – including technological – circumstances.

Looking Ahead

Following this analysis, the question that then arises is: can cross-state learning/borrowing in service delivery, for which there is clearly an electoral incentive, be more formalised and institutionalised to contribute to development through the quicker spread of innovations and best practices? What are the possible institutions and processes for this?

One possible institutionalised process is to formalise cross-state learning/borrowing in the mid-career training programmes of

IAS officers (Phases III, IV and V) conducted at the LBSNAA, Mussoorie.

A second possible institutionalised process is to incentivise, at the technical level, the NIC to transfer lessons and applications, and their modifications across states. As of now, NIC personnel doing ICT development work for states' service delivery programmes work in silos unless modification by a borrowing state or in the context of a CSS demands a change in orientation.

A third possible institution is the NITI Aayog, the successor institution of the Planning Commission abolished in 2014. Its agenda and structure are still evolving and being defined but early statements indicate that it seeks greater involvement of the states and a move away from a top-down model. The formal acceptance by the government of the recommendations of the Fourteenth Finance Commission, to increase the states' share of the divisible pool of central tax revenues from 32 per cent to 42 per cent, the biggest ever one-time jump, would have precisely this effect, making for greater state autonomy and experimentation with projects and programmes tailored to the particular needs of individual states in tandem with the announced whittling down of CSS. This could yield a crop of successful experiments in service delivery that could be adopted by other states as best practices. However, smooth and effective adoption would require some sort of institutionalised cross-state learning mechanism. NITI Aayog's mandate states that it will provide "strategic and technical advice to the states". This mandate and declared intentions would seem to allow scope for institutionalisation of cross-state learning processes and promotion of adoption and adaptation of best practices across states and also from international experience to take what has so far been informal and tacit learning to a more systemic and systematic level. Although later in Modi's first and early second term there have been mixed signals on state autonomy, with the Finance Ministry directly negotiating with states since the Planning Commission mechanism has been replaced by a NITI Aayog without that mandate, there appears to be growing scope for experimentation in inter-state learning processes.

The larger goal would be to create a virtuous cycle, in the macro-political economy, of competing for electoral success on the basis of performance in governance and service delivery, more broadly, developmental outcomes rather than patronage/clientelist politics, or identity politics, with cross-state learning processes, as well as international learning processes, incentivised and institutionalised as part of the effort to deliver better outcomes.

Acknowledgements

I would like to thank two anonymous referees and Vikram Chand for feedback and twenty-two interviewees for their co-operation. This is a much-revised version of a paper originally written for the World Bank, whose earlier support I acknowledge.

References

Anderson, C. J. (2007). "The End of Economic Voting? Contingency Dilemmas and the Limits of Democratic Accountability", *Annual Review of Political Science, 10*, pp. 271–96, https://doi.org/10.1146/annurev.polisci.10.050806.155344.

Chandra, K. (2004). *Why Ethnic Parties Succeed: Patronage and Ethnic Headcounts in India* (Cambridge: Cambridge University Press).

Chawla, R., and S. Bhatnagar (2004). *Online Delivery of Land Titles to Rural Farmers in Karnataka, India* (World Bank, http://web.worldbank.org/archive/website00819C/ WEB/PDF/INDIA_BH.PDF).

Chockalingam, S. (2013). *Preventing Frauds in Property Transactions: A Study of the Possibility of Preventing Frauds Using the Centralised Registration Module i-SARITA*, September.

Chockalingam, S., B. Gangopadhyay, and P.K. Sharma (n.d.). "Protecting the Property Rights of People of India: Putting the Pieces Together to Ensure Clarity of Land Ownership in India".

Garg, S. (2013). *Systems of Public Food Distribution and Procurement of Rice: Experiences from Chhattisgarh state of India*, http://www.ipc-undp.

org/conference/south-south- learning-event/presentations/Samir%20Garg.pdf.

Gupta, P., S. Kumar, and S. Sardesai (2013). "The Weakening of Electoral Anti-incumbency", *Economic and Political Weekly*, *48* (13), pp. 128–31, https://www.epw.in/journal/2013/ 13/notes/weakening-electoral-anti-incumbency.html.

Keefer, P., and S. Khemani (2004). "Why Do the Poor Receive Poor Services?", *Economic and Political Weekly*, *39* (9), pp. 935–43, https://www.epw.in/journal/2004/09/special- articles/why-do-poor-receive-poor-services.html.

Khemani, S. (2001). *Decentralization and Accountability: Are Voters More Vigilant in Local than in National Elections?* (World Bank Working Paper, 2557).

Lewis-Back, M.S., and M. Stegmaier (2000). "Economic Determinants of Electoral Outcomes", *Annual Review of Political Science*, *3*, pp. 183–219, https://doi.org/10.1146/ annurev.polisci.3.1.183.

Mishra, V. (2011, February 6). "The Sharing Parivar, *Indian Express*.

Niedzwiecki, S. (2016). "Social Policies, Attribution of Responsibility, and Political Alignments: A Subnational Analysis of Argentina and Brazil", *Comparative Political Studies*, *49* (4), pp. 457–98, https://doi.org/10.1177/0010414015612392.

Pacek, A., and B. Radcliff (1995). "The Political Economy of Competitive Elections in the Developing World", *American Journal of Political Science*, *39* (3), pp. 745–59, https://doi.org/10.2307/2111652.

Planning Commission, Govt. of India (2012). *Mid-term Appraisal of the Eleventh Five Year Plan, 2007–12*, http://planningcommission.gov.in/plans/mta/11th_mta/chapterwise/ list_boxes.pdf.

Ravishankar, N. (2009). "The Cost of Ruling: Anti-incumbency in Elections", *Economic and Political Weekly*, *44* (10), pp. 92–8.

Segatto, C. (2018). "Policy Diffusion in Subnational Governments: State–Local Relationships in the Brazilian Education Policy", *Regional and Federal Studies*, *28* (1), pp. 79–100, https://doi.org/10.1080/13597566.2017.1409732

Srinivas, A.K., and B. Ghatge (2014). *Case Study on Department of Registration and Stamps: Project i-SARITA, National e-Governance Division, Ministry of Communications and Information Technology*, http://nisg.org/files/documents/UP1399464092.pdf.

Sugiyama, N.B. (2008). "Theories of Policy Diffusion: Social Sector Reform in Brazil", *ComparativePolitical Studies, 41* (2), pp. 193–216, https://doi.org/10.1177/0010414007300916.

Vaishnav, M., and R. Swanson (2015). "Does Good Economics Make for Good Politics? Evidence from Indian States", *India Review, 14* (3), pp. 279–311, https: //doi.org/ 10.1080/14736489.2015.1066218.

Wallner, J. (2017). "Cooperation Without the Leviathan: Intergovernmental Policymaking in Canadian Education", *Regional and Federal Studies, 27* (4), pp. 417–40, https://doi.org/ 10.1080/13597566.2017.1327429.

Yadav, Y., and S. Palshikar (2009). "Between Fortuna and Virtu: Explaining the Congress' Ambiguous Victory in 2009", *Economic and Political Weekly, 44* (39), pp. 33–46.

6

The Growth and Sectoral Composition of India's Middle Classes

Its Impact on the Politics of Economic Liberalisation

THIS PAPER AIMS TO analyse the growth of the middle classes in India since the 1980s, in order to understand its implications for the process of economic liberalisation which began in 1991. The case that is usually made is that over the period of the early 1980s, when the Gross National Product (GNP) grew at a higher rate of above 5 per cent, as compared to 3.5 per cent in the 1950–80 period, the growth of the middle classes to a substantial size between 100 and 250 million, the exact number depending on where and on what criteria one draws the cut-off point, has fundamentally changed the social structure of Indian society. From a social structure characterised by a sharp contrast between a small elite and a large impoverished mass, Indian society has shifted to being one with substantial intermediate classes. The first type of social structure supported a broadly socialistic ideology while the second type has created a mass base for capitalism and liberalisation.[1]

The debate centred on the middle class has focused on the size of

[1] See, for example, Atul Kohli's (1989) argument that the growth of the number of shareholders in India provides a mass base for capitalism.

this class (whether it is, say, 50 million or 150 million or 250 million), and the criteria to be used in drawing boundaries. This paper focuses on a criterion that is politically more salient: the sectoral and occupational composition of the middle classes whether they are largely in the broadly defined public sector, the (entirely private) agricultural sector, or the non-agricultural private sector. My hypothesis is that the orientation of the middle classes towards economic liberalisation, especially towards continued or "second-generation" economic reforms involving the privatisation of public enterprises, reduction of the scope of the government, and desubsidisation of a range of activities and interest groups, depends on two factors: (i) the magnitude of the public-sector component, and the publicly subsidised component, of the middle classes; and (ii) how this component is being affected by these reforms. Public-sector employment in India means total job security and publicly determined, not market-determined, pay scales. Public-sector employees have a vested interest in the size and scope of the state and in the periodically increased public-sector wages. Similarly, nearly all of the better-off agrarian population has a vested interest in a variety of central and state-level subsidies, including those relating to fertilisers, electricity, water, and credit. Thus, these two segments of the middle classes have vested interests that militate against fiscal-stabilisation measures such as downsizing, public-sector wage restraints, central-and state-level de-subsidisation, and structural changes like privatisation, with consequential implications for continued reform. Their attitude can largely be expected to be oriented towards the benefits of liberalisation while being unprepared to accept the painful but inevitable costs of the process. This is not to say that all segments of the non-agricultural private sector middle classes can be expected to be pro-liberalisation. Non-competitive segments, such as those in sick industries or protected industries, could well be opposed, while groups employed in other sectors have much to gain from continued liberalisation.

Theories of the Middle Classes and India's Political Economy

There is a vast conceptual, theoretical and empirical literature on class and class structure, both Marxist and non-Marxist, that deals with the "middle classes" or the "intermediate strata" in capitalist societies (Bechhofer and Elliott 1981; Johnson 1982, 1985; Wright 1985). I do not attempt to summarise it here. There is also a considerable body of literature, overwhelmingly Marxist, on the class analysis of Indian society, which too I shall not summarise. However, there is very little on the Indian middle classes, particularly in the context of the post-1991 economic liberalisation period. In the approach to this paper, I will selectively refer only to the main points in the debate on the "middle classes" in the general literature on class that may be usefully be applied to the Indian context. Likewise, I only refer to developments in the Indian literature on class and class structure that refer to the "middle classes" or the "intermediate strata", and which are of relevance to understanding the relationship between the middle classes and economic liberalisation since 1991.

But who are the middle classes? How does one define them? The Marxian category of class, to begin with the paradigm which gives it central importance, defines class in relation to ownership of the means of production. In capitalist societies, the core classes are those of capitalists and workers, that is, the owners of the means of production and those who sell their labour power to the former for a wage. The only other class significant in the Marxian schema, aside from the landlords and peasants, is the petty bourgeoisie, an intermediate stratum of small producers and proprietors, typically shopkeepers, independent artisans and small manufacturers. But while the Marxian schema may be heuristically useful for certain purposes, it is of limited use for the empirical analysis of the class structure of societies, particularly in developing countries. For since the middle of the nineteenth century, the growth of capitalism, dependent on science and technology, and the growth of regulatory state apparatuses has meant the growth of an intermediate strata in white-collar occupations and professions, both salaried and self-employed, particularly the former, characterised by increasing degrees of education, and as a class which is intermediate in income between capitalists and manual workers. The middle classes have not only become a large fraction of the population in capitalist societies, but are the classes which throw up intellectuals and politicians, and thus play an important political and ideological role. Their importance grows as economies the world over, including developing economies, shift towards the services sector, in terms of both the share of the Gross Domestic Product (GDP) and employment.

Erik Olin Wright did not consider the middle class a true class but a "contradictory location within class relations" (Wright 1985: 19, 24–57). In a detailed analysis of the horizontal fractionisation and vertical layering of the middle classes, he argued that the "new middle class" of professionals and white-collar workers differed from the "old middle class", or petty bourgeoisie of small independent producers and shopkeepers, in that the latter shares the surplus produced by the working class and accruing to the capitalist class, because of their control of scarce knowledge and skills and their supervisory role in the labour process. However, they are also employees and sellers of mental labour power, and therefore exploited. For our purpose, what is useful is that the middle classes are highly fractionalised and layered and have a deeply contradictory relationship to capitalism, although they are largely allied to the capitalist classes. Some scholars, writing about the middle classes in developing countries, emphasised their relative autonomy from the principal property-owning classes, the industrial bourgeoisie and the landowners, due to a combination of their control of the state and their possession of scarce skills. Aijaz Ahmad argued that far from being mere "agents" of the ruling classes or a mere "vacillating mass" the intermediate and auxiliary classes of the periphery occupy a strategic field in the economy and politics of their countries, thus obtaining power and initiatives which make it possible for them to struggle for political dominance over other classes, including the bourgeoisie (Ahmad 1985: 44).

Here, Ahmad is referring to the sections of the middle class that play a role in politics. As for the traditional or "old middle class" or petty bourgeoisie in developing countries, especially at the lower end of the scale, it can be argued, as Chris Gerry and Chris Birkbeck (1981) have done, that the petty commodity producer is a proletarian in disguise. Pranab Bardhan also shared the view that the middle classes or "professionals", including all white-collar workers, are one of the "dominant proprietary classes" on the basis of their possession of human capital in the form of education and skills, especially those in the state apparatus, who have a rentier role in the control of state decisions on disbursements and patronage (Bardhan 1994: 51).

The classic work on the historical development of the Indian middle classes remains that of B.B. Misra (1960), though it is not useful for our purpose in this essay. Satish Deshpande (2003), while discussing possible alternative definitions of the middle class in the Indian context, privileged both cultural capital and the middle classes' role in the developmental state and, historically, in the ruling Congress party. While emphasising the highly differentiated character of the middle classes (including linguistic, English–non-English speaking, differentiation), he stated that cultural capital may consist of identities (caste, community, region) or competences (educational credentials, linguistic and other social skills), and that it has three attributes of property – tangible and psychological benefits; the ability to exclude others; and transmissibility across generations. Referring to Gramsci, Deshpande argued that the main function of the middle classes is to build hegemony, and further, that the elite fraction of the middle class specialises in the production of ideologies, while its mass fraction "engages in the exemplary consumption of ideologies thus investing them with social legitimacy" (ibid.: 141). These ideas are potentially useful in analysing the growing legitimacy of economic liberalisation as a policy paradigm and also, perhaps, of the Hindutva ideology and the Bharatiya Janata Party (BJP) as a political party (see also Hasan 2001; Palshikar 2001).

Ashok Rudra (1989), in a Marxian framework, conceived of the "intelligentsia", along with industrial capitalists and landlords, as a "ruling" class. He defined the intelligentsia, generally meaning non-manual labourers, as consisting of the following groups or strata:

- all white-collar workers in the organised private sector, including clerks, but excluding peons (messengers), drivers and sweepers
- all public servants from the top to lower-division clerks, excluding Group D of public-sector employees (peons, sweepers, etc.)
- teachers, doctors, lawyers, engineers, architects, and nurses in the organised sector or private practice
- writers, journalists, artists, advertising and entertainment industry professionals in both sectors and the self-employed
- professionals, politicians and trade-union leaders

All of these categories belong to the "intelligentsia" and share in the surplus produced by direct producers. The members of the intelligentsia all belong to the middle classes, but not all the latter belong to the former. This last point is somewhat cryptic, but one assumes that in stating this Rudra was referring to the "old middle class" or petty bourgeoisie of small shopkeepers and artisans, perceived as belonging to the middle classes, but not to the intelligentsia.

Pranab Bardhan objected to the use of the term "intelligentsia", considering them instead a ruling class (Bardhan 1989). His "professionals" generally match Rudra's five types of non-manual workers. Bardhan's framework conceived of state power as being dominated by a coalition of three dominant proprietary classes – the industrial capitalists, the rich farmers, and the "professionals (both civilian and military), including white-collar workers". Bardhan's definition of professionals appears to be restricted to professionals in the public bureaucracy; he explained in a footnote: "I have kept a conceptual distinction between white-collar workers in the public bureaucracy (which I include among the proprietary classes in civil society) and the political leadership representing the state (sometimes I have referred to it as the 'state elite')" (Bardhan 1994: 51). However, in work following his original use of the term "professionals" in Bardhan (1994 [1984]), he clarified that his definition of professionals included all white-collar workers, not just those in the public bureaucracy (Bardhan 1989). The basis for including professionals as one of the dominant proprietary classes was their possession of human capital in the form of education, skills and technical expertise. The economic interests of this class, particularly state professionals, lay in maintaining the state's economic empire for rent-extraction. Public policy was driven by the internal conflicts within this coalition, with each of the proprietary classes being able to defend its own interests without prevailing over the others. The result was protection (for import-substituting industrialists), subsidies (for all segments of the ruling coalition and food subsidies for the poor), over-regulation, and a bloated public sector (for the state professionals). The politics of competitive rent-seeking and populism pre-empted deregulation and growth complementing infrastructural investment, had a deficitary logic, retarded growth, and implied a deteriorating conflict-management mechanism.

Bardhan's work was a late offshoot of the debate on slow industrial growth in India since the mid-1960s. As far as the relationship between economic liberalisation and the middle classes was concerned, in Bardhan's framework, public enterprises were used to distributing patronage such as contracts and jobs, raising political finance, and were generally subjected to rent-seeking activities by the professionals, from politicians down to white-collar workers. The net result was both fiscal deficits and slow and inefficient growth.

Bardhan's political sociology was a modification of Marxism, one that incorporated insights from neo-classical political economy. His coalition of dominant proprietary classes sounded Marxian, but in his scheme of things policy outcomes were the result of the internal conflicts of this coalition, rather than of class struggle between the exploiting and exploited classes. The dominant coalition included not only the bourgeois–landlord alliance but also professionals, including white-collar workers, in the public sector as one of the dominant proprietary classes in themselves, with their own corporate class interests, distinct from, and to some extent conflicting with, those of industrialists and landlords. Bardhan argued that there was, at the beginning of the 1991 reform period, greater overlap and "increasing social and economic interpenetration" between the rich farmers and the urban industrial and professional classes, as well as between all of these and non-resident Indians, which led to reduced conflict within the dominant coalition (Bardhan 1989: 156; see also Bardhan 1992). He also argued that" [a]lmost all of this so-called 'middle class' . . . belongs to the top two deciles, if not the top decile, of the income pyramid. Its members certainly belong to different parts of what I have described earlier as the three dominant classes in India" (Bardhan 1992: 333).

Both these were departures from the traditional Marxian model in the direction of liberal-pluralist interest group theory and neo-classical political economy. For the state, in Bardhan's analysis, was not merely relatively autonomous in Poulantzas' sense (1973: 256–74) and structurally constrained but standing above the fractions of the dominant class(es) and managing public policy in the interest of "capital as a whole". Its personnel were a proprietary class in themselves, based on their possession of relatively scarce (in the Indian context) human capital in the form of education and by way of de facto possession of public capital assets. Their interest was to maximise rents from discretionary controls which constrained, and to some extent militated against, both industrial capitalist and land-owning interests.

Atul Kohli (1989) assigned the origins of the liberalizing impulse in the late 1980s to Prime Minister Rajiv Gandhi and his inner circle of advisors, and not to the supporting groups, of which he identified two – business groups and the middle classes. Of the former group, he argued that the business community of India had tended to react to rather than lead economic policy. Its power was closer to being one of veto than of agenda-setting. There was middle-class support for liberalisation, Kohli argued, because it offered them concrete benefits such as direct tax reduction and more consumer goods. Kohli also noted an emerging structural link between the growing middle classes and big business via the booming capital market, as business increasingly financed itself by raising capital from the public. Big business thus acquired a mass social base, while the middle class acquired a stake in corporate profitability.

The literature since 1991 indicates a shift from state-driven to society-driven reforms. E. Sridharan (1993), in a state-centric rather than society-centric analysis, argued that all liberalisation initiatives had originated not from the business community but from the top political leadership, and the former had merely reacted to it, largely supportive so long as the initiatives did not threaten them with foreign competition. Vanita Shastri (1997) also focused on the elite policy circle. Jorgen Dige Pedersen (2000) argued that the reforms were society-led in that the business community had been reconfigured and led by a new breed of entrepreneurs with an interest in reform. However, this work still focused on groups which would form a thin upper stratum, though outside the state.

Subsequently, Arun Shourie, as Minister for Disinvestment, Communications and Information Technology in the National Democratic Alliance (NDA) government, made the same point about the "society"-drivenness of reform in another way:

> Reforms are not the whim or fancy of some individuals. They are dictated by the compulsions that our polity and economy face on the one side and are propelled by the opportunities that have opened up on the other . . . Indeed, one Reform creates pressure that other Reforms be put through. Import-export licensing is abolished. Trade increases.

> Traders and manufacturers demand that ports be improved so that turnaround time comes down to Singapore levels, that the DGFT [Directorate General of Foreign Trade] accepts electronic filing of forms.[2]

The tone and tenor of the Bharatiya Janata Party's (BJP) election campaign in 2004, with its "India Shining" and "feel-good" slogans, seemed aimed at the middle classes, whose support for both reforms and the BJP seemed to be assumed.

Ashutosh Varshney (1999) distinguished between elite politics and mass politics, but focused on identity politics in the latter sphere, arguing that economic reforms largely remained an elite affair, while mass politics was driven by communal and caste passions. There was no detailed discussion on the growth of the middle classes per se and the implications of this growth for the politics of economic reform in any of these analyses.

At the end of this theoretical discussion, we are still left with considerable theoretical and conceptual ambiguity about the middle classes. I, therefore, adopt a pragmatic and eclectic definition (admittedly arbitrary) combining income levels with non-manual occupational status, following Andre Beteille's position (2001) that occupational function and employment status are the two most significant criteria for defining the middle classes, although education and income are also widely used. The most important occupational division is between manual and non-manual work, with typical middle-class occupations being non-manual ones. This would also roughly agree with Rudra's definition of the intelligentsia, except that I include the self-employed "old middle class" or petty bourgeoisie of shopkeepers, artisans and small businessmen above a certain income level. Therefore, we need an income cut-off level that would include all non-manual workers, even if it includes some manual workers.

[2] Arun Shourie, "When Spirit is Willing, Flesh has a Way", *Indian Express,* 4 February 2004.

Estimating Shifts in the Size and Composition of the Middle Classes in India

My definition is constrained by the availability of data and therefore I have adjusted my definition to fit the best available data for such an exercise, viz. the Market Information Survey of Households (MISH) data set of the National Council for Applied Economic Research (NCAER). This data set is more appropriate for our purpose than the National Sample Survey (NSS) data based on consumption; it is more appropriate for estimating middle-class size as income distribution data are better for this purpose than consumption data, though consumption of durables and consumables is extremely well covered by the MISH too.[3] Also, the MISH provided data is based on very large samples of 300,000 (compared to 120,000 of NSS), on both income distributions and occupational distributions over time since 1985-86, in a form that makes comparisons of income distribution across time possible:

> Households are classified into five income groups, namely, low, lower-middle, middle, upper-middle and high. Since the income data are collected at current prices, the cut-off points of each income group for each year are adjusted to allow for inflation so that they are comparable over time. Thus, these surveys provide comparable income distributions at different points of time. Such a unique data set is not available from any other source. (NCAER 2003: 5)

Another important point is that since the MISH surveys accounted for approximately 70 per cent of the GDP, survey incomes turned out to be less than the national income estimated by the Central Statistical Organization (CSO).

> The reason for this is that the CSO uses the economic concept of income, which includes imputed incomes, unrealised accruals, etc., while estimating the GDP. In surveys, on the other hand, the res-

[3] Lal, Mohan and Natarajan (2001) compared the MISH and NSS data with

> pondents report what they consider to be their income. Also, in surveys, income is invariably understated. This, however, does not underestimate the importance or usefulness of the MISH data. MISH surveys use the same method to estimate the household income and the underlying income distribution. The trends are therefore likely to be reliable. (NCAER 2003: 5)

One limitation that needs to be noted is that the five income groups used were not quintiles from bottom to top, but were based on arbitrary cut-off points. This constrained me to work with these arbitrary cut-offs-based income groups to estimate the middle class, although I combined the MISH data with other data in an eclectic manner. However, these five income classes very roughly lent themselves to this exercise.

This paper estimates the size and growth of the middle class in the post-reform (post-1991) period by merging the MISH data with other sources of data, primarily data on organised-sector employment, particularly public employment. My attempt is not merely to attempt to estimate the growth of the middle classes in horizontal income slabs using this data, but also to try to divide the horizontal income slabs into sectoral occupational categories such as the public-sector middle class, the non-agricultural private sector middle class, including its self-employed components, and the agricultural middle class, to the extent that such mergers of data are feasible.

There has been very little systematic work on the Indian middle classes despite the general feeling that the middle classes have increased in their thickness as strata. An alternative to Marxian classifications based on relations to the means of production, elaborated in great complexity by Wright, was to look at the middle classes in terms of income classes, or income-cum-occupation defined classes, beginning from the top, thereby working with categories

---

respect to the debate on the post-reform decline of poverty, and argued that NSS data in the 1990s was less reliable and greatly overstated poverty.

broadly similar in principle to Rudra's intelligentsia, and endorsed by Bardhan. In other words, the alternative was to view them as intermediate income groups in non-manual occupations, situated between a tiny rich upper class and a majority of low-income and manual occupation groups. This was admittedly extremely ambiguous and everything depended on theoretically or policy determined cut-off points for classification.

The MISH data-derived distribution of households by five income groups (Tables 6.1 and 6.2) provided the following picture of the growth of the income-defined middle class: the MISH data set's arbitrary cut-offs, which I was constrained to work with, divided the population of 171.92 1 million households in 1998-99 into five income groups (in rupees per annum) on the basis of the income reported by the respondent head of household:

- High Above (Rs 140,000)
- Upper Middle (Rs 105,001 – Rs 140,000)
- Middle (Rs 70,001 – Rs 105,000)
- Middle (Rs 35,001 – Rs 70,000)
- Lower (upto Rs 35,000)

Based on this classification, I differentiated between three ways of conceiving of the middle class:

- Elite middle class (i.e., including the very rich) – this corresponded to the High Income group mentioned earlier.
- Expanded middle class – this corresponded to the High and Upper Middle Income groups mentioned earlier.
- Broadest middle class – this corresponded to the High, Upper Middle, and Middle Income groups mentioned earlier.

Tables 6.1 and 6.2 show that from 1989–90 to 1998–9, there were significant increases in the percentage and number of households in each of the three top categories overall, as well as in both the urban and rural components, combined with a decline in the percentage of households falling in the Lower Income group, and in the Lower Middle Income group (except for an increase in this

Table 6.1: Estimated Distribution of Households by Income Groups (in percentage)

Annual Income (at 1998–9 prices)	*1989–90*	*1992–3*	*1996–7*	*1997–8*	*1998–9*
Urban					
Up to 35,000 (L)	37.14	38.44	24.46	21.87	18.96
35,001–70,000 (LM)	34.76	32.97	34.69	34.42	33.76
70,001–105,000 (M)	17.89	16.07	21.33	22.11	22.59
105,001–140,000 (UM)	6.46	7.62	10.55	11.29	12.16
Above 140,000 (H)	3.75	4.90	8.98	10.30	12.53
Total	100.00	100.00	100.00	100.00	100.00
Broadest Middle Class (M + UM + H)	28.10	28.59	40.86	43.70	47.28
Expanded Middle class (UM + H)	10.21	12.52	19.53	21.59	24.69
Elite Middle class (H)	3.75	4.90	8.98	10.30	12.53
Total no. of households ('000)	40,106	42,114	47,375	48,161	49,111
Rural					
Up to 35,000 (L)	67.34	65.49	52.80	50.69	47.94
35,001–70,000 (LM)	23.89	22.61	31.79	33.17	34.83
70,001–105,000 (M)	7.07	8.22	9.54	9.87	10.41
105,001–140,000 (UM)	1.16	2.30	3.44	3.61	3.85
Above 140,000 (H)	0.54	1.37	2.43	2.65	2.97
Total	100.00	100.00	100.00	100.00	100.00
Broadest Middle Class (M + UM + H)	8.77	11.89	15.41	16.13	17.23
Expanded Middle class (UM + H)	1.70	3.67	5.87	6.26	6.82
Elite Middle class (H)	0.54	1.37	2.43	2.65	2.97
Total no. of households ('000)	1,02,334	1,13,203	1,19,289	1,21,046	1,22,810
Total					
Up to 35,000 (L)	58.84	58.16	44.75	42.49	39.66
35,001–70,000 (LM)	26.95	25.42	32.61	33.53	34.53
70,001–105,000 (M)	10.11	10.35	12.89	13.35	13.89
105,001–140,000 (UM)	2.66	3.74	5.46	5.80	6.22
Above 140,000 (H)	1.44	2.33	4.29	4.83	5.70
Total	100.00	100.00	100.00	100.00	100.00
Broadest Middle Class (M+UM+H)	14.21	16.42	22.64	23.98	25.81
Expanded Middle class (UM+H)	4.10	6.07	9.75	10.63	11.92
Elite Middle class (H)	1.44	2.33	4.29	4.83	5.70
Total no. of households ('000)	1,42,440	1,55,317	1,66,664	1,69,207	1,71,921

Source: NCAER (2003: 123).

Note: L=Low Income, LM=Lower Middle Income, M=Middle Income, UM=Upper Middle Income, H=High Income.

Table 6.2: Estimated Distribution of Households by Income Groups (in millions)

Annual Income (at 1998–9 prices)	*1989–90*	*1992–3*	*1996–7*	*1997–8*	*1998–9*
Urban					
Up to 35,000 (L)	83.414	90.656	64.892	58.984	52.144
35,001–70,000 (LM)	78.069	77.756	92.033	92.831	92.847
70,001–105,000 (M)	40.180	37.899	56.588	59.631	62.127
105,001–140,000 (UM)	14.509	7.620	27.989	30.449	33.443
Above 140,000 (H)	8.422	11.556	23.824	27.779	34.460
Total	100.00	100.00	100.00	100.00	100.00
Broadest Middle Class (M+UM+H)	63.111	57.075	108.402	117.860	130.030
Expanded Middle class (UM+H)	22.931	19.176	51.813	58.229	67.903
Elite Middle class (H)	8.422	11.556	23.824	27.779	34.460
Total no. of households ('000)	40.106	42.114	47.375	48.161	49.111
Rural					
Up to 35,000 (L)	385.906	415.165	352.714	343.606	329.701
35,001–70,000 (LM)	136.907	143.333	212.363	224.845	239.538
70,001–105,000 (M)	40.516	52.110	63.729	66.905	71.593
105,001–140,000 (UM)	6.648	14.581	22.980	24.471	26.478
Above 140,000 (H)	3.095	8.685	16.233	17.963	20.426
Total	100.00	100.00	100.00	100.00	100.00
Broadest Middle Class (M+UM+H)	50.258	75.375	102.942	109.338	118.497
Expanded Middle class (UM+H)	9.742	23.265	39.213	42.434	46.904
Elite Middle class (H)	3.095	8.685	16.233	19.963	20.426
Total no. of households ('000)	102.334	113.203	119.289	121.046	122.810
Total					
Up to 35,000 (L)	469.345	505.861	417.660	402.618	381.830
35,001–70,000 (LM)	214.97	221.097	304.355	317.717	332.440
70,001–105,000 (M)	80.644	90.022	120.305	126.499	133.727
105,001–140,000 (UM)	21.218	32.530	50.959	54.958	59.884
Above 140,000 (H)	11.486	20.266	40.039	45.767	54.877
Total	100.00	100.00	100.00	100.00	100.00
Broadest Middle Class (M+UM+H)	113.348	142.817	211.303	227.225	248.488
Expanded Middle class (UM+H)	32.704	52.795	90.999	100.726	114.761
Elite Middle class (H)	11.486	20.266	40.039	45.767	54.877
Total no. of households ('000)	142.440	155.317	166.664	169.207	171.921

Source: NCAER (2003: 123).

Note: L=Low Income, LM=Lower Middle Income, M=Middle Income, UM=Upper Middle Income, H=High Income.

category in rural areas). This was buttressed by data on the penetration of consumer durables in both urban and especially rural areas over the period (NCAER 2003: Chapter 5, Annexure 4).

However, even with these increases in incomes, the percentages of the population in the three upper-income groups (that is, in the broadest middle class), overall and in both rural and urban areas, remained in a minority. The great majority of the population, overall and in both rural and urban areas, fell in the lowest two income groups. Thus, by 1998–9, the elite middle class was only 6 per cent, the expanded middle class was only 12 per cent, and the broadest middle class was only 26 per cent of the population. The remaining 74 per cent of the population fell below these levels in terms of income (Table 6.1). In other words, depending on how expansively the middle class is conceived, it consisted of 55 million people (the elite definition), 115 million people (the expanded definition) or 248 million people (the broadest definition) out of almost a billion in 1998–9.

Shifts in occupational composition in the period from 1989–90 to 1998–9 were not dramatic (Table 6.4). The most significant change was the fall in cultivator (by definition, self-employed cultivators in agriculture) households from 38 per cent to 30 per cent of all households, and the rise in wage-earner households from 24 per cent to 31 per cent. (The MISH survey made a distinction between wage earners and salary earners, the latter being paid a monthly or annual salary, the former presumably being paid in less than a month. However, it is important to remember that salary earners can be manual workers too.) This shift was particularly marked in rural areas, where cultivator households fell from 50 per cent to 41 per cent, and wage-earner households rose from 26 per cent to 35 per cent. However, the overwhelming bulk of this shift was outside the broadest middle class, i.e. in the Low and Lower Middle Income groups.

In the largely non-manual broadest middle-class occupations, i.e. salary earners and self-employed categories (see Table 6.4), the

Table 6.3: Distribution of Population into Income Classes by Household Heads Occupation in 1999–2000 (in millions)

Occupation	*L*	*LM*	*M*	*UM*	*H*	*All*
Housewife	2.86	3.42	1.87	0.86	0.52	9.53
Cultivator	113.57	108.15	39.49	18.35	16.87	296.43
Wage Earner	173.02	104.00	25.87	3.32	1.41	307.62
Salary earner	29.24	65.25	47.30	25.92	28.38	196.12
Professional	0.96	2.58	3.65	3.91	4.34	15.44
Artisan	14.22	17.30	9.13	2.02	1.06	43.73
Petty Shopkeeper	19.03	29.15	16.80	8.19	7.81	80.98
Businessman	0.06	0.62	3.22	4.56	5.34	13.80
Self employed sub-total	34.27	49.65	32.80	18.68	18.55	153.95
Others	6.59	7.63	5.34	2.99	2.40	24.95
Total	359.55	338.13	152.67	70.12	68.13	988.60

Source: Computed from NCAER (2003: 22), using a multiplier of 5.6 to convert households into people (176.535 million households would yield 988.596 million persons in 1998-99, compared to 1,027 million in the census of 2001).

Note: (1) L==Low Income, LM==Lower Middle Income, M==Middle Income, UM==Upper Middle Income, H==High Income.

(2) The numbers in boxes are those for the self-employed by income class.

shifts were relatively marginal. Salary-earner households increased from 18.32 per cent to 19.61 per cent over the period from 1989–90 to 1998–9, and the self-employed remained the same at 16 per cent. Even for urban areas, the shifts were marginal, if any, with salary earners increasing from 40 per cent to 41 per cent, and the self-employed remaining stable at just over 30 per cent. In fact, the percentages of professionals and of businessmen households in total households declined marginally (Table 6.4).

However, during 1999–2000, in the broadest middle class, the salary earners were 35 per cent, in the expanded middle class they were 39 per cent, and in the elite middle class they were 42 per cent (Table 6.3). Taking urban areas only, in the broadest middle class in 1999–2000, the salary earners were 49 per cent, in the

Table 6.4: Estimated Distribution of Households by Occupation (in percentage)

Occupation	*1989–90*	*1995–6*	*1996–7*	*1998–9*
Urban				
Housewife	0.98	1.07	0.96	0.88
Cultivator	5.79	3.39	3.47	3.54
Wage Earner	18.37	20.74	20.77	20.87
Salary earner	39.91	40.69	40.51	40.64
Professional	3.92	3.42	3.55	3.31
Artisan	6.87	7.01	7.08	6.77
Petty Shopkeeper	15.33	15.92	15.96	16.68
Businessman	4.13	3.46	3.63	3.77
Others	4.70	4.30	4.08	3.53
Total	100.00	100.00	100.00	100.00
Total no. of Households ('000)	40,106	46,699	47,375	48,750
Rural				
Housewife	0.63	1.12	1.07	1.04
Cultivator	50.52	41.02	40.86	40.89
Wage Earner	26.45	35.30	35.23	35.22
Salary earner	9.86	11.11	11.20	11.26
Professional	1.01	0.64	0.70	0.72
Artisan	3.20	3.45	3.51	3.44
Petty Shopkeeper	5.37	4.86	4.95	4.99
Businessman	0.81	0.37	0.43	0.44
Others	2.15	2.13	2.03	2.00
Total	100.00	100.00	100.00	100.00
Total no. of Households ('000)	102,335	118,173	119,290	122,810
Total				
Housewife	0.73	1.11	1.04	0.99
Cultivator	37.93	30.36	30.23	30.28
Wage Earner	24.18	31.18	31.12	31.15
Salary earner	18.32	19.49	19.53	19.61
Professional	1.83	1.43	1.51	1.45
Artisan	4.23	4.46	4.53	4.38
Petty Shopkeeper	8.17	7.99	8.08	8.31
Businessman	1.74	1.24	1.34	1.39
Others	2.87	2.74	2.61	2.44
Total	100.00	100.00	100.00	100.00
Total no. of Households ('000)	142,441	164,872	166,665	171,560

Source: NCAER (2003: 147).

expanded middle class they were 51 per cent, and in the elite middle class they were 54 per cent.[4]

The self-employed categories in 1999–2000 were 24 per cent of the broadest middle class, 27 per cent of the expanded middle class, and 27 per cent of the elite middle class (computed from Table 6.3; please note that the broadest middle class in 1999–2000 was 291 million compared to 248 million in 1998–9). Taking urban areas only, the self-employed categories in 1999–2000, were 34 per cent of the broadest middle class, 35 per cent of the expanded middle class, and 35 per cent of the elite middle class.[5] That is, the salary earners and the self-employed, in that order, dominated the top three income categories, with the former constituting about half of the broadest urban middle class, and the self-employed over a third. However, it should also be noted that of the self-employed categories, the businessmen and the professionals, though much less in number than petty shopkeepers and artisans (the traditional petty bourgeoisie or old middle class), increased in percentage as one went up the ladder. Nearly three-quarters of the artisans and nearly 60 per cent of the petty shopkeepers were in the two lowest income groups, below the broadest middle class, and even in urban areas, the bulk of both these categories was below the broadest middle class.[6]

To sum up, in 1999–2000, out of a broadest middle class of 291 million, salary earners (both manual and non-manual) totalled 102 million (35 per cent), the self-employed totalled 70 million (24 per cent), cultivators, the emerging agricultural middle class in the rural areas (which is not the same as the rural middle class, which was very disproportionately non-agricultural), totalled 75 million (26 per cent), and the rest, mostly wage earners, totalled 30 million (10 per cent).

It would appear that while the share of the salary earners and the

[4] Computed from Table 4.3 in NCAER (2003: 22).

[5] Ibid.

[6] Tables 3 and 4.3 in NCAER (2003: 22).

self-employed in the elite middle class expanded and the broadest middle classes did not change much, what did change were their absolute numbers and their income levels over the period 1989–99. The question that arises is: Were these salary earners all non-manual? In that category, were they professional-managerial-technical or clerical workers? And how did these shares in the salary-earner category shift? Furthermore, how many of the non-manual salary earners were public employees, i.e. how large was the public-sector middle class by the income-cum-occupation (non-manual) criteria? Or alternatively, purely by the income criterion, how large was the public employee component of the broadest middle class?

According to National Sample Survey Organisation (NSSO) data (Table 6.5), the percentage of non-manual, i.e. the first three categories in Table 6.5 consisting of professional, technical, and related workers; administrative, executive and managerial workers; and clerical and related workers, in that order, in total employment, increased from 1977–8, particularly in urban areas, and particularly over the period from 1987–8 to 1999–2000.

These non-manual workers in urban areas increased from 20.5 per cent in 1977–8 to 23.2 per cent in 1987–8, and further to 26.5 per cent in 1999–2000. If one took the first (higher) two of the three categories of non-manual workers, i.e. excluding clerical and related workers, the increase in urban areas was sharper, moving up from 10.3 per cent in 1977–8, to 13 per cent in 1987–8, to 17.3 per cent in 1999–2000. In absolute numbers, this was impressive at over one-sixth of urban employment, at 15.97 million, or a maximum of 89 million persons in such households at the maximalist assumption that each such employee heads an independent household. If we were to deflate this by one-sixth, assuming that all these were in the organised sector and assuming that the one-sixth of the women employed in the organised sector (Table 6.7) all belonged to male-headed households, we would still arrive at a modern professional—managerial-technical middle class

Table 6.5: Percentage Distribution of Total Employment by Occupation

	Rural				
Occupational Division	*1977–8*	*1983*	*1987–8*	*1993–4*	*1999–2000*
Professional, technical and related workers	1.50	2.10	1.70	2.30	2.10
Administrative, executive and managerial workers	0.30	0.40	0.70	0.90	1.40
Clerical and related workers	0.90	1.20	1.30	1.40	1.50
Non-Manual workers	2.70	3.70	3.70	4.60	5.00
Sales workers	3.10	3.30	3.90	4.20	4.10
Service worker	2.50	2.40	2.30	2.00	2.50
Farmers, fishermen and related workers	82.40	79.80	75.10	76.70	74.20
Production and related workers, transport equipment operators and labourers	9.30	10.80	12.70	12.40	14.20
Workers not classified by occupation	–	–	2.40	–	–
Total	100.00	100.00	100.00	100.00	100.00
Total employment (in millions)	197.50	213.60	224.00	255.00	273.80

Table 6.5 (*Contd.*)

Table 6.5 (*Contd.*)

Urban				
1977–8	*1983*	*1987–8*	*1993–4*	*1999–2000*
7.30	8.20	8.00	9.00	8.90
3.00	4.00	5.00	5.90	8.40
10.20	9.90	10.20	9.70	9.20
20.50	22.10	23.20	24.60	26.50
16.30	15.80	16.80	17.00	16.70
11.00	10.40	9.90	9.20	9.70
13.70	12.70	10.70	10.70	8.30
38.50	39.10	38.50	38.70	38.90
–	–	0.80	–	–
100.00	100.00	100.00	100.00	100.00
46.10	56.00	65.10	76.90	92.30

Source: IAMR (2001: 154).
Note: (a) Totals may not tally due to rounding off.
(b) This table is based on NSSO data provided by IAMR.

of 75 million (at 5.6 persons per household) in urban areas alone! Deflating by a quarter, we still get 67.5 million persons in such urban households! Adding clerical workers, for the period 1999–2000, we get 26.5 per cent in urban employment, which when deflated by a quarter brings us to a figure of 103 million persons in urban non-manual households, or approximately a little over a third of the urban population. This figure, it must be noted, is roughly consistent with the figures derived from the MISH survey data noted earlier to the effect that salary earners (but only if we assume them to be non-manual, which is definitely not the case) constitute 35 per cent of the broadest middle class, itself 26 per cent of the population in 1998–99, and 49 per cent of the broadest middle class in urban areas, itself 47 per cent of the urban population of 275 million, or 63 million, or about 23 per cent of the urban population. It appears that we will have to deflate the NSSO-derived figures by much more than a quarter by assuming that not only all women employees, but also many other employed family members lived in joint households, thus reducing the number of households before applying the multiplier of 5.6.

Because this paper is concerned with differences among middle-class groups in terms of their support for economic liberalisation, and because my hypothesis is that it is the degree of reliance on the public sector (whether for direct employment or subsidies) that will best explain differing levels of support for liberalisation, I must now, to come to the core of the essay, try to estimate the extent of the public-sector middle class. That is, what is the share of non-manual public-sector employees, broadly defined, in the middle class, especially in the broadest middle class? Employment data for the organised sector, consisting of all establishments in the public sector and non-agricultural private establishments employing 10 or more persons, indicate the following: organised sector employment at 28 million persons in 2000 was only 7–8 per cent of the total employment throughout 1973–2000 (Table 6.6), the bulk of total employment being agricultural employment, and

Table 6.6: Employment in Organised and Unorganised Sectors

Year	*Organized*	*Unorganised*	*Employment in millions total*	*Organized as percentage of the total*
1973	18.82	217.48	236.30	7.96
1978	21.24	249.46	270.70	7.85
1983	24.01	278.69	302.70	7.93
1988	25.71	296.29	322.00	7.99
1991	26.73	315.17	341.90	7.82
1994	27.38	344.72	372.10	7.36
2000	28.07	368.73	396.80	7.07

Source: IAMR (2000: 158)

Note: The organized sector includes all establishments in the public sector and non-agricultural private establishments employing 10 or more persons in the private sector. This table is based on NSSO and Directorate-General of Employment and Training's Employment Review data, various years, according to the source given here.

a large part being small-scale industry employment that is not in the organised sector (though the larger small-scale factories, of over 10 employees, are in the organised sector).

Public-sector employment, which is, by definition, entirely in the organised sector, consistently dominated over private-sector employment in the organised sector (Table 6.7), being double the latter, if not more, since 1981. However, public-sector employment levelled off in the post-reform period – 19.057 million in 1990–1 to 18.773 million in 2001–2, after peaking at 19.559 million in 1996–7. This decline was largely due to recruitment freezes and Voluntary Retirement Schemes in public enterprises, not due to layoffs, privatisation or their closures. Private employment in the organised sector, on the other hand, increased slightly from 7.676 million in 1990–1 to 8.432 million in 2001–2, decreasing after peaking at 8.748 million in 1997–8. In a country having the size of labour force as in India, these shifts in both organised private and public employment were marginal (for a break-up of public employment in the post-reform period into central government, state governments, quasi-government [central and state public

Table 6.7: Employment in the Organised Sector

Year	Employment **(in lakhs) Public	Private	Total	Percentage of Women employed to total
1971	107.31	67.42	174.73	11.00
1981	154.85	73.95	228.79	12.20
1982	159.46	75.47	234.93	12.30
1983	164.57	75.52	240.09	12.50
1984	168.69	73.46	242.15	12.60
1985	172.70	73.09	245.79	12.90
1986	176.84	73.74	250.58	13.00
1987	180.24	73.64	253.88	13.20
1988	183.20	73.92	257.12	13.40
1989	185.09	74.53	259.62	13.60
1990	187.72	75.82	263.54	14.10
1991	190.57	76.76	267.33	14.10
1992	192.10	78.46	270.56	14.40
1993	193.26	78.51	271.77	14.80
1994	194.45	79.30	273.75	15.20
1995	194.66	80.59	275.25	15.40
1996	194.29	85.12	279.41	15.80
1997	195.59	86.86	282.45	16.40
1998	194.18	87.48	281.66	16.90
1999	194.15	86.98	281.13	17.20
2000	193.14	86.46	279.60	17.80
2001	191.38	86.52	277.90	
2002	187.73	84.32	272.05	

Source: IAMR (2001: 159).
**Sikkim, Arunachal Pradesh, Dadra & Nagar Haveli and Lakshadweep are not covered under the Employment Market Information (EMI) Programme.

Note: This table is based on Directorate-General of Employment and Training's Employment Review data, various years, provided in IAMR (2001).

enterprises, universities and autonomous bodies], and local bodies [municipalities and panchayats], see Table 6.8). An additional point is that public employment here does not include employment in the armed forces, which totalled 1.3 million, the great bulk of about 1.1 million being in the army, of whom the vast majority were soldiers, only a relatively small minority being officers.

The question that now arises, as far as the estimation of the middle class is concerned, is: what was the composition of public and

Table 6.8: Estimated Employment in Public and Private Sector (in thousands)

	Public Sector							
	Central govern-ment	*State govern-ment*	*Quasi Government*		*Local bodies*	*Total Public Sector*	*Private Sector*	*Total Employment*
Year			*Central*	*State*				
1990–1	3,410	7,113	3,564	2,658	2,313	19,058	7,675	26,733
1991–2	3,428	7,190	3,554	2,839	2,198	19,209	7,846	27,055
1992–3	3,383	7,293	3,592	2,898	2,160	19,326	7,850	27,176
1993–4	3,392	7,337	3,566	2,948	2,202	19,445	7,930	27,375
1994–5	3,395	7,355	3,574	2,946	2,197	19,467	8,058	27,525
1995–6	3,366	7,414	3,538	2,920	2,192	19,430	8,511	27,941
1996–7	3,295	7,485	3,586	2,950	2,244	19,560	8,658	28,245
1997–8	3,253	7,458	3,536	2,925	2,246	19,418	8,748	28,166
1998–9	3,313	7,458	3,472	2,914	2,259	19,416	8,698	27,114
1999–2000	3,273	7,460	3,413	2,913	2,255	19,314	8,646	28,960
2000–1	3,261	7,425	3,291	2,901	2,261	19,139	8,652	27,791
2001–2	3,195	7,384	3,195	2,824	2,175	18,773	8,432	27,205

Source: CSO (1999: 5; 2003: 5); GoI (2005: S-49, S-50).
Note: (a) Totals may not tally due to rounding off; (b) central government employment does not include the defence services.

private organised-sector employment? How much of this was non-manual? How much of this was professional-managerial-technical? And have these categories, which one could be certain would fall in the broadest middle class at least, increased in share? And, more importantly, what was the share of non-manual public-sector employees in the middle class?

One way of arriving at a rough estimate of non-manual public-sector employees is to exclude public-sector employees in Group D (peons, drivers, sweepers, etc.) for the manual nature of their work, and their hence not being middle class by the income-cum-occupation criteria *a la* Rudra, Beteille, and Bardhan, although purely by the income criterion many of these households, if they have several earning members, would be in the broadest middle class, at the least. It is important to add here that by the self-identification criteria, Group D or manual employees may also be identified as middle class because they were sharply aware of the vast numbers below them in society; for example, in conversations with me, peons and police constables identified themselves as middle class. However, I have no data on self-identification in general, and have limited myself to the income-cum-non-manual occupational criteria in this exercise. I have included only public-sector employees in Groups A, B and C, the last being clerical and, hence, white-collar workers. In central government employment, 28 per cent were Group D employees.[7] The bulk of central government employees (65 per cent) fell in the clerical Group C category. Only a mere 6.65 per cent were in the executive-managerial-technical Groups A and B. In the government as a whole, this figure would be even less since the central government is relatively top-heavy. Assuming a similar distribution in the private sector, or an even more manual composition, this casts doubt on Table 6.5's figure of 17.3 per cent employees being in the top two occupational categories in 1999–2000, and 10 per cent as far back as 1977–8. Including only the Group A, B, and C categories by taking 72 per cent of the central government employment in 1998–9 (to match the MISH data), we get 2.385 million central-government public employees. There are no ready figures to give us a state-wise break-up of employees of state governments, quasi-governments (central and state), which includes public enterprises and autonomous bodies like universities, and local bodies into Groups A to D. However, in central public-sector enterprises, which in 1998–9 employed 1.9 million of the 3.47 million central quasi-government employees, the managerial and clerical workers amounted to only 30 per cent, the rest being highly skilled, skilled, and unskilled workers (highly skilled workers, though manual, may well be in the broadest middle class by the income criterion alone). If one eliminated 70 per cent of the central public sector employees, assuming likewise for state public enterprises, extended this assumption to the whole state

[7] See Table 6, Ministry of Labour, Directorate General of Employment and Training, *Census of Central Government Employees, 2003*, p. 7.

quasi-government sector, assumed the same 28 per cent share for Group D in the central quasi-government sector other than public enterprises, and assumed a 50 per cent share of Group D in local bodies, then from Table 6.8 we arrive at, for 1998–9, 11.459 million non-manual public employees.[8] Assuming that the 17 per cent women employees were evenly distributed among Groups A, B, C, and D, and assuming that each of them was part of a male-headed household, not necessarily in public employment, we get 9.5 million non-manual public-sector employee households or over 53 million people.

How many of these would fall into the broadest middle class? Using the pay-scale for the lowest non-manual category of Group C employees following the Fifth Pay Commission report, at the bottom of the scale of Rs 3200 basic pay, plus two increments of Rs 85 by 1998–9, plus 30 per cent house rent allowance, plus city compensatory allowance and travelling allowance, the total emoluments came to Rs 4781 per month, or Rs 57,372 per annum, at the bottom of the scale. Actually, this was not the bottom of the scale, but I used it because some technical/skilled workers in the scale had to be eliminated to keep to the non-manual criterion of middle classness. For this problematic issue of non-manual character and skilled workers, I used a rough approximation to apply this cut-off on the scale.[9] This would mean that the overwhelming majority of Group C public-sector employees, especially if there is more than one earner in a household (joint families being the norm even in urban India as one goes down the income ladder),

[8] For making this assumption, I drew upon information from the Institute of Social Sciences, New Delhi, which specialises in local government. My assumption, in turn, was based on the fact that (urban) municipalities, not Panchayats (rural local bodies), dominated local bodies, and in the former about 60 per cent of the employees would be in Group D. There are no consolidated figures for employment in local bodies or a break-up by Groups A to D. Taking local bodies as a whole, I used an estimate of 50 per cent for Group D.

[9] See Government oflndia, Ministry of Finance, January 1997, *Report of the Fifth Central Pay Commission*, vol. 1, pp. 452–61.

would be in the 1998–9 MISH-derived definition of the broadest middle class, constituting 26 per cent of the population and 47 per cent of the urban population in 1998-99 (Table 6.1). If one deflated the roughly estimated 9.5 million non-Group D public employee households by a quarter to eliminate female-headed and some additional households to get, say, 7.13 million households headed by non-manual public-sector employees, we arrive at 40 million non-manual public employees in 1998–9, excluding those in the armed forces, or about a sixth of the broadest middle class of 248 million. Assuming that the ratio of non-manual employees is the same in the organised private sector and applying the ratio of two-thirds public employees in the organised sector, we get 60 million people in the organised sector non-manual households. This would make public-sector employees and non-manual private-sector employees, taken together, about 24 per cent of the broadest middle class of 248 million in 1998–9. This is a much smaller figure than one would expect from the calculations based on NSSO figures on occupational composition mentioned earlier, of 103 million public-cum-private urban non-manual employees alone, and 160 million overall, since public-sector employment is over two-thirds of the organised sector employment. I probably underestimated the number of non-manual public-sector employees by eliminating too large a share for Group D and too small a share for Group C outside of the central government, and/or the NSSO percentage estimates of non-manual employment, particularly in urban areas, was much too high, particularly of the professional-managerial category, since these were much higher than Groups A and B in central government and hence in the government as a whole.

Those who were not public-and private-sector non-manual employees in the broadest middle class of 248 million were either self-employed or the better-off agriculturists or manual workers, public or private, including Group D public-sector employees. The 24 per cent of the broadest middle class which was self-employed totalled around 62 million persons. Taken together with the estimated 40 million non-manual public-sector employees, the total number of non-agricultural, non-manual household members would rise to 102 million. The remaining 146 million in the broadest middle class of 248 million would be either agriculturists or, very importantly, a considerable number of Group D public employees, skilled manual workers (and soldiers) who may not be middle class by the income-cum-occupation criteria of non-manual work, but would qualify by income alone. If, for example, out of 19.4 million public-sector employees plus 1.3 million defence services employees, or a total of 20.7 million, 15 million households, or about 84 million persons, including therefore a large portion of Group D, skilled manual workers in public enterprise and soldiers were included in the broadest middle class, public-sector employees would amount to one-third of this class. In this case, eliminating the 62 million non-manual self-employed household members leaves us with 102 million farmers and others, including manual employees, public and private.

Therefore, from the point of view of support for economic reforms, we need to estimate the share of public-sector employees and public subsidy-dependent farmers. Going by the above-mentioned estimates, the numbers of these two groups would total approximately from 144 million to 186 million, or 58 per cent to 75 per cent, of the 248 million broadest middle class. Thus, the majority of the broadest middle class would be persons whose livelihoods depend on state employment or state subsidies.

The Caste Composition and Political Leanings of the Middle Classes

Finally, we must examine the sociological composition, in terms of caste and, relatedly, the emerging political leanings, of the middle class in the post-1991 period, as these two parameters have an important bearing on the relationship of the middle class to economic liberalisation. Historically, the very narrow middle class was almost entirely dominated by the traditional, i.e. "twice born", upper castes, especially outside South India. That has been changing, although the traditional upper castes still have a hugely disproportionate representation in the upper and middle classes, howsoever defined. As Deshpande pointed out, the Hindu upper castes accounted for 59 per cent of the top-most Monthly Per Capita Consumption Expenditure (MPCE) class in urban areas (Rs 1950 or more), and 40 per cent in rural areas (Rs 950 or more), according to NSSO data for 1999–2000 (Deshpande 2003: 112–13). However, as D.L. Sheth (1999a, 1999b) commented, the new middle classes of the 1990s, as revealed by the Centre for the Study of Developing Societies (CSDS) survey of 1996, were increasingly being constituted by non-traditional caste groups, particularly middle-caste, non-"twice born" farmer castes who would fit M.N. Srinivas' category of dominant castes. The middle class in the CSDS survey was defined (more restrictively than in my estimates from the MISH data) by five indicators: (i) respondents identifying themselves as middle-class; (ii) ten years or more of schooling; (iii) residence in a brick-and-cement house; (iv) white-collar occupation; (v) ownership of at least three of the following four assets: car/jeep/tractor, scooter/motorcycle; television set; electrically operated, water pump-set; and non-agricultural land. Twenty per cent of the CSDS' survey sample was identified as middle class. It was found that while the upper castes (defined as the "twice born" upper castes and the non-"twice born" dominant castes) were a quarter of the sample, they constituted nearly half of the middle class. However, this signified a reduction in the representation of the upper castes in the middle class, which was earlier almost totally dominated by them. The findings of the survey also represented a rise in the share of the non-"twice born" dominant castes, as well as of the Scheduled Castes, Scheduled Tribes, Other Backward Classes or OBCs (lower castes) and religious minorities, which together constituted half the middle class and three-quarters of the sample.

As far as the emerging political leanings of the middle class were concerned, Yogendra Yadav, Sanjay Kumar and Oliver Heath argued that during the 1990s there was a distinct shift in the political preferences of the upper and middle classes, as also of the upper castes, away from the Congress and towards the BJP. They argued that the BJP "created a new social bloc, a new coalition of various social groups, that now lays claim to political power . . . The new social bloc is formed by the convergence of traditional caste-community differences and class distinctions . . . defined by an overlap of social and economic privileges."[10] In 1999, according to the CSDS' post-poll survey, the BJP got 60 per cent of the upper-caste Hindu votes, 52 per cent of the votes of the dominant Hindu peasant castes such as Jats, Marathas, Patidars, Reddys, and Kammas, which were not classified as OBCs, and less and less down the caste hierarchy. Likewise, the BJP's vote share was clearly related to class, its vote share falling linearly as one went down the ladder of economic status and educational attainment. The BJP's base, though spreading to rural areas, remained disproportionately urban. The new social bloc leaning towards the BJP largely comprised upper castes and dominant castes, who also made up a disproportionately large part of the upper income groups.

Mirroring Sheth's, and Yadav, Kumar, and Heath's survey data from the elections of 1996, 1998 and 1999, Radhika Desai (2002) argued that in the more prosperous states there was an emerging top-middle convergence of interests and political preferences between the traditional upper castes and the rising dominant peasant castes, particularly in western and southern India. This explained the powerful social bloc behind the BJP in Gujarat and the support of the dominant caste-based regional parties for the NDA, led by

[10] Yogendra Yadav, Sanjay Kumar and Oliver Heath, "The BJP"s New Social Bloc", *Frontline,* 19 November 1999, p. 32.

the BJP, through the worst communal riots of 2002. "The greater the economic fortunes of these middle castes, the more they tended to see the possibility of integration into Hindutva's predominantly upper caste/class fold as inviting" (ibid.: 146).

This evidence of a new social bloc, disproportionately upper caste and upper class, in support of the BJP and the BJP-led NDA coalition for essentially social reasons would seem to indicate that the largely upper- and dominant-caste middle classes, which overlapped very substantially with this bloc, would have tended to support the BJP-led NDA's economic-liberalisation programme for reasons other than purely economic – in fact, may have supported the programme because they supported the BJP and/or its coalition for essentially social reasons. Therefore, the NDA was able to take a strong pro-reform line, as it did in the 2004 election campaign, because it could rely on this "new social bloc" for social, i.e. caste-cum-class, reasons. In fact, the views of white-collar workers and those of BJP supporters on economic reforms were very mixed, with a significant section disapproving of various aspects of the reforms (S. Kumar 2004: Tables 2.1 and 2.5).

The CSDS post-poll survey data supported the middle-class character of the BJP despite its defeat in urban areas in 2004. In the cities which accounted for the predominantly urban constituencies, the Congress-led United Progressive Alliance parties won 43 per cent of the votes of the very poor, while the BJP-led NDA parties won just 25 per cent, while among the urban upper middle class the NDA parties enjoyed a 14 per cent lead.[11] This underscores the proposition that support for economic reform among the middle class was not due to any ideological shift in favour of reform or any understanding of reform policies – the survey data showing very poor awareness and understanding of reform policies even among the middle class – but due to the class identification of the rich and the middle class with the BJP.

[11] Yogendra Yadav, "Urban India more Polarised", and "Economic Reforms in the Mirror of Public Opinion", *The Hindu*, 13 June 2004.

It would appear that the change in India's social structure from an elite-mass structure to one with a substantial middle-class presence emphasised the political vacuum in the centre-right after the demise of the Swatantra party in the 1970s. That is, there was no right-of-centre party specifically articulating the interests of the emerging middle class in a context where there was a sociological and political convergence between the top and the middle, like there is in most capitalist democracies, the Congress party being a catch-all party catering to the lower castes, the minorities and the poor. The BJP and its NDA allies seemed to have occupied this political space created by the emergence of the middle class in the past two decades, going beyond the BJP's narrow Hindu communal agenda, although by no means abandoning, at most temporarily downplaying, it.

If the recent (2004 pre-election) survey data indicating that the 18–24 age group was disproportionately inclined towards the BJP is correct, it would seem to indicate that, in a country where 60 per cent of the population is under 30, there is also an "aspirational" middle class beyond the economically defined middle class, particularly among the young of all castes and classes.[12] This section, though it may fall below the middle class, does not share solidarity with the class into which it is born, but aspires to leave it behind and therefore identifies with classes, social groups, parties, and policies that seem to promise upward mobility. The middle class would, then, appear to have a wider socio-political and economic policy impact than its actual numbers suggest.

Conclusion

I conclude, contrary to the case usually made, that while the growth of the middle classes is a development that does not explain liberalisation itself, what it does explain is the particular character of liberalisation since 1991, which I will call "sustained gradualism".

[12] See opinion poll in *Outlook*, 15 March 2004.

This is in contrast to the spurts of liberalisation following each International Monetary Fund (IMF) stand-by episode earlier (1957, 1966, 1973, 1981), which petered out very soon in the import substitution industrialisation regime (DeNoon 1998). The post-1991 liberalisation, by contrast, has been sustained but, unlike in a whole range of countries, has been gradual to the point of being glacial, with the economy remaining one of the more closed economies, at least in terms of trade. This can perhaps be explained by, among other things, the growth of the broadest middle class since the 1980s, leading to the formation of a support base for liberalisation while at the same time being constrained by the weight of public-sector employees and publicly-subsidised agriculturists in it.

Looking to the future, what are the implications of the relative size and composition of the middle class as estimated in this paper? If we categorise economic reform into three broad types of policies – deregulation, macroeconomic stabilisation, and public-sector reform, including privatisation – we can expect varying responses from different components of the middle class. Deregulation and macroeconomic stabilisation are "first generation" reforms, while public-sector reforms, including (centrally) privatisation, are "second generation" reforms. However, the backlog of "first generation" reforms must also be considered part of the agenda of "second generation reforms", and that backlog is considerable. The economy still remains fairly heavily regulated and fiscal stabilisation remains to be achieved with the combined fiscal deficit of the centre and the states at over 10 per cent of GDP, which is where it was in 1990–1. As for public-sector reform and privatisation, there has been only a marginal fall in total public-sector employment, largely due to recruitment freezes and Voluntary Retirement Schemes, and barely half a dozen central public enterprises have been truly privatised with government ownership falling below 50 per cent of equity.

Deregulation can be expected to command widespread support, as regulation is identified with corruption and inefficiency.

Regional capital and medium-scale businesses would welcome deregulation, especially central deregulation. However, there is likely to be a contrary pull from the rising backward-caste component of the middle classes, who may not want to give up statist regulation for patronage, especially at the state level.

Macroeconomic stabilisation would also bring forth mixed responses, particularly de-subsidisation. The urban middle class would tend to resist giving up high administered interest rates on the savings schemes of public-sector banks and financial institutions, and the rural rich would resist giving up subsidies to agriculture. Likewise, the removal of subsidies to higher public education would invite middle-class protest. On the closely related issue of public-sector reform and privatisation, the public-employee component of the middle classes could be expected to resist downsizing and wage restraints, although it is possible that a snowballing support effect could occur after a certain point among those who are not laid off but who stand to gain in the increasingly privatised public enterprises, and among those whose family members gain from the growth of the private sector. All in all, given the largely public-employee and publicly subsidised farmer character of the broadest middle class, support for second-generation reforms of the de-subsidisation and privatisation type can be expected to grow only very gradually.

Acknowledgements

A shortened version of this paper, written in nearly-identical language, was published in *India Review*, 3 (4), pp. 405–28. I thank the publishers of the journal, Taylor & Francis Publishers, for permission to publish this earlier and lengthier version. I thank Pranab Bardhan for detailed comments; Vijay Joshi for useful conversations; D.L. Sheth, George Mathew, and Pronab Sen for pointers to data; and Sucharita Sengupta for research assistance.

7

Where is India Headed? Possible Future Directions in Indian Foreign Policy

THE NATIONAL Democratic Alliance (NDA) government of Prime Minister Narendra Modi, led by his Bharatiya Janata Party (BJP), has been extraordinarily active in foreign affairs during its first two years in power, logging as many as forty-eight foreign visits up to June 2016, for both bilateral and multilateral meetings, as well as hosting a plethora of high-level visits to India by world leaders, including the heads of state or government of the United States, China, the UK, France, and Japan. Among these have been seven meetings with President Obama, including a visit by him to India and an address by Modi to a joint session of the US Congress. What have been the drivers of this extraordinary foreign policy dynamism, and what does it portend for possible future directions in Indian foreign policy, not only under the current government but into the future? In addressing the latter question, this paper will inevitably be speculative; but it will be a reasoned speculation, building on recent foreign policy developments. I shall pose two questions: first, what kind of power is India – an emerging Great Power or a middle power? Second, what kind of foreign policy can we expect to see following from the answer to the first question?

After years of sustained high growth, and having weathered

the 2008–9 world financial crisis relatively well, India became the focus of much extravagant talk among its own elite and in sections of the global media as a rising power, even as an emerging superpower.[1] Is the emergence of India – with the world's second-largest population, projected to overtake China's in the next few years at current rates of growth – as one of the Great Powers of the world system a realistic possibility? The maintenance of high rates of economic growth would certainly be a necessary condition for such an outcome, but is it a sufficient condition? And even if that were to happen, are there other obstacles to such an outcome? In other words, are there factors specific to India that might impede the conversion of economic power and nuclear capability into true Great Power capabilities?

Alongside growth, and facilitated by its fuelling of higher defence budgets, there has been a gradual but systematic attempt at military modernisation in India since the 1998 nuclear tests, primarily by importing arms – to the point where the country is now one of the world's largest arms importers. India is seeking to buttress these capabilities by entering into strategic partnerships. Its improved relationship with the United States in particular, and the concomitant relative shift in arms procurement away from Russia to the US has seen the latter emerging as India's leading supplier in 2014, not counting Russian-licensed production in India.[2] Looking ahead from this point, then, what are the future possibilities? In attempting to answer this question, I begin by outlining a typology of power.

[1] For more scholarly assessments, see Stephen P. Cohen, *India: Emerging Power* (Washington, D.C.: Brookings Institution Press, 2001); Baldev Raj Nayar and T.V. Paul, *India in the World Order: Searching for Major-Power Status* (New York: Cambridge University Press, 2003); David M. Malone, *Does the Elephant Dance? Contemporary Indian Foreign Policy* (New Delhi: Oxford University Press, 2011).

[2] Rajat Pandit, "US Set to Be India's Biggest Arms Supplier", *Times of India*, July 13, 2015.

Great Powers, Middle Powers, Regional Powers and Rising Powers in Today's World

In this section, I discuss the ingredients of and constraints on power, and the world's hierarchy of powers, as a necessary prelude to discussing what kind of power India is, what its future foreign policy might look like, and what kind of power it has the potential to become.

The standard ways of measuring power and comparing powers involve counting the indicators of military, economic, and other forms of power – for military power, nuclear warheads and delivery vehicles, size of armies, air forces and navies, numbers of foreign bases and power projection capabilities, space-based assets and cyberspace capabilities; for economic power, absolute and relative GDP, world trade shares, foreign exchange reserves, tax revenues, military budgets, industrial production, possession of vital energy and other resources; for "soft power", scientific, technological, intellectual, ideological, and cultural prowess, presence and power position in international organisations, institutional power, and so forth. The Chinese use the concept of comprehensive national power combining a range of indicators.[3]

Bearing all these aspects in mind, how does one understand terms such as super- power, Great Power, middle power, regional power and rising power in today's world? And where does India fit in? Without embarking on a detailed review of typologies, we can build on useful definitions set out by Buzan and Wæver, and by Mearsheimer. Buzan and Wæver define a superpower as a state that, first, has broad spectrum of capabilities – military, economic, etc. – that are exercised globally, that is, a power with comprehensive global reach; and that, second, is acknowledged by others as such in their calculations.[4] Mearsheimer asserts that a superpower,

[3] Yan Xuetong, "The Rise of China and Its Power Status", *Chinese Journal of International Politics* 1:1, 2006, pp. 5–33.

[4] See Barry Buzan and Ole Wæver, *Regions and Powers: The Structure of*

in addition to comprehensive military capabilities and their implied economic and technological underpinnings, needs not just to dominate its own region comprehensively but to extend beyond any one region in its reach and influence.[5]

A Great Power for Buzan and Wæver is one that, first, is greater than regional but smaller than global; second, does not need to have great capabilities in all spheres – for example, economic capabilities alone will do, as will nuclear capabilities; third, is considered a Great Power in other powers' calculations. For Mearsheimer, Great Power status is largely determined by relative military capabilities, but these in turn imply economic, industrial, and technological power. Additionally, for Mearsheimer, a Great Power dominates its region, and it is implied that this is a necessary but not sufficient condition.

For Buzan and Wæver a regional power (by either dominance or consent or both) is one whose power is confined to its home continent; whose regional power status is more security-related than economy-related; and that is defined by both relative military capabilities and the historically inherited, path-dependent dynamic of amity and enmity in the region.

For Mearsheimer, any discussion of superpower, Great Power or regional power status is incomplete without consideration of geographic features such as size, resources, and bodies of water separating powers. For him, land power is of paramount geostrategic importance owing to the stopping power of water, it being more difficult by an order of magnitude to project power across oceans or seas than to threaten a land invasion. Hence, powers separated by significant bodies of water are both more secure in a world of conventional wars and less able to project power.

International Security (Cambridge: Cambridge University Press, 2003), for their arguments summarised here.

[5] See John J. Mearsheimer, *The Tragedy of Great Power Politics* (New York: Norton, 2001), for the arguments summarised here.

The concept of middle power is a nebulous one.[6] Middle powers can be seen as those that lack system-shaping capabilities but nevertheless cannot be "ignored", however that is defined. That is, while they cannot challenge Great Powers, they do have the capabilities to resist the imposition of Great Power diktats and behaviour under compulsion. It is also important to distinguish between middle powers and regional powers. A middle power may or may not be a regional power. A regional power can be a Great Power and even a superpower: for example, the United States is both a superpower and the regional power of the Americas.

What is a rising power? There is no agreed definition in the limited literature on rising powers, but by implication a "rising power will, in the near future, become a great power".[7] Again, by implication rising powers can be considered a subset of middle powers that in the future could evolve to be Great Powers or powers of some rank above the general run of middle powers.

The literature on power transitions informs some of the work on rising powers. Power transition theories seek to answer larger questions about war and peace and find balance of power theory too static. Organski and Kugler, for example, attribute power transitions to the worldwide spread of the industrial revolution increasing the relative power of newly rising nations relative to Great Powers.[8] They found a "recurring pattern", that is, that the rise of a

[6] For theoretical discussions of middle powers, see Andrew Fenton Cooper, Richard Higgott, and Kim Richard Nossal, *Relocating Middle Powers: Australia and Canada in a Changing World Order* (Vancouver: University of British Columbia Press, 1993); Eduard Jordaan, "The Concept of a Middle Power in International Relations: Distinguishing Between Emerging and Traditional Middle Powers", *Politikon: South African Journal of International Relations* 30: 1, 2003, pp. 165–81.

[7] Manjari Chatterjee Miller, "The Role of Beliefs in Identifying Rising Powers", *Chinese Journal of International Politics* 9: 2, 2016, p. 216.

[8] A.F.K. Organski, *World Politics* (New York: Knopf, 1958); A.F.K. Organski and Jacek Kugler, *The War Ledger* (Chicago: University of Chicago Press, 1980).

challenger almost guarantees a major war. However, there are exceptions: for example, leading power status passed peacefully from Britain to the United States; not all rising powers are necessarily dissatisfied (again, the United States serves as an example); and a challenger can surpass the dominant power through growth without a war. Kennedy argues that every major power occupying the number one position has to face two major tests which challenge its long-term hold on the top rank: first, maintaining a balance between perceived defence requirements and the means to maintain those commitments; second, preserving the technological and economic bases of power from relative erosion due to shifting patterns of global production.[9] Nye argues that such erosion might be uneven, in that while military power might remain unipolar, economic power might become multipolar and the universe of cross-border interactions might see power widely dispersed.[10]

Some later authors in the power transition literature, such as Lemke, have extended the theory to regional sub-systems, distinguishing between regional and global activities of powers.[11] Thompson argues that proximity and similarity are among five variables which are said to be especially critical to the intensity of challenges to the dominant power, with proximity magnifying threat perceptions and similarity alleviating them.[12] Thus, region and regional power dynamics are very important for understanding rising powers; this is important for the Indian case, as I shall show.

These are useful perspectives – particularly the notion that the spread of industrial and technological power lies behind the emer-

[9] Paul Kennedy, *The Rise and Fall of the Great Powers* (London: Fontana, 1989).

[10] Joseph S. Nye, Jr, *The Paradox of American Power* (New York: Oxford University Press, 2002).

[11] Douglas Lemke, *Regions of War and Peace* (Cambridge: Cambridge University Press, 2002).

[12] William R. Thompson, "The Evolution of Political-Economic Challenges in the Active Zone", *Review of International Political Economy* 4:2, 1997, pp. 286–318.

gence of the current rising powers. Of more limited use in understanding the current rising powers (with the possible exception of China's predicted overtaking of the United States during the first half of the present century) are power transition theories focused on the causes of war and based largely on long-term historical shifts in the balance of power over the centuries preceding the mid-twentieth century, a pre-nuclear era, and one that was much less tightly integrated in economic and communication terms than the present.

More recent work on rising powers departs from power transition theories that see them as challengers to the existing order. Narlikar defines rising powers as "states that have established themselves as veto-players in the international system, but have still not acquired agenda-setting power."[13] In other words, they cannot be ignored. Mohan sees India's interests converging with those of the existing order through its growing integration with the world economy and through a process of socialisation.[14] Miller stresses the ideational aspect of rising powers, arguing that all rising powers have historically been characterised not only by growing material capabilities but by a vigorous internal debate among elites about their possible role; they saw themselves as Great Powers or similar in the making.[15] On India specifically, Pardesi argues that it is already a Great Power because it has security-related and economic interests outside its home region (in south-east Asia) and the requisite capabilities to deploy there, and demands that this status be accepted both by other Great Powers, notably the United States, and by regional states.[16]

[13] Amrita Narlikar, "Introduction: Negotiating the Rise of New Powers", and idem, "India Rising: Responsible to Whom?", both in *International Affairs* 89: 3, May 2013, pp. 561–2, 595–614.

[14] C. Raja Mohan, *Crossing the Rubicon: The Shaping of India's Foreign Policy* (Delhi: Viking, 2003), pp. 261–4.

[15] Manjari Chatterjee Miller, "The Role of Beliefs in Identifying Rising Powers', *Chinese Journal of International Politics* 9:2, 2016, pp. 211–38.

[16] Manjeet Pardesi, "Is India a Great Power? Understanding Great Power

Given the importance of region to my argument, I would supplement the above literature review by arguing that a country can, broadly speaking, be a regional power in three ways, not mutually exclusive.[17] First, it can be a regional power by consent: that is, it can be accepted by the countries of a region as their natural leader and spokesperson. Some possible examples are South Africa in southern Africa, Saudi Arabia in the Gulf Cooperation Council, or Brazil in South America. Second, it can be a regional power by virtue of having the power of compulsion over its neighbours. Third, it can be a regional power simply by virtue of relative size, without necessarily being able to impose its will or get its way – that is, simply by bulking larger than its neighbours in area, population, GDP and size of its armed forces.

From this discussion two factors emerge as of particular importance in understanding power in the contemporary international system: material capabilities and geography. The latter defines the relationship between the power projection capabilities necessary for compulsion and the stopping power of water. Further, it covers not just the physical (mountains impeding land power, oceans impeding power projection) but what I will call the geostrategic features of a country's international environment: that is, the extent to which a country's relative power is defined not just by its own capabilities but by those of its neighbours and opponents. Together, the geographic features that surround a country and the capabilities of its neighbours constrain the conversion of economic, conventional, and nuclear capabilities into meaningful power, particularly power projection necessary for compulsion. Hence, a power with considerable capabilities could be unable to project it

---

Status in Contemporary International Relations", *Asian Security* 11:1, 2015, pp. 1–30.

[17] Here and in the next section I build on and extend the argument on regional geostrategic constraints in Eswaran Sridharan, "Rising or Constrained Power?', in David Malone, C. Raja Mohan, and Srinath Raghavan, eds, *The Oxford Handbook of Indian Foreign Policy* (New Delhi: Oxford University Press, 2015).

and might be frozen into a defensive or purely deterrent posture if its neighbours have effective deterrence capabilities against it and/or if geographic features such as mountain ranges or oceans impede effective power projection.

What Kind of Power is India?

Following on from this discussion we may turn to address the question: what kind of power is India today? It is definitely not a Great Power, despite its possession of nuclear weapons and intermediate-range ballistic missiles (Agni V), since it lacks a global strike capability, lacks serious extra-regional power projection capabilities, does not decisively dominate its own region, and is not a system-shaping power in either economic or military balance terms. India is neither one of the Great Powers nor a minor power; but it is one that cannot be ignored, and in this sense fits the most general definition of a middle power. It is, moreover, one whose relative weight and influence in material terms have been increasing over the past decade and more. Hence, India is a rising power – a middle power moving up in the global power hierarchy. It is also one whose status as a regional power is contested. Will India go from rising power to Great Power by proving itself capable of projecting power beyond its region in the long term? As we saw, the later literature on power transitions and rising powers attaches importance to regional factors such as proximity. In India's case the region is important, as I shall show below, and we need to consider regional dynamics to understand the constraints under which India operates and their substantial effects on India's foreign policy, accentuated by the rise of China.

India is constrained as a regional power by geostrategic factors, specifically, the possession of nuclear weapons by its neighbour Pakistan, a de facto ally of China. Geostrategically speaking, then, India is blocked along its entire continental north by nuclear Pakistan and China. It is thus reduced to a purely defensive and deterrent posture that not only is incapable of preventing even the systematic use of terror by non-state actors based in Pakistan but is also limited in its potential for military modernisation by the preponderance of its army (over 50 per cent) in its defence budget, when the forces of the future will be those of the air and sea. To the south, the vast expanses of the Indian Ocean hamper the development of power projection capabilities of a kind that would count in the global strategic calculations of the major powers. Hence, geostrategic and geographic constraints box India into South Asia in a way that make it a contained power. India will find it very difficult to overcome these constraints, even with sustained high growth and greater missile and naval reach. To count globally, it will need to make a massive jump in both economic weight and military reach.

India is not accepted as South Asia's natural leader or spokesperson – except perhaps by Bhutan: certainly not by Bangladesh, Pakistan, or Sri Lanka, nor even by the Maldives or Nepal, all of which have resisted India's demands and wishes to varying degrees. It does not have the power of compulsion over Pakistan, given the latter's nuclear deterrent. Indeed, it is doubtful whether it has decisive compulsion capabilities over even its other, smaller, neighbours should it ever attempt intervention for whatever reason, given the enormous military and diplomatic costs and risks and their capacity to resist. India's intervention in Sri Lanka and counter-insurgency operations there from 1987 to 1990 was a failed adventure that had to be abandoned. Hence, measured by the criterion of being able to dominate and impose its will on its neighbours, it does not qualify as a regional power. India can, therefore, be called a regional power in South Asia only by the third criterion of relative size, since its area, population and GDP are over three-quarters, roughly speaking, those of the region, and its armed forces are commensurately large. India has regional weight and influence, but not dominance or the capacity to change the policies of its neighbours that it would like to see changed.

I would argue that while a high-growth India could possibly induce bandwagoning behaviour towards itself in South Asia, it would still find it difficult to become a regional power in the sense of dominance, let alone an extra-regional power in a strategic sense. India would face the problem of converting its economic or nuclear capabilities into meaningful regional or extraregional power, owing to the geographical and geostrategic constraints outlined earlier.

Economists, particularly those writing on emerging economies, often tend to assume that economic weight converts smoothly into power and tend to project economic trends in a linear fashion, ignoring geography and military capabilities and their ingredients.[18] While economic power might easily convert into political power above certain economic thresholds, one needs to distinguish between weight and influence on the one hand and, on the other, power in the hard sense of compulsion or the ability to achieve desired geopolitical outcomes, including inducing others to change their policies in the direction desired. The capacity to convert economic and/or nuclear capabilities into meaningful geopolitical power depends on the geographic and geostrategic constraints that countries face.

Three major examples of the problems of converting economic and/or nuclear power into commensurate geopolitical power are Russia, Japan, and contemporary China. Russia has the world's second largest nuclear arsenal and global strike capabilities, but finds it difficult to convert such a capability into meaningful influence even in its "near abroad". It has been forced to retreat into a purely defensive/deterrent mould (barring exceptional developments

[18] See e.g. the argument by economist Arvind Virmani in "Tri-Polar World: India, China and the United States in the 21st Century", Carnegie Endowment for International Peace, 9 Feb. 2011, http://carnegieendowment. org/ 2011/02/09/tri-polar-world-india-china-and-united-states-in-21st-century/247d. (Unless otherwise noted at point of citation, all URLs cited in this article were accessible on 6 Nov. 2016.)

such as the interventions in Georgia in 2008, and in Crimea/Ukraine in 2014). This is because the post-Cold War expansion of NATO to its borders and the fact that its economy and technological base cannot support a conventional power projection capability such as that wielded by the former Soviet Union. Similarly, Japan, although the world's second largest economy for much of the later Cold War and post-Cold War periods, could not, even had it wanted to, convert its massive economic power into geopolitical power, even in its own neighbourhood. It faced the geostrategic constraint of having two nuclear neighbours in Russia and China, besides the geographical constraint of being a resource-poor island. Even China, now with the world's second-largest and system-shaping economy and a global nuclear strike capability, faces the geostrategic constraints of a US presence off its shores and US allies around it including Japan, South Korea and – in effect, if not formally – Taiwan.

All three powers are examples of conversion problems, whereby they enjoy less geopolitical power and are more defensive than might be expected from their nuclear and/or economic capabilities.

These conversion problems apply to India too. In addition to being boxed in by geographic features and the capabilities of the neighbours on its northern borders, India is subject to other significant power constraints. It is heavily dependent on energy and resource imports; it has a weak manufacturing and technological base; and, more specifically, it is an arms importer, heavily dependent on external suppliers for all major platforms – combat aircraft, surface ships, submarines, tanks and artillery, not to speak of electronic force multipliers – despite joint development efforts with Russia and Israel, and it has a qualitatively and quantitatively limited nuclear arsenal. Hence, India is constrained by its regional situation, including the rise of China.

So what kind of power *is* India? From the above analysis we can conclude that it is currently still a middle power, albeit a rising one;

that it is increasing its global weight but not yet able to leverage its relative weight in its own region. The Indian Ministry of External Affairs' *Annual Report 2015–16* seems to indicate this, speaking as it does of India's potential to "act as a leading power" without defining what that means, while also referring to China, France, Germany, Japan, Russia, the United Kingdom and the United States as "major powers of the world",[19] thereby implying a current middle-power status but with aspirations to something more, that is, reflecting a rising power mindset.

Middle-Power Status, Rising-Power Aspirations, and Recent Indian Foreign Policy Behaviour

Given the analysis above, what can we expect in the future foreign policy of India as a rising middle power? Recent Indian foreign policy has seen both change and continuity; I shall examine both here, and then briefly consider India's relations with the United States and the US–China dynamic, before turning to possible future directions.

Elements of Continuity

The main elements of continuity have been continued antagonism with Pakistan and China, with unresolved disputes over border/territorial issues, and the continued arms supply relationship with Russia. Both of these have continued to define India's national security environment and capabilities.

The focus on security threats arising from Pakistan and China, both nuclear armed and in effect mutually allied, and with both of which India has been in armed conflict in the past, has been a constant of Indian foreign policy and makes regional relations central

[19] Ministry of External Affairs (MEA), Government of India, *Annual Report 2015–16* (New Delhi, 2016), p. 1.

to any understanding of India's prospects as a rising power. There is no sign of any resolution of these conflicts. The only progress has been in putting in place limited confidence-building measures to prevent the outbreak of war by misperception or accident. These include the 1992 agreement between India and Pakistan not to attack each other's nuclear facilities and the linked exchange of a list of such facilities at the start of each year, and the 1999 agreement to give prior warning of ballistic missile tests, later extended to cruise missiles. With China, there have been four border defence management agreements (1993, 1996, 2005, and 2013) to prevent the start of a border war due to the undemarcated and disputed nature of the Line of Actual Control (LAC).

Relations with Pakistan have been deadlocked on terrorism since the Mumbai attacks of November 2008 and other lesser attacks since then. Kashmir, beneath a surface normality, remains a tinderbox that could explode at any time. On the LAC between India and China, minor incursions without casualties take place frequently. China is modernising its forces and military infrastructure on its side of the border at a pace that makes it difficult for India to keep up. Despite the rapid growth of trade – with a huge surplus on the Chinese side – over the past decade and a half, security relations with China remain fraught.

A more serious longer-term threat lies in plans by China to divert part of the waters of the river Brahmaputra in Tibet eastwards and northwards, a development that would have serious downstream effects on India's north-east and yet about which India would be unable to do anything significant. China is also actively wooing all of India's neighbours, among them Afghanistan and Myanmar, and has made diplomatic inroads in all of them, including taking control of the Pakistani port of Gwadar near the mouth of the Gulf. More ominously, China is building two additional nuclear reactors at Chashma in Pakistan in a deal that it claims was "grandfathered" by agreements signed before it joined the Non-Proliferation Treaty (NPT) in 1992 and the Nuclear Suppliers Group (NSG) in 2004 –

although it did not declare any such commitment at the time of joining the NSG – and the United States has been passive in accepting this state of affairs.

The only bright spot in South Asia for India has been the Modi government's pragmatic deal on settling the "ragged" border with Bangladesh and a general improvement in relations with that country. So while improved relations in the neighbourhood are seen as vital for creating a secure environment for growth, there has been little improvement so far. A US$2 billion aid investment in Afghanistan since 2002 has not paid off in that the Ghani government is negotiating with Pakistan for a settlement which will enable the Taliban to make some sort of comeback and hence provide Pakistan with a proxy in Afghan affairs. An India-centric South Asia is not coming into being.

Elements of Change

The main trajectory in post-Cold War foreign policy, however, has been a gradual shift since 1991 away from the legacy of a non-alignment tilted towards the then Soviet Union to a search for new partnerships that would boost economic growth and security. However, the underlying desire and goal of the non-alignment paradigm, the search for strategic autonomy, seems intact.[20] What is new is the means of pursuing this end: to realise strategic autonomy it is now necessary to forge strategic partnerships, particularly with the United States and its allies and partners. Even so, there has not been an explicit reconceptualisation of Indian foreign policy doctrine in the post-Cold War period, with the exception of the unofficial "Nonalignment 2.0" vision unveiled by a group of largely non- governmental policy intellectuals at the end of 2011.[21] This vision can be interpreted as a response to an incipi-

[20] See Harsh V. Pant and Julie M. Super, "India's 'Non-Alignment' Conundrum: A Twentieth-Century Policy in a Changing World", *International Affairs* 91:4, Sept. 2015, pp. 747–64.

[21] Sunil Khilnani, Rajiv Kumar, Pratap Bhanu Mehta, Prakash Menon,

ently multipolar world, away from the unipolar moment of the 1990s and early 2000s, in circumstances formed by the global financial crisis of 2008, the rise of China and a hydrocarbon-powered Russia, and the emergence of a cluster of middle powers – all developments tacitly recognised by the prominence after 2008 of the Group of 20 (G20), rather than the western-dominated G7 or G8, as the key forum for global coordination. "Nonalignment 2.0" signalled the need to pursue some sort of balancing among power centres even while building strategic partnerships for the ultimate goal of the achievement and maintenance of strategic autonomy. Nor has Indian foreign policy under the present Modi-led NDA government from 2014 seen the explicit articulation of a new vision, grand strategy or policy framework. Interestingly, there has to date been no explicit articulation of a foreign policy framework based on the Hindu nationalist concept of Hindutva – or, indeed, any sort of "Modi doctrine".[22]

The following patterns of change may be traced in the evolution of Indian foreign policy under successive governments since the end of the Cold War.

A major shift has been the establishment of full diplomatic relations with Israel in 1992 and the steady growth of that relationship, centred on defence equipment imports – without, however, a formal change in policy on Palestine, in respect of which India remains committed to the two-state solution supported by the international community (including Israel's indispensable supporter,

---

Nandan Nilekani, Srinath Raghavan, Shyam Saran, and Siddharth Varadarajan, *Nonalignment 2.0* (New Delhi: Centre for Policy Research, 2012).

[22] Although it has been argued, on the basis of the policies adopted by the BJP-led NDA government of 1998–2004, that a distinctive security orientation associated with the BJP and rooted in its worldview – consisting of explicit nuclear weaponisation, a tilt towards the United States, regional pragmatism and *realpolitik* – has come into being in practice. See Chris Ogden, *Hindu Nationalism and the Evolution of Contemporary Indian Security: Portents of Power* (New Delhi: Oxford University Press, 2014).

the United States). For several years in the 2000s, Israel was India's second-largest arms supplier, next only to Russia.[23]

The "Look East" policy, now called "Act East", launched in the early 1990s following economic liberalisation, also represents a departure from India's relative neglect of this region during the Cold War due to its own pro-Soviet tilt and the pro-US orientation of much of South East Asia and non-communist East Asia. Since then India has become a full dialogue partner of the Association of South- East Asian Nations (ASEAN), a member of the ASEAN Regional Forum, and from 2005 a member of the East Asia Summit (ASEAN plus six). The ASEAN–India Free Trade Area entered into force in July 2015. Since the new government came into office in 2014 India has participated actively in these forums, as well as in the ASEAN Defence Ministers Meeting Plus and the Expanded ASEAN Maritime Forum. ASEAN now accounts for a significantly larger share of India's trade than China does. There has also been a major improvement of relations with Japan as Chinese assertiveness in the East and South China Seas has grown since 2011, particularly under the Modi government. Japan is now committing itself to selling dual-purpose amphibious aircraft technology to India, a far cry from its strong reservations about India after the 1998 nuclear tests.[24]

India has also begun to look further beyond its traditional areas of concern. There has been an active attempt to build long-term relationships with Africa, an emerging continent rich in natural resources including oil and gas. There have been four India–Africa summits since 2008, most recently in October 2015. After that meeting, India made new long-term commitments of $10 billion in Lines of Credit (LOCs) on top of existing commitments of

[23] N.P. Ullekh, "$10 Billion Business: How Israel Became India's Most Important Partner in Arms Bazaar", *Economic Times*, 23 Sept. 2012.

[24] Press Trust of India, "'Make in India' Boost: Japan Offers to Set Up Plant in India for US-2 Amphibious Aircraft", *Economic Times*, 1 Feb. 2016.

US$6.77 billion.[25] The motivation is probably long-term access to resources, energy supplies, markets and UN General Assembly votes in support of India's global governance aspirations.

The Modi government has also broken new ground in courting Saudi Arabia and the United Arab Emirates with prime ministerial visits to drum up investment and credit, particularly for infrastructure and energy development. This balances both India's closer relations with Israel and Pakistan's close relations with the Gulf countries, and takes account of the large Indian diaspora in the Gulf, numbering some 6 million people, which accounts for a major part of India's inward remittance income.

One strand of the Modi government's foreign policy has been a vigorous search for foreign investment and the associated technology. Modi recognises that investment and growth are crucial both domestically, for creating the 10 million jobs a year that India needs in order to absorb new entrants to the labour market and maintain social stability, and in pursuit of its ambitions to be a leading power in a slow-growth world looking for new markets. It has accordingly sought to promote India as the next manufacturing platform. The high points of this search for investments in manufacturing and infrastructure so far have been the securing of a US$35 billion investment commitment from Japan over five years and of US$22 billion from China over a similar time-frame.[26]

The concomitant drive to acquire technology has focused particularly on the civil nuclear and defence sectors. India is well aware that attempts to acquire advanced nuclear, military, and dual-purpose technologies will be eased if it is seen to be playing by the

[25] For all data in this paragraph, see EXIM Bank database: http://www.eximbankindia.in/lines-of-credit.

[26] MEA, Government of India, "Joint Statement on India and Japan Vision 2025', 23 Dec. 2015, http://www.mea. gov.in/bilateral-documents.htm?dtl/26176/Joint_Statement_on_India_and_Japan_Vision_2025_Special_Strategic_and_Global_Partnership_Working_Together_for_Peace_and_Prosperity_of_the_IndoPacific_ Region. See also MEA, *Annual Report 2015–16*, p. iv.

non-proliferation rules valued by the major powers and their allies and partners, and hence has sought admission to the four major dual-purpose technology export control regimes. India under Modi amended its civil nuclear liability law to make investment in civil nuclear power generation attractive to US companies, enabling it to take full advantage of the Indo–US nuclear deal. Most recently, India applied to join the NSG, a move that failed in mid-2016 owing to resistance from China and some other countries with a strong attachment to non-proliferation. However, India was admitted into the Missile Technology Control Regime (MTCR) in June 2016 and is seeking to join the Wassenaar Arrangement and the Australia Group. On defence technology, India took the unprecedented step of opening up foreign direct investment in its defence industries to the extent of allowing 100 per cent foreign ownership; it remains to be seen whether this leads to investment that transfers advanced technologies. India has also, as part of the Defence Trade and Technology Initiative with the United States, been trying to shift progressively to acquisition of advanced US defence equipment and technologies.

Modi has also played an active role in promoting Indian participation in multilateral forums, including regional groupings, for both economic (trade, energy, connectivity, technology) and security reasons. India has most recently joined the expanded Shanghai Cooperation Organization (SCO) founded initially by China, Russia and Central Asian states. It has joined the Chinese-promoted, Shanghai-headquartered Asian Infrastructure Investment Bank and the New Development Bank promoted by the BRICS grouping[27] – both alternatives to western-dominated development finance institutions – and has played an active role in neighbourhood regional organisations, including the South Asian Association for Regional Cooperation (SAARC) and the Bay of Bengal Initiative for Multi-Sectoral Technical and Economic Cooperation (BIMSTEC), as well as in the East Asia summit and other groupings centred on ASEAN.

[27] Brazil, Russia, India, China and South Africa.

India has continued to push for permanent membership of a reformed UN Security Council, reflecting its desire to rise from middle to Great Power status. In UN debates, and on international crises including those in Libya, Syria, and Crimea/Ukraine, it has continued to play a more traditional "non-aligned" role, careful not to align itself with the West and alienate Russia and China or vice versa. Likewise, in the World Trade Organization, it has taken a nationalist rather than a liberal multilateralist stand on food subsidies; and it has taken a similarly nationalist and "Third Worldist" stand in its emphasis on equity and reluctance to commit to hard ceilings on emissions in global climate change negotiations, most recently at the 21st Conference of the Parties in Paris in 2015 (although it finally made the commitment in October 2016). Hence, while moving away from non-alignment and improving its relations with the United States and the West, India has kept its options open; there are limits to realignment that will be explored later in this paper.

Indo–US Relations and US–China Dynamics in Asia

The major change in Indian foreign policy has been the improvement of relations with the United States. This has come about only gradually, after a continuing period of uneasiness during the 1990s arising from the continuing American need for Pakistani co-operation in stabilising Afghanistan after the end of the Soviet occupation, a generally hyphenated US policy on India and Pakistan that tended to equate them, an intensified US concern about non-proliferation (particularly following the near-nuclear crisis of May 1990, India's veto of the Comprehensive Test Ban Treaty at the Conference on Disarmament in Geneva in 1996 and India's 1998 nuclear tests), and a generally tightening US policy on non-proliferation – together with some degree of sympathy for the Pakistani position on Kashmir in the early to mid-1990s.

Over the course of the 1990s and early 2000s, particularly after 9/11, two of the three major irritants in the Indian relationship with the United States declined in political significance: with Russia's relative decline, India's continued arms supply relationship with the former superpower was of less concern to the United States, and the United States became less closely bound to Pakistan after 9/11, despite its dependence on Pakistan for its Afghanistan operations. This left only the third major irritant – India's nuclear weapons capability, particularly after the 1998 tests – to be salved, if not resolved, in order that the relationship could move forward, a trend already favoured by India's economic liberalisation and closer integration with world markets, epitomised by the information technology sector. The eleven-round dialogue between US Deputy Secretary of State Strobe Talbott and Indian Foreign Minister Jaswant Singh on nuclear weapons following the 1998 tests laid the basis for what would become the Indo-US nuclear deal of 2005–8. While India has drawn significantly closer to the United States since at least 2005, and since 2011 significantly closer to US allies in the Asia–Pacific region such as Australia, Japan, and several ASEAN countries (as reflected in growing naval cooperation and joint exercises), it must be remembered that the overarching context for these developments, including the Indo–US nuclear deal, has been the shift in US security policy in the Asia–Pacific region driven by the rise of China. This is often understood as the Obama administration's "pivot" (later relabelled "rebalance") towards Asia, whereby 60 per cent of US air and naval assets would be deployed in the Pacific rather than the Atlantic. However, while formally declared in 2011, the pivot actually began much earlier, in ideational terms as early as 2001, and in practice from 2004 under the Bush administration.[28] The basic aim was to balance the rise of China, not by containment as practised towards the Soviet Union during the Cold War, but by both internal and external balancing, to maintain the superior strategic position of the United States in the Asia–Pacific while accepting the rise of China as a given. The external balancing component of the strategy was not a new NATO-

[28] See Nina Silove, "The Pivot Before the Pivot: US Strategy to Preserve the Power Balance in Asia', *International Security* 40:4, Spring 2016, pp. 45–88.

style alliance but a shift from the traditional hub-and-spokes pattern of defence relationships in the Asia–Pacific to a federated, network model in which Asian allies, themselves increasingly concerned about China's rise and assertiveness, were to be encouraged to establish stronger relationships with each other as well as increasing interoperability of forces, a trend fostered by the growth of military, particularly naval, exercises among the United States and its Asian allies and partners since 2001, on a multilateral basis.

In 2004 the Bush administration took the key decision to bring India into this federated network model as a new partner. Hence the Next Steps in Strategic Partnership framework agreement of 2005, and the Indo–US civil nuclear agreement negotiated over the following three years, which dealt with the major remaining irritant in Indo–US relations, bringing India into the global nuclear commerce regime while allowing it to retain its nuclear military capabilities. This would not have happened without a shift in US policy, and that in turn can only be understood in the context of US concerns about the long-term rise of China and the development of an appropriate response that combined balancing with continued engagement. The defence and foreign policies of countries in the Asia–Pacific region are significantly influenced by US strategy, and this is an important factor, creating both incentives for behaviour and windows of opportunity for a number of countries in the region.

Thus India's shift towards improved relations with the United States and its Asian allies and partners can be fully understood only by taking into account the context of US policy and its impact on foreign policy behaviour throughout Asia. From the US point of view, it made sense to include India in its federated network model to balance China's rise; in addition, India could be an ally against post-9/11 international terrorism and the threat of further nuclear proliferation. Thus the overarching and gradual shift in US policy, in addition to the economic rise of Asia, created opportunities for shifts in Indian foreign policy towards the United States and its allies and partners in South East Asia and East Asia.

These developments gathered momentum after 2005; again after the economic and financial crisis of 2008–9, in the aftermath of which China's relatively unscathed growth took it ahead of Japan to become the world's second largest economy; and yet again after 2011 as Chinese offshore assertiveness increased. Thus the United States supported a Japanese proposal in 2007 to create a "quadrilateral" security dialogue between the two countries plus Australia and India; this led to increased security interaction among all four states. Japan and India signed a defence co-operation agreement in 2008 and a Strategic and Global Partnership Agreement in 2014.[29] The United States, Japan, and India conducted their first trilateral naval exercises in the western Pacific in 2007, and since that year the Indo–US Malabar naval exercises were expanded to include Australia, Japan, and Singapore. Bilateral Indo–Japanese naval exercises started in 2012. The influence on Indian foreign policy, in terms of incentives and opportunities, of the context-changing shifts in US policy is clearly discernible, and will continue to affect its future evolution.

On the whole, recent foreign policy changes have been slow and incremental, building on past policies without dramatic breaks, but taking advantage of windows of opportunity such as those afforded by shifts in US policy. The Modi government's initiatives since 2014 seem to represent a more energised version of earlier foreign policy changes, such as one would expect from a middle power without system-shaping capabilities but with aspirations to a bigger role and higher international status.

Possible Future Directions in Indian Foreign Policy: Three Broad Scenarios

What does the discussion so far imply for future directions in Indian foreign policy? Clearly there are certain constant imperatives

[29] Silove, "The Pivot Before the Pivot", p. 78.

which will persist – the search for security against the perceived threats from the combination of Pakistan and China, as well as more generally the preservation and enhancement of capabilities, and the search for economic growth, and hence for capital, technology, and partners. The aspiration, shared across political parties, to become a leading power in the world, will remain, and alongside the desire for strategic autonomy. At a practical level of boosting institutional capacities for foreign policy, one can expect the rectification of certain weaknesses – such as the small size of the foreign service and its relatively weak links with academia and think-tanks – and the increasingly institutionalised involvement of India's states, reflected in the creation of the States Division in the Ministry of External Affairs in 2014, driven by the globalisation of the economies of states and their links with various parts of the Indian diaspora. The overall strategy – whether or not there is any declared grand strategy, paradigm, or doctrine – and specific foreign policies deployed to achieve these objectives will depend on the incentives and windows of opportunity offered by the global, extra-regional, and regional structural context. These contexts are in turn shaped by the dynamics of Great Power interaction, specifically, for the Asia–Pacific land and maritime context, the dynamics of interaction between China, Russia, and the United States, and the evolution of the world economic order. While India's relationship with Europe is critical to its economic growth, the EU is not a single political entity and plays a secondary role in the Asia–Pacific landmass and waters; hence my focus on the overarching relationships between China, Russia, and the United States in setting the geopolitical context for Indian foreign policy. Against this background, three possible broad scenarios can be identified for the next five to ten years.

The first is one of increased US dominance. In this scenario, the United States is able to balance the rise of China, aided by a slowdown of the Chinese economy, by a wholehearted rebalance to the Pacific and by a relatively declining Russia, possibly increasingly allied to China with the aim of countering US dominance. In these conditions one could expect India to align itself more closely with the United States and its federated network of allies and partners in Asia and elsewhere. However, even in this case there will be limits to any realignment or tilt towards the United States and the West. Even a slowing China will be growing faster than the West in the foreseeable future, starting from a baseline of about half the US GDP, and so will still be narrowing the gap, albeit more slowly. Also, China will be impossible to isolate, given that it is already a larger trading partner than the United States for almost all its Asian neighbours. Besides, if China's "one belt, one road" (OBOR) project is fully implemented, particularly in respect of pipelines, then it will have land connections with Europe, the Middle East, and much of South East Asia, reducing its dependence on seaborne trade and energy supplies.

As far as India is concerned, China will still control the headwaters of the Indus and Brahmaputra rivers, and could divert the latter's waters. It will still have a clandestine nuclear and missile partnership with Pakistan, bolstering the latter *vis-à-vis* India, along with the advantages of terrain, infrastructure, and superior forces along the border; and it will remain an important trading partner and potential source of capital for India, giving it leverage over Indian behaviour. There is nothing that the United States can do to protect India in the event of a border war in which China is well positioned to grab scraps or slices of territory, or in the eventuality of a diversion of river waters. So, even in this scenario India would have incentives not to alienate China by throwing in its lot definitively with the United States. Most likely would be a strategic partnership with the United States, with some limits on realignment, to increase India's leverage *vis-à-vis* the China–Pakistan combination. As far as Russia is concerned, given the fact that at present something like 70 per cent of major military platforms in the Indian armed forces (combat aircraft, submarines, ships, tanks) are of Soviet/Russian origin, and the fact that Russia is sharing key military technologies with India (the leasing of a nuclear-powered submarine, reported assistance for India's sea-based deterrent, collaboration on the Brahmos supersonic missile, and the fifth-generation fighter project), it will not be easy to make sudden and drastic changes in the relationship.[30] Hence, even in a US-dominant scenario there will be limits to a fully fledged Indian alignment with America.

The second possible broad scenario is the maintenance of the status quo. This would see the thrust of the Modi government's policies over the past two years continue in the same direction, that is, a continuing realignment towards the United States and its allies and partners in Asia, and a continuing but partial shift in defence acquisitions towards US and western sources and away from Russia, along with an attempt to sustain India's influence in neighbouring countries, the Middle East, Central Asia, and Africa, and a continued search for infusions of capital and technology. At the same time, India would retain its autonomy in the UN and on international crises, making independent decisions according to its assessment of the national interest in each case.

The third possible broad scenario is one of increasing Chinese ascendancy and US/western decline. This is possible if a slowing China still manages to grow significantly faster than the United States, increasing its weight in the world economy and in the Asia–Pacific region. In such a scenario, if the US rebalance towards the Pacific is incomplete and/or if Washington decides to accommodate the rise of China and its commensurately expanded definition of core national interest in the Pacific and Indian Oceans, and if China's OBOR project succeeds and reduces Chinese dependence on sea routes for trade and energy supplies, then China will loom larger as both a security threat and an economic opportunity for all its neighbours, including India. Such a scenario would also probably

[30] For Russian collaboration in India's submarine-based deterrent efforts, see Yogesh Joshi and Frank O'Donnell, "India's Submarine Deterrent and Asian Nuclear Proliferation', *Survival*, 56:4, 2014, pp. 157–74.

lead to a closer relationship between China and Russia, given Russia's frozen relationship with the West following the Crimea/Ukraine crises of 2014.

Given that China has an unresolved border dispute with India, a military advantage on the frontier and a close de facto alliance with Pakistan cemented by overland access to Gwadar port, this scenario could be a threatening one for Indian security. India would then have two contrasting options. One would be an even stronger alignment with the United States and the West for security against China, alongside increasing economic ties with China to maintain a stable relationship. If this angers China and the relationship becomes confrontational, and if the United States is not able to help balance China as far as the land border or possible river water diversion is concerned, India would face intensified pressure from the China–Pakistan combination all along its de facto borders. In such a scenario, several of India's South Asian neighbours could tilt towards China. The other option would be to attempt to accommodate/appease China while attempting internal balancing through a military buildup. However, China and Pakistan can be expected to demand a very high price, possibly the formal acceptance of the LAC in the western sector (Ladakh), concessions on Tawang, political concessions on Kashmir, and the like. This would be almost impossible to sell domestically in India. The only situation in which India would be able to fend off such pressures in this scenario would be if its economy were to grow much faster than that of a slowing China and its military modernisation to narrow the gap between the two countries' capabilities.

Conclusion

All three of the broad scenarios outlined above assume sustained high growth of the Indian economy and domestic political stability. In the absence of either, India's prospects of rising to the position of a leading power, if not a Great Power, in a more multipolar world are dim. It will remain a middle power and a struggling one at that. If, however, sustained high growth and the associated domestic political stability increase its weight and influence in the world economy, then various rising power possibilities open up.

If India's prospects for rising from a middle to a Great Power over the next decade or two appear limited, what other roles could it play, given its expanding relationship with the United States and its Asian allies? India has good prospects of building itself up as an important coalitional and bridging power between West Asia and Pacific Asia. It could, however, by virtue of its participation in broader US-led Asia–Pacific security (particularly naval security) partnerships, become something of an extraregional net security provider for South East Asia, and perhaps the Gulf and Indian Ocean, without being a fully fledged regional power in South Asia. It can increasingly be seen as an attractive coalition partner on a range of international economic and Asian regional issues, including regional and oceanic security, conflict resolution and environment, spanning different subregions and international coalitions from the Gulf to South East Asia and the western Pacific. And, as its economy grows, it can play a larger role in international and Asian regional institutions.

India could also potentially leverage its soft power, which derives from being a successful, diverse, secular, federal democracy, and its current non-threatening "good citizen" status to become an exemplar and promoter of democracy, human rights, and their subsets – minority rights and autonomy for minority regions: an ideological model and a promoter of regional co-operation in South Asia and indeed Asia more widely. Promoting a specifically Indian model of democracy could considerably increase its endowment of soft power. This possibility assumes that Indian democracy, secularism, federalism, and inclusiveness are not subverted by extremist forces within, and that the existing constitutional consensus is robust enough to survive.

The most probable future direction for India over the next five to ten years is a continuation of the gradual shift towards the United States and its allies and partners, but still within the context of a search for strategic autonomy via strategic partnerships and without full realignment. India is likely to gain greater weight and influence in the world due to faster-than-average growth, but to gain less than commensurate real geopolitical power owing to the conversion problems and geostrategic blockages impeding its becoming a regional and extraregional power. Hence, India will probably not be among the Great Powers in a decade, but could hope to be a leading power, that is, one level down in the global hierarchy of powers in an increasingly multipolar world.

Finally, to reconnect with the literature on power transitions and rising powers, and the question whether India will challenge the existing order, the trajectory of Indian policy projected into the future seems more in line with recent work on rising powers, which argues that they will be socialised into the existing US-led order, rather than with that of the classic power transition literature, which argues that rising powers mean challenge and conflict. This is largely because the rise of India is taking place against the backdrop of the much greater rise of China, which does potentially challenge US economic and at least Pacific strategic dominance, as well as posing a threat to India, pushing it towards the United States.

8

Foreign Assistance in India's Foreign Policy

Political and Economic Determinants

Introduction: Key Questions About India as an Emerging Donor

EMERGING ECONOMIES are also emerging as aid donors and players in the international aid architecture and in the use of aid as a foreign policy tool. India's development partnership policy has been little studied for a country that is a major emerging market and regional power that has given over $34 billion (bn) in aid since 2004. This paper attempts a detailed account and analysis of India as an emerging foreign aid donor, or development partner as it prefers to call itself while rejecting the former term (I will refer to Indian assistance rather than aid henceforth). It analyses India's development partnership programme within the framework of Indian foreign policy and relations rather than that of only the development aid literature. India is not a member of the Development Assistance Committee (DAC) of the Organization for Economic Cooperation and Development (OECD), the traditional coordination mechanism of the developed country donors and the international aid regime. This paper will analyse India's development partnership policy in the context of its foreign policy by asking and analysing five key questions:

(1) *How much?* Aid numbers have always been prone to massaging as donors attempt to show their largesse. A good handle on India's assistance numbers is an essential first step.

(2) *To Whom?* What have been the allocations by country and/or region? To what extent is Indian assistance directed to the "near abroad" versus more geographically distant countries? Is the assistance directed to the poorest countries or to resource-rich countries?

(3) *For what?* What are the purposes to which this assistance is directed? What are the sectors and types of projects being assisted? Is there a discernible philosophy regarding economic development in Indian assistance policy?

(4) *How?* What are the modalities and institutional mechanisms through which Indian assistance works? Is it through grants or loans? Is it tied to imports from the donor? Which arms of the government give the assistance and how is it co-ordinated and administered? Is India's assistance strategically planned, either for promoting development or for promoting its interests, or it is *ad hoc*, case by case, and evolving?

(5) *Why?* What are the motivations of this assistance? Is it to secure access to scarce natural resources, commercial expansion, or for geo-strategic goals or in response to geopolitical competitive dynamics? Is it co-ordinated with India's expanding trade and investment relationships? This paper links India's programme to its foreign policy toward all its major recipients with a section on each.

Emerging Donors in the International Aid Architecture

While the post-war global foreign aid regime has been largely constructed and driven by Western countries, other country groups also played a varying role. For a few decades, the Soviet Union (and

Maoist China despite low per capita income) was an important player in countries allied to its interests. After the first oil shock of 1973, some of the OPEC did so in the 1970s (especially Kuwait, Saudi Arabia, and Venezuela), through both bilateral and multilateral institutions (such as the OPEC Fund for International Development) targeted especially to members of the Organization of the Islamic Conference (OIC) and global membership multilateral institutions (notably IFAD and UNIDO). But, with the sharp decline in oil prices in the 1980s, the economic power of OPEC diminished and with it reduced any influence they might have on the global aid regime.

However, today the economic resurgence of non-Western countries, epitomised by the emergence of China and of the other BRICS (the Brazil–Russia–India–China–South Africa group), the BRICS-promoted New Development Bank (NDB), and the Chinese-promoted Asian Infrastructure Investment Bank (AIIB), is raising new questions, challenges, and perhaps even hope about the future of the global aid regime. India, like China earlier, graduated from International Development Association (IDA) – the largest multilateral concessional source of development aid – in 2014, and after a period of transitional support till 2017 is now off it completely, borrowing at standard World Bank interest rates. It is an emerging donor.

Currently, the international aid architecture is, to simplify a bit, constituted by two broad groups of donors (for useful outlines of the international aid regime and emerging donors, see Manning 2006; Naim 2007; Paulo and Reisen 2010; Six 2009; Walz and Ramachandran 2011; Woods 2008).

First, the traditional developed-country donors who co-ordinate their aid policies through the OECD's DAC, formed in 1960. The DAC defines Official Development Assistance (ODA or aid) as a concessional transaction (a minimum of 25 per cent must be a grant, calculated for loans at a 10 per cent preference rate), that is concessional loans and grants provided by governments for the promotion of economic development and welfare and including technical co-operation (Chaturvedi 2008, 5). DAC ODA enjoyed near-total dominance in the 1990s, but the pattern has changed since the 2000s. ODA from DAC donors in 2016 was $145 bn (Table 8.1). DAC ODA as a per centage of GNI declined from 0.51 per cent (1960) to 0.22 per cent (2000) before recovering to 0.32 per cent (2016) (Table 8.1).

Second, a diverse non-DAC group of emerging donors, which include China, India, Brazil, South Africa, Russia, and Venezuela, among others, have emerged in the 2000s. Manning (2006) has identified four subgroups of non-DAC donors: (i) OECD members not part of DAC; (ii) EU members from Central and Eastern Europe that are not part of the OECD; (iii) Middle East and other OPEC; (iv) "others" that do not fall into the above three categories (including China and India).

Table 8.1: DAC ODA
(Official Develpoment Assistance) 1960–2017

Year	*ODA (U.S.D. Mn)*	*ODA as a Percent of GNI*
1960	4,676	0.51
1970	6,713	0.33
1980	26,304	0.35
1990	52,808	0.33
2000	54,021	0.22
2010	1,28,484	0.32
2012	1,27,030	0.29
2013	1,34,847	0.30
2014	1,37,139	0.29
2015	1,31,563	0.30
2016	1,44,965	0.32
2017(p)	1,46,600	NA

Source: *OECD, accessed July 11, 2018*—http://www.oecd.org/dac/stats/data.htm.

Note: 1. (p) is for preliminary; NA is for not available.
2. The values are basis current prices (last updated April 9, 2018).
3. For raw data, see the file "Longterm-ODA" and "TAB01e".

Of the third subgroup above, mainly the oil-rich Arab donors, while these are not members of the OECD's DAC, most report their aid to the DAC although not necessarily according to DAC definitions or disaggregation (for example, do not report debt forgiveness as ODA unlike DAC). Arab aid started in the 1970s, with five aid agencies being established between 1971 and 1976, led by the United Arab Emirates (UAE), Saudi Arabia, and Kuwait. The average net aid for these three states between 1973 and 2008 was 1.5 per cent of GNI, and between 1973 and 1994 Arab aid accounted for 13.5 per cent of global ODA (Walz and Ramachandran 2011). Arab aid tends to flow to other Arab and Muslim countries, but in recent years to sub-Saharan Africa too.

The fourth subgroup of non-DAC donors referred to above tends to call their aid development assistance or co-operation, and to focus on infrastructure, particularly China, and particularly to Africa. The main southern donors tend to be regional powers – China, India, Brazil, and South Africa. Although aid from this group does not impose policy conditions, the majority of their aid is tied to the use of donor-country goods and services, contractors or oil imports, or packaged with commercial deals and foreign direct investment in an era when DAC aid is moving to untied aid. Aid from this group of countries is much less transparent as regards data and disaggregation. Non-DAC donor ODA in 2015 (excluding India and China) was $17.55 bn, of which $12 bn was from Saudi Arabia and UAE compared to DAC aid of $131 bn that year.[1]

The evolution of the international aid regime in the past quarter century can be summarised as ows. Following a decline in the 1980s, the era of Third World debt, aid flows began rising again in the 1990s. The traditional donors pledged to reform the aid architecture, creating the Paris Declaration on Aid Effectiveness in the Paris High-level Forum, 2005, followed by the Accra Agenda for Action in 2008. This was supposed to usher in a revised architecture

[1] Accessed August 4, 2018, https://stats.oecd.org/index.aspx?lang=en.

that prioritised commitments to improve (recipient) ownership, alignment, harmonisation, results, and mutual accountability. This is now the basis of the OECD-DAC approach to ODA. However, the Paris Forum was attended by many new donors (notably, not India, but India signed on in 2006). However, there has been not much progress in implementing all the commitments made in the Paris Declaration and Accra Agenda, even by DAC donors. Since the Fourth High-level Forum on Aid Effectiveness of November 2011 in Busan, South Korea, DAC donors have been trying to extend their lending norms to new donors but with diverse results to date.

These developments have led to the construction of the so-called Southern model (De Renzio and Seifert 2014) which does not impose DAC economic criteria, philosophies, and conditionalities. However, on a closer look, the Southern model collapses into a diversity of donors and practices. Comparatively speaking, Chinese assistance is much larger than India's and its motivations have shifted from ideological to mutual economic interests, resource access, and energy security (Gu, *et al.* 2016). Non-DAC aid on the whole tends to be geopolitically motivated somewhat like Western aid was at an early stage during the Cold War; perhaps it will evolve as it matures as Western aid did toward the current OECD-DAC approach referred to in the last paragraph, less nakedly geopolitical and more embedded in development economics, but that remains to be seen.

India: Emerging Development Partnership Policies

Historical Background and Evolution

Historically, India's assistance to fellow developing countries began in 1949 with scholarships and humanitarian assistance in cases of famine.[2] The Colombo Plan was the main channel for scholar-

[2] See Chaturvedi (2012a, 2012b, pp. 171–7) for a historical account until the 2000s.

ships, although India's own International Technical and Economic Cooperation (ITEC) programme started in 1964 for training and transfer of expertise. Nepal and Bhutan were the earliest recipients of Indian assistance and from 1959 India has been giving programme-based assistance as annual grants to these countries, worked into their and India's five-year plans.

Indian assistance has traditionally been co-ordinated by two ministries, the Ministry of External Affairs (MEA) and the Ministry of Finance's Department of Economic Affairs (DEA) (see Agrawal 2007; Chanana 2009; Chaturvedi 2012a, 2012b, 2008; Kragelund 2010; Mullen 2012, 2013; Naidu 2008; Price 2005, for accounts of India's emerging assistance policies). The MEA concentrates on neighbours like Nepal, Bhutan, and other South Asian countries for immediate geopolitical reasons of keeping them from aligning against India, and gave mainly grants and lines of credit (LOC) (through the Exim Bank since 2004–5), and also assistance through the ITEC programme.

ITEC, which came into existence in 1964, operates through four modalities: training in India, project assistance, study trips, and humanitarian assistance. The DEA (in the Ministry of Finance) gave LOC to a range of developing countries, especially South Asian neighbours.

Exim Bank LOC

There was a basic policy shift from 2003 to 2004 from government to government credit lines to government-supported LOC through the Exim Bank of India. As the Ministry of Finance put it:

> Policy on Lines of Credit: For about four decades, Department of Economic Affairs on behalf of Government of India had been extending lines of credit (LOCs) to friendly developing foreign countries. These LOCs were essentially "Government to Government" (G to G) credit lines as the credit agreements were signed between GOI and the Government of the recipient country. Till 2003–4, the LOCs were from

> Government to Government. Accordingly the full amount covered by the LOCs, used to be provided in the Budget. Since 2003–4, this system has been substituted by extending GOI supported Lines of Credit through Exim Bank of India.[3]

To address a question that can be raised, at the outset, viz. why should LOC be considered foreign assistance and not commercial activity? The answer is that it is government-subsidised and below market rates of interest. Furthermore, the Ministry of Finance continues:

> Q. What is the interest rate the overseas importer of Indian goods has to pay?
>
> A. The overseas importer of Indian goods has to approach the overseas borrower financial institution/recipient of Exim Bank's LOC, for approval of his proposal for import of Indian goods on deferred credit terms. The interest rate that the importer will need to pay to the recipient of Exim Bank's LOC, will depend on various factors such as the cost of fund, the currency of credit, tenure of credit, security offered by the importer, the risk perception of the importer and the interest rate structure prevalent in the country. It may however be mentioned that Exim Bank's interest rates on LOCs being competitive, the importer would normally have to pay interest rate lower than what he would otherwise pay to his Bank on similar credits.[4]

The last sentence indicates that the LOCs of the Exim Bank may be considered subsidised credit and hence foreign assistance. The interest subsidy on the Exim Bank's LOCs is given in the IDEAS line item in Statement 11 of the annual Expenditure Budget.

A key turning point in Indian foreign assistance was the decision in 2003 to repay its bilateral debt to all but four countries, not to accept tied aid in the future, and accept bilateral aid from only five

[3] Source: Accessed December 15, 2015, http://finmin.nic.in/the_ministry/dept_eco_affairs/ cie2sec/cie2sec_index.asp.

[4] See note 3, above.

countries and the EU, and simultaneously shift from a major aid recipient to donor (Chaturvedi 2008, pp. 26–9). Between 2003 and 2004 and June 2018, India provided $22,515 million (m) in 227 operative Exim Bank LOCs with another $1782 m in the pipeline to be operationalised, totalling 246 LOCs of $24,297 m (Table 8.2). The average worth of an operative LOC was $99 m.

Region-wise and country-wise (Table 8.3), 158 LOCs (of 227 operational) worth $9,229 m went to sub-Saharan Africa (henceforth, Africa refers to sub-Saharan, that is, non-Arab Africa, plus Sudan and Djibouti, and including the island states of Madagascar, Mauritius, and Seychelles), 15 LOCs worth $10,481 m to South Asian countries, 10 LOCs worth $539 m to Myanmar, 15 LOCs worth $538 m to South East Asia and Pacific (other than Myanmar), LOCs worth $1167 m to the (non-oil) Middle East and Central Asia, and 22 LOCs worth 405 m to Latin America and the Caribbean. Thus, 70 per cent of the number of LOCs went to Africa and 7 per cent to South Asia, 4 per cent to Myanmar, and 7 per cent to South East Asia and Pacific. By value, 47 per cent went to South Asia and

Table 8.2: Operating Exim Bank LOC as on June 2018

Level of Utilisation of LOC	*No. of LOCs*	*Amount ($Mn)*
Operating	227	22,515
Pipeline	19	1,782
Total	246	24,297
Of the operating		
Fully used*	142	5,762
Partly used**	43	4,793
Totally unsused***	42	11,960

*Assuming amount left for utilization is zero, where such data is missing in relevant columns.

**Of partly used, the amount left for utilization is $2,357.46 m.

*** "To be made effective" are clubbed under this.

Source: *EXIM Bank, accessed July 11, 2018*—http://www.eximbankindia.in/lines-of-credit.

Table 8.3: Region-wise (Operating) LOC as on June 2018

Country/ Region	*No.of LOCs*	*Amount ($Mn)*
Africa	158	9,229
Eurasia	2	156
LAC	22	405
Middle East and Central Asia	5	1,167
Myanmar	10	539
South Asia	15	10,481
South East Asia and Pacific	15	538
Total	227	22,515

Source: *EXIM Bank of India, accessed July 11, 2018*—http://www.eximbankindia.in/lines- of-credit.

41 per cent to Africa, these two regions getting 88 per cent of the total amount loaned.

By major purpose (Table 8.4), the largest single number of LOCs was 71 (of 227 operational LOCs, 31 per cent of the total num-

Table 8.4: Purpose-wise (Operating) LOC as on June 2018

Purpose	*No. of LOCs*	*Amount ($Mn)*	*Amount Left for Utilization ($Mn)*
General	40	11,070	10,580
Agricultural	29	1,162	455
Cement	6	157	46
Rural electrification	26	1,646	921
Power	27	1,688	653
Sugar Industry	11	905	29
Railway	14	1,979	816
Non-bilateral	3	500	155
Miscellaneous	71	3,409	666
Total	227	22,515	14,321

Source: *EXIM Bank, accessed July 11, 2018*—http://www.eximbankindia.in/lines-of-credit.

ber), covering a wide range of miscellaneous purposes too diverse to slot into sectors, worth $3,409 m, or 15 per cent of the total amount of credit extended. By identifiable purpose, the loans show a focus on power and electrification, railways, agriculture, and sugar, or more generally, electricity, transport, and agriculture. The largest amounts loaned by major sector were in power projects ($1688 m in 27 LOCs) and the related area of rural electrification ($1646 m in 26 LOCs), the latter two between them $3334 m or 15 per cent of the total amount equalling the Miscellaneous category. There was also a significant category of general purpose LOCs which the recipient could use for any purpose, amounting to $11,070 in 40 LOCs, or 18 per cent of the LOCs, totaling 49 per cent of the total loaned amount.

Grants and Loans Other Than Through the Exim Bank

Other than the LOCs extended by the Exim Bank and subsidised by the government since 2004–5, India provided a grand total of $15,030 m in grants and loans over the period from 1984 to 2018 (Tables 8.5A and 8.5B), of which $13,364 m was over 1997–2018, particularly since 2004–5 and more so over 2008–18. Grants have dominated this non-Exim Bank assistance (77 per cent) over the period 1997–2018 (Table 8.5A). Table 8.6 gives the amount of grant and loan assistance, other than Exim Bank, to South Asia. For the period since 2004–5, this totalled $7796.

Of the grand total, since 1997, or $13,364 m, $7796, or 58 per cent (Tables 8.5A and 8.6), went to its South Asian neighbours. Thus, India's non-Exim Bank Non-Plan grants and loans have gone mainly as grants, primarily to its South Asian neighbours, with Afghanistan registering a presence since 2008–9 and Africa since 2005–6. Infrastructure, health, and education are the main focus of Indian development assistance in South Asia while assistance tied to purchases of Indian goods and services and tech-

Table 8.5A: India's Bilateral Aid, Excluding EXIM Bank LOCs, 1997–2018 (U.S.D. Mn)

	Plan			*Non-Plan*			*Total*
Year	*Grant*	*Loan*	*Total*	*Grant*	*Loan*	*Total*	
1997–8	10	6	16	91	43	134	150
1998–9	44	27	71	100	30	131	202
1999	57	36	92	88	33	121	213
2000–1	76	44	120	88	38	127	247
2001–2	50	34	84	110	34	144	228
2002–3	69	44	114	56	113	169	282
2003–4	99	66	165	155	60	215	381
2004–5	101	62	164	208	65	273	437
2005–6	100	63	162	287	39	326	488
2006–7	41	8	49	305	28	333	382
2007–8	63	12	75	359	17	376	451
2008–9	73	25	98	313	177	490	588
2009–10	89	63	151	328	26	353	505
2010–11	69	106	175	495	–	495	670
2011–12	64	165	229	451	52	503	732
2012–13	86	209	296	601	129	729	1,025
2013–14	209	241	450	659	26	684	1,134
2014–15	231	380	611	678	–	678	1,289
2015–16	314	511	825	776	25	801	1,626
2016–17	–	–	–	810	–	810	810
2017–18	–	–	–	696	–	696	696
2018–19*	–	–	–	828	–	828	828
Total	1,845	2,102	3,947	8,482	935	9,416	13,364

Note: Rupee figures converted at average annual rupee–dollar exchange rates.
Source: *Ministry of External Affairs, accessed July 11, 2018*—http://indiabudget.nic.in/ previousub.asp.

*Budget estimates.

nical training of civil servants and public sector managers is the main focus in Africa. An Indian company, usually a public sector company, has to be the lead contractor and 75 per cent of goods and services should be sourced from India. However, there is an open bidding process among Indian companies and the choice of contractor among them is the host government prerogative.

Table 8.5B: India's Bilateral Aid, Excluding Exim Bank LOCs, 1984–97 (U.S.D. Mn)

Year	*Grant*	*Loan*	*Total*
1984–5	85	58	143
1985–6	81	59	140
1986–7	67	206	273
1987–8	129	36	165
1988–9	124	34	158
1989–90	96	10	106
1990–1	123	49	173
1991–2	67	15	82
1992–3	50	16	66
1993–4	53	22	75
1994–5	48	25	73
1995–6	78	31	110
1996–7	73	30	102
Total	1,074	593	1,666

Source: *Government of India, Ministry of Finance: Expenditure Budget, 1984–1997 accessed November 20, 2015.*

Note: Rupee figures converted at average annual rupee–dollar exchange rates.

Consolidated data on the number of scholarships and training slots offered under the ITEC programme and allied programmes like the Technical Co-operation Scheme (TCS) of the Colombo Plan, and the Special Commonwealth Assistance to Africa Program (SCAAP), and the amounts spent on these, are still unavailable. However, in 2017–18, 10,918 civilian and 2512 defence training slots were available for 161 partner countries including 4700 for African countries.[5]

Overall, it is not surprising, as we shall see later, that South Asia, as well as the "near abroad", including Myanmar and Afghanistan, has dominated Indian foreign assistance. However, Africa has emerg-

[5] Ministry of External Affairs, *Annual Report 2017–18*, pp. 193–4.

Table 8.6: Loans and Grants to South Asia, 1984–2019

Year	*South Asia Total ($Mn U.S.D)*
1984–5	107
1985–6	105
1986–7	110
1987–8	77
1988–9	82
1989–90	54
1990–1	77
1991–2	39
1992–3	47
1993–4	45
1994–5	34
1995–6	63
1996–7	59
1997–8	89
1998–9	79
1999	78
2000–1	84
2001–2	95
2002–3	92
2003–4	102
2004–5	116
2005–6	145
2006–7	188
2007–8	199
2008–9	328
2009–10	349
2010–11	463
2011–12	562
2012–13	788
2013–14	902
2014–15	929
2015–16	1184
2016–17	602
2017–18	481
2018–19*	560

Source: *Government of India, Ministry of Finance: Expenditure Budget, accessed July 12, 2018*—http://indiabudget.nic.in/previousub.asp. South Asia includes Nepal, Bangladesh, Bhutan, Maldives, and Sri Lanka.

*Budget estimates.

ed as a major focus particularly since 2008 (Duclos 2012; Kragelund 2010; Naidu 2008).

Recent Institutional and Policy Evolution: The Development Partnership Administration

In terms of institutions, organisation, and strategy, in common with many other donor countries, there was considerable bureaucratic competition between the Finance Ministry and the MEA on institutional control. A proposal for an integrated agency called the India International Development and Co-operation Agency, mulled over since 2003 and mooted in the budget for 2007–8, did not come into being immediately. However, since January 2012, a Development Partnership Administration (DPA) has been formed within the MEA, and started functioning from June 2012 in effect, co-ordinating the implementation of India's development partnership programme. It is a three-division department. The DPA currently has a staff strength of 75–80. This was a somewhat belated response to India's development assistance programme since 2003–4 outpacing the support infrastructure in the MEA. The creation of the DPA within the MEA to co-ordinate Indian assistance has to be seen in the context of the clear understanding in the MEA that a capital-hungry country like India can justify a foreign assistance programme only if it serves vital national interests, political, strategic, and economic.[6] Foreign assistance is clearly seen as a matter of foreign policy rather than disinterested development assistance despite it not laying down economic policy conditionalities.

The core DPA mandate consists of (a) focused attention on projects, the flagship project of the DPA being the construction of

[6] In fact, the former head of the DPA, Ambassador P.S. Raghavan, was explicit that aid by a low-income country like India could only be justified if it was clearly linked to foreign policy needs. Interview with Ambassador P.S. Raghavan, March 8, 2013, New Delhi.

50,000 houses for displaced persons in the North and East of Sri Lanka; (b) developing a skill base; (c) helping in policy formulation. However, it is an implementation agency, not a policy-making agency and does not propagate any particular development philosophy or strategy. Policy is handled by the country desk in the relevant political (territorial) division in the MEA. The traditional mechanism continues, that is, requests for assistance originate from the would-be recipient country. The Indian embassy, usually the ambassador or deputy chief of mission, is approached by the foreign government. This also happens very commonly on high-level visits to India either by heads of government or foreign ministers, or other cabinet ministers such as trade ministers, or when Indian leaders undertake high-level visits.

Four major examples are the India–Africa Forum summits of 2008, 2011, and 2015, the Afghan president's visit to India in 2011, and the Indian prime minister's visit to Bangladesh in 2017, all of which were followed by major increases in assistance commitments. The requests are processed by the country desk, i.e. the political (territorial) division of the MEA, which makes a decision on whether and how to respond. Assistance requests and hence, assistance decisions reflected in annual numbers are not – and cannot realistically be expected to be – a smooth affair but jerky and politically punctuated. Except for long-term Plan assistance to countries like Bhutan and Nepal, one can expect the numbers to jump up and down with events.

Once a policy decision is made by the relevant political division of the MEA, the DPA is then charged with implementing the decision. After the shift to Exim Bank LOCs for project loans, including import of Indian equipment, the MEA now gives 95 per cent of the total assistance, reflected in Statement 11 of the Government of India's Expenditure Budget, with about 5 per cent coming from some other ministries such as Science and Technology, Health, and Renewable Energy. The factors that will shape the likely mix of bilateral and multilateral modes of Indian development partnership are unclear and need better understanding, particularly with India's future participation in new institutions like the (BRICS') NDB and the AIIB.

The experience of various DAC donor agencies and their relationship to their respective foreign ministries is being studied, particularly the models of the Japan International Cooperation Agency (JICA), UK's Department for International Development (DFID), and the US Agency for International Development (USAID). The DPA has observed that the independently spun-off DFID in the UK developed tensions with the Foreign and Commonwealth Office, and that USAID is gradually being reintegrated into the State Department.

Internal issues that the DPA is currently addressing include: (a) budget allocations – funds are needed early in the financial year; (b) the approval process – an empowered committee is proposed to be set up to speed up LOCs selected by host countries; (c) efforts to move away from the monopolisation of projects by a few companies and reduce over-dependence on public enterprises; (d) streamlining contracting/procurement procedures.

India is striving to emerge as a South–South co-operation leader, cofounding the Global Network of Exim Banks and Development Finance Institutions in 2006, promoting the establishment of the Development Cooperation Forum in 2007, and becoming one of the largest contributors to the Commonwealth Fund for Technical Co-operation, and has now joined the NDB (which is based in Shanghai but headed by an Indian for its first five years) and the AIIB. Will it strive to marshal its limited foreign assistance resources through those multilateral institutions where it has a leadership role, but which might be relatively small, or try and leverage them through large global institutions where its voice is relatively limited? There has been some co-operation with DAC donor agencies which have expressed a desire to train Afghans and Africans in India as it is more cost-effective; this has been welcomed by DPA. Some DAC agencies have also expressed interest in joint project implementation in third countries. DPA has resisted this, fearing brand equity dilution and also wanting to avoid the terms and conditions of DAC aid. There has been a DAC attempt since the Fourth High-level Forum on Aid Effectiveness (Busan, South Korea meeting) Agenda of November 2011 to launch a global partnership on aid effectiveness in which DAC donors have been trying to envelop new donors under common norms for project selection, terms and conditions, etc., particularly for the post-millennium development goals (MDG) (post-2015) development agenda. India and China have been resisting this to avoid DAC conditionalities and also avoid having the global development aid burden passed on to them in part, which would reduce the flexibility of their own programmes.

India's Emerging Trade and Investment Relationships: Correlation with Development Partnership?

India's foreign assistance policy does not seem to be related to trade and investment relationships as far as its major thrust, South Asia, is concerned. Table 8.7 gives India's total trade with various regions and countries from 2004–5 to 2016–17 including with the countries of South Asia.

India's gross merchandise trade increased during the period of the new assistance policy from 23 per cent of GDP in 2004–5 to 43 per cent in 2011–12 before declining to 29 per cent in 2016–17, while its exports increased from 10 per cent to 17 per cent before declining to 11 per cent of GDP for the same years, indicating a rapidly globalising economy even after the global financial crisis of 2008.[7] India's trade with the countries of the South Asian

[7] See the Indian Ministry of Commerce database: http://commerce.nic.in/eidb/iecnttopnq.asp and the Reserve Bank of India database: http://dbie.rbi.org.in/DBIE/dbie.rbi?site=statistics and World Integrated Trade Solutions, World Bank – https://wits.worldbank.org/for the figures in this section. Accessed on August 4, 2018.

region, a major focus of Indian assistance with 47 per cent of Exim Bank credit, amounts to only 3.3 per cent of its overall trade in 2016–17, up from 2.8 per cent in 2004–5, and only 7 per cent of its exports in 2016–17, from only 5.5 per cent in 2004–5. India's trade with, and exports to, Afghanistan, remain tiny at 0.14 per cent and 0.2 per cent, respectively, as at 2016–17. Likewise, India's trade with, and exports to, Myanmar remain tiny at 0.24 per cent and 0.36 per cent, respectively, as at 2016–17.

India's outward private investment flows increased steadily, from a very low base, over 2001–2 to 2017–18, rising from $759 m to over $19 bn in 2008–9 then down to $9.1 bn in 2017–18, totalling $177.77 bn over the period (Table 8.8). As Table 8.9A shows, the bulk of Indian outward FDI since 2010 has gone to developed Western Europe ($44.7 bn) and North America ($24.5 bn), and to South East Asia (mainly, developed Singapore) ($36.6 bn), oil-rich West Asia ($14.3 bn), resource-rich South America, and not to the main aided regions with the sole exception of Eastern Africa. Private investment flows to South Asia of $2.33 bn (Table 8.9B) are very small (just over 1 per cent of all outward FDIs over 2010–17), although they are significant from the host country's point of view in the cases of Bhutan, Nepal, and Sri Lanka.[8] They are practically non-existent for Afghanistan, Myanmar, Nepal, and Bangladesh, all recipients of a significant chunk of Indian assistance since 2004–5.

As far as Africa is concerned, trade, exports, and imports show the following pattern over the past few years (2013–17). For sub-Saharan (non-Arab) Africa as a whole, India's trade from that continent has decreased from 9.2 per cent to 8.1 per cent of its total trade, exports decreased from 10.3 per cent to 8.3 per cent, and imports from 8.5 per cent to 8.1 per cent.[9] As of 2016–17, total trade with

[8] Ministry of External Affairs, *Annual Reports*, various years, pages for these countries.

[9] World Integrated Trade Solutions, World Bank – accessed August 3, 2018, https://wits.worldbank.org/.

Table 8.7: India's Foreign Trade, 2004–2005 to 2016–2017

Country/Division	*2016–17 Total*	*2015–16 Total*	*2014–15 Total*	*2013–14 Total*	*2012–13 Total*	*2011–12 Total*
Africa	**60,693**	**65,286**	**83,912**	**79,280**	**86,143**	**80,969**
South Africa	9,365	9,500	11,793	11,013	13,991	14,688
Nigeria	9,464	11,678	17,032	17,126	18,101	16,628
African Countries in OPEC (ex. Nigeria)	4,161	4,340	7,458	9,826	10,385	9,540
Rest of Africa	37,702	39,768	47,630	41,315	43,666	40,113
Asia-Developing countries (incl. SAARC)	**2,21,766**	**2,09,420**	**2,31,418**	**2,21,777**	**2,21,677**	**2,38,589**
SAARC	**21,636**	**21,587**	**23,437**	**20,056**	**17,786**	**15,968**
Afghanistan	801	835	686	689	630	637
Bangladesh	7,397	6,766	7,071	6,663	5,780	4,419
Bhutan	624	748	485	508	397	434
Maldives	207	183	157	110	129	144
Nepal	5,804	4,398	5,213	4,128	3,632	3,291
Pakistan	2,288	2,623	2,354	2,717	2,606	1,954
Sri Lanka	4,515	6,034	7,471	5,241	4,612	5,089
Latin American Countries	**26,071**	**24,988**	**32,075**	**30,355**	**31,185**	**25,279**
China	**71,527**	**70,721**	**72,409**	**66,123**	**65,826**	**75,886**
Russia	**7,487**	**6,170**	**6,337**	**6,016**	**6,527**	**6,454**
European Union	**88,770**	**88,516**	**98,744**	**1,01,704**	**1,02,844**	**1,11,181**
Canada	**6,080**	**6,263**	**5,953**	**5,186**	**4,845**	**4,997**
United States	**64,416**	**62,101**	**64,266**	**61,535**	**61,388**	**59,213**
Japan	**13,600**	**14,500**	**15,509**	**16,275**	**18,520**	**18,501**
World	**6,59,288**	**6,43,297**	**7,58,385**	**7,64,629**	**7,91,137**	**7,95,283**

Table 8.7 (*Contd.*)

Table 8.7 (*Contd.*)

2010–11 Total	*2009–10 Total*	*2008–9 Total*	*2007–8 Total*	*2006–7 Total*	*2005-06 Total*	*2004-05 Total*
59,128	**45,400**	**47,116**	**35,632**	**29,896**	**21,251**	**17,076**
11,064	7,725	7,366	5,860	4,718	3,999	3,182
12,058	9,451	9,972	7,469	6,316	4,328	3,486
6,918	5,423	5,721	4,285	3,624	2,483	2,000
29,088	22,800	24,057	18,018	15,237	10,441	8,409
1,85,770	**1,38,901**	**1,29,932**	**1,01,753**	**84,975**	**61,431**	**47,550**
13,807	**10,008**	**10,237**	**8,581**	**7,977**	**6,961**	**5,391**
567	589	525	291	216	201	–
3,684	2,678	2,769	1,885	1,856	1,791	1,691
377	271	260	252	199	188	156
132	83	132	73	72	70	48
2,680	1,981	2,046	1,556	1,235	1,240	1,089
2,364	1,848	1,783	1,637	1,673	869	616
4,004	2,559	2,722	2,887	2,726	2,602	1,792
18,903	**13,837**	**11,415**	**9,907**	**9,394**	**5,754**	**4,243**
58,928	**42,316**	**41,369**	**35,396**	**25,755**	**17,627**	**12,714**
5,295	**4,545**	**5,380**	**3,371**	**3,312**	**2,755**	**1,954**
90,658	**74,386**	**81,240**	**65,220**	**56,638**	**47,536**	**36,253**
3,376	**3,220**	**3,814**	**3,083**	**2,888**	**1,942**	**1,643**
45,338	**36,465**	**39,414**	**39,885**	**30,602**	**26,808**	**20,767**
13,716	**10,336**	**10,793**	**9,186**	**7,458**	**6,542**	**5,363**
6,20,905	**4,67,124**	**4,88,991**	**3,77,853**	**3,12,149**	**2,52,256**	**1,95,053**

Source: *RBI—https://dbie.rbi.org.in/DBIE/dbie.rbi?site=home—https://wits.worldbank.org/accessed on 13 July 2018 accessed on 13 July 2018; and World Integrated Trade Solutions, World Bank.*

Table 8.8: India's Outward Direct Investment Flows, 2000–2018 (U.S.D. Mn)

Year	*Gross Inflows/ Gross Invest-ments*	*Repatria-tion/ Disinvest-ment*	*Direct Invest-ment to India*	*FDI by India*	*Net Foreign Direct Invest-ment*	*Net Portfolio Invest-ment*	*Total*
2017–18	60,974	21,544	39,431	9,144	30,286	22,115	52,401
2016–17	60,220	18,005	42,215	6,603	35,612	7,612	43,224
2015–16	55,559	10,652	44,907	8,886	36,021	–4,130	31,891
2014–15	44,291	9,864	34,427	1,799	32,628	40,934	73,562
2013–14	36,047	5,284	30,763	9,199	21,564	4,822	26,386
2012–13	34,298	7,345	26,953	7,134	19,819	26,891	46,711
2011–12	46,552	13,599	32,952	10,892	22,061	17,170	39,231
2010–11	36,047	7,018	29,029	17,195	11,834	30,293	42,127
2009–10	37,746	4,637	33,109	15,143	17,966	32,396	50,362
2008–9	41,903	166	41,738	19,365	22,372	–14,030	8,342
2007–8	34,844	116	34,729	18,835	15,893	27,433	43,326
2006–7	22,826	87	22,739	15,046	7,693	7,060	14,753
2005–6	8,962	61	8,901	5,867	3,034	12,494	15,528
2004–5	6,052	65	5,987	2,274	3,713	9,287	13,000
2003–4	4,322	–	4,322	1,934	2,388	11,356	13,744
2002–3	5,095	59	5,036	1,819	3,217	944	4,161
2001–2	6,130	5	6,125	1,391	4,734	1,952	6,686
2000–1	4,031	–	4,031	759	3,272	2,590	5,862

Source: *RBI, accessed July 13, 2018*—https://dbie.rbi.org.in/DBIE/dbie.rbi?site=home.

Africa was about $61 bn, less than trade with China at $71 bn. If we look at Africa sub-regionally and country-wise in 2017, we see that $20 bn trade is with West Africa and $13 bn with Southern Africa out of a total of $61 bn. This is due to the dominant shares of just two countries in Indo-African trade – Nigeria with $9.46 bn and South Africa with $9.37 bn, totalling $18.83 bn. This is due to large imports from these energy- and resource-rich countries, India's trade profile with these two countries being dominated by imports. However, out of total assistance to Africa, these two countries are not at all dominant in the assistance profile, the overwhelming bulk of the assistance going to less developed or less resource-rich countries.

Table 8.9A: India's Outward FDI Region-wise, 2010–2017

(U.S.D Mn) *Continent*	*2010 Total*	*2011 Total*	*2012 Total*	*2013 Total*	*2014 Total*	*2015 Total*	*2016 Total*	*2017 Total*
Africa (total)	**5,116**	**2,661**	**1,829**	**3,679**	**8,320**	**3,991**	**4,970**	**2,759**
Eastern Africa	5,098	2,582	1,762	3,466	8,223	3,890	4,899	2,695
Western Africa	–	–	–	17	30	12	18	13
Central Africa	–	–	–	0	0	0	0	0
Southern Africa	–	–	–	19	33	62	28	29
Northern Africa	18	79	67	178	36	27	25	22
Asia (total)	**7,047**	**3,891**	**4,033**	**7,469**	**9,412**	**7,816**	**8,280**	**7,985**
South Asia	1,262	260	157	173	79	140	65	191
Southeast Asia	4,135	2,457	1,981	4,164	6,759	5,251	6,040	5,765
Western Asia	1,449	572	1,663	2,583	2,362	2,028	1,989	1,693
Eastern Asia	201	602	232	547	212	397	180	249
Central Asia	–	–	–	1	–	–	6	87
Caribbean	–	34	55	45	28	24	13	0
EU	2,551	1,955	1,835	0	0	0	0	0
Eastern Europe	–	–	–	62	70	46	107	545
Western Europe	2,255	2,028	2,263	5,479	15,030	5,011	7,531	5,089
South America	–	–	–	51	46	102	42	86
Central America	–	–	–	38	39	17	77	62
North America	893	835	745	4,928	5,213	3,340	4,034	4472
Oceania	–	–	–	1	3	5	9	10
Antartica	–	–	–	0	0	0	0	0
Australia	183	313	177	141	59	103	51	60
Unspecified	1,596	666	475	39	15	39	37	47
World	18,337	11,405	10,973	23,964	40,261	22,510	27,180	23,138

Source: *RBI, accessed July 13, 2018*—https://dbie.rbi.org.in/DBIE/dbie.rbi?site=home.

Outward FDI and assistance are also not correlated at all with respect to Africa except for East Africa ($32.62 bn, almost 98 per cent of the total to Africa of $33.33 bn), a somewhat suspect figure which needs to be further investigated, the rest of Africa getting under 2 per cent of Indian FDI commitments.

Programme Evolution and Motivations: Politico-Security Concerns in India's Assistance

If trade and investment relations have not been the prime drivers what have been the motivations behind India's development part-

Table 8.9B: FDI by India to South Asian Countries, 2010–2017

(U.S.D Mn) Country	*2010 Total*	*2011 Total*	*2012 Total*	*2013 Total*	*2014 Total*	*2015 Total*	*2016 Total*	*2017 Total*
Afghanistan	–	–	–	–	1	4	–	0
Bangladesh	–	–	–	26	10	19	9	30
Bhutan	–	–	–	6	1	0	0	0
Iran	–	–	–	–	–	–	–	–
Maldives	–	–	–	1	2	14	3	7
Nepal	–	–	–	10	3	5	2	22
Pakistan	–	–	–	–	–	–	–	–
Sri Lanka	1,262	260	157	130	63	98	52	131
Myanmar	–	–	–	16	4	1	13	50
Total	1,262	260	157	190	84	141	78	240

Source: *RBI, accessed July 13, 2018*—https://dbie.rbi.org.in/DBIE/dbie.rbi?site=home.

nership programme? To situate the programme in its politico-security and economic context, we situate it in the evolution of India's foreign policy with respect to the major regions of the programme's concentration, viz. South Asia, Afghanistan, Myanmar, and the African continent, in this section, based on detailed confidential interviews.[10]

Bhutan

The assistance relationship with Bhutan, along with Nepal, is the oldest and most consistent. India's relations with Bhutan have been governed by the India–Bhutan Treaty of August 8, 1949, and the updated and revised treaty called the India–Bhutan Friendship Treaty signed in February 2007, by which India *de facto* controlled its foreign relations, a carry-forward of the situation before

[10] All facts and figures in the country accounts in this section are from Indian Ministry of External Affairs, *Annual Reports*, various years, and anonymous conversations with nine senior Indian diplomats with experience of the various countries and regions covered, including two former heads of the DPA, and a former chairman and managing director of the Exim Bank of India, besides the foregoing sections.

Indian independence. Bhutan is a monarchy that inherited and continued its strategic status after India's independence as a Himalayan buffer state between India and China, and still does not have formal diplomatic relations with China, although relations are growing despite an unresolved border. India now accounts for 80 per cent of Bhutan's imports and 94 per cent of its exports, although the former figure is expected to be rapidly reduced by Bhutan's growing relations with China. Bhutan's export earnings are overwhelmingly from its export of hydro-electric power to India. India is the largest trade and development partner of Bhutan. Bhutan along with Nepal became a priority country after the October–November 1962 Sino–Indian border war. Assistance to Bhutan has been integrated into India's planning process and a number of grants are made under the head of Plan grants by the MEA.

After the shift in India's overall assistance policy from 2004, and stepped-up border management and security co-operation by Bhutan in December 2003–January 2004 in taking action against Indian insurgent groups (United Liberation Front of Assam) holed up in Bhutan, Bhutan's Ninth Plan assistance was reviewed. In March 2004, an Indo-Bhutan Group on Border Security and Management was established. The subsequent stepping up of assistance has to be seen in this context.

In 2005, it was decided to renew the bilateral Trade, Commerce and Transit Agreement for another ten years, and an umbrella agreement on power projects in Bhutan was finalised. In 2008, on the occasion of the centenary of the Wangchuck dynasty and the coronation of the fifth king, India agreed to double its assistance to Bhutan's 10th five-year plan (over the ninth plan) to Rs 34,000 m ($700 m). This would consist of Rs 20,000 m ($400 m) for 65 projects, mostly small development projects (SDPs), first introduced in Nepal and then in Bhutan, to be spread all over Bhutan. In March 2009, an Empowered Joint Group on Hydroelectric Power Development in Bhutan met to discuss the development of 10,000 MW of hydropower generation in Bhutan for export to India by 2020. Implementation agreements were signed later, indicating growing economic integration with India.

Nepal

Nepal, another Himalayan buffer state between India and China, is vital for India's border security, particularly after the 1962 border war with China. The 1850 kilometre Indo–Nepal border is a porous one with free movement of people. Nepal is a weak and unstable multi-party democracy that has been wracked by a Maoist insurgency since the mid-1990s. On February 1, 2005, the government was dissolved as the Maoist insurgency spread, triggering talks of the Joint Working Group on Border Management and the India–Nepal Bilateral Consultative Group on Security Issues. The Joint Committee on Water Resources also met in 2004–5, and an MOU was signed on an oil pipeline, and rail service commenced in July 2004.

The SDP programme is central to India's assistance to Nepal. It was introduced in 2003, and by 2010–11 there were 400 projects in all 75 districts of Nepal. The aim is to spread the impact of assistance and also local awareness of it in the host country. In 2011–12, an Indo-Nepal Bilateral Investment Promotion and Protection Agreement (BIPPA) and a Double Taxation Avoidance Agreement were signed. More recently, Indian Prime Minister Modi announced a $1 bn credit line for hydro-power, irrigation, and infrastructure in August 2014.

Over the entire period since the Emergency of 2005, India helped to politically stabilise Nepal, seen as vital for Indian security, by encouraging peace talks and the restoration of democracy and building up of a constitutional development process in Nepal at Nepal's invitation. Nepal agreed that it would not allow anti-India insurgent activities. Assistance to Nepal has to be placed in this context along with the fact that India now accounts for 60 per cent of Nepal's foreign trade and 44 per cent of its inward FDI, and India is the largest assistance provider and source of tourists. However, India faces stiff competition from China in economic assistance for political influence and Nepal has been adroitly playing the two off against each other.

Bangladesh

India–Bangladesh relations after the latter's independence in 1972 were governed by the 25-year India–Bangladesh Friendship Treaty, which was allowed to lapse in 1997 by the then Awami League government of Sheikh Hasina Wazed despite the signing of the watershed Indo–Bangladesh Ganga Waters Treaty in December 1996 which addressed Bangladesh's long-standing demands on river water-sharing.[11] The 1972 Treaty provided that neither country would harm the security of the other. The lapsing of this treaty removed this security feature from the Indian point of view, and in fact since then India has suspected Bangladesh, particularly during the Bangladesh National Party government of 2001–6, of conniving with terrorist activities directed against India by non-state actors. Despite starting on a promising note, relations have been bedevilled by a number of issues, including an unresolved "ragged" boundary, illegal immigration of Bangladeshis into India, sharing of waters of 54 common rivers, primarily the Ganges, the operation of anti-Indian insurgent, and terrorist groups from Bangladesh. Hence, Bangladesh is a neighbour with whom India's relations are sensitive. Assistance to Bangladesh has to be seen in this context.

Talks in 2004–5 between the new UPA government in India and the Bangladesh government included the biannual Director General-level talks between the two border guard forces, the issue of insurgent and radical Islamist groups, sharing of the Teesta river waters, illegal immigration, trade, investment and the possible

[11] See Kabir (2011) for a comprehensive overview of Indo–Bangladesh relations.

Myanmar–Bangladesh–India gas pipeline, and the annual meeting of the Joint Rivers Commission. The year 2006–7 saw a revised Trade Agreement. The Joint Boundary Working Group met after a gap of four years and discussed the Land Boundary Agreement of 1974. An Indo-Bangladesh Chamber of Commerce and Industry was inaugurated in 2007–8 and a trial run of the Kolkata (Calcutta)–Dhaka passenger train took place, leading to the start of rail services the next year. A trade agreement and a BIPPA were signed in February 2009.

The Grand Alliance (GA) government led by the Awami League of Sheikh Hasina Wazed was formed in January 2009 and took steps to improve relations with India. She visited India in January 2010, following which an LOC of $1 bn for infrastructure projects, including railways, was signed in August, as was a 35-year power transmission agreement. Indian Prime Minister Manmohan Singh visited Bangladesh in September 2011, resulting in the Land Boundary Demarcation Agreement, an increase in the annual duty-free export quota of garments to India, a joint venture agreement for the 1320 MW Khulna power plant, increased defence co-operation, and an increased number of ITEC and Colombo Plan training slots. More recently, Prime Minister Modi announced an additional $2 bn credit line focused on infrastructure in his 2015 visit, which also saw the resolution of the long-festering boundary issue. The stepping up of assistance is clearly linked to the co-operative attitude of the GA government and the perceived importance of its stability for Indian security. However, Indo-Bangladesh trade remains sluggish, with India accounting for only 13 per cent of Bangladesh's imports, in sharp contrast to dominating the imports of landlocked Nepal and Bhutan.

Sri Lanka

Sri Lanka, which was in the throes of a long-drawn out separatist war over 1983–2009 between the government and the Liberation

Tigers of Tamil Eelam (LTTE), a separatist guerrilla group of the hitherto discriminated-against Tamils of the North and East of the island, signed a free trade agreement with India in 1998, operational from 2000, called the India–Sri Lanka Free Trade Agreement. This gradually liberalised trade ahead of the South Asian regional trade liberalisation process, and also had the effect of encouraging Indian investment in Sri Lanka to take advantage of lower tariffs on raw materials, and consequent export of products back to India. The free trade agreement and the domestic peace process between the Tamil rebels and the government, marked by the Ceasefire Agreement of 2002, led to an improvement of Indo–Sri Lanka relations, and Sri Lanka supported India's bid for a permanent UNSC seat. There were the beginnings of moves to upgrade the FTA to a Comprehensive Economic Partnership Agreement (CEPA). India had become the biggest FDI source by 2004 and the fourth largest cumulatively.

In November 2005, Mahinda Rajapaksa was elected president of Sri Lanka and visited India in December. India stressed the importance of political dialogue and pressed its view that there was no military solution, and offered to share its constitutional experience. By 2007, India became the largest single source of tourists, the largest single source of imports and third largest destination for Sri Lankan exports. The civil war ended in May 2009 with the elimination of the LTTE, and President Rajapakse was re-elected in January 2010. India stressed the importance of reconciliation and a devolution-based political solution to the conflict, and gave assistance for relief and rehabilitation of the internal refugees.

India opened two new consulates-general, resumed ferry services, renewed the MOU on SDPs, signed a new MOU on Interconnection of Electricity Grids, increased defence co-operation focused on army and navy chief visits and training, an LOC of $415 m for the Northern Railway line, a de-mining team, a package for relief and rehabilitation, and a commitment to build 50,000 houses for internally displaced persons in the Northern, Eastern, and Central provinces. Sri Lanka assured India that political proposals for devolution of power building on the 13th Amendment to its constitution would be discussed with the Tamil leadership but has dragged its feet even under the new government that took power in 2015. India remained the largest trade partner, largest FDI, and tourist source, and sees engagement as vital for leverage. Assistance is part of this engagement and leverage on both internal reform and for providing an incentive to maintain a distance from a China that has emerged as the largest donor to Sri Lanka since the end of the civil war in 2009. India has stepped up its aid since then in response to the geopolitical competition for influence from China, signified most dramatically in Sri Lanka giving the southern Hambantota port, overlooking the main Indian Ocean sea lanes, to China on a 99-year lease in 2017.

Afghanistan

Afghanistan has emerged as one of the largest single-country assistance programmes for India. The political background to this is as follows, in brief. After the 9/11 attacks in the United States, and the subsequent invasion, overthrow of the Taliban regime and occupation of Afghanistan by U.S.-led NATO forces in late 2001, and the Bonn Agreement of December 2001, India made assistance commitments to the post-war reconstruction of Afghanistan. This began with $100 m in January 2002 at the Tokyo Donors Conference. This needs to be seen in light of the erstwhile Taliban regime's complicity in the hijack of an Indian aircraft in December 1999 and its closeness to the Pakistani military. It was in India's security interests to stabilise a moderate and democratic alternative in Afghanistan.

Indian assistance was focused on three major infrastructure projects:

(i) upgradation of the Zaranj–Delaram highway of 218 kilometres;
(ii) the Salma Dam project in Herat province in the west;
(iii) the 220 kV double circuit transmission line from Pul-e-Khomri to Kabul, and the 220/110/20 kV substation at Chimtala to bring power from Uzbekistan to Kabul, all completed by 2010.

Apart from this, India undertook to build the new Afghan parliament building, contributed to the Afghan Reconstruction Fund, and to a broad SDP programme, which paralleled similar SDP programmes that were in existence in Bhutan and Nepal, including assistance in the agriculture, education, healthcare, and medical sciences areas.

In 2006–7, the security situation worsened with increasing attacks by the Taliban insurgents through most of the country. Two Indians working in the country were killed. MOUs in rural development and education were signed, and India participated in the November 2006 second Regional Economic Cooperation Conference in Afghanistan and the parallel Regional Business Conference on Afghanistan hosted by the Federation of Indian Chambers of Commerce and Industry (FICCI), the Confederation of Indian Industry (CII), and the Associated Chambers of Commerce and Industry (Assocham). Cumulative Indian assistance rose to $750 m by 2006–7. The year saw new project commitments like expansion of TV coverage, and the training of Afghan diplomats in the Foreign Service Training Institute in Delhi. About a thousand training slots were given to Afghans in the ITEC programme. India supported the admission of Afghanistan to the South Asian Association for Regional Cooperation (SAARC) at the 14th SAARC summit in Delhi in April 2007 as its eighth member.

India welcomed the Obama speech of December 2009 on strengthening the Afghan government and security forces as preparation to the eventual U.S. drawdown and pullout, and participated in the UN International Conference on Afghanistan in London in January 2010. This was a prelude to the stepping up of India's security co-operation with Afghanistan from the next year. President Karzai's visit in October 2011 resulted in an Agreement on Strategic Partnership, the first such with any country for Afghanistan. This included political and security co-operation, and an MOU on hydrocarbons and minerals. An additional $500 m of assistance was announced during the visit, taking the cumulative total assistance by then to $2 bn.

India's assistance strategy, to some extent, mirrors its assistance experience in countries like Bhutan and Nepal in that it focused not just on a few major high-profile projects but on a range of widespread small projects and capacity building by offering scholarships to students and trainees, and thereby building long-term human contacts.

India's assistance strategy in Afghanistan is geared to supporting and stabilising the Afghan government in both political and economic terms to secure India's perceived long-term security interests, against a possible future re-conquest of the country by the Taliban operating with covert backing from Pakistan. In recent years, China too has increased its level of activity in Afghanistan, something not to India's comfort given the *de facto* Pakistan–China alliance.

Myanmar

Myanmar is India's neighbour, bordering four north-eastern Indian states, with a 1650 kilometre border, and an ethnic Naga insurgency that overlaps that border. It also has about 400,000 people of Indian origin, mostly very poor. India has followed a policy of engagement with the military regime in Myanmar from the mid-1990s, its policy being based on cultivating Myanmar to prevent it from going entirely into the hands of China politically and to gain Myanmar's co-operation in tackling the Naga insurgency, de-prioritising democracy, and the Indian minority. In return, Myanmar supported India's bid for UNSC permanent membership and has been cooperative on the Naga insurgency issue. Annual foreign office consultations began in 1995.[12]

Assistance to Myanmar increased gradually over the past decade. An MOU for the Chindwin hydroelectric project was signed in 2004–5, and one on the India–Myanmar–Thailand trilateral highway project following the Myanmar foreign minister's visit in July 2004. This was followed by MOUs on railways and energy co-operation *inter alia* a possible Myanmar–Bangladesh–India gas pipeline. The idea was to work toward the integration of India's north-eastern states with Myanmar and further afield with booming South East Asia and South West China.

A BCIM group (Bangladesh–China–India–Myanmar) co-operation meeting was held in March 2006. A Double Taxation Avoidance Agreement and a BIPPA were signed in 2008–9. Emergency humanitarian assistance was rushed to Myanmar following Cyclone Nargis in May 2008.

Co-operation was significantly stepped up in 2010–11, mainly LOCs for oil and gas, power, railways, and highways. A delegation from north-eastern India visited Myanmar to promote sub-regional co-operation. The Myanmar president Thein Sein visited India in October 2011 (coincidentally coinciding with Afghan President Karzai's visit), an LOC of $500 m was extended and a target was set for $3 bn in trade by 2015. The stepping up of assistance is part of a strategy to support Myanmar's democratisation and relative shift away from dependence on China.

Africa

Indian foreign policy has traditionally supported decolonisation, and opposed racism and apartheid. India had been offering training and expertise to Africa under the ITEC programme since the

[12] See Egreteau (2011) for an account of contemporary India–Myanmar relations.

1960s. In the period of the 1990s and in the twenty-first century, in the context of the liberalisation and faster growth of India's economy, the end of apartheid in South Africa in 1994, the liberalisation and faster growth of African economies since 2002, Indian policy has come to pay greater attention to Africa. At the start of India's new foreign assistance policy from 2004 to 2005 onwards, the Indian president addressed the Pan-African Parliament in 2004, India was part of UN Peacekeeping Forces in four countries, and most of Africa had endorsed India's candidature for a permanent UNSC seat.

In 2004, India declared its intent to build a fiber-optic E-connectivity network for Africa. There was also close co-operation with the ECOWAS group of West African states (established 1975). In 2005, India engaged with COMESA (Common Market for Eastern and Southern Africa, established 1994) based on an India-COMESA MOU. An India–Africa Conclave was held in Delhi in March 2005, and the SADC-India Forum was approved by the (14 nations) SADC (Southern Africa Development Community, established 1992) Council of Ministers. The TEAM-9 Initiative (India plus eight West African countries) was launched at the margins of the UN General Assembly in New York in September 2005 and a $500 m LOC offered to TEAM-9. An LOC of $200 m was extended to several countries for execution of projects and purchase of equipment under the New Partnership for African Development (NEPAD). India joined the African Capacity Building Foundation (based in Harare) as a full member. Four thousand ITEC and SCAAP slots were allotted to Africa, spanning thirty-nine institutions in India.

A landmark event in India's assistance policy to Africa was the India–Africa Forum Summit held on April 2008 in Delhi. It ended with the Delhi Declaration, a new architecture and framework for Africa–India co-operation, and a doubling of LOCs to Africa to $5.4 bn over the next five years (2008–13), concentrated in agriculture and food, small and medium enterprises, irrigation, infrastructure, IT, energy, and pharmaceuticals. Scholarships were doubled, and a Duty Free Tariff Preference scheme for access to products from African LDCs was initiated. A second India-Africa Forum Summit was held in 2011 and a third in 2015, both marked by step-ups of assistance.

Four Indo-African institutions were established as part of the follow-up to the India-African Forum Summit. These were the India–Africa Institute of Foreign Trade, India-Africa Diamond Institute, India-Africa Institute of Educational Planning and Administration, and the India-Africa Institute of Information Technology.

The Duty Free Tariff Preference scheme was offered to 33 African Least Developed Countries, of which 18 acceded to it. The Pan-African E-network was implemented in 34 out of 47 states in 2010–11.

In May 2011, the second Africa–India Forum Summit was held in Addis Ababa, resulting in the Addis Ababa Declaration and Africa–India Framework for Enhanced Cooperation, another step-up in the level of co-operation. The Declaration was a political document covering UN reform, WTO, climate change, and terrorism among other things.

The second meeting between India and African Regional Economic Communities was held in November 2011. India has MOUs with four such entities – COMESA, ECOWAS, ECCAS (Economic Community of Central African States, established 1985), and SADC. South Africa joined the BRIC grouping, making it BRICS, in April 2011 and the fifth IBSA summit was held in Pretoria. Africa is the second largest recipient ($9.23 bn) among regions (after South Asia) of the $22.52 bn in LOCs extended by India till June 2018.

India's attractiveness to Africa lies in its ability to produce soft infrastructure like IT goods and services and pharmaceutical products relatively cheaply and some see it as offering an alternative to Chinese assistance and trade (Naidu 2008). Access to African oil and gas resources for long-term energy security and as an alternative to the volatile Middle East also remains a goal of India's

Africa policy (Naidu 2008). Assistance also complements the growing footprint of Indian companies in Africa and helps promote trade and investment, including in minerals.

Development assistance to Africa is not a case of immediate economic benefits or of short-term security competition with China but more of investment in long-term relationship-building with a resource-rich continent with close to fifty UN General Assembly votes that promises to be increasingly important in the future in both economic and political terms. All African countries have been visited by Indian ministers during the Modi government's tenure and Indian Ocean maritime security co-operation has also been discussed with several African states.[13]

Discernible Patterns

Among the major recipients of Indian assistance, the following patterns are discernible.

First, in the cases of Bhutan and Nepal, India bulks large in their trade, inward investment, and tourism profiles, while they are of marginal significance in India's trade and outward investment profile. They matter to India's security calculations in a major way as they are neighbours with porous borders and buffer states between India and China. Hence, India's assistance to them is primarily motivated by political and security considerations but is important to the recipients in economic terms. An important point here is that India's assistance is widely distributed in the form of a large number of small projects, thus maximising popular awareness and impact. Also that India being the principal destination for higher studies and training creates an alumni network in both countries. India's assistance is one of long-term commitment as signified by the fact that it comes from its Plan budget as well as Non-Plan budget for decades.

[13] Ministry of External Affairs, *Annual Report 2017–18*, pp. xi–xii.

Second, Bangladesh and Sri Lanka, which are neighbours in which India perceives competition for diplomatic influence from Pakistan and China, are both insignificant to India's trade and outward investment profile but of considerable importance to the recipients' trade, inward investment, remittances (for Bangladesh), and tourism (for Sri Lanka) profile. In both cases, Indian assistance is fairly recent, becoming significant over the past half-decade, and relatively concentrated in large LOC. Scholarships and training are significant in both cases.

Third, Afghanistan and Myanmar are again recent cases of assistance, motivated primarily by political and security considerations with perceived competition for political influence from Pakistan and China, respectively. In both cases, the recipient country is of marginal economic but major geopolitical significance to India, although both can be of significance for India's natural resource needs in the future. This is because if the democratically elected Afghan government is not stabilised, and if there is a Pakistani-backed Taliban takeover after an eventual U.S. pullout, then a regime backing terrorism against India might get entrenched in Kabul. Likewise, a Myanmar overwhelmingly dependent on China is not in India's security interests, given the growing Chinese presence in the Indian Ocean. India does not bulk large in Afghanistan's or Myanmar's trade and inward investment. The pattern of assistance is one of large LOCs rather than small projects, although this is beginning to happen in Afghanistan, where scholarships and training are also significant.

Fourth, in the case of Africa, assistance again is recent in its growth, particularly after the India–Africa summits of 2008, 2011, and 2015. It consists of 158 of 227 operative LoCs, with an average worth of $58 m, to thirty-six countries and the ECOWAS Bank of Investment spread across the continent, and is concentrated in fairly large to medium projects in infrastructure and agriculture, although scholarships and training are important. Within Africa, there has been a shift of Indian assistance from Eastern and Southern Africa to West Africa, recognized to be energy- and mineral-rich. However, in 2016–17 as noted earlier, $18.83 bn of the $61 trade was with Nigeria and South Africa only, and these are not where the LOCs go. Assistance is not driven by immediate trade and resource considerations but by long-term relationship-building, plus close to fifty UN General Assembly votes factored in.

Fifth, comparing the Modi government with the previous Manmohan Singh government, one sees more continuity than change and a stepping up of LOCs from the Exim Bank as India's economic capacity increases. The major areas of focus remain South Asia and Africa as before. However, India now faces increased economic and political competition from China in its South Asian neighbourhood with all countries other than India having signed up for the Belt and Road Initiative including its maritime component, and China having gained influence in Nepal, Sri Lanka, and the Maldives during the tenure of the Modi government.

An Overall Assessment

Four major points emerge from an overall assessment of the Indian development partnership programme.

First, India eschews terms like aid and donor, and prefers to use the term "development partner" as a fellow developing country and DAC aid recipient. It is only with the formation of the DPA, that India's "demand-driven" and politically punctuated assistance can be said to have acquired the character of a programme. As the amounts increased, it gradually acquired the character of a programme in two shifts – the shift to LOCs through the Exim Bank from 2004, and the formation of the DPA as an implementation agency in 2012.

Second, while the purpose of partnership is admittedly political, it is meant to cultivate goodwill toward India and long-term relationships rather than immediate payoffs, either political or economic, particularly in the case of Africa.

Third, the MEA considers the ITEC programme the most cost-effective and the one that had yielded the best returns in terms of long-term goodwill because it trains key personnel in India and builds long-term human relationships. These are considered important as money alone is not enough to buy influence. India, because of English language education, is seen to have a comparative advantage in education and training of developing country personnel.

Fourth, there is no clear economic development philosophy or macroeconomic policy prescription that emerges from a scrutiny of the development partnership programme. The basic philosophy seems to be seen as a fellow developing country partner that fits in with what the recipient wants except that the assistance is largely tied to India-sourced supplies, similar in this respect to early-stage Western aid. However, if the development partnership programme acquires a more programmatic rather than a jerky, politically punctuated, and *ad hoc* character, one might expect a prescriptive development strategy to emerge over time either on its own or in learning/partnering processes with established Western aid programmes or in the context of new, South-led lending institutions like the NDB and the AIIB. However, this might possibly be in tension with the explicit policy position at present that the development programme is to serve national, that is, foreign policy interests, although these have been seen so far in a long-term perspective.

Overall, India appears to have operated on the realist assumptions of power politics and interest-orientation in its assistance policies, particularly with its neighbours, and especially energy security as regards Africa, as argued by Six (2009) and Fuchs and Vadlamannati (2013), and in line with the earlier work on developed donor motivations by Alesina and Dollar (2000). However, as we said earlier, the Indian focus is on the long run more than for immediate gains. India's partnership relationships with Bhutan, Nepal, Bangladesh, and Sri Lanka, and with Afghanistan and Myanmar, remain essentially determined by the objective of having its neighbours favorably inclined toward India. However, assistance seems to be more a defensive than a coercive or control strategy, to incentivise bandwagoning toward India or at least not incline toward India's geopolitical competitors, faced with competition in recent years from a China that can deploy much greater resources in development assistance. From a practitioner's standpoint, as emphasised in interviews, the Indian programme is about building long-term relationships and not about immediate benefit. This is particularly the case in South Asia but also applies to Africa.

Acknowledgements

The authors acknowledge the financial support from the International Development Research Centre (IDRC), Ottawa, Canada. The authors are solely responsible for the facts, figures, and interpretations in this article.

References

Agrawal, S. 2007. "Emerging Donors in International Development Assistance: The India Case", IDRC, accessed April 2, 2016, http://www.idrc.ca/EN/ Documents/Case-of-India.pdf.

Alesina, A., and D. Dollar. 2000. "Who Gives Foreign Aid to Whom and Why?", *Journal of Economic Growth* 5 (1), pp. 33–63.

Brautigam, D. 2009. *The Dragon's Gift: The Real Story of China in Africa* (Oxford: Oxford University Press).

Chanana, D. 2009. "India as an Emerging Donor", *Economic and Political Weekly* 44 (12), pp. 11–14.

Chaturvedi, S. 2008. "Emerging Patterns in Architecture for Management of Economic Assistance and Development Cooperation: Implications and Challenges for India", *RIS-Discussion Paper, 139*, accessed April 2, 2016, http://www.ris.org.in.

Chaturvedi, S. 2012a. "India and Development Cooperation: Expressing Southern Solidarity", in *Development Cooperation and Emerging Powers*, ed. S. Chaturvedi, T. Fues, and E. Sidoropoulos, pp. 169–89 (London: Zed Books).

Chaturvedi, S. 2012b. "India's Development Partnership: Key Policy Shifts and Institutional Evolution", *Cambridge Review of International Affairs* 25 (4), pp. 557–77.

Chin, G.T., and B.M. Frolic. 2007. "Emerging Donors in International Development Assistance: The China Case", IDRC, accessed April 2, 2016, http://www.idrc.ca/EN/Documents/ Case-of-China.pdf.

De Renzio, P., and J. Seifert. 2014. "South–South Cooperation and the Future of Development Assistance: Mapping Actors and Options", *Third World Quarterly* 35 (10), pp. 1860–75.

Duclos, V. 2012. "Building Capacities: The Resurgence of Indo-African Techno-economic Cooperation", *India Review* 11 (4), pp. 209–25.

Egreteau, R. 2011. "A Passage to Burma? India, Development, and the Democratization in Myanmar", *Contemporary Politics* 17 (4), pp. 467–86.

Fuchs, A., and K.C. Vadlamannati. 2013. "The Needy Donor: An Empirical Analysis of India's Aid Motives", *World Development* 44, pp. 110–28.

Govt. of India 2015. "Government of India Portal on Development Assistance", accessed April 2, 2016, http://www.externalassistance.gov.in/ portal/.

Gu, J., Y. Chen, and W. Haibin 2016. "China on the Move: The New Silk Road to International Development Cooperation?", in *The BRICS in International Development*, edited by J. Gu, A. Shankland, and A. Chenoy (London: Palgrave Macmillan).

Kabir, M.H. 2011. "Obstacles to Bangladesh–India Cooperation: An International Relations Theory Perspective", in *International Relations Theory and South Asia: Security, Political Economy, Domestic Politics, Identities and Images*, vol. 1, edited by E. Sridharan, pp. 329–68 (New Delhi: Oxford University Press).

Kragelund, P. 2010. "India's African Engagement", Real Instituto Elcano, accessed April 2, 2016, http://www. realinstituoelcano.org.

Lagerkvist, J. 2009. "Chinese Eyes on Africa: Authoritarian Flexibility versus Democratic Governance", *Journal of Contemporary African Studies* 27 (2), pp. 119–34.

Lancaster, C. 2007. "The Chinese Aid System", Center for Global Development, accessed April 2, 2016, http://www.cgdev.org.

Manning, R. 2006. "Will 'Emerging Donors' Change the Face of International Cooperation?", *Development Policy Review* 24 (4), pp. 371–85.

Ministry of External Affairs, India. *Annual Reports*, 1991–2 to 2014–15, accessed December 15, 2015, http:// htm?57/Annual_Reports.

Ministry of Finance, India. *Economic Survey*, 1984–5 to 2014–15, accessed.

December 15, 2015, http://finmin.nic. in/the_ministry/dept_eco_affairs/dea. asp.

Ministry of Finance India. *Annual Budget*, 1991–2 to 2014–15, accessed December 20, 2015, http://indiabudget. nic.in/glance.asp.

Mullen, R.D. 2012. "India Flexes Its Foreign Aid Muscle", *Current History* 111 (744), pp. 154–6.

Mullen, R.D. 2013. "Holding Back on Soft Power", *Indian Express*, March 4.

Naidu, S. 2008. "India's Growing African Strategy", *Review of African Political Economy* 35 (115), pp. 116–28.

Naim, M. 2007. "Rogue Aid", *Foreign Policy* 159 (March–April), pp. 95–6.

Paulo, S., and H. Reisen. 2010. "Eastern Donors and Western Soft Law: Towards and DAC Donor Peer Review of China and India?", *Development Policy Review* 28 (5), pp. 535–52.

People's Republic of China 2011. "China's Foreign Aid", Information Office of the State Council, People's Republic of China.

Price, G. 2005. "Diversity in Donorship: The Changing Landscape of Official Humanitarian Aid: India's Official Aid Programme", Overseas Development Institute, accessed April 2, 2016, http:// www.odi.org.

Reilly, J. 2012. "A Norm-Taker or Norm-Maker? Chinese Aid in Southeast Asia", *Journal of Contemporary China* 21 (73), pp. 71–91.

Reserve Bank of India 2015. "Database on the Indian Economy", accessed December 20, 2015, http://dbie.rbi.org. in/DBIE/dbie.rbi?site=statistics.

Six, C. 2009. "The Rise of Postcolonial States as Donors: A Challenge to the Development Paradigm?", *Third World Quarterly* 30 (6), pp. 1103–21.

Walz, J., and V. Ramachandran 2011. "Brave New World: A Literature Review of Emerging Donors and the Changing Nature of Foreign

Assistance", *CGD Working Paper 273*, accessed April 2, 2016, pp. 1–23, http://www.cgdev.org/ content/publications/detail/1425691.

Woods, N. 2008. "Whose Aid? Whose Influence? China, Emerging Donors and the Silent Revolution in Development Assistance", *International Affairs* 84 (6), pp. 1205–21.

9

Economic Co-operation and Security

Theory, India and Pakistan

INDIA AND PAKISTAN have had a strained security relationship ever since they emerged as sovereign nation-states after Independence and Partition in August 1947. The period since 1989, in particular, has been one of continuing tension between India and Pakistan due to the ongoing Pakistan-supported insurgency in Kashmir. Pakistani policy on India under all governments since 1989 has remained conditional on the resolution of the Kashmir issue. In this sense, and in its clandestine military support of the Kashmir insurgency, Pakistan remains an actively revisionist power. India, while formally claiming Pakistan-occupied Kashmir, has never actively sought to press its claim and is de facto in favour of the status quo. Following the 1998 nuclear tests by both countries, relations plummeted due to the 1999 Kargil border war and India's ten-month border mobilisation called Operation Parakram in 2002, before improving to an uneasy calm following the Vajpayee–Musharraf meeting on the sidelines of the Islamabad summit of the South Asian Association for Regional Co-operation (SAARC) in

Originally published as "Improving Indo-Pakistan Relations: International Relations Theory, Nuclear Deterrence and Possibilities for Economic Co-operation", *Contemporary South Asia*, vol. 14, no. 3 (2005), pp. 321–40. This is a revised and updated version.

January 2004, worsening again after the terrorist attacks in Mumbai in November 2008. Notwithstanding progress in regional economic co-operation in South Asia since the 1990s, little economic co-operation has taken place apart from one major treaty on sharing the Indus basin waters. Why has this been so? Why has the Indus Waters Treaty not had positive spillovers into the security relationship? Can increased economic co-operation lead to an improved security relationship? Or is such co-operation dependent on prior improvement in the security relationship? If so, under what conditions can it take place and have positive security spillovers? While there is abundant literature on the nuclear programmes of India and Pakistan, and virtually nothing on India–Pakistan economic co-operation, there is nothing, post-1998, on the *relationship between the two countries' nuclearisation and economic co-operation.*[1] This paper focuses on this relationship and the prospects for conflict mitigation through economic co-operation, and tries to answer the above questions in the light of recent international relations (IR) theory.

Unlikely as it may seem, economic co-operation is more possible than before, and with greater potential for further economic and security spillovers, after the 1998 nuclear tests, Kargil, and Operation Parakram. Economic co-operation in this tense bilateral relationship is contingent *either* on prior security co-operation to pre-empt the possibility of war, *or* nuclear deterrence as a substitute. The 1998 nuclear tests and the failed attempt to alter the status quo by force in Kargil and the fact that India was effectively deterred from exercising its limited punitive conventional strike option in 2002, implied a state of de facto deterrence.[2] Pakistan's options

[1] See Sumit Ganguly, "India's Pathway to Pokhran II: The Prospects and Sources of New Delhi's Nuclear Weapons Program", *International Security*, 23 (4), 1999, pp. 148–77; and Samina Ahmed, "Pakistan's Nuclear Weapons Program: Turning Points and Nuclear Choices", *International Security*, 23 (4), 1999, pp. 178–204, for post-tests analyses.

[2] While there is no doubt that India was effectively deterred, it is also likely

have changed in two ways, both of which would probably make it less inclined to resist greater economic co-operation in the future. First, explicit nuclearisation with a demonstrated missile capability has assured Pakistan's security in a way that reduces the sensitivity to relative gains in the military sphere. Second, the Kargil and 2002 confrontations and the US role in ending the former and scaling down the latter have demonstrated to Pakistan that using nuclear capability as a shield to launch a military offensive to force India to come to the table on its terms on Kashmir is no longer a feasible option.

Following from these two points, Pakistan is *more* secure vis-à-vis a possible Indian military threat than ever before, as well as *less* able to threaten conventional force to resolve the Kashmir dispute. It therefore has less to fear and much to gain from greater economic engagement with India. When viewed through the prism of cumulative relative gains, there are incentives for economic co-operation for both countries, without having to fear an adverse security fallout, particularly in common projects such as gas pipelines and interlinkages of electricity grids. Such common projects can create stakes in continuing co-operation and can catalyse trade and investment over time, and remove some issues from the arena of conflict, as the Indus Waters Treaty did for river waters, while enlarging the areas of common interest, and contributing to forward movement on conflict resolution.

The paper is organised as follows. The first section lays out a basic framework, drawn from recent IR theory, focusing on relative gains sensitivity, cumulation, the relationship between economic interdependence and war, common projects as a means of conflict mitigation, and the stability of nuclear deterrence between the new

---

that the restraint exercised was also partly self-imposed in order to keep the focus on Pakistan as an aggressor in Kargil. Whether the de facto deterrence in place *is* stable can be debated, but the fact is that existential and then explicit deterrence has demonstrably been demonstrated in the three major eyeball-to-eyeball crises – 1990, Kargil 1999, and 2002 – none of which escalated into a full-scale conventional war.

nuclear states in South Asia. The second section outlines their pattern of economic co-operation, particularly over the past decade. The third section analyses how the Indus Waters Treaty of 1960, the longest lasting economic co-operation agreement, came about and why it did not lead to security co-operation. The fourth section applies the theory outlined in the first section to analyse why past economic co-operation remained so limited, why it did not spill over into security, and whether the post-1998 nuclear face-off, reinforced by other factors, can now lead to increased economic co-operation, and whether such co-operation can lead to positive security spillovers.

A Framework for Viewing the Inda–Pakistan Conflict

In this section, India-Pakistan economic and security co-operation is viewed through the prism of IR theory; specifically, the concepts of relative gains, cumulation, the relationship between economic interdependence and war, common projects as a means of conflict mitigation, and the stability of nuclear deterrence. The first two concepts, and the theorising based on them, emerged in the evolution of the debate between neorealism and neoliberalism in IR theory. The neorealist-neoliberal debate led to a focus on what drives states' behaviour.[3] For our limited purposes and for the India–Pakistan case, what is most important are the debate on absolute versus relative gains, the impact of nuclearisation on relative gains sensitivity, and following from that, how the incentives for behaviour towards the other country are affected.

Neorealists hold that states are more sensitive to relative gains than absolute gains in co-operation.[4] That is, even if a co-operative deal were to yield absolute gains to a state, it would still be willing

[3] See Robert Powell, "Anarchy in International Relations Theory: The Neorealist-Neoliberal Debate", *International Organization*, 48 (2), 1994, pp. 1303–20, for a detailed discussion on the neo-realist–neoliberal debate.

[4] Joseph M. Grieco, "Anarchy and the Limits of Cooperation", in David

to forgo co-operation if it believed that other states, especially if potentially threatening, would gain relatively more. Hence, co-operation can be successful only if it does not upset the perceived power balance to which states are sensitive, no matter what absolute gains one can point to as the fruits of co-operation. This does not necessarily mean they are relative gains maximisers. They can be defensive positionalists seeking to defend their relative position,[5] and co-operation can also occur under conditions of sensitivity to relative gains.[6]

Neoliberals, while agreeing with neorealists that the anarchical nature of the international system creates a security dilemma for states which will incline them towards relative gains sensitivity, nevertheless do not privilege the latter to the point of devaluing the possibility of co-operation. They argue that the degree of a state's concern for relative gains is conditional, and depends on the intensity of the security dilemma it faces. A predominant concern with relative gains is an effect of the state's perceived strategic situation. Citing Grieco, Robert Powell argues that a state's sensitivity to relative gains depends upon six factors, two of which are: (i) whether relative gains or losses occur over the military or the economic sphere, and (ii) the fungibility of power across issues. Where relative gains occur over the military sphere, and the greater the fungibility of power across issues, the greater the degree of sensitivity to relative gains. Relative gains sensitivity is part of the outcome or effect of the perceived strategic setting influenced by several factors.

Peter Liberman has shown that sensitivity to relative economic gains in trade, even between powers engaged in political-military

---

Baldwin, ed., *Neorealism and Its Critics: The Contemporary Debate* (New York: Columbia University Press, 1993).

[5] Grieco, "Anarchy and the Limits of Cooperation".

[6] Duncan Snidal, "Relative Gains and the Pattern of International Cooperation", *American Political Science Review*, 85, September 1991, pp. 701–26.

rivalry, is very low in a multi-polar regime.[7] He shows that the hypothesis of sensitivity to relative economic gains between rival military powers which perceived each other as a potential military threat failed in the case of trade between Britain and Germany during 1890–1914, and the US and Japan during 1931–41, with both Britain and the US not restricting trade with their perceived military rivals *despite their perception that their rivals were gaining relatively more from the trade,* until the outbreak of war. He, however, argues that under bipolarity, and when economic gains can, over time, translate into military power, relative gains sensitivity becomes important. This is because relative gains under bipolarity can only benefit the one other significant rival and security threat whereas in multi-polar rivalry the gaining power is only a fraction of a constellation of possible threats. This was the case during the Cold War when the US restricted trade with the Soviet Union in the 1950s and 1960s, believing that trade would provide greater benefits to the less developed Soviet economy.

A key factor affecting the perceived strategic setting, and hence relative gains sensitivity, is whether the relationship is based on nuclear or conventional military technology, and the perceived offense-defence balance.[8] Nuclear weapons being "absolute" weapons create new incentives for restraint. Under nuclear weapons, balancing may not occur despite anarchy; rather, co-operation to prevent war may be the outcome. Nuclear weapons shift the balance toward defensive advantage as they enable a state to survive an attack and retaliate, inflicting unacceptable damage, far in excess of that of conventional weapons. Hence, a relative gain in the security sphere,

[7] Peter Liberman, "Trading with the Enemy: Security and Relative Economic Gains", *International Security,* 21 (1), 1996, pp. 147–75.

[8] For an overview of the offense–defence balance debate, see Stephen Van Evera, "Offense, Defense and the Causes of War", *International Security,* 22 (4), 1998, pp. 5–41; and Sean M. Lynn-Jones, "Offense–Defense Theory and its Critics", *Security Studies,* 4 (4), 1995, pp. 660–91.

or an economic gain that may translate to military capability, will not lead to an unassailable advantage over the other side. Therefore, one can expect relative gains sensitivity in both the security and economic spheres to be reduced as a factor of state behaviour under a nuclear deterrence regime.

John C. Matthews III advanced the discussion on relative gains sensitivity by introducing the concept of cumulation.[9] He defines cumulation as occurring when "a relative gain in a current round of interaction creates advantages that allow additional gains in future rounds . . ." When this occurs, relative gains will be more important in states' behaviour, whereas when "a relative gain on a current round produces only absolute gains in that round and does not have implications for the future interactions", relative gains will be less important and absolute gains will be more determinative of states' behaviour.[10] This greater sensitivity to relative gains when there are cumulation effects, and more to absolute gains when there are no cumulation effects, applies to both the economic and security spheres.

In a military-technological regime where the offense-defence balance favours defence, such as in a nuclear stand-off (above a certain level of survivability of one's forces), relative gains sensitivity would be reduced precisely because, in terms of the above argument, an assured second-strike capability ensures that the cumulation effect is reduced. The current round loser (in a surprise attack) will still be able to retaliate and resist the winner, unlike the current round loser in a war between conventionally armed states, in which a current round winner, destroying or overrunning the other state's forces and making territorial gains, would have an increased probability of victory in an immediately succeeding round. Matthews contrasts the growth of arms control agreements in the nuclear

[9] John C. Matthews III, "Current Gains and Future Outcomes: When Cumulative Relative Gains Matter", *International Security*, 21 (1), 1996, pp. 112–46.

[10] Ibid. p. 114.

sphere between the US and the Soviet Union over 1970–90 with the relative failure of the Mutual and Balanced Force Reduction talks in Europe, to show that relative gains sensitivity in the former case being less due to the prevalent defensive advantage, made agreements possible, while it was exactly the opposite in the latter case.[11]

Similarly, when commerce in non-strategic technologies and industries is involved, the current round loser is not going to lose competitiveness in critical products, firms, and underlying technologies. Matthews argues that there was much greater tension in US–Japan bargaining over supercomputer market access than over steel. This was because it was perceived that loss of market share in supercomputers, believed to be a strategic technology affecting future competitiveness in general, was far more serious because it was cumulative in its effects. Hence, loss of market share in supercomputers had greater relative gains implications than was loss of market share in steel.[12]

On the relationship between economic interdependence and the likelihood of war, Dale Copeland has advanced a theory of trade expectations which argues essentially that economic interdependence will be conducive to peace if both states expect the level of trade to rise in the future.[13] He factors in not just the actual level of economic interdependence and its trend, but expectations for the future, into the incentives and behaviour of states. Citing the cases of Japan and Germany before World War II, neorealists argue that, if highly interdependent states expect trade to be restricted some time in the future, or existing restrictions will not be lifted, then the most interdependent states may go to war, fearing econom-

[11] Ibid., pp. 135–40, 143–6.

[12] Ibid., pp. 130–4, 140–3.

[13] See Dale C. Copeland, "Economic Interdependence and War: A Theory of Trade Expectations", *International Security*, 20 (4), 1996, pp. 5–41, for a survey of the neo-realist-neoliberal debate on the relationship between economic interdependence and the likelihood of war.

ic losses. Copeland shows that in the case of Germany before both the world wars, the expectation of declining trade and fear of economic strangulation despite high interdependence was explicitly factored into the war decision.[14] On the other hand, if expectations of future trade are positive, interdependence is conducive to peace.

An important theory on conflict resolution that may be useful in the India–Pakistan context is that of the common project school.[15] Mircea Malitza, outlining the common project school of thought on conflict resolution, draws a distinction between "distributive bargaining" and "integrative bargaining", the latter being less a question of mutual concessions as in distribution, but of a search for mutually profitable alternatives. He argues that this approach is particularly suited to the resolution of persistent conflicts based on identity, values, and culture. These are central to the India–Pakistan conflict over Kashmir because of the role of Muslim identity in Partition and the separatist movement, and more generally flow from the constitutional self-definition of the emergent states of India and Pakistan as, respectively, secular and Islamic states. The key is the adoption of an integrative, interaction-generating project, and the stabilisation and institutionalisation of such interaction between India and Pakistan, not necessarily in or involving Kashmir, leading ultimately to a transcendence of the values that dominated the confrontation, thus helping to resolve the Kashmir issue. This transcendence, or at least temporary bypassing/shelving, is vital, for arguments about historical wrongs, values, and culture can continue to eternity. Malitza cites France and Germany as the key example, the common project being European economic integration. In practical terms, the approach means finding a common project that can produce common interests, *overlap diverging interests*, and have *minimal* cultural, value, or belief consider-

[14] Ibid., pp. 26–39.

[15] Mircea Malitza, "Ten Thousand Cultures, A Single Civilization", *International Political Science Review*, 21 (1), 2000, pp. 75–89.

ations. This common project would need to *generate long-term interaction without prejudicing the distinct cultures* of the parties, and also result in tangible material advantages from the standpoint of the global, or at least extraregional, arena.

Eventually, such projects create economic integration and political trust in a way that may make mutual concessions over vital security issues such as territory and borders less difficult, because "when a country joins a common entity with others, territorial possession becomes less relevant."[16]

Lastly, in a unique situation like the India–Pakistan nuclear standoff, with the complicating factor of a close strategic relationship in nuclear and missile technology transfer between Pakistan and China, will deterrence work? Devin Hagerty's analysis of the 1990 crisis supports the view that opaque but perceived nuclear capabilities did deter both sides from escalating the crisis.[17] Sumit Ganguly and Devin Hagerty conclude that perceived nuclear capabilities, opaque or explicit, were the principal factor checking escalation in all six crises from 1984 to 2002, especially since 1990.[18] This supports the view that the logic of nuclear deterrence – even existential deterrence based on the perception of the existence of nuclear capabilities – works even in the case of two states having a history of wars, ideological and territorial tensions, a common border, and

[16] Ibid., p. 83. One can view the peaceful break-up of Czechoslovakia, the devolution of powers to Scotland, and the possible resolution of Northern Ireland to be nested in the commitment or aspiration of existing states to a larger European unification.

[17] Devin T. Hagerty, "Nuclear Deterrence in South Asia: The 1990 Indo-Pakistani Crisis", *International Security*, 20 (3), 1995–6, pp. 79–114. Hagerty outlines the differences between the two logics: that of non-proliferation, and that of nuclear deterrence, and their opposite predictions of the likelihood of war between small and new nuclear powers with insecure second-strike capabilities.

[18] Sumit Ganguly and Devin T. Hagerty, *Fearful Symmetry: India-Pakistan Crises in the Shadow of Nuclear Weapons* (New Delhi: Oxford University Press, 2005), pp. 188–92.

a conventional military imbalance, all of which should, according to the logic of non-proliferation, conduce to the incentive to pre-emptive strikes. The lack of willingness of either side to escalate to conventional conflict despite a decade of low-intensity warfare in Kashmir, and Indian restraint in Kargil and in 2002, further support the effectiveness of nuclear deterrence over the logic-of-nonproliferation view that proliferation creates incentives for preventive or pre-emptive attack on a fledgling nuclear power with an insecure second-strike capability.

The neorealist–neoliberal debate has thrown into relief the effects of anarchy and the degree of concern about relative gains. The challenge is to specify more rigorously, in the India–Pakistan relationship, the kinds of economic co-operation that are feasible, given sensitivity to relative gains and cumulation under conditions of territorial and ideological conflict and military, including nuclear, confrontation, and how these can mitigate conflict over time.

Economic Co-operation Between India and Pakistan

Economic relations between India and Pakistan over the past sixty yeats have been marginal to both countries' economies.[19] India adopted an import-substitution industrialisation strategy led by the public sector, with a highly protectionist trade policy, five-year plans, and comprehensive government controls on economic activity, despite the existence of large-scale private manufacturing industry.

This strategy helped create a broader industrial, scientific, and technological base than existed in most developing countries. It also promoted nuclear, space, missile, and defence production programmes, and food self-sufficiency. However, it led only to a modest Gross

[19] I thank Mahendra P. Lama, Y.R. Panchamukhi, Nagesh Kumar, Shabnam Pareek, and Nisha Taneja for help with material, and Mahendra P. Lama, Vineet Virmani, and Tariq M.A. Rangoonwala for conversations on India–Pakistan trade.

Domestic Product (GDP) growth rate of about 3.5 per cent during 1950–80, picking up to 5.8 per cent in the 1980s, and 5.8 per cent during 1990–2002, and nearly 9 per cent over 2003–8, still leaving large masses in absolute poverty and marginalising India in the world economy until the 1990s. Serious liberalisation of the economy began only in 1991. The peak import tariff was then 300 per cent, the average tariff about 100 per cent, and there were broad import quotas. This has been reduced to a peak tariff of 30 per cent, an average tariff of 14 per cent by 2007, and withdrawal of quotas from April 2001.

Pakistan's economy remained relatively more open and less oriented to import-substitution than India's but failed to create a diversified, modern industrial sector. Its leading industries and exports remained cotton textiles and apparel.[20] In 1948–9, 56 per cent of Pakistan's exports went to India while the percentage of Indian imports was 80 per cent for East Pakistan and 50 per cent for West Pakistan. By 1958, only 4 per cent of Pakistan's exports went to India, as both countries actively disengaged and embarked on import-substitution strategies.[21] Pakistan's economy grew at 6.8 per cent in the 1960s, 4.8 per cent in the 1970s, 6.5 per cent in the 1980s, 4.6 per cent in the 1990s, dipping below 3 per cent thereafter before recovering to over 5 per cent since 2002–3, the 1988–2008 period coinciding with the return of democracy until General Musharraf's coup in 1999, restored again in 2008, and the beginning of an extended period of stabilisation and structural adjustment policies. A key element relevant to India–Pakistan relations in this process has been the lowering of tariff barriers from a maximum of 225 per cent to 25 per cent over the period 1988–2008 with a weighted average tariff of 11 per cent by 2007, and the reduction of quota restrictions. The trade deficit has been contained through an increase in

[20] I am indebted to S. Akbar Zaidi, *Issues in Pakistan's Economy*, 2nd edn (Karachi: Oxford University Press, 2000), for the capsule account of Pakistan's economy since Independence in this section.

[21] Ibid., pp. 159, 165–6.

non-traditional exports and a significant inflow of foreign direct and portfolio investment.

These patterns of development, together with the political antagonism over half a century, have resulted in extremely weak economic ties between India and Pakistan despite the gradual growth of preferential trade since the 1990s among the countries of South Asia under the auspices of SAARC. The South Asian Preferential Trade Area (SAPTA), initiated in 1995, went through four rounds of negotiations toward intra-regional trade liberalisation based on a commodity approach. The SAARC summit of January 2004 led to a Framework Agreement to achieve a South Asian Free Trade Area (SAFTA) beginning in January 2006, which will include further cuts in tariff and non-tariff barriers.[22]

However, India–Pakistan bilateral trade has remained at a very low level (Tables 9.1 and 9.2).

Pakistan allowed only 573 products to be imported from India until the list was expanded to 615 at the end of SAPTA-III, with a further seventy-eight added in March 2004 following the thaw after the successful SAARC summit of January 2004 at which the Indian and Pakistani heads of government met and agreed to promote economic co-operation with a schedule of talks on all issues.[23] This was subsequently expanded to 1075 items by 2008. It accounts for only a miniscule fraction of each country's imports and exports (Tables 9.1 and 9.2).[24] In 2007 (Table 9.1), only 0.1 per cent of India's imports came from, and 0.68 per cent of India's exports went to, Pakistan. Even for a smaller Pakistan, only 2.26 per

[22] Government of India (GoI), *Annual Report 2004–2005* (New Delhi: Ministry of External Affairs, GoI, 2005), pp. 129–30.

[23] "List of Items Exportable from Pakistan to India" (New Delhi: Federation of Indian Chambers of Commerce and Industry, 2005).

[24] *Direction of Trade Statistics Yearbook 2004* (Washington DC: International Monetary Fund, 2004). These are the only comparable statistics since Indian and Pakistani statistics do not tally, the drawback being that they have been updated only to 2003.

cent of its imports came from and 2.67 per cent of its exports went to India. However, the estimated trade through third countries (primarily the Gulf countries) was estimated to be three times the official trade in 2003.

In fact, neither India nor Pakistan imports any of each other's major exports. This is true even for products involved in their bilateral trade, except perhaps for products like tyre imports by Pakistan. This will probably remain true even if unrecorded cross-border trade and trade through third countries like the United Arab Emirates (UAE) and Singapore are factored in. The difficulties of trading directly due to tariff and quota problems, border controls, transport and visa problems, and other non-tariff barriers have induced a diversion of trade through third countries which was estimated to be about US$ 1.5 billion, three times the official trade.[25] Furthermore, the Indian and Pakistani economies are competitive rather than complementary, with the exports of both being largely in the same product categories, including textiles and apparel, leather goods and footwear, marine products, and other labour-intensive manufactures. While India–Pakistan trade has not grown significantly as a share of their overall commerce despite the SAPTA process, the same holds true in general for intra-regional trade in SAARC, with the exception of Bangladesh.[26]

Lastly, direct investment and joint ventures are non-existent. However, between 1947 and the outbreak of the 1965 war, when each country confiscated "enemy property", half a dozen Indian business groups owned controlling shares of public limited companies in Pakistan, employed Pakistani managers, and held board meetings

[25] Interview with Vineet Virmani, a businessman long involved in India–Pakistan trade, currently a member of the executive committee of the India–Pakistan Chamber of Commerce and Industry, and former president of the Punjab, Haryana, Delhi Chamber of Commerce and Industry, 3 August 2000.

[26] For SAARC intra-regional trade, see *SAARC Survey of Development and Cooperation 2003–2004* (New Delhi: Research and Information System for Developing Countries, 2004), pp. 47–61.

Table 9.1: India-Pakistan Trade by IMF Statistics

	IMPORTS (CIF) (US$mn) India from Pakistan			EXPORTS (FoB)(US$ mn) Pakistan to India		
Year	*DoTS World Total (of India Imports)*	*Indian Imports from Pakistan*	*Percentage of Imports from Pakistan to Total Indian Imports*	*DoTS World Total (Pakistan's Exports to World)*	*Pakistan's Exports to India*	*Percentage of Exports to India to Total Exports to World*
1997	40,897	42	0.10	8,647	33	0.38
1998	42,162	172	0.41	8,446	203	2.40
1999	47,901	105	0.22	8,449	87	1.03
2000	50,336	65	0.13	8,883	58	0.65
2001	59,151	73	0.12	9,217	66	0.72
2002	58,913	50	0.08	9,884	49	0.50
2003	74,078	54	0.07	11,928	84	0.70
2004	99,898	86	0.09	13,285	158	1.19
2005	1,34,690	157	0.12	16,053	337	2.10
2006	1,86,618	194	0.10	16,989*	417*	2.45
2007	2,49,577	241	0.10	19,363*	517*	2.67

Table 9.1 (*Contd.*)

Table 9.1 (*Contd.*)

	IMPORTS (CIF) (US$mn) Pakistan from India			EXPORTS (FoB)(US$ mn) India to Pakistan		
Year	*DoTS World Total (of Pakistan's Imports)*	*Pakistan's Imports from India*	*Percentage of Imports from India to Total Pakistan's Imports*	*DoTS World Total (India's Exports to World)*	*India's Exports to Pakistan*	*Percentage of Exports to Pakistan to Total Exports to World*
1997	11,612	142	1.22	35,008	147	0.42
1998	9,303	154	1.65	33,437	115	0.34
1999	10,299	134	1.30	35,667	96	0.27
2000	10,723	178	1.66	42,379	163	0.38
2001	10,166	241	2.37	43,361	219	0.51
2002	11,239	163	1.45	50,372	191	0.38
2003	13,048	226	1.73	58,963	267	0.45
2004	17,756	455	2.56	76,649	451	0.59
2005	25,412	577	2.27	99,620	642	0.64
2006	33,869	714	2.11	1,20,861	793	0.66
2007	39,208	886	2.26	1,45,393	984	0.68

Source: IMF, Direction of Trade Statistics, 2009
Note: *Indicates tentative estimate

Table 9.2: India's Non-Petroleum Trade with Pakistan (Values in US$ Million)

Year	*2003–4*	*2004–5*	*2005–6*	*2006–7*	*2007–8*
Export	286.94	521.05	689.023	1348.55	1,944.17
Percentage Growth		81.59	32.28	95.66	44.17
India's total export	63,842.55	83,535.95	1,03,090.54	1,26,262.67	162,904.15
Percentage Growth		30.85	23.41	22.48	29.02
Percentage Share	0.45	0.62	0.67	1.07	1.19
Import	57.65	94.97	179.56	323.01	287.80
Percenatge growth		64.75	89.06	79.89	-10.90
India Total Imports	78,149.11	1,11,517.44	1,49,165.73	1,85,604.10	251,439.17
%Growth		42.70	33.76	24.43	35.47
Percentage Share	0.07	0.09	0.12	0.17	0.11
Total	344.59	616.03	868.79	1671.55	2,231.97
% Growth		78.77	41.03	92.40	33.53
India's total trade	1,41,991.66	1,95,053.38	2,52,256.27	3,11,866.78	414,343.32
Percentage Growth		37.37	29.33	23.63	32.86
Percentage share	0.24	0.32	0.34	0.54	0.54
Trade balance	229.29	426.08	509.67	1025.54	1,656.37
India's trade balance	–14,306.56	-27,981.49	-46,075.2	-59,341.43	-88,535.02
Exchange rate: (1US$=Rs)	45.9516	44.9315	44.2735	45.2849	40.2607

Source: Government of India, Ministry of Commerce and industry, Department of Commerce, Export-Import Data Bank

Note: India's Total import since 2000 – I do not include import of petroleum product (2,71,00,093) and crude oil (2,70,90,000)

in Pakistan right up to the 1965 war. Likewise, a Pakistani business group owned tanneries in Kanpur.[27] The SAARC Chamber of Commerce and Industry, formed in 1994, has not been particularly successful in promoting regional trade or investment or in influencing the SAPTA negotiations. The India–Pakistan Chamber of Commerce and Industry, formed in March 1999 after Prime Minister Vajpayee's Lahore visit, has had its agenda frozen since Kargil, reviving only after the successful SAARC summit of January 2004 and the accompanying India–Pakistan thaw.

[27] I am indebted to Vineet Virmani and Shabnam Pareek, Punjab, Haryana, Delhi Chamber of Commerce and Industry (PHDCCI), for this historical information.

There has been much talk in recent years of economic co-operation in the laying of gas pipelines from Iran, the Persian Gulf, and Turkmenistan through Pakistani land or continental shelf territory to India, and of export of electricity from Pakistan to India. Several pipeline proposals have been under discussion from as early as 1993.[28] Two proposals discussed in recent years are the Iran–India pipeline and the Turkmenistan–Afghanistan–Pakistan or Trans-Afghan Pipeline (TAP) extending to India. Natural gas, which is abundant in these countries and far less so in India and Pakistan, is an economical and environmentally cleaner fuel than coal or fuel oil for thermal power plants. Both countries currently depend largely on thermal power and will continue to depend upon it in the foreseeable future. It would make both economic and environmental sense for India and Pakistan to phase in greater use of gas as opposed to coal or fuel oil for thermal power. Pipeline technology is mature and would be more economical than the import of liquefied natural gas (LNG) for both countries. A joint pipeline would make possible greater economies of scale and lower unit costs than a separate pipeline for Pakistan alone and cost much less than importing LNG for Pakistan and northern India.

Against the projection of increasing energy demands, particularly for electricity, both countries, and anticipated shortfalls, particularly during peak demand in India, and foreign direct investment in the petroleum and power generation sectors, the stage had been set by the late 1990s to consider such gas pipelines. A joint pipeline as a shared project between India and Pakistan and

[28] I am indebted to the detailed work on this subject in Rahul Tongia and V.S. Arunachalam, "Natural Gas Imports by South Asia: Pipelines or Pipedreams", *Economic and Political Weekly*, 34 (18), 1999; Toufiq Siddiqi, "India-Pakistan Cooperation in Energy and Environment", in Dipankar Banerjee, ed., *CBMs in South Asia: Potential and Possibilities* (Colombo: Regional Centre for Strategic Studies, 2000), pp. 95–108; Mahendra P. Lama, "Integrating Stakeholders in Energy Cooperation", *South Asian Journal*, July–September 2005, pp. 6–20; Mohammad Ramzan Ali, "Gas Pipelines and Regional Cooperation", *South Asian Journal*, July-September 2005, pp. 21–9.

the country of origin would also make it much easier to attract the necessary foreign direct investment by multinational energy majors and, in turn, provide better financial terms from international capital markets, than a Pakistan-only project. Pakistan would also gain from transit fees that are estimated at around US$ 700 million.[29] The only problem is a political one relating to economic and military security fallouts. From Pakistan's point of view, any such co-operation would run counter to its policy since 1994 of holding economic co-operation hostage to the Kashmir issue. It also fears somehow getting locked into a relationship with India and thus losing political leverage. From India's point of view, a pipeline through Pakistan runs the risk of disruption, whether deliberate or due to attacks by non-state groups. Such disruption could hold hostage its necessarily massive complementary investments in the power and other industrial plants at the receiving end of the pipeline.

There are however mechanisms for enforcement of compliance. Since the project, the cost of which is estimated at between US$ 4–7 billion, will necessarily involve Iran and/or some other country of origin as well as international firms and private and multilateral agency lenders, Pakistan would surely not want to antagonise them and lose their confidence through uncooperative behaviour.[30] In any event, international capital will be made available only if security of supply is guaranteed. It is possible to involve Japan and Korea as stakeholders if surplus gas is piped to India for conversion to LNG destined for these countries. It may even be possible to have a mutually interlocking agreement as a confidence-building measure, with part of the gas being used to supply thermal power stations

[29] For transit fee estimates, see Tayyab Qazi, "Pipe Dream", *Asian Age*, 27 August 2005; Ravi Batra, "The Peace Pipe, or a Pipe in Pieces", *Economic Times*, 9 November 2004.

[30] For the pipeline cost estimates, see Arnitav Ranjan, "We Will Pay for Gas We Get, Pak Stretch Your Lookout: India to Iran", *Indian Express*, 20 December 2004; Sanjeev Sharma and G. Ganapathy Subramaniam, "India Wants WTO Shield for Pipeline", *Economic Times*, 24 August 2005.

near the Pakistan border for export of power to Pakistan.[31] There are clauses that can be incorporated in any agreement requiring Pakistan to take or pay for the entire volume of supplies if there is any disruption in transmission to India, something it would be unable to do. In June 2000, Pakistan agreed in principle, following Iranian persuasion, to an Iran–India gas pipeline through its territory. After Kargil, India lost interest in the plan and contemplated alternatives, including the LNG import route and a deep-sea pipeline, both costlier options.

A meeting of the Indo–Iran Joint Commission in August 2000, in which Iran attempted to persuade India to consider the more economical and technically sound trans-Pakistan pipeline, was inconclusive. Iran was sensitive to Indian concerns regarding security of supply through Pakistan and undertook to bring Pakistan on board. Iran also outlined various measures in the design of the agreement and project to ensure Pakistan's co-operation. Nevertheless, the Indian side remained unconvinced about the credibility of Pakistani assurances cited by Iran. India is, however, clear that Iran is the ideal supplier in the long term, especially for gas-fuelled thermal power for the northern grid, and has not closed the door on a possible deal since the alternatives are much more expensive.[32] The Iran–India pipeline would not need to traverse US-occupied Afghanistan and can therefore be insulated from possible US opposition to a deal with Iran.

However, since January 2004, Pakistan has ceased linking the pipeline as well as trade and other co-operation to movement on Kashmir, and following the assumption of power by the United Progressive Alliance government in May 2004 there were renewed negotiations on the pipeline, notwithstanding opposition from the US. By August 2005, it appears that actually investing in the

[31] For R.K. Pachauri, "Not a Pipedream: Back to Iran Gas Pipeline Option", *Times of India*, 17 August 2000, for these suggestions.

[32] Interview with K.V. Rajan, Secretary (East), Ministry of External Affairs, who led the Indian delegation in the Indo–Iran Joint Commission talks in August 2000, New Delhi, 7 September 2000.

pipeline as against merely taking delivery of gas at the border was being considered as it was felt that this might help ensure pipeline security.[33] As of 2009, while Iran and Pakistan have agreed to go ahead with the pipeline with the door left open for India, Indian participation seems unlikely given the new tensions in India–Pakistan relations since the Mumbai terror attacks of November 2008 and political instability within Pakistan.

The other potential co-operative pipeline project is the TAP project relating to which Turkmenistan, Afghanistan, and Pakistan signed an agreement of intent to construct a 1500-kilometre pipeline from the former's Daulatabad field to Multan in Pakistan, extendable by another 650 kilometres to India at US$ 2 billion plus US$ 600 million. This will depend both upon Afghanistan's normalisation and Indian acceptance as the economic viability of the pipeline depends upon deliveries to the Indian market. It would also need US concurrence given its control over Afghanistan since late 2001. The US is known to be in favour of the TAP and Russia can be persuaded provided it is given a stake. The TAP project does not face political obstacles other than India's fears about Pakistan's reliability and the normalisation of Afghanistan. India has indicated official interest in reviving the idea of a TAP project, not as a substitute for but in addition to the Iran–India pipeline during Prime Minister Manmohan Singh's visit to Afghanistan in August 2005.[34] This seems most unlikely as of 2009 given the unsettled situation in Afghanistan and Pakistan.

Will a gas pipeline have positive security spillovers? What if Pakistan uses the revenues from such a pipeline to boost the insurgency in Kashmir? This would not be surprising given that gas pipelines from the former Soviet Union to Western Europe would probably not have ended the strategic antagonism had the Soviet Union and its bloc not collapsed. It is most likely that Pakistan

[33] "India May Invest In Gas Pipeline Project", *The Hindu*, 5 August 2005.

[34] Siddharth Varadarajan, "Manmohan, Karzai Moot Gas Pipeline Project", *The Hindu*, 29 August 2005.

will continue to support the insurgency, as it is a low-cost option and its principal bargaining chip in trying to get India to talk about Kashmir on Pakistani terms. Nevertheless, co-operation on a gas pipeline will still help to narrow the conflict by removing a major issue area, energy co-operation, from the arena of conflict as the Indus Waters Treaty removed river waters as an area of contention. This would narrow the scope of conflict to Kashmir-related issues while simultaneously building co-operation and mutual interests in the key energy sector. One can plausibly argue that the narrower the scope of conflict and the broader and deeper the areas of co-operation, the more likely it will be that mutual concessions on the really difficult issues will be reached.

The proposal for the export of surplus electricity from Pakistan to northern India has been under discussion since 1996. Prime Minister Nawaz Sharif made a formal proposal to Prime Minister Vajpayee when they met at the United Nations in September 1998.[35] A power surplus for years to come was anticipated for Pakistan from the end of the Pakistani Eighth Plan in 1998. A proposal to export power from Pakistan to the Power Grid Corporation of India to meet the shortfall in India's northern grid was backed by the Independent Power Producers (IPPs), multinational corporations who had come on stream in Pakistan with the liberalisation of the power sector in the 1990s. The Vajpayee government set up a high-level committee to examine the deal shortly after the proposal was made. The estimate was that if Pakistan had a surplus capacity of 200 megawatts for export it could earn as much as US$ 1.2 billion per year for perhaps up to twenty years.[36] The deal however fell through over the price sought, with India expecting the power to cost less than heavily subsidised domestic power. Pakistan's IPPs disagreed with the Indian demand and wanted counter-guarantees as

[35] Nadeem Iqbal, "Working for a Regional Energy Supply Network", in Dipankar Banerjee, ed., *CBMs in South Asia: Potential and Possibilities* (Colombo: Regional Centre for Strategic Studies, 2000).

[36] Lama, "Integrating Stakeholders In Energy Cooperation", pp. 30–1.

they had no confidence in the ability of India's bankrupt State Electricity Boards, who distributed the power, to pay. It also fell through because of a quarrel between the IPPs in Pakistan and the Nawaz Sharif government over high power tariffs within Pakistan.

The important point to note here, though, and a reason why a deal can still be struck, is the fact that, from October 1998, both governments were keen on quickly finalising the deal so that it could "considerably rev up the then ongoing foreign secretary-level talks . . ."[37] The 1998 nuclear tests were apparently *not* an obstacle to the deal being proposed and seriously considered. More significantly, the tests were not an obstacle to the proposal being made by Pakistan, traditionally the party resisting greater economic co-operation. The relative thaw since January 2004 has also cleared the political obstacles to a revival of such co-operative projects, although this situation has been reversed since late 2008 due to terrorism and political instability within Pakistan.

To sum up, there are several reasons for the low level of economic co-operation so far.

First, quite apart from political conflict, the principal reason appears to be the fact that low-income economies, following import-substitution strategies, are largely not complementary. Such economies do not need each other much, barring some raw materials or agricultural products. Thus, intra-South trade tends to remain very low until a certain level of industrialisation and product differentiation is reached.[38] The low volume of India–Pakistan trade is, therefore, not surprising and parallels the low volume of each country's trade with other developing countries with whom they have no political conflict.

[37] Siddiqi, "India–Pakistan Cooperation in Energy and Environment", ref. 25, p. 162.

[38] The best example of such intra-South trade is the growing intraregional trade within ASEAN (Association of South-East Asian Nations), and between China, Hong Kong, and Taiwan. In the 1980s, Japanese and other multinationals relocated labour-intensive manufacturing to Southeast Asia. With rising wages, Hong Kong and Taiwanese companies relocated such industries to coastal China.

Second, due to political conflict, Pakistan has been unwilling to grant India "most favoured nation" status (although this is just a matter of time under its World Trade Organization [WTO] commitments), and both countries have created other obstacles to trade, resulting in the growth of trade through third countries.

Third, this pattern is beginning to change, as is reflected in the growth of such trade beginning in the early 1990s and accelerating from 2004. This has more to do with the general growth of their trade, India's in particular, as a result of economic liberalisation and a higher rate of GDP growth rather than as a result of the SAPTA or SAFTA process.

Fourth, the real potential for growth in trade is in the future. This is because of the inevitable liberalisation of both economies coupled with perhaps sustained 7 per cent plus growth in India and industrial diversification. Potential complementarities are in areas such as agricultural and mineral products, including tea, coffee, cotton, sugar, edible oils, spices, rock salt, iron ore and phosphates, and some manufactures such as fertiliser, cement, tyres, auto-components, textile and tannery chemicals, pharmaceuticals, and plastic raw materials.[39] These complementarities will surely grow as both economies, particularly the much larger Indian economy, lower tariffs and phase out quantitative restrictions under their WTO obligations. This trend will be reinforced if both, particularly India, attract foreign direct investment which will increasingly be interested in expanding from single-country to regional markets. One can also expect these trends to be reinforced by the spread of telecommunications and the internet. It will, however, be some time before trade diverted through third countries will be redirected to the direct cross-border (Lahore–Amritsar) or Bombay–Karachi

[39] For details, see "Trade and Economic Cooperation between India and Pakistan" (New Delhi: Federation of Indian Chambers of Commerce and Industry, 1999), and "Minutes of the First Meeting of the Executive Committee of India-Pakistan Chamber of Commerce and Industry" (New Delhi: Federation of Indian Chambers of Commerce and Industry, 1999); *South Asian Development and Cooperation Report 2004* (New Delhi: Research and Information System for Developing Countries, 2004), p. 57.

routes. This will follow only when confidence is built in the politics-proof reliability of trans-border trade procedures.

Fifth, it is unrealistic to visualise trade having spillovers that may be a driver of security co-operation as it is most unlikely that either country, particularly Pakistan, will bulk large in the total trade of the other. The private sector participants will be firms that are unlikely to co-operate or have the collective economic and political muscle to drive policy on core security and non-economic foreign policy issues.

Sixth, even more than trade, the real potential for complementarities and economic co-operation in the longer term is in energy infrastructure, particularly gas pipelines from Turkmenistan, Iran, and the Gulf, and the joint development and distribution of electric power. In these areas, deals leading to further economic co-operation, such as downstream gas-based fertilizer, petrochemical and power plants, and, eventually, security co-operation, look possible as, to begin with, these will have to be major inter-governmental initiatives.

The Indus Waters Treaty: Economic Co-operation Shrinking the Arena of Conflict

The Indus Waters Treaty, signed in 1960, has been the only major economic co-operation agreement between India and Pakistan.[40] It has survived the 1965 and 1971 wars, Siachen, Kashmir, and Kargil. This is remarkable given that three of the six rivers of the Indus basin flow from Jammu and Kashmir into Pakistan. The treaty has however failed to lead to further economic or security co-operation.[41]

[40] Niranjan D. Gulhati, *The Indus Waters Treaty: An Exercise in International Mediation* (Bombay: Allied, 1973), for a comprehensive account of the origins and negotiation of the treaty.

[41] I am indebted to Ramaswamy R. Iyer, former secretary, Water Resources, and to S.K. Singh, former foreign secretary, for conversations on this issue.

How did the Treaty come about in the 1950s despite the dispute over Kashmir? Why has the Treaty survived despite subsequent wars and tensions? Why did India, notwithstanding its inherently strong position as the upper riparian, agree to the division of waters? Why did India not try to use its position for leverage in the dispute over Kashmir by employing cross-issue linkages? The answer to this is not entirely clear but it appears to comprise the following factors.

First, the Indian leadership could not have been unaware of the fact that India was the lower riparian of the Brahmaputra and Sutlej which rose in Tibet, and of several smaller rivers in Nepal. Second, both India and Pakistan needed World Bank and Western, particularly American, aid for their development, something that might have induced co-operation. Third, despite Partition and the Kashmir dispute, the Indian leadership in the 1950s did not see and did not want to write off Pakistan as a permanent enemy. They saw the Kashmir dispute as perhaps solvable, and were aware that from 1954 Pakistan was a recipient of US military aid, later joining US-led Cold War pacts such as SEATO (South-East Asia Treaty Organization) and CENTO (Central Treaty Organization). India probably wanted to avoid the possibility of Pakistan approaching the International Court of Justice or otherwise internationalising the dispute more widely. Fourth, it was technically not possible to turn off river waters like turning off a tap.

As to why the Treaty has been successful despite wars and tensions, the following factors provide some explanation. First and foremost is the technical feature of the Treaty that divided up the waters into three rivers each to India and Pakistan for their separate and independent development rather than joint development. This removed the scope for protracted conflict that is typical when river waters are shared between upper and lower riparian countries or provinces.

Second, the Treaty can be significantly violated only by the upper riparian, India, which is a status quo power, and not by the revisionist power, Pakistan. India has no incentive to violate the Treaty, as any such violation will provoke war and internationalise the Indo–Pakistan dispute, which India has always wished to avoid. Violation would also render India, in the long term, vulnerable to non-co-operation by China and Nepal.

Third, the wars between India and Pakistan have been of relatively brief duration in which India did not feel pushed to the wall to the extent of attempting desperate measures like abrogating the Treaty and attempting cutting off river water flows.

Why has the Indus Treaty not produced spillovers of economic co-operation in related areas, or in negotiations on confidence-building and war-prevention measures, let alone conflict resolution in relation to territorial claims? The answer is that the Treaty was *specifically designed at the insistence of both parties* in order to facilitate separate development of river waters, hydroelectric power, and the resulting agricultural and industrial development rather than joint development.

Taken together, the Treaty came about and has lasted despite wars (and notwithstanding the dispute over the Baglihar project referred to the World Bank for arbitration in 2005) because, in our framework it did not threaten relative gains to either state in a form that could be translated into military gains. What it has done is to wall off an issue area from the larger conflict, shrinking the arena of the conflict. Similarly, agreements on gas pipelines or electricity grids can wall off these issue areas and further shrink the arena of conflict while expanding the arena of institutionalized co-operation, thus reducing the likelihood of war.

The Impact of Nuclear Deterrence on Economic Co-operation Between India and Pakistan in the Light of IR Theory

Viewing India and Pakistan through the concepts and theory outlined in section I, and in the light of the material in the following sections, I advance the following propositions on why past economic co-operation was very limited, why the situation today has both incentives and imperatives for growing economic co-operation *because of, rather than despite,* nuclear confrontation, and why such co-operation, particularly certain common projects, will have positive security spillovers.

First, economic co-operation in terms of trade and investment did not occur over the past fifty years, not so much because of political conflict as because of the inherently limited scope for such co-operation between two import-substituting low-income countries with high trade barriers, in line with the limited growth of South–South trade in general. The Indus Waters Treaty was specifically designed to separate, not join, the two economies, and could not in the short run be used as a military or political weapon.

Second, one cannot expect either country to become a major trading partner of the other, even larger India for smaller Pakistan, given their competing rather than complementary endowments. The real potential of economic co-operation today is in energy, for example, a gas pipeline and the export of electricity, preferably in the context of South Asian grids. Such co-operation on common projects can catalyse the growth of trade in the future, integrate the two countries, develop common interests, and foster continuing interaction.

Third, given the tension over Kashmir, the state of confrontation in a covert nuclear weapons regime since 1987, overt from 1998, one can expect sensitivity to relative gains in the security sphere to be very high, especially from the point of view of the weaker state, Pakistan. The major obstacles to the gas pipeline and electricity export possibilities are politico-military and concern security fallouts.

Fourth, the issue for the Pakistani establishment is not only national defence, but the sustenance of its revisionist territorial ambitions. To the extent that Pakistan considers economic gains translatable into security gains, it could also be highly sensitive to economic gains by India, such as possible Indian trade surpluses and threats to Pakistani industry from Indian products. This sensitivity would be accentuated if economic gains are believed to be of a cumulative nature leading to additional economic gains in further rounds of interaction. Pakistan would also be sensitive to the emergence of economic interests with a stake in increased economic co-operation, and implicitly, a political interest in scaling down its confrontation with India. The latter development would threaten to undermine, from within, its revisionist ambitions relating to Kashmir. This is probably a factor in resisting trade co-operation.

Fifth, as mentioned briefly at the outset and crucial to my argument, the developments following the 1998 nuclear tests, especially Kargil and Operation Parakram, have changed Pakistan's options in two ways, both of which would probably make it less inclined to resist greater co-operation in trade and energy infrastructure in the future, *provided* the *economic gains are neither of the cumulative relative gains type, nor translatable into security gains.*

One, explicit nuclearisation with a demonstrated missile capability has assured Pakistan's security in a way that reduces the sensitivity to relative gains in the military sphere.

Two, the Kargil and 2002 confrontations, and the US role in ending the former and scaling down the latter, have demonstrated to Pakistan that using nuclear capability as a shield to launch a military offensive to force India to come to the table on its terms on Kashmir is no longer a feasible option.

Following from these two points, Pakistan is *more* secure vis-à-vis a possible Indian military threat than ever before, as well as *less* able to threaten conventional force to resolve the Kashmir dispute. It therefore has *less* to fear and *much* to gain from greater economic engagement with India, especially given the growing complementarities deriving from the momentum of industrial diversification, general liberalisation, and regional integration, and hence less need to be sensitive about relative gains. This is particularly true given that the regional security system structure is multi-polar in view of the roles played by China and the US, particularly post

9/11. In economic terms, the system is highly multi-polar, both states being minor players in the world economy and in each other's economies. Thus, nuclear deterrence, Kargil, and 2002 may have actually removed disincentives to greater trade and infrastructural co-operation on common projects. The January 2004 agreement on a composite dialogue, including trade and energy co-operation, is a reflection of this logic, which will probably continue, albeit jerkily with hiccups over terrorist incidents.

Sixth, the only possible snag is whether the expansion of trade poses a threat to Pakistan or India in the form of relative economic gains for one or the other which could translate into relative security gains, especially if the gains are cumulative. This seems most unlikely as the bulk of the trade is, and will continue to be, in agricultural, mineral, and relatively labour-intensive, standard-technology manufactures which have nothing to do with military or dual-purpose technologies. Relative gains in one round of interaction, say, a given year's trade surplus, are not cumulative and can be reversed in succeeding years, unlike in cases where strategic technological capabilities and research and development (R&D) bases in leading national firms are eroded. In any event, both countries' military industries and R&D establishments remain in the public sector, and both import rather than develop most of their major classes of armaments, apart, of course, from the nuclear and missile areas. Therefore, there will be no threatening conversion of gains from economic co-operation into direct military capability, let alone cumulation of either. As for the much-feared large Indian trade surplus that is evident in India's trade with its other SAARC neighbours, Pakistan's trade with India will most probably remain relatively small in terms of Pakistan's overall trade, at under 10 per cent, making any Indian surplus non-threatening.

Seventh, will a gas pipeline from points west through Pakistan to India, or the interconnection of power grids for the import or export of electricity, generate risks of a slide towards war due to politically motivated cut-offs of gas or power supplies? I would argue that the risks are minimal. There are ways, outlined earlier, of ensuring Pakistan's compliance, which would deter the stoppage of gas supplies as a political weapon. The disruption of a gas pipeline or power supplies could hurt Pakistan's economy in the event of a cut-off. It would also hurt foreign power-producing firms and gas supplier countries and shake international investor confidence. A pipeline could also function as an additional insurance against an Indian attack from the point of view of the smaller country, Pakistan. However, interlinked electricity grids could be more prone to misunderstandings in the event of power shortages, even if not politically motivated, and have more of a tradelike, arms-length character than the binding character of a gas pipeline. However, Indian dependence on Pakistani electricity exports will, at best, be only a small part of the deficit, and a smaller part of total supply, even for the northern grid.

Copeland's theory that high interdependence conduces to peace given positive trade expectations would lead to the conclusion that such common projects in energy will stabilise peace. This is because, unlike in the Indus Waters Treaty, where separation was aimed to be achieved, common energy projects can be expected to have positive multiplier effects on economic growth and on the growth of trade between the two countries both directly and indirectly for many years into the foreseeable future. This expectation would be reinforced by three factors. One, such projects, especially a pipeline, would create a situation in which both states are locked into an economic relationship from which there can be no easy disengagement, at least not without huge costs for both, including the state that may seek to disengage, roughly analogous to the difficulty of cutting off river waters for short-term political purposes. Two, India and Pakistan are entering an era in which the level of economic interdependence can only rise given the multilateral WTO commitments of both to economic liberalisation. Three, even an expanded economic relationship, because it builds on a very low base, would not lead to critical dependence, even sectoral, on the other. Besides, if both have nuclear capabilities, one can expect this factor to override any war-like tendency deriving from potential economic disengagement. Indeed, de facto nuclear deterrence would also deter both countries from contemplating disruptive disengagement.

Would co-operation in gas and power produce a lock-in effect where dependence on the other's economy or decisions could translate directly into relative security gains, or indirectly, through relative economic gains translating into relative security gains? This is a more complex question. Both the gas pipeline and the electricity export proposal, especially the former, will lock Pakistan and India together in great economic interdependence that will be difficult to sever. Both proposals will require more joint management than entailed by the Indus Waters Treaty. While the Indus Waters Treaty walled off the issue area of waters from the sphere of conflict by separation, with both parties to the Treaty committed to merely refraining from negative actions, cross-border pipelines and power grids are about integration. They require positive action in the form of an everyday commitment by the parties to co-operate, but can be designed with disincentives to counter negative actions such as cut-offs of gas or power. Pipelines and power grids could constitute archetypal new common projects that bind the countries together. In the long run, a gas pipeline could integrate co-operation in both gas and electricity if it extends to downstream gas-based power plants. It would be somewhat analogous to post-war Franco-German economic integration under the umbrella of the US, in that the US is friendly to both and desires conflict mitigation.

Who the relative gainer may be is an open question, but such interactive interdependence will certainly have a cumulative character. The interdependence would spur trade, perhaps beginning with joint development of gas-based power and fertiliser industries, and lead to the emergence of groups in each country with an economic stake in trade with the other. This may, over time, lead to a greater relative dependence of Pakistan on India, although the level of dependence may be small in comparison to the totality of Pakistan's external economic relationships. It may erode the political feasibility of the option of withholding economic co-operation in the future as a bargaining chip over the Kashmir issue. However, and this is crucial to the argument, *given that the option of forcing a military solution is no longer feasible after Kargil and 2002, and that insurgency can in any case be supported at low cost, this is more a notional than a real loss of flexibility, and not a security threat.* In a scenario in which there is an interconnection of their economies by a gas pipeline and an electricity grid, there is nothing that India can do unilaterally to threaten Pakistan. *Again, this is not a loss of a military option, for nuclearisation has in any case removed such possibilities.*

Eighth, following from the above, the relative gains sensitivity of states locked in a military confrontation over territory and ideology does not lead to economic co-operation, particularly if relative gains are cumulative, unless there are significant security pacts to begin with, *or as a substitute,* assured nuclear deterrence. In the case of India and Pakistan since 1998 it is the latter that greatly removes the fear of, and the option of, a major conventional or nuclear attack. Deterrence has, therefore, enabled the conditions for the growth of economic co-operation without fear of adverse security spillovers. In other words, the potential for spillover is from nuclear deterrence to growing economic co-operation.

The spillover effects would be analogous to the growth of economic detente between the US and the Soviet Union after the Strategic Arms Limitation Treaty (SALT I) accords. Nuclear deterrence and the failure of the Kargil adventure have set the stage for assured security, *but without an offensive option.* This, in turn, sets the stage for economic co-operation on infrastructure and trade, which, over time, could lead to further economic co-operation, eventually spilling over to some resolution of the Kashmir problem, whatever form that may take, and security co-operation.

Unlikely as it may seem, the nuclear tests and Kargil have actually created enabling conditions for economic co-operation when viewed through the prism of cumulative relative gains sensitivity. For this process to begin, Pakistan has to change tack on its "Kashmir first" policy, shifting gear to building co-operation in other areas without necessarily giving up its position on Kashmir. The signs of change have been there, with Pakistan initiating the electricity export proposal in 1998 and finally agreeing to a possible gas pipeline in mid-2000. The turnaround in the Indian position from April 2003 following the no-talks stance during 2002, and the successful SAARC summit in Islamabad in January 2004 at which Indian Prime Minister Vajpayee and Pakistan President Musharraf met on the sidelines, and continued progress since then, supports the argument of this paper, as does the resumption of contacts at the highest level despite the November 2008 terrorist attacks. They agreed to a schedule of talks for a composite dialogue which would include all issues, including economic co-operation, a significant shift in Pakistan's position. Subsequently, the list of 615 items that Pakistan allows to be imported from India was expanded to 1075. India too has to build confidence to sustain the momentum by remaining, most importantly, a secular, pluralistic state in which minority rights are assured in law and justice is done in practice, and taking the lead in economic openness to its smaller neighbours.

10

International Relations Theory and the India–Pakistan Conflict

Deterrence Theory, International Relations Theory, and South Asia

THE TESTING OF nuclear weapons by both India and Pakistan in May 1998 marks the explicit nuclearisation of an existing dyadic conflict that has existed since 1947. The period since 1998 has been marked by a fragile nuclear deterrence that has been in periodic crisis, particularly the Kargil conflict of May–July 1999 and the ten-month full mobilisation on the border between the end of 2001 and October of 2002, following a terrorist attack on the Indian parliament by armed militants. The period has also seen continuous low-intensity warfare and terrorism in Jammu and Kashmir where a rebellion against the Indian state has been actively backed by Pakistan. Conflict resolution therefore assumes a new urgency. Scholars who seek to understand the problem must begin by addressing the basic issue of survival, that is, the stability of deterrence in a dynamic context in South Asia, factoring in China and the American presence in the extended region. But they need to go beyond the nuclear deterrence relationship to understanding the underlying political conflict between the two states. The questions I attempt

I thank the two anonymous referees for their comments. However, the responsibility for all facts, figures, and opinions is solely mine.

to answer are: how adequate is the theory of deterrence when applied to South Asia? How good is international relations theory (henceforth IR theory), particularly the dominant paradigm of neorealism? What explanatory alternatives can be constructed from existing theoretical resources?

As the lead essay of a collection of South Asian subcontinental perspectives on nuclear deterrence in the region, this essay is an attempt at theorising, within the framework of IR theory, the larger conflict within which the post-1998 nuclear confrontation and deterrance relationship between India and Pakistan is situated, rather than on deterrence theory and its applicability per se. It argues that the best explanatory theory for the India–Pakistan conflict is a combination of Mohammed Ayoob's subaltern realism and the regional security complex theory put forward by Barry Buzan and Ole Waever. It ends by posing and attempting to answer a larger question: whether the stabilisation of deterrence in South Asia, necessary for the prevention of future wars, will merely lock both states into conflict over the long term or whether, under certain conditions, it can be a driver of conflict resolution. If the latter, then what are those conditions and policies?

Nuclear deterrence strategy consists of specific military deployments and threats, with the objective of deterring potential attackers. Deterrence theory consists of the underlying principles and logic. There are six key elements to the theory according to Patrick Morgan: "The assumption of a very severe conflict, the assumption of rationality, the concept of a retaliatory threat, the concept of unacceptable damage, the notion of credibility and the notion of deterrence stability."[1] In a dyadic nuclear relationship the core of nuclear deterrence theory is that a state will be de-

[1] Patrick M. Morgan, *Deterrence Now* (Cambridge: Cambridge University Press, 2003), p. 8. Other examples of relatively recent works on deterrence theory are Frank C. Zagare and D. Marc Kilgour, *Perfect Deterrence* (Cambridge: Cambridge University Press, 2000); Robert Powell, *Nuclear Deterrence Theory: The Search for Credibility* (Cambridge: Cambridge University Press, 1990).

terred from launching a nuclear attack against another state, or a major conventional attack that carries the risk of escalation to the nuclear level, if it has good reasons to fear retaliation. Deterrence theory assumes the centrality of survival as a core value. This is subsumed in the assumption of rationality, i.e. states will not want to suffer the risk of extinction or the enormous devastation that is inevitable in absorbing nuclear strikes. Assumptions of rational, cost-benefit calculating, risk-assessing behaviour by decision-makers and a survivable second-strike capacity on the part of a state vis-à-vis its antagonist are the bases of nuclear deterrence.

Deterrence theory is also closely related to the realist paradigm in IR theory. As in realism, particularly structural or neorealism, deterrence theory assumes a fundamentally anarchic international system in which states have to rely on self-help for their survival. They thus face a security dilemma which they try to resolve by either or both of two strategies: arming themselves and/or forming alliances, both with the objective of accumulating the power to deter potential threats (and/or exert compellant threats, depending on one's assumptions about states' behaviour). Neorealism and deterrence theory, however, have both focused on the level of the global system and on the great powers. During the Cold War, when deterrence theory developed, attention was focused specifically upon the two superpowers, since these states determined the distribution of capabilities at the systemic level. Deterrence theory and realism are similar in this respect.

In assessing the utility of deterrence theory and the neorealist approach to explaining the nuclear behaviour of India and Pakistan, particularly since 1998, I focus on the issue of deterrence stability in particular. India and Pakistan both possess fission weapons and the aircraft and short-, medium-, and intermediate-range land-based missiles to deliver them. Does their relationship have the ingredients of stable deterrence? Does their nuclear behaviour conform to expectations derived from deterrence theory? From the realist paradigm, I argue that in three important ways the nuclear behaviour of India and Pakistan do not conform to the expectations of deterrence theory or of neorealist theory.

First, one would expect a state facing a threat from a neighbour (China) with which it has had a border dispute and a war and which is itself a nuclear power (China), to arm itself at the earliest with a nuclear deterrent. But India's first nuclear test in 1974 came ten years after China's and, *more importantly*, did not result in further testing for the rapid development and deployment, even de-mated, of a nuclear delivery capacity against the main Chinese cities. Nor has this happened after the 1998 nuclear tests in the past seven years, despite China being cited as the prime threat to India both in 1998 and before that by advocates of the bomb. As of the time of writing, India has deployed only the short-range Pakistan (or Tibet)-specific Prithvi missile. The medium-range (700–800 km) Agni-I and intermediate range (2000 km-plus) Agni-II missiles are only now being inducted into the army.[2] Even if the ten-year gap between China's and India's first nuclear tests was due to technological and economic constraints, the lack of follow-through after 1974, and indeed after 1998, contradicts deterrence and neorealist theories in explaining the pattern of nuclearisation.

Second, despite an immediate nuclear threat from Pakistan on at least four occasions (during Operation Brasstacks in early 1987, during the May 1990 crisis, during Kargil, May–July 1999, and during the border mobilisation in most of 2002 especially in May–June), India has adopted a very slow process of weaponisation and deployment, preferring the adoption of a non-weaponised or recessed-deterrent approach and altogether eschewing attempts at compellance or the development of compellant capabilities.[3] This again is hard to explain by the logic of deterrence theory or neorealism.

[2] Times News Network, "Prithvi's naval variant is successfully test-fired", *Times of India*, October 28, 2004.

3 For non-weaponised deterrence, see George Perkovich, *India's Nuclear Bomb: The Impact on Global Proliferation* (New Delhi: Oxford University Press,

Third, India has not taken any steps to protect itself against the possibility of a disarming counter-proliferation strike by one or more of the established nuclear powers despite it being clear that all of them, even China, can, theoretically, undertake such a strike expending only a fraction of their stockpile of warheads without India having any retaliatory capability as it lacks long-range missiles. India is not known to have located its nuclear reactors and other assets deep underground. Even if this could be explained by bureaucratic politics and keeping up of the appearance of a peaceful programme, one would have expected India, post-1998, to have increased the risks and costs for potential pre-emptive strikes by rapidly making and deploying nuclear devices far away from its nuclear plants. This has not been the pattern. This behaviour cannot be explained by either deterrence theory or neorealism. India's nuclear behaviour seems to assume an attitude of acceptance of its nuclear capability by the five permanent, nuclear-armed members of the UN Security Council. *Its strategic mental horizon seems to be limited, from its actions or lack of them, to South Asia despite invoking the Chinese threat.* This has theoretical implications that I draw out later.

These three aspects of Indian nuclear behaviour are not in consonance with either deterrence theory or with neorealist theory.[4]

2000), pp. 3 and 317; for recessed deterrence, see Jasjit Singh, "A Nuclear Strategy for India", in Jasjit Singh, ed., *Nuclear India* (New Delhi: Knowledge World, 1998), p. 318.

[4] See Perkovich, *India's Nuclear Bomb*, pp. 455–6; Itty Abraham, *The Making of the Indian Atomic Bomb* (New Delhi: Orient Longman, 1998), pp. 16–17; Ashley J. Tellis, "Reconstructing Structural Realism: The Long March to Scientific Theory", *Security Studies*, vol. 5, no. 2 (Winter 1995/96), pp. 3–94, pointing out how India's nuclear behaviour does not fit the realist paradigm. For detailed analytical histories of the Indian nuclear programme, see Bharat Karnad, *Nuclear Weapons and Indian Security: The Realist Foundations of Strategy* (New Delhi: Macmillan India, 2002); Ashley Tellis, *India's Emerging Nuclear Posture: Between Recessed Deterrent and Ready Arsenal*

Pakistan too, has been totally focused on India and has not taken steps to develop missile capabilities to deter other possible threats, such as a possible Israeli strike or an American counter-proliferation strike – the latter a possibility given Pakistan's closeness to the Taliban before 9/11 and its proliferation of nuclear technologies and materials to North Korea, Iran, and Libya. It too has not located its reactors or other assets deep underground, although its programme is purely military, and despite the existence of a precedent in the Israeli attack on Iraq's Osirak facility in 1981. India's deterrence behaviour would appear to approximate a desire for nuclear weapons as a currency of power and for generalised security in the long term rather than one of a state facing a real and imminent threat of nuclear or major conventional attack.

As far as the key survival issue of deterrence stability is concerned, stable deterrence would be expected from a relationship in which both sides had survivable second-strike capabilities, both knew and accepted this, and both accepted as credible the threat to use nuclear weapons if struck with nuclear weapons, or faced with defeat in a conventional war, or faced with impossible political demands amounting to extinction, severe truncation of the state, or compromised sovereignty.

However, despite the known nuclear capabilities on both sides, there have been three crises since Pakistan revealed its nuclear capabilities in A.Q. Khan's interview to Indian journalist Kuldip Nayar in January 1987,[5] in which major conventional war threatened to break out with the possibility of escalation to the nuclear

---

(Santa Monica, CA: RAND, 2001); Ashok Kapur, *Pokhran and Beyond: India's Nuclear Behavior* (New Delhi: Oxford University Press, 2001); Perkovich, *India's Nuclear Bomb*; Raja Menon, *A Nuclear Strategy for India* (New Delhi: Sage Publications, 2000); Abraham, *The Making of the Indian Atomic Bomb*; Sumit Ganguly, "India's Pathway to Pokhran II", *International Security*, vol. 23, no. 4 (Spring 1999), pp. 148–77.

[5] "We have the bomb, says Pakistan's Dr. Strangelove", *Observer*, London, 1 March 1987.

level. Of these, two post-dated the 1998 nuclear tests. While one can argue that during the Cold War there were numerous instances of US–Soviet brinkmanship, including major ones such as Berlin (1961) and Cuba (1962), this does indicate that deterrence stability, even non-crisis stability, is fragile.

As far as crisis stability is concerned, there was an Indian threat, articulated at the highest level, to launch a limited conventional thrust in May–June 2002 and an implicit threat of crossing the Line of Control (LoC) during the Kargil operations in 1999. Both times there was *de facto* American mediation without which it is possible that deterrence might have broken down. Deterrence stability so far has been based on a second-strike capability deriving from technological backwardness of the nuclear weapons infrastructure on both sides. In a static sense, for the period 1998–2005, this fragile stability has been based on the lack of satellite monitoring capability, lack of knowledge of the opponent's nuclear asset numbers, types, location at any given time, a recessed posture, few deployed missiles of sufficient range and accuracy, and so forth, hence removing first-strike options but ensuring a second-strike capability. This does not bode well for the stability of deterrence in the future as both states move up the technological ladder and develop more accurate missile capabilities and other infrastructure, including possibly spy satellites by India, airborne early warning and theater missile defenses, fuller deployment of weapons, and rapid-reaction command, control and communication systems. To move from second-strike capability based on the technological backwardness of both sides to US–Soviet-type second-strike capability, assured and credible over the decades, will need huge technological advances and investments, and an arms race that could be destabilising militarily and politically. In the intermediate stages of development, one or both states could feel an imbalance and vulnerability to a disarming strike or the development of escalation dominance by India.

Apart from deterrence stability there are theoretically important questions about the larger conflict between India and Pakistan that need explanation. These are: whom does the nuclear capability demonstrated in 1998 deter? And deter from doing what? The answer to the first question is that to date their nuclear capabilities credibly deter only each other. The credibility of India's deterrence of China is doubtful given no deployed missiles other than the short-range Prithvi and China's capacity to, in theory, take out India's assets using only a fraction of its arsenal. In answer to the second question, to date nuclear deterrence in South Asia has not deterred sub-conventional warfare or limited conventional warfare (Kargil) but only full-scale conventional warfare (2002) and nuclear strikes. Given the Kashmir dispute, Pakistan has an incentive to carry out low-intensity warfare (insurgency) against India as a cost-effective, low-risk option behind the shield of its nuclear capability. India does not have the escalation dominance that could be used to threaten escalation to conventional warfare since this could escalate further to nuclear use, due to a lack of adequate conventional capability and diversified nuclear capability. Hence, it lacks compellance vis-à-vis Pakistan, and this will work against it as the numbers of Pakistani devices increase and as they are dispersed and perhaps delegated as regards the authority to use them in certain crisis conditions. If the capabilities developed deter only each other from nuclear or major conventional warfare this reveals again a regionally bounded and dyadic other-focused mindset. How does one explain this behaviour pattern in the framework of deterrence and IR theory? I shall explore this in the next two sections.

Some Pointers from Critiques of Mainstream IR Theory

The starting point for assessing the usefulness of IR theory for analysing conflict between states in South Asia is the neorealist–neoliberal debate, and its recent evolution which seeks to transcend the terms of both sides of the debate.[6] The extended debate between neorealism and neoliberal institutionalism saw considerable criticism of neorealism.[7] First, unlike neorealism's assumption that preferences are exogenous, it was widely argued that it is necessary to explain the origins of states' preferences. Most fundamentally, anarchy does not necessarily mean neorealist assumptions and imply neorealist conclusions. Robert Keohane showed that a repeated prisoner's dilemma game could lead to cooperation under anarchy.[8] Joseph Grieco responded that Keohane assumes that absolute gains drive behaviour; what is relevant are relative gains.[9] To elaborate (since this point is very important for South Asia), neorealists like Grieco hold that states are sensitive to relative gains more than to absolute gains in cooperation. In neorealist theory, states in an anarchic world system seek power and the balance of power to safeguard their security, and since power is relative, they are sensitive to relative, not absolute, gains. Hence, co-operation can be successful only if it does not

[6] For an excellent critical survey of the neorealist–neoliberal debate see Robert Powell, "Anarchy in International Relations Theory: The Neorealist–Neoliberal Debate", *International Organization*, vol. 48, no. 2 (Spring 1994), pp. 313–44. For two book-length collections on the debate, see Robert O. Keohane, ed., *Neorealism and its Critics* (New York: Columbia University Press, 1986), and David A. Baldwin, ed., *Neorealism and Neoliberalism: The Contemporary Debate* (New York: Columbia University Press, 1993). For the best statement of traditional realism, see Hans J. Morgenthau, *Politics Among Nations* (New York: Alfred A. Knopf, 1948), and for the classic statement of neorealism, see Kenneth Waltz, *Theory of International Politics* (Reading, MA: Addison Wesley, 1979). For an early and classic statement of neoliberal institutionalism, see Robert O. Keohane, *After Hegemony* (Princeton: Princeton University Press, 1984).

[7] The structure of the argument and the classification of criticisms of neorealism in the next few pages draw heavily on Powell, "Anarchy in International Relations Theory".

[8] Keohane, *After Hegemony*.

[9] Joseph Grieco, "Anarchy and the Limits of Cooperation", in Keohane, ed., *Neorealism and its Critics*, pp. 116–42.

upset the relative gains balance, no matter what absolute gains one can point to as the fruits of co-operation.[10]

Robert Powell argues that neorealists have mistaken effects for causes, arguing that concern for relative gains is primarily an effect not a cause.[11] While neorealists assume that states under anarchy are preoccupied with relative gains in transactions with other states, neoliberals argue that the degree of a state's concern for relative gains is conditional, and depends on the intensity of the security dilemma it faces. A predominant concern with relative gains is an effect of the state's *perceived* strategic situation. Citing Grieco, Powell argues that a state's sensitivity to relative gains depends on six factors, two of which are: the fungibility of power across issues, and whether relative gains or losses occur over the military or the economic sphere. Thus, Powell argues that the degree of sensitivity to relative gains is part of the outcome or effect of the *perceived* strategic setting, influenced by several factors: an effect but not a cause or an explanation of the presence or absence of international cooperation. Thus it is not just structure but perceptions and what goes into their shaping that are critical to policy and hence to outcomes.

The neoliberal criticism that the origins of states' preferences needs to be explained gets scholars into the territory of ideologies, beliefs, experiences, and knowledge, all hitherto neglected by neoliberal as well as neorealist theories but emphasised by the constructivist approach to international relations which emerged as a dissatisfied reaction to both neorealism and neoliberalism.[12] Most importantly, constructivism stresses the force of norms upon agents and hence, interactively, on international structures. Norms

[10] However, it has been shown that co-operation can take place under conditions of sensitivity to relative gains too. See Duncan Snidal, "Relative Gains and the Pattern of International Cooperation", *American Political Science Review*, vol. 85, no. 3 (September 1991), pp. 701–26

[11] Powell, "Anarchy in International Relations Theory".

[12] See for example, Alexander Wendt, "Constructing International Politics", *International Security*, vol. 20, no. 1 (Summer 1995), p. 73.

are collective understandings important for behaviour. They constitute actor identities and interests and not just regulations or constraints upon behaviour.

The constructivist approach, and its social construction of "legitimate" and "illegitimate" norms, would appear to be particularly relevant to the study of ethnic conflict and conflict between states perceived by each other to have an ethnic (including religiously defined ethnic) character.[13] Following from this, states based on ethnicity/religion have potential for conflict with states of different or overlapping ethnicities/religion and with states that seek to build inclusive civic and territorial nations that do not place much importance on ethnicity/religion.[14]

Neorealism's focus on structure and outcomes, and its indeterminacy as regards policy, make it useless for foreign policy analysis and conflict resolution. Neorealism is a theory of outcomes or, if one follows Powell, a theory of preference over actions, not over outcomes – pursuit of power as the means to whatever ends is assumed to be the operational motive. Neorealists like Stephen Krasner argue that in the long run rational power calculations will prevail whatever ideas and internal processes determine short-term foreign

[13] Sagarika Dutt, citing Lapid and Kratochwil, argues that as homogeneous nation-states are a dwindling minority, national identity based on territory and that based on "ethnicity"/culture have become contradictory. See Sagarika Dutt, "Identities and the Indian State: An Overview", *Third World Quarterly*, vol. 19, no. 3 (September 1998), pp. 411–33, at p. 412; Yosef Lapid and Friedrich Kratochwil, "Revisiting the 'National': Toward an Identity Agenda in Neorealism", in Yosef Lapid and Friedrich Kratochwil, eds, *The Return of Culture and Identity in IR Theory* (Boulder, CO: Lynne Rienner, 1997).

[14] Constructivist approaches also enable approaches to understanding identity conflict that have the potential to transcend and resolve such conflicts. Jonathan Mercer argues that identities being malleable, identity conflicts can be overcome by giving transcendence to larger identities, for example, national to pan-European identity in the case of European integration. See Jonathan Mercer, "Anarchy and Identity", *International Organization*, vol. 49, no. 2 (Spring 1995), pp. 229–52.

policy.[15] But power alone does not explain action as traditional realism acknowledges. Power and situation set limits on options but almost never reduce the number of options to one. In this context, Robert Keohane and Judith Goldstein argue that ideas and internal processes have independent causal significance.[16] As Stephen Walt argues, whether states balance or bandwagon depends *inter alia* on *perceived intentions* of the adversary, which brings us to the importance of images.[17] Perceptions/images thus connect structure to foreign policy. But images are formed through repeated interaction. Therefore, images, and hence perceived intentions, are crucially linked to the history of interaction of states-in-the-making and nations-in-the-making, leading us to the perspectives discussed in the next section.

Subaltern Realism, Regional Security Complex Theory and South Asia

If deterrence theory and neorealism do not explain the nuclear behaviour of India and Pakistan, how well do they explain the India–Pakistan conflict? Let us first examine how well they explain, in general, the international relations of the newer and less powerful states in the contemporary world system. A number of scholars have expressed dissatisfaction at the inadequacies and/or Eurocentrism or superpower/Great Power focus of IR theory.[18] It has been

[15] Stephen Krasner, "Global Communication and National Power", in Baldwin, ed., *Neorealism and Neoliberalism.*

[16] Judith Goldstein and Robert O. Keohane, "Ideas and Foreign Policy: An Analytical Framework", in Robert O. Keohane and Judith Goldstein, eds, *Ideas and Foreign Policy: Beliefs, Institutions and Political Change* (Ithaca, NY: Cornell University Press, 1993.

[17] Stephen M. Walt, *The Origins of Alliances* (Ithaca, NY: Cornell University Press, 1987).

[18] See Mohammed Ayoob, "Subaltern Realism: International Relations Theory Meets the Third World", pp. 31–49, Carlos Escude, "An Introduction to Peripheral Realism and its Implications for the Interstate System: Argentina

argued that a number of concepts central to mainstream IR theory do not fit, or only imperfectly fit, Third World realities. These include key concepts such as anarchy, the state, and the international system.

A common criticism has been that the international order for Third World countries is characterised more by hierarchy than anarchy, and the internal order by anarchy more than by well-defined hierarchy. Third World countries face a world in which the informal hierarchical realities of power differentiation severely constrain their freedom of action, and generate systemic pressures on them to modify their behaviour in accordance with the interests of powerful states. Conversely, the domestic politics of Third World states are not characterised by agreed rules, but often exist in a condition more akin to anarchy, or rather in a state where politics is an arena for making rules between contending forces.

Following from this, the "state" in the Third World does not neatly fit the Westphalian Western state characterised by inviolable boundaries, a monopoly on the use of force within those boundaries, effective government and, latterly, constitutional political institutions based on consensus and democracy. Rather, Third World states are really states-in-the-making, the process of which is inevitably violent, particularly because *inter alia* the boundaries of most such states are colonial legacies cutting across ethnic, tribal, linguistic, and cultural divides.[19]

Mohammed Ayoob's conceptualisation of Subaltern Realism is

---

and the Condor II Missile Project", pp. 55–76, and Amitav Acharya, "Beyond Anarchy: Third World Instability and International Order After the Cold War", pp. 159–212, all in Stephanie G. Neuman, ed., *International Relations Theory and the Third World* (London: Macmillan, 1998). Also for a detailed critique of neorealism see Powell, "Anarchy in International Relations Theory".

[19] Ayoob, "Subaltern Realism", and Sumit Ganguly, *The Origins of War in South Asia: Indo–Pakistani Conflicts Since 1947* (Boulder, CO: Westview, 1986), emphasise the importance of the nature of partition and the British exit in post-colonial India–Pakistan conflict.

a step forward that does not altogether reject neorealism, anarchy, or the idea that there is only one international system of which the Third World is a part.[20] Subaltern realism, according to Ayoob, drawing on the classical realism of Machiavelli and Hobbes, addresses the absence of any theory of the state in neorealism (a criticism equally applicable to neoliberalism, both being ahistorical system-level theories) and its neglect of the domestic variables affecting conflict and order. The proliferation of international conflict is an extension of the proliferation of internal conflicts in developing states and can only be explained as a product of the process of state-making and nation-building (and its obverse, state-breaking and state failure). The process of state-making interacts with the dynamics of regional balances as well as with global power rivalries and international norms, exporting domestic conflicts to the international system. Such export takes place because "favourable regional balances are perceived by state elites as essential to the success of their state-building enterprise especially since this is an activity usually undertaken concurrently by neighbouring states . . ."[21] A realist logic operates on the behaviour of such states but is distorted by their subaltern status in the international system where international norms require them to be effective and humane in their domestic politics, and where they lack effective control over economic resources and are at the receiving end of the export of conflict between major power centres to the periphery of the system. Subaltern realism, argues Ayoob, requires the strengthening of the Westphalian order at the level of the unit (state) for the effective management of conflict in the international system.

This brings us to the relevance of the concept of the international system. IR theory assumes the unitary nature of the international system. However, given the poor fit of concepts like the state, sovereignty, and anarchy, for Third World countries, is it

[20] Ayoob, "Subaltern Realism".

[21] Ibid., pp. 42–3.

not possible that there are two or more international systems, following different political norms and practices? Or perhaps, more meaningfully, a multilevel international system governed by different norms and practices at each level, with a regional system intervening between the world system and the unit states?

Barry Buzan and Ole Waever argue for the conceptual recognition of regional security subsystems or complexes as an intermediate level between global dynamics and internal dynamics, comprising the level of the dynamic of security relations between local sub-systemic states.[22] This was an attempt to deal with the problem of the seamless web in security studies, security being relational. IR theorising, however, tends to be global-systemic and does not recognise sub-systemic levels as distinct levels of analysis except for the very traditional notion of local or regional balances of power. However, there is no widely accepted definition of region. For forming a regional security complex, a region does not have to be economically or politically integrated, since a regional security complex is not an alliance, merely a geographically adjacent set of states that affect each other's security even if antagonistically.

A useful regional sub-system concept can be based on security itself. As Buzan and Waever put it, "Security complexes are regions as seen through the lens of security. They may or may not be regions in other senses, but they do not depend on, or start from, other conceptualizations of regionness."[23] And, "The formation

[22] Barry Buzan and Ole Waever, *Regions and Powers: The Structure of International Security* (Cambridge: Cambridge University Press, 2003). Also see Barry Buzan, "Conclusion: System versus Units in Theorizing About the Third World", in Neuman, ed., *International Relations Theory and the Third World*, pp. 213–34.

[23] Buzan and Waever, *Regions and Powers*, pp. 43–4. Perhaps the earliest and most comprehensive IR-theoretic accounts of South Asia's international relations are those by Barry Buzan, "A Framework for Regional Security Analysis", Gowher Rizvi, "Pakistan: The Domestic Determinants of Security", and idem, "The Rivalry Between India and Pakistan", all in Barry Buzan and Gowher

of RSCs derives from the interplay between, on the one hand, the anarchic structure and its balance-of-power consequences, and on the other the pressures of local geographical proximity . . . *Adjacency is potent for security because many threats travel more easily over short distances than long ones.*"[24]

For a useful definition of security for the purpose of identifying a regional security sub-system or complex, we need to consider power in combination with the historical dynamic of amity and enmity, which is only partly related to balances of power: "RSCs are defined by durable patterns of amity and enmity taking the form of subglobal, geographically coherent patterns of security interdependence."[25] This historical dynamic is much more rigid than the more fluid balance of power, even where it is related. Thus, a regional security complex is a regionally bounded historical pattern of amity and enmity as well as distribution of power. Cultural and racial ties too are important in constituting regional security complexes insofar as these focus states' attention on each other. "South Asia provides a clear example where the wars and rivalries of the subcontinent constitute a distinctive pattern that has been little affected by events in the Gulf or in South East Asia."[26]

An important point is that external actors have a much lesser impact on the historical patterns of amity and enmity than they do on the distribution of power. Indeed, they tend to acquiesce in local patterns of amity and enmity. "The specific pattern of who fears or likes whom is generally not imported from the system level but generated internally within the region by a mixture of history, politics and material conditions."[27]

Rizvi, eds, *South Asian Insecurity and the Great Powers* (London: Macmillan, 1986).

[24] Buzan and Waever, *Regions and Powers*, p. 45 (emphasis added).

[25] Ibid.

[26] Ibid., p. 46.

[27] Ibid. p. 47.

There can be a hierarchy of higher- and lower-level security complexes, ideal-typically four levels in the Cold War era: domestic, regional, super-regional, and global. For example, for India, the four levels can be India, South Asia, South Asia plus China, and the global level. Or, to conceive of India's situation during the Cold War in another way, the South Asian regional security complex can be said to be surrounded by three other regional security complexes or super-complexes: the South East Asian complex to the East, the Sino-Russian–Central Asian supercomplex to the North and the Middle East and Gulf super-complex to the West, with Afghanistan and Myanmar occupying ambiguous or multiple positions. Post-Cold War, it can be reconfigured as India, the South Asian RSC, abutted to the north and east by the Asian Super-complex consisting of the North East Asian sub-complex and the South East Asian sub-complex, the former dominated by China.

Buzan's argument that territorial disputes such as Kashmir are not just territorial but reflect political tension derived from the history and very principles of Partition in 1947 fits well with Ayoob's subaltern realist emphasis on state-making processes as a source of conflict. India and Pakistan have been engaged in building very different states and nations, one an Islamic state for the Muslims of the subcontinent, an explicitly ethno-religious state that defines itself in contrast to India in terms of the two-nation theory that Muslims and Hindus constitute two different nations, and the other a secular, multicultural state that rejects the two-nation theory. Once locked in conflict from birth due to the Partition and even more, the Kashmir events of 1947–8, the logic of enmity and of state- and nation-building based on contrasting principles plays itself out according to the realist logic of arming oneself for defence. Over time and after nuclear capabilities have been developed, it follows the logic of nuclear deterrence albeit in non-weaponised and then recessed form and with a focus on each other, while tacitly accepting subalternity within the world system and even vis-à-vis China. Hence India and Pakistan pose systemic threats to each other. India's secular federalism threatens Pakistan with dismemberment or absorption while Pakistan's subcontinental Muslim nationalism threatens India with the secession of Kashmir.

Rizvi reinforces these points, directly bringing in domestic, ideological and psychological factors: The polarisation (between Hindus and Muslims in undivided India) occurred not so much because of irreconcilable incongruities or any deep-seated animosities but merely because of irritants and apprehensions which the minority community suffered. It was largely psychological. Minority groups in all societies perceive a threat and are anxious to preserve their separate identity and culture. Whether such perceptions by the Indian Muslims is real or imagined is immaterial. Fears can be genuine without being well-based. What is important is that the Muslims harboured such anxieties and the majority community, or their leaders, did little to disarm them.[28]

He argues, about Pakistan, that three factors contribute to national insecurity (as a state of mind): a narrow and weakly defined purpose in terms of the concept of Islamic state; the absence of consensus on the evolution of national institutions; and the heterogeneous nature of the state. The rivalry between India and Pakistan is also because of *inter alia* viewing the rivalry as a zero-sum game, thus perpetuating it. Rizvi views the South Asian complex as a lop-sided bipolarity – bipolar because Pakistan is able to back up its claims militarily.

Several other scholars theorising about South Asia's international relations reinforce the point about the domestic political, ideological, and psychological roots of the conflict between India and Pakistan, which can be extended to the uneasy relationship in most of the postcolonial period between India and its smaller South Asian neighbours. Sumit Ganguly argues that three structural factors – the messy nature of the British colonial disengage-

[28] Rizvi, "The Rivalry Between India and Pakistan", p. 94.

ment policy, the ideological commitments of the leaderships of India and Pakistan, and the strength of the irredentist/anti-irredentist relationship (about Kashmir) between the two countries, influenced at various times by other situational factors (immediate political compulsions) – account for the enduring nature of the conflict between India and Pakistan.[29] He brings in ethnicity (religiously defined in this case) through the concept of irredentism – the desire on the part of a state to revise some portion of its international boundaries to incorporate the ethnic/religious/linguistic minority of a contiguous state and the territory it occupies.

Kanti Bajpai and Stephen Cohen also emphasise, besides power asymmetry, territorial and border problems, ideological differences over nation-building strategies and ethnic conflict and its international fallout.[30] Maya Chadda roots the conflicts between states in domestic politics, ethnicity, and separatism.[31] She rejects the separation of the domestic from the international and argues, very much like Ayoob, that international conflict, to a considerable degree, is rooted in the process of nation-building, especially when ethnic groups straddle borders. Rajat Ganguly addresses the same problem in great detail, analysing the motivations and consequences of "kin state" intervention in ethnic conflicts.[32]

From the foregoing I argue that the best explanation of Indian and Pakistani conflict behaviour and their dyadic focus on each other is from a combination of the Subaltern Realist perspective and the Regional Security Complex approach, building on the approaches of Ayoob, and Buzan and Waever. It would appear from the apparent subaltern and regionally bounded mindsets of both

[29] Ganguly, *The Origins of War.*

[30] Kanti P. Bajpai and Stephen P. Cohen, eds, *South Asia After the Cold War: International Perspectives* (Boulder, CO: Westview, 1990).

[31] Maya Chadda, *Ethnicity, Security and Separatism in India* (New Delhi: Oxford University Press, 1997).

[32] Rajat Ganguly, *Kin State Intervention in Ethnic Conflict: Lessons from South Asia* (New Delhi: Sage, 1998).

India (despite its formal invocation of the Chinese nuclear threat) and Pakistan as regards their nuclear postures, that what is happening is a playing out of Ayoob's subaltern realism *within the bounds* of the South Asian regional security complex: capabilities, state-making processes rooted in domestic politics and in history (the partition of the subcontinent), and the resultant patterns of enmity determining outcomes in a South Asia nested in a larger extra-regional supercomplex that includes China and a world system dominated by far more powerful countries, that are taken for granted by the subaltern actors.

However, while the subaltern realism of state-making processes within the bounds of a regional security complex goes a long way to explain the pattern of conflict between India and Pakistan, does it explain nuclearisation and its specific timing and pattern of follow through or lack of it? I would argue that while the specific timing of the 1974 and 1998 tests cannot have been predicted or cannot be explained by subaltern realism and regional security complex theory, they do explain the lack of urgency on the Indian side at least, to a greater extent than mainstream deterrence theory or neorealism. The pattern of state-making and nation-building has historically linked India and Pakistan, not India and China or India and the West, in a pattern of enmity rooted in the partition and the contrasting principles on which the nation-building process in India and Pakistan were based. This would explain the regionally bounded mindset of India, its obsession with Pakistan and its relatively relaxed attitude to China despite 1962 and the latter's nuclearisation. It would also, when the nuclearisation issue is viewed through this lens, explain its slow-motion character, since India's nuclear capability was always adequate to deter Pakistan because it was the main perceived threat and ideological antithesis of India. Add to this regional security complex theory's emphasis on adjacency rooted in the fact that military threats, given the two states' plains frontiers and conventional capabilities, travel more easily between the two than over the Himalayas, and one can understand why weaker Pakistan is seen as the more immediate threat. Therefore, even in explaining the pattern of nuclearisation subaltern realism and regional security complex theory give us greater purchase.

As far as developing possible theories of India–Pakistan conflict resolution processes is concerned, what emerges from the foregoing is a need to incorporate at least three other perspectives. The first would be constructivist perspectives on the shaping of state behaviour not only by threats arising from territorial/border disputes and the balance of power, but also perceptions of such threats and of other states shaped by historically evolved domestic and international norms, including state ideology and patterns of amity and enmity. Incorporation of cognitive psychology and the imagery of the various "others" would need to be a part of such theorising.

The second would be the incorporation of domestic politics. To come to grips with the roots of conflict in South Asia, this would need to go beyond party politics and their impact on foreign policy but critically examine the very way the state has been historically constructed, including the rights of different groups in the society and the ideology and rhetoric of the state and political leaders as regards its identity, and the position taken, explicitly or implicitly, towards different ethnic groups. The focus would need to be the impact of the domestic political system on inter-group power-sharing with a focus on minorities and minority regions. Viewing India and Pakistan historically and contemporaneously in the light of consociational theory, which focuses on group rights and representation in power, could be fruitful.[33]

The third, not explored in the literature, is the asymmetry between large and small states in a regional security complex, the scale

[33] See Katherine Adeney, "Constitutional Centring: Nation Formation and Consociational Federalism in India and Pakistan", *Commonwealth and Comparative Politics*, vol. 40, no. 3 (November 2002), pp. 8–33, for a historical analysis of the Partition movement using consociationalist categories.

of which is unique in South Asia, combined with special emphasis on understanding the implications for relative gains from the standpoint of all the states concerned. The implications of this are only dealt with in passing as the recourse to alliances or "cliency" on the part of small states to resolve their security dilemma, particularly superpower protection vis-à-vis regional threats, and subsumed under superpower/external power intervention in the context of South Asia.[34] What must be incorporated into an understanding of the dynamics of stable co-operation-building in situations where there is a structural asymmetry of power is a rational choice-theoretic approach to international coalitions and alliances that focus on the interactions between larger and smaller partners/players, drawing on but not limited to economic cooperation arrangements.

After Nuclear Deterrence: Locked into Conflict or Moving Toward Peace?

To shift gears to implications for the future, will nuclear deterrence lead to peace in a gradual manner, now that military options for achieving political and territorial goals are no longer feasible? Or will it only lock India and Pakistan into a permanent conflict and slow arms race? But first, what is peace? Non-war? Cold war? The ugly stability of violent peace of low-intensity warfare? Bajpai and Cohen have categorised the competition between states into five categories: war, cold war, détente, entente, and integration.[35] They envisage the most likely path as being from the present regional cold war to a future regional détente via confidence-building measures (CBMs). While it is vital to go beyond deterrence (that is, cold war or détente) via CBMs to viable and stable regional entente and integration, what are the policies/conditions necessary

[34] For a classic case of a small state resorting to "cliency" as a strategy to protect its security interests, see Mary-Ann Treteault, "Autonomy, Necessity and the Small State: Ruling Kuwait in the Twentieth Century", *International Organization*, vol. 45, no. 4 (Autumn 1991), pp. 565–91.

[35] Bajpai and Cohen, eds, *South Asia After the Cold War*.

for this to happen? I will argue that three broad sets of policies – military, regional, and domestic political – are needed.

In the military sphere, the process of institutionalising CBMs and managing deterrence between two antagonists can itself, as during the Cold War, lead to the institutionalised interaction of co-operative security management that stabilises deterrence and leads to some sort of détente.[36] However, it is essential for a broad vision of the eventual future to be agreed upon first in order for interim CBMs to work, at least in political relationships. Progress on difficult issues in bilateral relationships can be made only when there is overall progress on other issues and a common vision of the future is developed.[37]

The relative gains calculus can, arguably, shift in favour of the smaller/weaker state in the case of a nuclear face-off, as in the case of India and Pakistan after 1998. This is because in the case of nuclear weapons the offense–defence balance shifts in favour of defence. Since a state with a nuclear deterrent above a certain threshold of survivability has an assured retaliatory capacity (at least in the South Asian eyeball-to-eyeball context), the weaker state would not necessarily find the relative gains security calculus shifting against it if the stronger state builds up its nuclear or even conventional capabilities (perhaps vis-à-vis a third state). Also, relative gains in the economic sphere are not easily convertible to those in the security sphere under nuclear deterrence. It may be possible to live with asymmetry without jeopardising the weaker state's security, as has been the case with China and the Soviet Union during the Cold War, China and the United States today, and Pakistan and India. Thus, if stable deterrence can be established in a managed way, the relative gains barrier to cooperation can, arguably, be overcome. However, the issue of whether deeper integration can pose

[36] Morgan, *Deterrence Now*, p. 4.

[37] For a survey of the then-existing CBMs in South Asia, see Dipankar Banerjee, ed., *Confidence Building Measures in South Asia* (Colombo: Regional Centre for Strategic Studies, September 1999).

long-term threats to security, or deprive a threatened state of an exit option, needs to be thought through.

In building regional co-operation, apart from the self-evident importance of economic co-operation in creating mutual stakes, (1) consensus among partner countries on a common regional political and rights regime based on values such as respect for democracy, human rights and, derivatively, treatment of minorities, and (2) willingness to be judged by a supranational body on these matters, can create confidence both at a state-to-state and people-to-people level. Effective power-sharing arrangements and minority rights may positively impact the assessment of *intentions* by neighbouring states and peoples where the majority group may be in a minority and vice versa, instead of their going by capabilities alone. The European Union, which has gone furthest down the road to regional integration despite a historical pattern of amity and enmity that led to two world wars, is a good example. The EU emphasises democracy as an eligibility criterion for membership. The much broader Council of Europe whose membership has expanded in the post-Cold War period, has had a European Convention for the Protection of Human Rights and Fundamental Freedoms, and associated institutions of a European Commission of Human Rights and European Court of Human Rights, now merged into a single European Court of Human Rights. In 1998, a Framework Convention for the Protection of National Minorities came into effect as a derivative of the former agreements and institutions, and is the first-ever legally binding instrument devoted to the general protection of national minorities. These are the sorts of agreements that create confidence in the goodwill of partner states *towards each other's peoples*, and need to be studied for their lessons for South Asia.

Finally, domestic political change that institutionalises the rights of minorities and minority regions and some sort of power-sharing between various groups and regions is needed. This is very important given the importance of perceptions, including perceptions of intentions, in shaping foreign policy and cooperative behaviour, including their importance in shaping sensitivity to relative gains over absolute gains. Edward Kolodziej's argument about post-Cold War security studies, viz. that security studies must extend *inter alia* to consideration of denial of rights and illegitimate order within a state as factors vitally affecting security, is relevant here.[38] This perspective places the issue of majoritarianism in domestic political power structures and processes squarely on the security and inter-state conflict resolution agenda. One can add that this should have been an integral part of security studies all along, particularly in South Asia.

Crucial to the success of the policies outlined above is what the largest state in a regional sub-system would need to do to build a viable regional alliance or co-operative arrangement. It would need to induce the smaller states to bandwagon rather than attempt to balance them. What is critical here is the willingness and ability of the largest state, and one which is seen as an actual or potential threat by its neighbours, to accept a disproportionately high share of the costs of alliance, and gain a disproportionately lower share of the immediate benefits, e.g. accept non-reciprocal trade liberalisation in categories of goods in exchange for long-term increase in regional and global status as a result of being the largest country in a political and/or economic bloc.

To sum up, one can conceive of deterrence moving toward peace in three overlapping stages and sets of policies on nuclear deterrence management, regional and domestic political regimes. First, the stabilisation of deterrence by co-operative security management including the organising of orderly build-ups in parallel is needed. Second, the building of economic co-operation and regional political regimes leading to economic interpenetration and mutual stakes as well as to a EU/Council of Europe-type of shared political value framework of democratic and multicultural priorities. And third, political co-operation including domestic reconstitution in

[38] Edward A. Kolodziej, "Whither Security Studies After the Cold War?", in Bajpai and Cohen, eds, *South Asia After the Cold War*, pp. 15–46.

line with non-discriminating citizenship, a secular state, minority rights, federalism, power-sharing, and so forth, would be required.

This is not to say that nuclear deterrence need necessarily lead to this outcome, only that given the right policies it can arguably do so. It can freeze the relationship into a conflictual mould with each side ratcheting up tensions by arms-racing. Deterrence need not stabilise South Asia. It could heighten and freeze conflict. If India attempts to threaten Pakistan, as in 2002, or if hardline Hindu chauvinism becomes dominant in India, unconstrained by coalition politics, Pakistan could feel a permanent threat from India. Parties subscribing to the explicitly Hindu chauvinist and anti-Muslim Hindutva ideology got 20–27 per cent of the vote in the five elections India had from 1991 to 2004. And if India adopts hegemonic objectives, it could feel permanently constrained and frustrated due to its inability to exercise a dominance or hegemony it might feel natural given its size. That is, it could feel that Pakistan de facto achieves strategic parity due to nuclear deterrence, diminishing India and turning a "naturally" unipolar region into a de facto bipolar situation, which in turn means a huge defeat for India's larger ambitions seen in a 50- to 100-year time frame as it remains locked into South Asia in a defensive posture by Pakistan and China.

There are, broadly and schematically speaking, four possible combinations of the domestic political situation in both countries, each of which has implications for whether deterrence can lead to peace. These are:

India under secular, liberal parties, Pakistan under hardline Islamism.
India under secular, liberal parties, Pakistan under moderate Islamism.
India under Hindutva parties, Pakistan under hardline Islamism.
India under Hindutva parties, Pakistan under moderate Islamism.

It would appear that the positive outcome of deterrence leading to peace, via the kinds of military, regional, economic, and domestic policies outlined above, stands the best chance under combination (b) which appears to fit the situation obtaining under the Congress-led United Progressive Alliance government in India and the Musharraf regime in Pakistan.

Lastly, does conflict resolution between India and Pakistan require denuclearisation? Not necessarily, I would argue. From India's South Asia and Pakistan-centric nuclear behaviour and deterrence pattern and the fact that severe political conflict preexisted the 1974 nuclear test, it is clear that nuclearisation is more a manifestation of deeper underlying conflicts (including between India and China, and between India and the global non-proliferation regime) than their cause. Therefore, while the nuclear issue has become one of the points central to India–Pakistan conflict, it need not be a stumbling block, and might even be a driver of conflict resolution given the pressing importance of nuclear war avoidance and, as argued earlier, reducing the relative gains problem to co-operation due to the shift in the offense–defence balance towards defence, enabling security despite asymmetry. This is supported by the fact that, post-1990, the Cold War between the USSR/Russia and the NATO bloc ended without substantial denuclearisation, the strategic capabilities and targets not being significantly changed.

What conflict resolution requires in South Asia is a resolution of territorial and ideological conflict. Regional conflict resolution need not mean moving toward denuclearisation in South Asia irrespective of the global nuclear situation. Indian nuclear policy, at least in the long run, is also officially motivated by perceived threats from China, from the discriminatory stands of the declared nuclear powers, and to secure India's long-term security in an uncertain world order. If this is meant seriously, then there should be no conflict between far-reaching moves to resolve conflict with Pakistan and the position of Indian nuclear nationalists. For the Indo-Pakistan conflict actually detracts from the stature of India in the wider world by reducing India's perceived and effective power to be India-minus-Pakistan, boxes India into South

Asia and reduces its leverage in international forums. Pakistan's potential is, arguably, similarly retarded by being locked into a nuclear confrontation with India. A fundamental resolution of conflict with Pakistan and associated moves towards greater non-hegemonic South Asian integration *a la* the EU or ASEAN, will surely improve the status of India and each of its neighbours in the larger world arena. Perhaps in the future, absurd (and outrageous to some) as it may seem today, a joint, back-to-back Indo-Pak or joint South Asian nuclear deterrent may be possible and desirable to the extent that nuclear weapons remain the currency of power in a continuingly conflict-ridden and uncertain world.

11

Indo–Sri Lanka Relations

Geopolitics, Domestic Politics, or Something More Complex?

Historical Background

INDIA'S RELATIONS with Sri Lanka began after the latter's independence from Britain on 4 February 1948. Relations with the island state have been determined by a number of factors that have shifted in relative importance over time. Some of these factors are the same as those that determine India's relations with its other neighbours – geography, the legacy of British colonial rule, the relationship inherited from the colonial period, geopolitical alignments, economic relations, and personal relationships between the leaders. In this paper, which is interpretative, I will analyse the evolution of India's Sri Lanka policy and its drivers in terms of three levels of analysis – the systemic, domestic, and personal. While all three factors have played a role, my argument will be that domestic politics has been the most significant factor in shaping Indian policy, but in a way that is different from most other analyses which share this conclusion.

Colonial Ceylon was directly ruled from Britain and was not part of the British Indian Empire.[1] During the colonial period, beginning from the 1830s, Indian indentured labour was taken to the

[1] For a very select list of works on India–Sri Lanka relations from varied perspectives, see Bhasin (2001), de Silva (2012), DeVotta (2004), Dixit (1998),

Central Highlands of Sri Lanka to constitute the labour force of the plantation sector. This population came to be called the Indian-origin Tamils or (tea, rubber) estate/plantation Tamils (numbering 842,000, or 4.2 per cent of the population in 2012). They are a community distinct from the native Sri Lankan Tamils (11.2 per cent of the population in 2011), who were a majority of the population in the Northern and Eastern Provinces of the island at independence, and are still the vast majority in the north and 40 per cent in the east (2011 Sri Lanka census). The deteriorating relationship between the majority Sinhalese, who are about three-quarters of the population, and the minority Tamils, since independence and especially since the early 1980s, has been a major factor in Indo–Sri Lanka relations, as has been Sri Lanka's shifting geopolitical alignment since the late 1970s and again in the 2000s.

Starting from shortly after independence, Sri Lanka (Ceylon till 1972) established itself under the 1948 Soulbury constitution as a unitary state under the effective control of the majority Sinhalese, who constituted three-quarters of the population, and who were overwhelmingly Buddhist. The official language policy of 1956 made Sinhalese the sole official language, threatening the prospects of the Tamils in public employment, a sphere in which they were then relatively overrepresented due to the early emergence of an English-educated professional class, in turn due to the impact of missionary education in the Tamil heartland, Jaffna, in the north. Sinhalese majoritarianism went from strength to strength from the 1950s onwards. Two important pacts between prime ministers and the leaders of the main Tamil party, the (S.W.R.D.) Bandaranaike–(S.J.V.) Chelvanayakam pact of 1957 and the Dudley Senanayake–Chelvanayakam pact of 1965, which made concessions to Tamil speakers on matters of language, education, public

---

Ganguly (1999: chapter 6), Ghosh (2003), Gokhale (2009), Krishna (1999), Mehrotra (2011), Swamy (1994, 2003, 2010), and the annual reports of the Ministry of External Affairs, Government of India, over the years.

employment, and limited regional autonomy in the Tamil-majority Northern and Eastern Provinces, were not honoured.[2] Tamil speakers were progressively marginalised in public employment, and from the early 1970s in university admissions, under a "standardisation" policy that favoured the backward provinces, in effect the Sinhalese. State-sponsored colonisation schemes settled Sinhalese in considerable numbers in the Tamil-majority Eastern Province, significantly altering its demography such that, by 2011, Tamil speakers were down to about three-quarters of the population overall and less than that in the Trincomalee district that connects the Northern and Eastern Provinces. The 1972 republican constitution officially established Buddhism as having a special status and removed the 1948 Soulbury constitution's protection of minority rights, completing the establishment of a Sinhalese-Buddhist majoritarian unitary state. The 1978 constitution concentrated power in the hands of an executive president, inevitably a Sinhala Buddhist, against a weak parliament. Major anti-Tamil riots, in which state forces and politicians were involved, took place in 1956, 1958, 1977, 1981, and 1983.

From the late 1940s to the 1970s, Indo–Sri Lankan relations remained normal if not cordial, both being nonaligned, Third Worldist, and state-regulated economies. Sri Lanka's nonaligned geopolitical posture was not seen as a threat by India. The major tension in the first three decades was over the citizenship status and repatriation of the Indian-origin Tamils. In 1948 itself, immediately after independence, Ceylon refused citizenship to the Indian-origin Tamils, who at that time had actually come to outnumber the native Tamils, reducing them to statelessness and therefore vulnerability in terms of lacking citizens' rights. It also wanted their repatriation to India, which Nehru resisted because he did not want to set a precedent for other overseas Indian populations (Sahadevan 1995). This was a point of tension in the relationship. However, India agreed

[2] See Ghosh (2003: Appendix III and IV, pp. 440–4), for the two pacts.

to consider repatriating some of them, and long-drawn-out negotiations took place resulting in two major agreements spaced ten years apart, the 1964 Sirimavo–Shastri accord, and the 1974 Sirimavo–Indira accord, that fixed the exact numbers to be repatriated, the rest being granted citizenship. These accords were of a piece with the broad Nehruvian policy on overseas Indians, which was to encourage the Indian communities to be good citizens of the countries they found themselves in, and to encourage the host countries to accord them full citizenship with commensurate rights, thus avoiding conflict with a range of countries that India sought to build relations with as part of the nonaligned and broad Third World grouping in world politics and at the United Nations. This strategy worked so long as the host country followed an accommodative policy. In the case of Ceylon this was not so.

India helped, short of military force, with the quelling of the uprising by the radical, then-Maoist as well as paradoxically Sinhalese-nationalist Janatha Vimukthi Peramuna in 1971. Despite Sri Lanka allowing Pakistani aircraft to refuel at its airports during the December 1971 war, India concluded the 1974 and 1976 agreements that completed the process of repatriation of Indian-origin Tamils in agreed numbers, and also recognised Sri Lankan sovereignty over the barren Kachchativu islet, against objections by the Dravida Munnetra Kazhagam (DMK) government in Tamil Nadu, without adequate safeguards for traditional fishing rights of Tamil Nadu fishermen.[3] However, Chief Minister Karunanidhi chose not to exercise the option of moving the Supreme Court, unlike West Bengal Chief Minister B.C. Roy over the Beru Bari enclave that was agreed to be ceded to the then East Pakistan in the 1960s. These developments were partly because of the personal relationship between Indira Gandhi and Sirimavo Bandaranaike, a move to keep Sri Lanka well disposed to India, but also a complete lack of foresight that

[3] See Suryanarayan (2005) for an account of the Kachchativu and maritime boundary issue.

relations with Sri Lanka could deteriorate due to the latter's domestic policies of discrimination against the Tamil minority and its fallout in India, and, likewise, that in the future the depletion of fish stocks could lead to trans-maritime boundary poaching and its political fallout.

However, it certainly cannot be interpreted as being due to any conscious bias against Tamil Nadu, as evidenced by the decision by the Congress government during the first DMK government, 1967–71, to locate one of the most vital strategic nuclear facilities at Kalpakkam in Tamil Nadu, the first fully indigenous, unsafeguarded plutonium producing reactor and reprocessing plant (and later, the crucial fast breeder reactor project at the same location). This was an act of inclusion and participation of Tamil Nadu in the most secret and sensitive core of national security, indicating trust and confidence in the leadership and people of the state whose ruling DMK party had abandoned separatism less than a decade earlier (in November 1963).

The Deterioration of Relations from the Early 1980s

Indo-Sri Lankan relations worsened from the early 1980s under the combined impact of three developments, and sharply after the July 1983 riots against the Tamil minority, widely considered a pogrom, which resulted in about 200,000–250,000 refugees crossing over to India in a short period of time (Dixit 1998: 13). The three developments were the following. First, the election of J.R. Jayawardene of the United National Party (UNP) in 1977, and his election as executive president under the new 1978 constitution, led to a distinct shift to the right in economic policy as well as a pro-American tilt in foreign policy. In the next few years, despite Indian misgivings expressed at the diplomatic level, Sri Lanka was negotiating with the US over naval facilities in Trincomalee and a Voice of America broadcast relay station on the west coast, which India suspected could be used for electronic intelligence gathering and monitoring of communications. At that time, following the strain in Indo–US relations after the US tilt towards Pakistan during the Bangladesh war of 1971, the Indian nuclear test of 1974, and the pro-Soviet tilt in Indian policy in the early 1980s after the Soviet invasion of Afghanistan, India was very sensitive to a possible US presence in Sri Lanka.[4]

Second, Sri Lanka's discriminatory and majoritarian treatment of its Tamil minority had led to the beginnings of Lankan Tamil separatism from the late 1970s with the passage of the separatists' Vaddukoddai declaration in 1976 by the Tamil United Liberation Front. The 1977 anti-Tamil riots elicited expressions of concern by India at the diplomatic level (Bhasin 2001, 3: 1077–8). The 1981 riots and the burning down of the Jaffna Public Library and its priceless collection of manuscripts in June 1981 by the Lankan security forces, and finally the massive anti-Tamil riots of late July 1983, with the participation of government ministers, led to an eruption of sympathy in Tamil Nadu and in India generally, which the government could not ignore.[5] Covert assistance, including arms and training, to Lankan Tamil rebel groups, which had been in existence from the early 1980s, was stepped up, the support being spread across a number of groups (Dixit 1998: 23; Swamy 1994: 93–114). The Sri Lankan government in its counterinsurgency policy also drew upon the support of Israeli advisers at a time when India did not have diplomatic relations with Israel, saw the latter as a surrogate for a US with whom relations were cool, and had sensitivities about neighbouring countries inviting a security presence from third countries without consulting India.

Third, President Jayawardene's relations with Prime Minister Indira Gandhi, re-elected in January 1980, were cool. During the

[4] Interview with former High Commissioner S.J.S. Chhatwal, 10 September 2013.

[5] See Bhasin (2001, 3: 1466–536) for official statements and parliamentary debates.

Janata government, he had made gratuitous remarks about her role in the Emergency, and in general was seen as disregarding Indian sensitivities.[6]

Following the July 1983 riots, clandestine Indian support to Tamil insurgent groups, including the Liberation Tigers of Tamil Eelam (LTTE), was stepped up so as to put pressure on the Sri Lankan government to accommodate the Tamils, to mollify public outrage in Tamil Nadu, and respect Indian security sensitivities (Swamy 1994: 93–114). India also offered its good offices to arrange an accommodation between the government and the rebel forces. Indira Gandhi designated a special envoy, G. Parthasarathi, to talk to both the government and the Tamil parties and groups and try to arrive at a solution to devolve and share power. Parthasarathi made three visits to Sri Lanka in late 1983 and early 1984.

Despite a draft agreement in late 1984 (called Annexure C) modelled on Indian federalism, which arguably went beyond the later 1987 Indo-Sri Lanka Accord (ISLA), which was to be but eventually was not accepted by a (Sri Lankan) All Party Conference due to Jayawardene's machinations, this mediation did not bear fruit.[7] India then arranged, under Prime Minister Rajiv Gandhi, two rounds of talks between the Tamil parties and militant groups and the government in July–August 1985 in Thimphu, Bhutan. But that too did not bear fruit as the government rejected Tamil demands, which centred on their recognition as a nation, recognition of a Tamil homeland, and self-determination for Tamils. In the meantime, the government hardened its stand and, during 1986 and 1987, made a push for a military solution by sending the army to crush the rebel groups. By May 1987, it appeared as if the main rebel group, the LTTE, then supported by India, would be defeated by the army in the Jaffna peninsula.

[6] An internal Emergency was declared by Prime Minister Indira Gandhi on 26 June 1975, which lasted until the March 1977 elections which she lost, on dubious grounds of threats to internal security.

[7] See Dixit (1998: 22–3 and Annexure V, pp. 368–70 for the text of Annexure C proposals).

Rajiv Gandhi, under pressure of circumstances, made a decision to intervene. On 4 June 1987, the Indian air force dropped food packets in the Jaffna peninsula, violating Lankan airspace and sovereignty, ostensibly to offer relief to the civilian population in response to the government's blanket cut-off of civil supplies to the peninsula. Over June and July 1987, India pressured Sri Lanka to permit a mediatory military intervention under the ISLA of 29 July 1987, although in a separate exchange of letters India would send contingents of its army called the Indian Peace Keeping Force (IPKF) to disarm the Tamil rebel groups. And in return for this Sri Lanka would amend its constitution to provide for a meaningful devolution of power to the Tamil-majority, with north and east merged into a combined North-Eastern Province, and make Tamil an additional national language. Rajiv Gandhi went to Colombo to sign the agreement only after asking and getting the concurrence of the entire opposition including the All India Anna Dravida Munnetra Kazhagam (AIADMK), then ruling Tamil Nadu, as well as its main rival DMK, although he did not, constitutionally, have to seek any such concurrence (Bhasin 2001, 3: 1943; Dixit 1998: 150).[8]

Specifically, ISLA had the following components.[9] While supporting the territorial integrity and unity of Sri Lanka, it recognised Sri Lanka as a multi-religious, multi-lingual society in which each group's identity had to be carefully nurtured. It recognised

[8] The DMK did not initially criticise the accord, but after Prabhakaran's speech of 4 August 1984 criticising the accord while only grudgingly accepting it, N.V.N. Somu of the DMK echoed this criticism in the Lok Sabha on 18 August 1987, while not disowning the accord (Bhasin 2001, 4: 2019–21). The criticism that the accord should not have been signed by India but by the Sri Lankan government and the LTTE, and that Prabhakaran was kept in the dark till the last moment, has been contested by Indian diplomat Hardeep S. Puri, who discussed the terms with Prabhakaran in Jaffna in July prior to the accord. He maintains that Prabhakaran agreed to the main points, but also that he wanted India to sign it with Sri Lanka and did not want to sign an agreement himself. Interview with Ambassador Hardeep S. Puri, 9 May 2014.

[9] See Dixit (1998: Annexures II and III, pp. 355–61) for the texts of ISLA and the letters exchanged.

the Northern and Eastern Provinces as the historical habitation of the Tamil-speaking peoples. It provided for the devolution of power, including the subjects of land, police, and finances, to the provinces, and the recognition of Tamil as an official language. In exchange for this, India undertook to deploy a peace-keeping force to disarm the rebel groups, while the Sri Lankan army was to be confined to the barracks in the merged North-Eastern Province. In addition, there was a supplement to the agreement consisting of an exchange of letters that addressed Indian security interests, in that Sri Lanka undertook not to allow its territory, including Trincomalee port, to be used by third powers to the detriment of India's security, and India undertook to not allow its territory to be used for separatist militancy in Sri Lanka.

The Tamil rebel groups were not a party to the agreement, although it was very grudgingly accepted with explicit reservations by Prabhakaran on 4 August 1987 in Jaffna, and with equally great reluctance by the Sinhalese. The IPKF was deployed immediately starting from 30 July 1987, and initially a token surrender of arms by the Tamil groups including the LTTE was arranged in early August. However, Prabhakaran soon went back on his initial acceptance of the accord, and afterwards began to provoke the IPKF by organising demonstrations and a fast unto death (in September by Dileepan) against it.

The situation deteriorated after the 3–5 October incident in which the Sri Lankan navy arrested over a dozen LTTE guerrillas smuggling arms and transported them to Colombo against the appeal of Indian High Commissioner J.N. Dixit. They committed suicide by swallowing cyanide capsules. High Commissioner Dixit had tried to stop the movement of the captured LTTE cadres to Colombo, but the IPKF commander in Jaffna, Major-General Harkirat Singh, refused to take orders from him, saying Dixit was not in his chain of command. On the Sri Lankan side, Minister Lalith Athulathmudali, an opponent of the accord, acted pre-emptively before President Jayawardene's instructions not to take the prisoners to Colombo (in response to Dixit's plea) could reach him. The LTTE blamed the IPKF for this, unfairly from India's perspective, announced a pullback from the accord, and began firing on the IPKF on 6 October, including from crowded civilian locations, killing half a dozen Indian soldiers. This led India to order an operation (Operation Pawan) against the LTTE on 6 October, commencing from 10 October. In turn, this led to a long-drawn-out guerrilla war by the LTTE against the IPKF (Dixit 1998: 209–14). The inconclusive guerrilla war lasted until the IPKF's withdrawal by 24 March 1990. The losses suffered by the IPKF were over 1100 men dead and a few thousand wounded.

In the meantime, in November 1987, the Sri Lankan parliament passed the 13th Amendment to the (1978) constitution, setting up a devolutionary arrangement in which nine provincial councils with limited devolved powers were to be set up, including a merged North-Eastern (Tamil-speaking majority) Province. The permanence of the merger was to be decided by a referendum in the Eastern Province.[10] This was meant to give effect to the ISLA (although India has always maintained that the 13th Amendment only partially and in a diluted form reflected the agreement, and has pressed for "full implementation" of the agreement, though taking the 13th Amendment as a useful starting point).[11] Elections to the North-Eastern Provincial Council were held in November 1988, despite a boycott and armed obstruction by the LTTE. A North-Eastern Provincial Government headed by a chief minister (A. Varadaraja Perumal) was set up and began to function, however ineffectively given the LTTE's guerrilla war, under the protection of the IPKF, although without the still-to-be-devolved land, police, and fiscal powers.

[10] The text of the 13th Amendment is available at: http: //www. satp.org/satporgtp/countries/shrilanka/document/acts and ordinance/13th_Amendment.pdf, accessed 19 February 2015.

[11] Interview with former High Commissioner L.L. Mehrotra, 11 September 2013.

Understanding the Nature and Motivations of the Intervention

A crucial question is why India, after taking the risk of violating Sri Lankan sovereignty, and over the previous few years clandestinely arming and training the Tamil militants, opted for a relatively weak devolutionary solution in the ISLA that fell far short of even India's then relatively centralised federalism or even Annexure C of 1984. This is part of the reason why the agreement was rejected by the LTTE as falling far short of its aspirations. There was also a trust deficit in the Sri Lankan government that made the LTTE loath to surrender arms in exchange for vague promises and mere devolution within a still-unitary state. It appears that Jayawardene was not willing to go any further for fear of his own overthrow and opposition from his cabinet, party, parliament, and public opinion. Hence, India had to either settle for the terms of devolution as they emerged in the accord, or not have an agreement, which would result in a resumption of military action against the Tamils (Dixit 1998: 149).

What is crucial to understand about the 1987–90 military intervention and the subsequent trajectory of developments is the circumstances of the withdrawal ("de-induction") of the IPKF (Mehrotra 2011).[12] President Ranasinghe Premadasa, elected in December 1988 and an opponent of the ISLA and the IPKF's deployment, announced on 1 June 1989 that he wanted the IPKF withdrawn by the second anniversary of the ISLA, that is, by 29 July 1989. This resulted in a long-drawn-out battle over the withdrawal of the IPKF over the final six months of Rajiv Gandhi's term as prime minister. Gandhi, while agreeing in principle to eventually withdraw the IPKF, refused to commit to a date and kept linking withdrawal to the implementation of devolution to the North-Eastern Provincial Council as part of the agreement. The Premadasa government began covertly arming the LTTE, which also wanted an

[12] Ibid.

immediate withdrawal of the IPKF, calculating that it could then overthrow the seen-to-be-inadequate North-Eastern Provincial Council run by the pro-India Eelam People's Revolutionary Liberation Front (EPRLF) led by Perumal, as well as defeating the Sri Lankan army and gaining an independent Tamil Eelam. The demand for the IPKF's withdrawal also began to be supported by the DMK government in Tamil Nadu, elected in January 1989, and by the Janata Dal–led opposition to the Congress in the November 1989 national election, of which electoral alliance the DMK was a partner (Swamy 1994: 310–16). This position was motivated by the perverse and unexpected outcome of the Indian intervention, intended to secure Tamil rights, that of the IPKF ending up fighting the main Tamil rebel group.

After the victory of the Janata Dal-led National Front government, supported by the Bharatiya Janata Party (BJP) and the Left Front, Prime Minister V.P. Singh and Foreign Minister I.K. Gujral initially stuck to the stand that IPKF withdrawal was tied to the implementation of the agreement, that is, devolution (the North-Eastern Provincial Council constantly complained that Colombo had not devolved even the limited land, police and financial powers that were in the 13th Amendment). But on 6 January 1990, the V.P. Singh government agreed to unconditionally withdraw the IPKF by the end of March 1990 (it was actually withdrawn by 24 March 1990), thereby delinking withdrawal from devolution (Mehrotra 2011). Karunanidhi, who was asked to help bring the various Tamil groups including the LTTE under one umbrella to stabilise the North-Eastern Council, tried to do so but failed. The result was that the EPRLF leadership fled to India with the IPKF, the North-Eastern Provincial Council collapsed, and very soon war resumed between the LTTE and Colombo's army and continued in three different phases (1990–5, 1995–2001, 2006–9) until the defeat and liquidation of the LTTE in May 2009.

What were India's motivations for the intervention of 1987–90? Was it strategic, driven by concern about the international and security alignment of the Sri Lankan government in the 1980s? Or was it driven by domestic politics, that is, by pressure from Tamil Nadu public opinion and the regional parties of Tamil Nadu (AIADMK, DMK) in their concern for the Sri Lankan Tamils? The best answer seems to be that it was a combination of overlapping and mutually reinforcing motivations in a situation where security concerns and domestic politics coincided and led to an intervention of the type that was undertaken, subject to international structural constraints.

To elaborate, the belief that Sri Lanka might permit a US naval facility in Trincomalee, and an electronic intelligence facility on its west coast, caused great concern and was one of the motivations for destabilising the government by supporting the Tamil rebels even before the watershed July 1983 riots (de Silva 2012: 63; Krishna 1999: 223–4). Second, the enormous concern and pressure to do something that arose in Tamil Nadu, including from Congress Party MPs from the state, was also a factor in the post-riots period (Krishna 1999: 223–4). This has to be placed in context. While neither the Indira nor Rajiv government's majority depended on either the MPs of its regional ally the AIADMK, nor even on the Congress MPs from Tamil Nadu, the state's importance derived also from concerns about the possible long-term alienation of public opinion in Tamil Nadu if the Indian government ignored atrocities against Tamils in Sri Lanka.

The DMK had until 1963 been a party with a separatist platform. And although this had been decisively repudiated by the party in November 1963, and was never revived after it came to power in 1967, making Tamil Nadu a successful case of India's unofficial nation-building strategy of unity through accommodation, there remained an underlying concern about the revival of separatism due to a feeling that the centre and the Congress Party were not sensitive to Tamil Nadu's concerns about the Lankan Tamils. Hence, it was not possible to ignore the anti-Tamil policies of Sri Lanka.

Additionally, at the time of the July 1987 agreement, Rajiv Gandhi had decided to try to revive the fortunes of the Congress Party in Tamil Nadu by capitalising on a pro-Tamil intervention in Sri Lanka. Thus, from late 1987, in the context of the political vacuum after the death of two-term chief minister and AIADMK leader M.G. Ramachandran in December 1987, Gandhi visited Tamil Nadu every month in 1988 to rebuild his party.[13] The Congress contested the January 1989 state assembly elections on its own without an electoral alliance for the first time since 1967, and did creditably in terms of vote share (20 per cent) given this background, even though it picked up relatively few seats.

Thus, security concerns, domestic concerns at the centre about alienation in Tamil Nadu (something distinct from policy being driven by Tamil Nadu or regional party pressures, demands, or threats), and Congress revival plans in Tamil Nadu, all coincided and reinforced each other.

Indo-Sri Lanka Relations 1991–2009: Post-IPKF, Post-Assassination, Post-Cold War

The assassination of the then former prime minister Rajiv Gandhi at Sriperumbudur near Chennai on 21 May 1991 by the LTTE, while he was on an election campaign in Tamil Nadu, and the subsequent banning of the LTTE in India in 1992 after the act was traced to it, marked the beginning of the next phase in Indo–Sri Lanka relations. To set the latter in its larger context, Indian foreign policy underwent a gradual shift in the post-1991 period. Starting from the election of the Congress government of P.V. Narasimha Rao in June 1991 just after the assassination, India launched a long-term economic liberalisation programme that would gradually globalise the economy, with the merchandise trade–GDP ratio rising from 15 per cent in 1990 to about 43 per cent (57 per cent including trade in services) by 2012, and foreign investment bulking much larger in the economy. Parallel to this would be a pro-

[13] Interview with Mani Shankar Aiyar, a key aide to Rajiv Gandhi in the late 1980s, 30 April 2012.

US shift in foreign policy for both economic and strategic reasons. In economic terms, India's growth strategy needed Western capital and technology, overwhelmingly from private sources. Strategically, the collapse of the Soviet Union removed the implicit guarantee against China that the Indo–Soviet Friendship Treaty of 1971 represented. And since the Kashmir insurgency supported by Pakistan erupted from December 1989, an Indo–Pakistan war over Kashmir was always a possibility. In this larger context, Indian policy followed a dual track on South Asia, particularly from the time of the United Front government of I.K. Gujral, 1997–8, that had emphasised South Asian regional co-operation, particularly trade promotion, both for growth and to conduce to peace, as well as regional co-operation-building, both bilateral and via the South Asian Association for Regional Cooperation (SAARC), for improved relations and security. In this larger context, again, and in the context of domestic policy and political shifts in Sri Lanka, India's policy moved towards greater co-operation with Sri Lanka, particularly from the late 1990s (Basrur 2011).

This shift over the 1990s and 2000s was helped by shifts in public opinion in Tamil Nadu. Shocked by the assassination of Rajiv Gandhi, public opinion in Tamil Nadu underwent a distinct shift, in that there was a cooling off towards the LTTE from 1991 to 2008–9. In the 1991 Lok Sabha and state assembly elections, the Congress–AIADMK alliance swept to power, AIADMK's Jayalalitha forming the government in the state and cracking down hard on the LTTE. The LTTE was banned by the centre in 1992 after it was determined that the organisation had been behind the assassination. Jayalalitha remained uncompromisingly tough on the LTTE and carried the public with her, winning the 2001 assembly election, and arresting pro-LTTE apologists like Vaiko (V. Gopalaswamy) of the Marumalarchi Dravida Munnetra Kazhagam (MDMK), a minor party in Tamil Nadu that was a coalition partner of the 1998–9 BJP-led government. Incidentally, the pro-LTTE MDMK remained a minor party in Tamil Nadu, and other pro-LTTE fringe groups also remained marginal in Tamil Nadu politics, with the Sri Lankan Tamils issue remaining at best a second-order issue. However, the LTTE continued to operate a low-profile arms smuggling network using the Tamil Nadu coast and a local support network of sleeper cells, with apparent toleration of this by Indian intelligence, provided the LTTE did not create any internal problems for India.[14] This was not a policy, but apparently a low-level informal understanding, and was apparently violated by the LTTE by the training of (separatist) United Liberation Front of Assam cadres, support to separatist fringe elements in Tamil Nadu, and links with the bandit Veerappan. In retrospect, the LTTE made its biggest blunder ever in plotting the assassination, in that it seemed to have taken Tamil Nadu public support for granted on the assumption of blind ethnic solidarity, and also seemed to have made the bizarre assumption that subsequent governments at the centre could and would continue to deal with it as if the assassination of a former prime minister amounted to nothing.

Sri Lankan policy on its Tamil minority also underwent a shift under President Chandrika Kumaratunga from 1994, which helped the process of improvement of relations with India. Kumaratunga put forward proposals for resolution of the conflict, which went halfway towards a federal solution, in 1995, 1997, and 2000, the last of which can be read as an improvement on the 13th Amendment (Ghosh 2003: Appendix 6, pp. 450–8). These proposals were rejected by the LTTE, which was then bent on a sovereign Tamil Eelam and would not consider anything short of that.

The Indo–Sri Lanka Free Trade Agreement of 1998 signed by the BJP-led government of 1998–9, operational from 2000, was part of a larger shift in both foreign economic policy, South Asia policy, and Sri Lanka policy, as well as running parallel to the process of trade liberalisation in SAARC (in the form of the SAARC Preferential Trading Arrangement and the South Asian Free Trade

[14] Interview with former High Commissioner N.N. Jha, 2 October 2013.

Area) initiated in the mid-1990s. On the trade, investment, and tourism fronts, Indo-Lanka relations grew rapidly during the 2000s, particularly during the boom years for the Indian economy of 2003–8. Sri Lanka emerged as India's largest trading partner and largest investment destination in South Asia by 2012.

The gradual liberalisation of trade was reinforced by the policies of President Kumaratunga and, in the early 2000s, Prime Minister Ranil Wickramasinghe, which were felt to be serious in exploring accommodative solutions to the Tamil minority's demands. The National Democratic Alliance (NDA) government broadly followed the approach of the ISLA in encouraging a negotiated solution based on devolution of power and discouraging a military solution. It refused to intervene despite the appeal for help by Kumaratunga in the April–May 2000 crisis, when the LTTE captured Elephant Pass, the access point to the Jaffna Peninsula, and cut off some 40,000 troops. Defence co-operation, except for training slots in Indian military academies for Sri Lankan officers and the leasing of an offshore patrol vessel to the Sri Lankan Navy in 2000, was kept in abeyance.[15] This was partly because of opposition from its alliance partner, the DMK. This was the high point of the LTTE's military power. The NDA government, in a sophisticated behind-the-scenes operation, encouraged the Ceasefire Agreement (CFA) of February 2002 and the subsequent negotiations, in which Norway played the role of mediator between the Sri Lankan government and the LTTE. The process was co-chaired by the USA, the European Union, and Japan (Swamy 2010). India did not participate directly as it could not talk to the LTTE, a banned organisa-

[15] Anonymous interviews with Indian diplomat and journalists in 2014; also see Fernando. This leasing of a patrol vessel, which was renewed later by the UPA government in 2007 along with that of another such vessel, has to be seen in the context of a perception by both the NDA and UPA governments that – in the context of the 1995, 1997, and 2000 proposals for power-sharing by the Sri Lankan governments and the LTTE walkout from the Cease Fire Agreement in 2003 – the LTTE was the intransigent party to the conflict.

tion. However, it was kept fully informed and played a behind-the-scenes role in trying to arrange a federal solution. This was, however, rejected by the LTTE, which walked out of the dialogue process after six rounds, in April 2003, leaving India and the Western world with the impression that it, not the government, was the intransigent party in the process.

Three important developments changed the context of Indo–Sri Lankan relations in 2004. First, in March 2004, the LTTE split, with the bulk of its fighters in the Eastern Province defecting to the breakaway group led by Vinayakamoorthy Muralidharan, nicknamed Karuna, namely, the Tamil Makkal Viduthalai Puligal, which revolted against Prabhakaran's leadership and co-operated with the regime. Second, the UNP lost the parliamentary election, and the co-habitation arrangement between the UNP prime minister Ranil Wickramasinghe and the Sri Lanka Freedom Party (SLFP) president Kumaratunga came to an end. The relatively hawkish Sinhala nationalist Mahinda Rajapaksa became the prime minister, signalling a shift to a more hardline strategy vis-à-vis the LTTE. Third, the NDA government lost the May 2004 election and the Congress-led United Progressive Alliance (UPA) government of Manmohan Singh came to power. In Sri Lanka, although the CFA was still officially in force, negotiations were in effect frozen since the LTTE's walkout in 2003.

Meanwhile, in Sri Lanka, Mahinda Rajapaksa was elected president in November 2005, crucially helped in his victory over the dovish Ranil Wickramasinghe by the LTTE-enforced boycott of the election by Tamil voters in the Northern Province. The already hawkish Rajapaksa was provoked by LTTE actions such the Mavil Aru incident in the Eastern Province in July 2006, and the assassination attempts on the army chief Sarath Fonseka and the president's brother and defence secretary, Gotabaya Rajapaksa, in 2006. The ensuing final phase of the conflict, called Eelam War IV, 2006–9, led to the rollback and defeat of the LTTE by an army that had used the period of the CFA to modernise itself, particularly since

2005, beginning with the recapture of the Eastern Province with the help of the LTTE rebel group led by Karuna in July 2006, and ending with the decimation of the LTTE in May 2009.

The UPA minority government, in which the DMK was a key partner enjoying its highest-ever representation in the cabinet and council of ministers, followed a hands-off policy on the Sri Lankan ethnic conflict while promoting trade and investment. On forming a minority government in Tamil Nadu with Congress support in May 2006, it also declared that the centre's policy on Sri Lanka would be the state's policy. In 2008–9, while threatening to quit the UPA coalition unless the centre stopped the war in Sri Lanka, which the LTTE was losing, but not carrying out the threat, the DMK co-operated with the centre in that the state's intelligence branch actively co-operated with the Intelligence Bureau to break up the LTTE's smuggling network during the final phase of the war (Swamy 2010).[16] A key part of the reason for the DMK's co-operation in 2008–9 was that, firstly, it had a huge stake in the UPA government since it controlled key economic ministries. Secondly, bargaining power favoured the Congress, since a DMK withdrawal would not unseat the Congress as it could draw on the external support of the Samajwadi Party and Bahujan Samaj Party as it did after the Left withdrew support over the Indo-US nuclear deal in July 2008, and since the DMK minority government in Tamil Nadu depended on Congress support. In the 2009–11 period, key DMK ministers and Karunanidhi's daughter Kanimozhi, a member of parliament, were under investigation for corruption in the 2G (telecom) scam.

The UPA I government also kept defence co-operation in abeyance except for officer training, and continued to advocate a negotiated political solution right through to the defeat of the LTTE in 2009.[17] However, sometime during its tenure, possibly as early

[16] Interview with M.R. Narayan Swamy, 30 May 2014.

[17] The annual reports of the Ministry of External Affairs record a consistent official position throughout on urging Sri Lanka to go for a negotiated solution

as 2004 when J.N. Dixit was the national security adviser, but certainly after President Rajapaksa came to power in late 2005, it seems to have made a strategic decision that the LTTE was the intransigent party in the conflict, as well as a threat to Indian security due to its support to separatist fringe elements in Tamil Nadu, and hence that India would not intervene in the event of a war breaking out on the island.[18] In the event, India supplied non-lethal defensive equipment such as radars, and personnel to man the same, in response to the LTTE's use of micro-light aircraft, five Mi-17 transport helicopters (though these were used to transport troops, and hence in combat, although they were not used as gunships), and naval intelligence, along with US intelligence, to help the Sri Lankan navy sink the LTTE's arms smuggling fleet of ten ships in the final phase of the war, 2006–9, although without participation in the action (Gokhale 2009: 121).

Indo–Sri Lanka Relations after the LTTE: 2009 to 2015

The defeat of the LTTE and the decimation or surrender and capture of its entire leadership in a massive bloodbath took place in May 2009, just a couple of days after the Indian election results, in which the UPA, which included its partner DMK, was re-elected both nationally and in the seats from Tamil Nadu. This happened despite increasing public concern in Tamil Nadu from late 2008, as the Sri Lankan army used massive aerial and artillery bombardment to roll back the LTTE, about large-scale civilian

---

based on accommodating the legitimate aspirations of all communities. On defence co-operation, the UPA renewed the lease of an offshore patrol vessel transferred earlier by the NDA as well as another vessel in 2007; see note 28 for the context of such decisions.

[18] Interview with M.R. Narayan Swamy, 30 May 2014. Also see Swamy (2010) for an account of this phase. The post-2005 phase of Indian policy is the least transparent to researchers so far.

casualties among the Tamil population and the possible denial of Tamil rights and autonomy by the government in the event of an LTTE defeat. However, public opinion in Tamil Nadu, while concerned about civilian casualties and Tamil rights, cannot be interpreted as having become pro-LTTE. Nor can the stand of either the DMK, then a Congress ally, or the AIADMK, whose leader Jayalalitha urged Indian military intervention to stop the war in its closing months as the election campaign in India was in full steam, be interpreted as being pro-LTTE. In fact, neither party took a pro-LTTE or pro-Prabhakaran stand even while expressing acute concern about civilian casualties and apprehensions about Tamil rights in the event of the Sri Lankan government forcing a military solution to the ethnic conflict. In fact, the DMK–Congress alliance won the majority of Lok Sabha seats from the state (18 DMK including 1 Viduthalai Chiruthaigal Katchi, 8 Congress); the AIADMK, which had called for Indian military intervention, lost; and Vaiko's party, the pro-LTTE MDMK, lost all the seats it contested, with Vaiko losing his own election. Hence, at that point in time, public opinion in Tamil Nadu could be interpreted as being concerned about the Sri Lankan Tamils' rights, equality, and autonomy, including a separate Tamil Eelam in case these demands were denied, but not for anti-India or pro-LTTE/Prabhakaran positions, or for any separatist sentiments as regards the separation of Tamil Nadu from India. Indeed, in the period since then, as at all times since 1963, no significant party or politician in Tamil Nadu, even those expressing the strongest sympathies for the Sri Lankan Tamils or the strongest criticism of India's Sri Lanka policy, has claimed that Tamilians in India are discriminated against or expressed separatist sentiments.

The major developments after May 2009 are the following. In geopolitical terms, China and, to a much lesser extent, Pakistan established a diplomatic presence in Sri Lanka. Pakistan supplied pilots and arms during the final phase of the Eelam War (2006–9), and China supplied arms on a larger scale, while India exercised restraint due to its earlier bad experience of fighting the LTTE, its uncertainty about the Sri Lankan government's ultimate goals and intentions regarding the Tamils, and public sentiment in Tamil Nadu. Sri Lanka has since then played the "China card" against India to ward off pressures to accommodate the Tamils in a political solution based on the full implementation of the 13th Amendment involving the devolution of land, police, and fiscal powers to the north and east. China has also emerged as the largest aid donor to Sri Lanka even while India has emerged as the largest trade partner, source of tourists, and one of the major direct investors. China is also building the Hambantota port, a pet project of President Rajapaksa, which India initially turned down for financial reasons, and which India is keeping under observation in case it is used to service the growing Chinese naval presence in the Indian Ocean. However, Sri Lanka has repeatedly assured India that they will respect Indian security interests and concerns.

Second, economic integration between India and Sri Lanka has proceeded apace and constrained political options. India has become Sri Lanka's largest trading partner, with trade reaching $5 billion in 2011–12 (0.6 per cent of India's trade), with India enjoying a huge trade surplus. India has also become the largest direct investor in recent years ($800 million cumulative, $160 million in 2012), and the largest single source of tourists (176,000 or one-sixth of the influx).[19] This both gives leverage with Sri Lanka and at the same time constrains options to put pressure on Sri Lanka due to the fact that Indian economic interests have a stake in smooth trade relations with Sri Lanka.

Third, domestic politics in India has evolved since May 2009 in response to the Rajapaksa regime's policies towards the Tamil minority. While Tamil Nadu was initially quiescent, and the ruling DMK in the state, allied to the Congress Party and dependent on

[19] See http://www.mea.gov.in/Portal/ForeignRelation/India-SriLankaRelations.pdf and http://www.mea.gov.in/Portal/ForeignRelation/Sri_Lanka_January_2014.pdf, both accessed 15 February 2015.

it for its majority in the assembly, did not make an issue of the Sri Lankan Tamils, tacitly accepting the assurances of the Rajapaksa regime that it would implement the 13th Amendment and more, that is, 13++, left undefined, public opinion in the state gradually became more concerned about the regime's non-implementation, indeed, its movement backward on its promises. India's decision to vote against Sri Lanka in the United Nations Human Rights Council (UNHCR) twice in succession, in March 2012 and March 2013, despite such a vote potentially having an impact on India itself due to the fact that the Kashmir issue could similarly become internationalised, was due to mutually reinforcing factors, namely, pressures from Tamil Nadu parties and from the Congress' own Tamil Nadu unit, and the increasingly blatant reneging on commitments made to India at the highest level by the Rajapaksa regime.[20] Since the AIADMK's victory in the state assembly election of May 2011, Chief Minister Jayalalitha has chosen to raise the issue of the Sri Lankan Tamils forcefully, and a process of ratcheting up of demands on the centre on this issue by both the AIADMK and the DMK due to political competition has unfolded. Resolutions have been passed in the Tamil Nadu assembly demanding a UN referendum on self-determination by the Tamils in Sri Lanka's Northern and Eastern Provinces; there have been demands for an economic boycott, for cancellation of defence training and joint naval exercises (which were commenced after the defeat of the LTTE), and for condemnation of Sri Lanka in the UNHCR. The issue of fishing rights and the ceding of Kachchativu in the 1970s has been revived due to frequent Sri Lankan shooting and arrests of Indian fishermen over the past decade and particularly after the war, and efforts are on to reduce tensions. All

[20] However, the lame-duck UPA II government abstained on the US-moved UNHCR resolution on Sri Lanka in March 2014 because the resolution called for an international inquiry, something that would have set an uncomfortable precedent for India in that it could have been cited by Pakistan vis-à-vis Kashmir.

this reflects a combination of political competition and frustration with the non-implementation of the Rajapaksa regime's promises on sharing of power with the Tamils, and its ill-concealed intent to move backward rather than forward on the Tamil issue, including perhaps even gradual state-sponsored colonisation of the Tamil-majority provinces. Paradoxically, or perhaps not – see my argument later in this paper – India took a tougher stand on the Tamil issue with Sri Lanka *after* the DMK left the UPA II coalition in March 2013, at the time of India's UNHCR vote against Sri Lanka, on the grounds that the US-sponsored resolution was not strong enough, and that the centre had tried to dilute it. (The truth was that the US was against a stronger resolution that might not pass, as a number of non-Western states would have reservations in backing a stronger and more intrusive human rights resolution.) As a reaction to moves by the Rajapaksa regime, signalled by Defence Secretary Gotabaya Rajapaksa in May–July 2013, to either do away with the 13th Amendment and the provincial council system altogether, or dilute its devolutionary provisions, India intervened in the form of a telephone call on 17 May 2013 from Foreign Minister Salman Khurshid to his Sri Lankan counterpart G.L. Peiris, warning against any dilution of the 13th Amendment's provisions or cancelling the first-ever elections to the Northern Provincial Council (NPC) that were scheduled for September 2013 (*Sunday Times* 2013). National Security Adviser Shiv Shankar Menon reinforced this message in early July on his visit, pressing for full implementation of the 13th Amendment and for holding of the NPC elections.[21] The implicit threat was that of a boycott of the Commonwealth Heads of Government Meeting (CHOGM) that was scheduled to be held in Colombo in November 2013, and/or further action at the UNHCR. This led to the NPC elections being held on schedule on 21 September 2013,

[21] Interview with Harsh Vardhan Shringla, Joint Secretary (Bangladesh, Sri Lanka, Maldives), 30 September 2013.

which resulted in a sweeping victory for the main Tamil political coalition, the Tamil National Alliance, which had been in regular dialogue with the Indian government, and a resounding defeat for Rajapaksa's ruling United People's Freedom Alliance (UPFA) coalition. The NPC is now the only one of the nine provincial councils not controlled by the ruling UPFA. Prime Minister Manmohan Singh did not attend the Colombo CHOGM summit, sending another signal.[22]

The defeat of Rajapaksa and the coming to power of the new president, Maithripala Sirisena, in the January 2015 presidential election has improved relations. The Sirisena government has been attempting to correct the diplomatic tilt towards China to a greater orientation towards the West and India, and in this context the new president visited India in February 2015 and hosted a return visit by Prime Minister Narendra Modi in March 2015. Sri Lankan domestic politics and foreign policy are in flux and it remains to be seen how the relationship evolves.

Interpreting the Motives Behind India's Sri Lanka Policy

Taking a historical overview of India's Sri Lanka policy, what have been the key motivations and drivers? Has it been driven by systemic considerations? Has it been motivated by strategic concerns

[22] A critical view of India's Sri Lanka policy is that of former Foreign Secretary (2009–11) Nirupama Rao who was also High Commissioner to Sri Lanka (2004–6) who holds that Sri Lanka is a major foreign policy failure for India in that the policy was passive and reactive and no attempt to combat the LTTE narrative and champion the Tamil cause from an alternative perspective during both NDA and UPA, and in the case of the UPA there was no Plan B in case the Rajapaksa regime reneged on its promises to share power with the Tamils in exchange for diplomatic support against the LTTE despite there being grounds for suspecting his bona fides due to his repeated double speak on the issue of power-sharing. Interview with Ambassador Nirupama Rao, 9 January 2015.

about the possible acquisition of facilities by the US (in the early 1980s), or by China under the Rajapaksa regime? Undoubtedly, India is extremely sensitive to any third-power presence in Sri Lanka, and Indira Gandhi's decision to exploit Tamil grievances to destabilise the Jayawardene government in the early 1980s had this motivation among others. Likewise, concern about the Rajapaksa regime's proximity to China during Eelam War IV (2006–9) and since, at a time of a growing Chinese naval presence in the Indian Ocean, has undoubtedly led Indian policy towards the competitive wooing of Rajapaksa with aid, defence training, and other inducements. However, strategic concerns alone do not explain policy. If this was so, then India could well have abandoned the Tamil minority to woo successive Sri Lankan regimes to induce bandwagoning towards itself. This has not been the case either in the 1980s or since, whether at the height of the LTTE's power at the time of the CFA in the early 2000s, or even after the LTTE's defeat. Hence, it is necessary to factor in domestic politics for a fuller and more holistic explanation.

But what precisely does domestic politics mean, as a determinant in the context of Sri Lanka policy? Does it mean pressure to support the Lankan Tamil minority from the Tamil Nadu regional parties as a part of coalition politics? This might partly explain some developments, like the vote against Sri Lanka at the UNHCR in 2012 and 2013, or the decision to hold full defence co-operation in abeyance under both the NDA and UPA, but it is again only a partial explanation. As pointed out earlier in this paper, the strongest pro-Tamil intervention took place in the 1980s when coalition politics was not on the horizon, and when both Indira Gandhi and Rajiv Gandhi enjoyed ample majorities on the Congress's own strength in the Lok Sabha, even if one subtracted the Congress MPs from Tamil Nadu. Likewise, the strongest intervention in the post-LTTE phase came in May–July 2013 after the DMK left the UPA II government, and the latter survived without depending on either Tamil Nadu regional party and also not being dependent on the Congress MPs from Tamil Nadu. It was in May–July 2013 that the UPA II government pressured the Rajapaksa regime, against its will, to keep the 13th Amendment intact and hold elections to the NPC.

The most recent development in Indo–Sri Lanka relations, the bilateral meeting between newly sworn-in prime minister Narendra Modi and President Rajapaksa, reinforces this argument. Modi called for "full implementation of the 13th amendment and beyond" even when his party, the BJP, enjoys a majority on its own, and neither the ruling AIADMK in Tamil Nadu nor the DMK are its alliance partners and it has only one member of parliament from the state (Bastians 2014). On his visit to Sri Lanka in March 2015 at the invitation of the new government of President Maithripala Sirisena, he not only repeated this advice but also advocated "co-operative federalism" in a speech to the Sri Lankan parliament and visited Jaffna and met NPC Chief Minister C.V. Wigneswaran to show India's support for Tamil aspirations.

Hence, while coalition politics in the form of pressure from Tamil Nadu's regional parties is a factor, this is an incomplete explanation. Rather, one needs to interpret domestic politics more broadly and holistically in terms of the basic nature of the Indian state and its implicit nation-building strategy to be able to explain the Indian state's preference for accommodation of the Lankan Tamil minority. Basically, we need an explanation of why Indian governments across parties, coalitions, and personalities since 1983 have preferred an accommodative solution in Sri Lanka even when they were not dependent on Tamil Nadu's regional parties, and even when purely strategic and economic interests would dictate turning a blind eye to Sri Lankan treatment of the Tamils. In the case of Bangladesh, for example, India has turned a blind eye to the gradual colonisation of the Chittagong Hill Tracts by the Bengali Muslim majority and the reduction of the Buddhist Chakmas to a minority in that tract (their homeland) or to refugee status in India. And in the case of Myanmar, India has turned a blind eye to the problem of stateless Indians while cultivating the military regime for essentially (counter-Chinese) strategic and (Nagaland) counterinsurgency reasons over the past decade and more. Besides, the role of the states in foreign policy has often been misinterpreted as being a case of states proactively demanding a role. Actually, it was the centre that initially drew in the states, particularly the border states, so as to implement foreign policy more effectively.[23]

Foreign policy towards Sri Lanka and the issue of the Sri Lankan Tamils cannot be understood without taking into account the nature of the Indian state and its unstated nation-building project, as manifested in its constitution and political practices over the past six decades. The Indian state inherited vast heterogeneity at independence, being multi-religious, multi-caste, multi-lingual, and multi-cultural, de facto federal, and, after the linguistic reorganisation of states from 1956, linguo-federal, in effect, ethno-federal. It adopted a secular, federal, multi-lingual constitutional dispensation with explicit minority rights and protection against caste discrimination, in addition to equal rights and non-discrimination in general.

Political practice has flowed from this constitutional dispensation and from the inclusive, umbrella character of the Congress Party that ruled India for over four decades since independence, in that the unity of the nation and the inculcation of a sense of identification with the nation and the state have been based on policies of accommodation and inclusion. Hence, the resolution of the language conflict of the 1950s and 1960s, centred on whether Hindi should be the sole official language at the centre, was resolved in an accommodative manner with the reorganisation of states on linguistic lines, establishing self-ruled homelands for all major linguistic groups, and by the retention of English as an official language

[23] Interview with former High Commissioner S.J.S. Chhatwal, 10 September 2013.

by the central government and by the judiciary all over India, and from the 1960s by the creation of new states for ethnic groups in the north-east, starting with a separatist Nagaland in 1963. This a-commodative strategy has been by and large successful in integrating India as a nation, most notably in the Tamil Nadu case where the DMK dropped the separatist part of its platform in 1963 and has never raised it again since, nor have even minor parties in Tamil Nadu. The foreign policy counterpart of such a national integration strategy (and national unity is the foundation of internal security and hence national security) would inevitably be a policy of sensitivity to the feelings of any section of the people of India, if agitated or mobilized, as far as discrimination or maltreatment of ethnic kinfolk is concerned.[24]

I would argue, from the track record analysed in this chapter, that it is this – the centre's own sensitivity to the perceived requirements of national unity as the foundation of national security, and not only pressure from Tamil Nadu parties – that explains the broadly Tamil-sympathetic policy stance of India's Sri Lanka policy since the July 1983 riots. Underlying this sensitivity is the shadow of the possibility of alienation leading to the revival of separatism in Tamil Nadu, a crucial state from a strategic and economic standpoint, the danger being that alienation from the Indian state and the perception of the latter as an anti-Tamil, discriminatory state could arise, at first among fringe groups, if India went along with Sri Lanka's anti-Tamil policies. While this has not happened, and while Tamil Nadu political parties and public opinion have not turned anti-India or separatist or pro-LTTE, there is genuine concern about the fate of the Sri Lankan Tamils and a lack of trust in Sri Lankan parties and governments. The complication for Indian policy has been that the LTTE, the group nurtured by India in the mid-1980s, turned anti-India because it felt that the ISLA was far too weak, and it wanted nothing less than an independent

[24] For the concept of kin state, see Ganguly (1999: chapter 1).

Eelam. The assassination of Rajiv Gandhi made it impossible for India to deal with the LTTE. Indian policy has therefore proceeded by making a distinction between sympathy for the situation of the Lankan Tamils and antipathy to the LTTE as a group, which roughly mirrored post-assassination public opinion in Tamil Nadu.

In broader theoretical terms, the dissonance between India and Sri Lanka since 1983 has been founded on their contrasting nation-building and state-building strategies, which have been almost polar opposites. Sri Lanka has followed, almost from the outset, a Sinhala-Buddhist majoritarian state-building process, which contrasts sharply with India's inclusive and accommodative approach. As Mohammed Ayoob argues, the state-building process in its early stages impinges on relations with neighbouring states, and hence domestic politics cannot be separated from foreign policy (Ayoob 1995). Hence, it is necessary to move theoretically beyond not only realism to understand Indian policy on Sri Lanka, but also beyond extensions of it, like neoclassical realism, which merely incorporates domestic inputs. For while realism is clearly inadequate for the reasons just explained, even neoclassical realism can at best accommodate domestic inputs such as pressures from Tamil Nadu, but cannot explain why Indian policy has been sympathetic to Lankan Tamils even when the centre is not beholden to Tamil Nadu. The best fit would be a theory of the Ayoobian type that roots foreign policy behaviour in the state-building exercise and its external fallouts, in this case in the contrast between inclusive and majoritarian strategies for state building and nation building. This would explain Indian policy by the Indian state's sensitivity to Tamil Nadu's concerns about Sri Lankan Tamils because of the implications for alienation, and hence for the nation's psychological unity, and hence for long-term national security.

To conclude, in a larger perspective, India's relations with Sri Lanka raise three general issues for Indian foreign policy that need to be thought through to evolve a broad set of principles/guidelines. First, what position should India take on normative issues concerning democracy, human rights, and the treatment of minorities? Second, what should be the role of the states in foreign policy? Third, what should be the role of ethnic links, if any, in foreign policy? Guidelines for the last two need to be evolved in a way that do not undermine national unity and domestic harmony; that is, in the event that states and ethnic links are given a place in foreign policy, no state or group within India should feel that this is done on a discriminatory basis. Thus, India's relations with Sri Lanka, although seemingly an isolated relationship, have much broader implications in a world of discriminatory states and ethnic links instantaneously magnified by modern communications, increasing federalisation of Indian politics, and the growing strength of democratic and human rights norms.

References

Ayoob, M. 1995. *The Third World Security Predicament: State-Making, Regional Conflict, and the International System* (Boulder, CO: Lynne Rienner).

Basrur, R. 2011. "Foreign Policy Reversal: The Politics of Sri Lanka's Economic Relations with India", in E. Sridharan, ed., *International Relations Theory and South Asia*, vol. 1 (New Delhi: Oxford University Press), pp. 242–59.

Bastians, D. 2014. "Modi–Mahinda Talks: Indian PM Renews 13 Plus Call", *Daily FT*, 28 May 2015.

Bhasin, A.S., ed. 2001. *India–Sri Lanka Relations and Sri Lanka's Ethnic Conflict, 1947–2000*, 5 vols (New Delhi: India Research Press).

de Silva, K.M. 2012. *Sri Lanka and the Defeat of the LTTE* (New Delhi: Penguin).

DeVotta, N. 2004. *Blowback: Linguistic Nationalism, Institutional Decay, and Ethnic Conflict in Sri Lanka* (Stanford: Stanford University Press).

Dixit, J.N. 1998. *Assignment Colombo* (New Delhi: Konark).

Fernando, Shamindra. "India's Warships to remain with Sri Lanka", *The Island Online*, 1 May 2015.

Ganguly, R. 1999. *Kin State Intervention in Ethnic Conflict* (New Delhi: Sage).

Ghosh, P.S. 2003. *Ethnicity versus Nationalism: The Devolution Discourse in Sri Lanka* (New Delhi: Sage).

Gokhale, N.A. 2009. *Sri Lanka from War to Peace* (New Delhi: Har Anand).

Krishna, S. 1999. *Postcolonial Insecurities: India, Sri Lanka and the Question of Nationhood* (New Delhi: Oxford University Press).

Mehrotra, L. 2011. *My Days in Sri Lanka* (New Delhi: Har Anand).

Sahadevan, P. 1995. *India and Overseas Indians: The Case of Sri Lanka* (New Delhi: Kalinga).

Sunday Times. 2013. "Govt. Going Ahead with NPC Polls; 13th A intact", 26 May.

Suryanarayan, V. 2005. *Conflict over Fisheries in the Palk Bay Region* (New Delhi: Lancer).

Swamy, M.R.N. 1994. *Tigers of Lanka* (New Delhi: Konark).

———. 2003. *Inside an Elusive Mind: Prabhakaran* (New Delhi: Konark).

———. 2010. *The Tiger Vanquished: LTTE's Story* (New Delhi: Sage).

12

Eastward Ho? Indian Foreign Policy in the Indo-Pacific in the Context of Trade Integration and Security Rivalries

THIS PAPER TAKES a broad overview of the political and security context of the growing economic integration of Asia, which we have defined as East, Southeast, and Eastern South Asia, that is, excluding Pakistan and Afghanistan. It poses the two significant questions below, and attempts to arrive at a few tentative answers in order to layout a broad canvas that constitutes the context for Indian foreign policy.

Two Significant Questions: What Are the Strategic Consequences of Economic Integration for Asia? Also, What Are the Economic Consequences of the Absence of a Security Consensus for Asia

If one looks at the larger picture of the post-Cold War period in Asia, there are two overarching trends that can be observed: First, there is the growing economic integration of the Asia–Pacific region through trade and investment, and to a lesser extent, through

This paper draws heavily on two of my earlier papers: E. Sridharan, "The Political Context of Economic Cooperation in Asia: The Relation between Trade Integration and Security Rivalries", *Millennial Asia*, vol. 5, no. 2 (2014), pp. 129–36; and E. Sridharan, ""Where Is India Headed? Possible Future the movement of people, all helped by the multilateral and regional liberalisation of trade within Asia, which, as stated earlier, we have defined as East, Southeast, and South Asia. This has led to the growing intermeshing of the economies in the larger Asian region, and even more so in East Asia (China, Japan, South Korea, Taiwan, and Hong Kong), as well as in the 10-member Association of South-East Asian Nations (ASEAN).

The rise of China to the position of the worlds second-largest economy, and the country's growing importance in the trade profiles of all Asian countries, have made Asia's trade increasingly China-oriented over the past decade. Some of the major features as of 2018, the latest year available for comprehensive trade figures, are as follows.[1] Without delving into excessive details, the following facts point to the growing importance of intra-Asian trade. In 2018, out of (mainland) China's total trade of $4.635 trillion, its trade with its immediate East Asian neighbours, Japan, South Korea, and Taiwan, was $867 billion or more than its trade with either the US ($637 billion) or the European Union (EU) ($660 billion). If one adds its trade with the ASEAN ($589 billion), its trade with East and Southeast Asia exceeded its trade with the US and EU combined. Even if one takes exports alone, China's exports to its East Asian and ASEAN partners adds up to more than its exports to either the US or the EU. Conversely, China, and even more so, East. Southeast and South Asia as a whole bulk larger than either the US or the EU in the trade profiles of Japan, ASEAN, and India. Thus, Japan's trade with China in 2018 was more than its trade with either the US or the EU. Its trade with ASEAN was also more than that with either the US or the EU. As for ASEAN, its trade with

---

Directions in Indian Foreign Policy", *International Affairs,* vol. 93, no. 1 (2017), pp. 51–68. I am grateful for the research assistance of Aashik Jain and Devyani Chaturvedi.

[1] All figures are from the International Monetary Fund (IMF), Direction of Trade Stallstics, available at data. imLorg!7sk =9D6028D4-F14A-464C-A2 F259B2CD424B85.

China just exceeded its trade with the US and EU combined. For India, while the US was the largest trading partner, China was a strong second partner, and its trade with Asia as a whole exceeded trade that with the US and the EU. Such intra-Asian trade integration, driven to a large degree by the rise of China as a manufacturing and trading power, has its obvious geopolitical consequences in the fact that it will not be possible for the West to isolate and contain China in the way that the Soviet Union was contained during the Cold War.

This Asian trade integration was driven by both multilateral trade liberalisation under the rules of the General Agreement on Tariffs and Trade (GATT), the World Trade Organization (WTO) since 1996, and bilateral and plurilateral (multi-country, which can be both regional as well as cross-regional) free trade agreements in the Asian region. To give an indication of the growth in the number of such bilateral agreements between 2000 and 2017, the number of WTO-notified bilateral agreements within Asian sub-regions (for example, within East and South Asia) grew from one to eight, and the number of bilateral agreements across sub-regions (for example, between an East Asian and a South Asian country) grew from zero to seventeen. If one takes both WTO-notified bilateral free trade agreements (FTAs and those not yet notified), including those under negotiation, between 2000 and 2017, the number of FTAs within Asia grew from 1 to 43.[2] If one looks at the Asian plurilateral FTAs between 2000 and 2017, the number of such WTO-notified FTAs grew from 4 to 10, and the number of FTAs between an Asian plurilateral organisation, such as ASEAN, and individual Asian countries grew from 0 to 5. If all Asian plurilateral FTAs, both WTO-notified and those not yet notified (including those under negotiation) from 2000–17 are counted, then the number of Asian plurilateral FTAs grew from 4 to 14, and the number of FTAs between an Asian plurilateral grouping like ASEAN

[2] See Asian Development Banks Asia Regional Integration Centre Database, available at www.aric.adb.orglfta for these and other figures on bilateral and plurilateral FTAs in Asia.

and individual Asian countries grew from 0 to 8. These figures are indicators of the rapid proliferation of Asian FTAs, both bilateral and plurilateral, since 2000, which have been the drivers of trade integration within the region.

Second, the Trans-Pacific Partnership (TPP) has been diminished, following the Trump Administration's withdrawal of the US from it despite the remaining countries (which excludes China) signing a Comprehensive and Progressive Agreement for TPP. However, the Regional Comprehensive Economic Partnership (RCEP) was signed in November 2020 and it consists of the ASEAN plus Japan, China, South Korea, Australia, New Zealand, and India, or in other words the countries of the East Asian Summit held since 2005, excluding the US. In November 2019, India opted out of this pact at the Bangkok summit. Closer to India, the Bay of Bengal Initiative for Multi-Sectoral Technical and Economic Cooperation (BIMSTEC) has also been undergoing a new momentum, perhaps replacing the moribund South Asian Association for Regional Cooperation (SAARC) in an eastward tilt, away from South Asia, towards a hybrid South and Southeast Asian grouping.

Such trade integration also was a driver of, and conversely was also driven by, foreign direct investment (FDI) flows, although the latter would be more politically influenced than influenced by trade alone. FDI data from the United Nations Conference on Trade and Development (UNCTAD) database indicates a massive increase in outward FDI flow from five major Asian countries/blocs (Japan, China, Korea, ASEAN and India) between 2001 and 2018, a leap from $70 billion to $393 billion, of which non-Japan FDI outflows increased from $31 billion to $250 billion, led by a Chinese jump from $7 billion to $130 billion. This can be compared with a slippage of combined US+EU FDI outflows for the same years, from $935 billion to $691 billion.[3] A large part of Asian outward

[3] See UNCTAD database on FDI, available at www. unctad. orglfdistatistics.

FDI flows would have been to Western countries, but it can safely be assumed that an increasing part of it would have also been intraregional and closely correlated with the growing intra-Asian trade integration, also driving the latter by the internationalisation of production chains.

However, the striking fact about the security/strategic situation in Asia is the absence of a security consensus and an overall security treaty or regional cooperation treaty analogous to the North Atlantic Treaty Organisation (NATO) and the EU in the European continent. In the post-1945 Asia–Pacific region, the strategic alignments have been of a hub-and-spokes type. The US as the security provider for non-communist Asia has been the hub. It has had spokes – like individual security guarantee treaties with Japan, South Korea, and Australia, and less formalised arrangements with other states/entities, from Taiwan to Indonesia. Over the past decade, the rise of China – touted as the peaceful rise until recent assertive actions in all directions since 2011 – has led to the aggravation of existing and new territorial and maritime boundary disputes, and strategic, particularly naval, rivalries all around China, from the East China Sea to the South China Sea to the Sino–Indian Line of Actual Control (LAC). Apart from the tension over Taiwan, China has now asserted itself aero-navally in the East China Sea over the Diaoyul Senkaku islands and has made sweeping maritime territorial claims in the South China Sea over the Paracel and Spratly islands. It has also asserted that its vital national interests extend to the second Pacific island chain, thus bringing it into conflict with Vietnam, Philippines, Malaysia, Indonesia, and Brunei. It has built artificial islands in the South China Sea, with military facilities to assert its maritime claims. China's economic growth has had strategic consequences, and it is redefining its core interests, most recently expanding its reach to the second Pacific island chain and the Indian Ocean, much further afield, linked to the protection of energy and raw material supplies. China now has military supply and port construction relationships, plus substantial trade and aid, with Pakistan, Sri Lanka, Bangladesh, and Myanmar in the Indian Ocean, and has a naval base at Djibouti, along with naval facilities at Gwadar, Pakistan on the Arabian Sea.

The major question in the political economy of Asia is: how will these two contradictory tendencies will play out over the coming years? Will growing economic interdependencies provide the ballast for building political and security cooperation, thereby resulting in regional or pan-Asian security consensus embodied in a treaty or treaties? Or will the absence of a security consensus, and growing strategic rivalries and distrust prevent the political integration that usually follows increasing economic integration? These questions frame India's relationships with countries in the Indo-Pacific and shape India's options.

Can Asia-Wide Political/Security Co-operation Be Built as a Consequence of Economic Integration?

At the regional, all-Asian level, or even at the East Asian or Southeast Asian level, despite the existence of the US–Japan and US–South Korea security treaties, the existence of ASEAN as a political grouping – although not a situation of political integration unlike the EU – since 1968, and that of SAARC since 1985, there has been no institutionalisation of security relations, even after the Cold War. Indeed, the rise of China and its assertiveness since 2011 has led the US to announce a planned "rebalance" or "pivot" of its aero-naval forces to the Pacific from the Atlantic in the ratio of 60:40, favouring the Pacific, a clear indication of the intention to balance the rise of China.

This is partly the legacy of the history of the Cold War in Asia, and partly a question of fundamental differences in regime type between a democratic/democratising Asia and an authoritarian communist party-led China. However, it is also a consequence of unresolved territorial, including maritime, disputes. Recently, the democratic peace theory, widely popular in the West, has itself been questioned, with Douglas M. Gibler arguing that democracy and peace are symptoms and not causes of the removal of territorial issues between neighbours.[4]

The first objective that China and India need to diligently pursue, is a settlement or freezing/shelving of outstanding border issues, including maritime borders, with smaller neighbours. As Gibler shows, territorial settlement treaties are more likely than anything else to end the incidence of war. The next most important idea is to promote economic co-operation in a way that creates *incentives without the fear of being dominated,* losing one's autonomy, etc., for the smaller states.

The literature indicates that the largest state typically has to be prepared to bear a disproportionately large share of the costs of regional co-operation building and maintenance, and obtain only a disproportionately small share of the benefits, at least in the short run, for example, through non-reciprocal economic openness, in order to be able to make the usually necessary side payments to smaller partner countries. This insight is derived from coalition theory, as applied to states in an anarchic world system, which suggests that it is in the interest of smaller partners to coalesce with a larger partner, both in a legislative setting and in international politics, mainly, when the larger partner is willing and able to make side payments that make the sharing of the pay-off disproportional. As Bruce Bueno de Mesquita puts it,

> If the benefits derived from a winning coalition are distributed so as to preserve the initial relative distribution of resources among the winners, then the largest member of the coalition must get the largest share of the benefits. Of course, the ratio of this actor's size to that of each of its partners remains constant . . . but its absolute size moves closer to the system's definition of the size required to win.[5]

[4] Douglas M. Gibler, 'Bordering on Peace: Democracy, Territorial Issues, and Conflict", *International Studies Quarterly,* vol. 51, no. 3 (2007), pp. 509–32.

[5] Bruce Bueno de Mesquita, *Strategy, Risk and Personality* in *Coalition Politics: The Case of India* (Cambridge: Cambridge University Press, 1975), pp. 9–10.

The argument is essentially that the largest partner, even when bearing and taking only a proportionate share of the costs and benefits, respectively, is making a disproportionate quantum gain by its *being enabled to cross an international size/power/status threshold that makes it a qualitatively more important international player* (author's emphasis). That is, an effective Asian regional security organisation would need to compensate the smaller and less secure countries more than proportionately with regard to cost and benefit-sharing for it to be in their interest to be in such a regional coalition, and for the same reason, it would be in the interest of the big country/countries in such a coalition to so compensate them. What needs to be analysed are the kinds of cross-issue linkages and trade-offs, such as those between economic and security issues, and foreign policy and domestic policy changes affecting international relations, which are involved in the role played by the largest states and the transactions between these and smaller states.

The incentives for regional economic co-operation building for leading regional states could be analogous to that of global hegemons, from the perspective of hegemonic stability theory, for building global economic co-operation regimes, as neoliberal institutionalists Robert Keohane and Joseph Nye, argue: "Stable economic regimes require leadership, that is, willingness to forgo short-term gains in bargaining in order to preserve the regime", and that an actor is most likely to provide such leadership when it sees itself as a major consumer of the long-term benefits produced by the regime.[6] And they further state: "When the hegemonial

[6] Robert Keohane and Joseph S. Nye, *Power and Interdependence: World Politics in Transition* (Boston: Little, Brown &. Co., 1977), p. 44. For hegemonic stability theory, see Stephen D. Krasner, "State Power and the Structure of International Trade", *World Politics* 28 (1976), 317–47. For a critical survey of hegemonic stability theory, disaggregating its strands, see David A. Lake, "Leadership, Hegemony and the Internalional Economy: Naked Emperor or Tattered Monarch with Potential?", *International Studies Quarterly*, vol. 37, no. 4 (1993), pp. 459–89.

power does not seek to conquer other states, but merely to protect its favoured position, other states may benefit as well."[7] This argument can be modified to be applied to regional economic co-operation regimes, in which there is a clear regional economic power, whose relative global or extra-regional status would be boosted by leading a regional group, and hence, would have incentives to be "generous" to smaller states, as argued by Bueno de Mesquita.[8]

Scholars looking at successful cases of regional economic integration would argue that there are political prerequisites for successful economic integration, leading in turn to political integration. The most successful case of this is the EU, despite the recent event of Brexit. The process of European integration began with the Schuman Plan (for the European Coal and Steel Community) presented in May 1950, the European Coal and Steel Community Treaty in 1951, ratified to bring it into effect in 1952. Helen Milner argues,

> The Schuman Plan called for countries and their firms to relinquish control of two vital economic sectors, coal and steel, to a supranational "High Authority" (HA). Since these sectors undergirded the rest of the economy and provided the means to make war, control over them was not just an economic issue . . . Once these sectors were integrated internationally, it was felt, war between these countries would never again be possible.[9]

[7] Ibid.

[8] See Mesquita, *Strategy, Risk and Personality*, ch. 1, for a survey of power maximisation theories of coalition politics, which shows that it is in the interest of smaller partners to coalesce with a larger partner, in a legislative setting mainly when the larger partner is willing and able to make side paynents that make the sharing of the pay-off disproportional. The argument is essentially that the largest partner is only compensating for the disproportionate quantum gain that it is enabled to make either by enabling government-formation or by enabling the crossing of a political threshold that makes it a qualitatively more important player in the system.

[9] Helen Milner, *Interests, Institutions and Information: Domestic Politics and International Relations* (Princeton: Princeton University Press, 1997), p. 180.

Thus, the treaty neutralised the Saar, Rhine, and Ruhr border areas between France and Germany, which produce coal and steel; it would, therefore, constrain Germany. It should be noted, moreover, that this Treaty was preceded by the formation of NATO as a security umbrella under US leadership, the Warsaw Pact as a common threat, and the Korean War as an ongoing regional hot war in the Cold War confrontation, in addition to which there was US pressure on both France and Germany to ratify the treaty. It is evident that the process of economic integration was built on political preconditions from its very inception, rather than being an economic process bringing about security and political integration.

However, the opposite view, that trade co-operation does not need prior political amity, but merely a truce-like deterrent capacity, also has empirical substance. The "cold politics but hot economics" scenario of East Asia since the 1980s was signified by trade booming among China, Taiwan, South Korea, and Japan, and now Vietnam and the rest of ASEAN, without any security pact, and in fact with territorial and maritime disputes and competitive arming. This, in turn, indicates that an effective and well understood deterrent capacity, including guarantees by an outside power like the US, can be a substitute for a formal political or security agreement, and that trade can flourish under such circumstances, leading, perhaps, in the long term to reduced political differences and mutual stakes in each others' economies.

In the context of Asia, there is no clear hegemonic power analogous to the US in the North Atlantic or the Americas, which can play the role of a benevolent hegemon or the nucleus of an Asian regionalism. Moreover, neither is there a common threat analogous to the perceived Soviet threat to the post-war West, nor is there a common political or economic ideology, or even a common cultural identity, other than being non-Western, still less a common racial, ethnic or religious identity. Hence, these preconditions for regional political or security integration, quite apart from disputed borders and territories, do not exist, unlike in the case of post-war European integration or the formation of the Western alliance.

However, as the literature on the trade–security relationship shows, trade and security are closely interlinked; FTAs are used as an instrument to bolster diplomatic and security ties, or to embed security ties, in addition to assisting trade promotion alone, particularly cross-regional FTAs or plurilateral FIAs involving significant powers. This is particularly so since the decade of the 1990s, due to what Vinod K. Aggarwal and Min Gyo Koo have called the triple shocks of the end of the Cold War, the Asian financial crisis of 1997, and the 9/11 shock to global security.[10] This has led to a search for regional, and sub-regional and cross-regional institution building in the form of not only both FTAs for trade integration and economic expansion, but also politico-diplomatic and security institutionalisation. This suggests a search for regional institutions that goes beyond the loosely structured US-centred hub-and-spokes system in place since the Cold War, and is intended to mutually bolster both security co-operation and economic integration. As of 2019, this is a still nascent and evolving architecture, which is in a state of flux due to the rise and newly assertive behaviour of China.

To sum up, Asian economic integration and the rise of China are both interrelated, and pose both opportunities and challenges for political and security integration. This is bound to be a long-term process, but is vulnerable to being derailed by short-term opportunistic behaviour on the part of both major and minor actors.

Implications for Indian Foreign Policy in the Indo-Pacific

Indo–US Relations and US–China Dynamics in Asia

In this scenario, what are India's foreign policy, security and economic options in Asia, or in the Indo-Pacific, the recently coined

[10] Vinod K. Aggarwal and Min Gyo Koo, "Asia's New Institutional Archi-

term in 2017, which stretches, for the purposes of this paper, from the eastern rim of South Asia to Southeast and East Asia?

The major change in Indian foreign policy, which has had implications for its Asia policy, earlier called Look East policy since the early 1990s, and re-labelled the Act East policy since 2014, has been the improvement of relations with the US. Relations with the US improved only gradually after a continuing period of uneasiness during the 1990s. This uneasiness happened due to the continuing American need for Pakistani co-operation in stabilising post-Soviet occupation Afghanistan, a generally hyphenated US policy towards India and Pakistan, and the fact of the stepped-up US concern about non-proliferation, particularly following the May 1990 near-nuclear crisis, India's veto of the Comprehensive Test Ban Treaty (CTBT) at the Conference on Disarmament in Geneva in 1996, the 1998 nuclear tests by India, and a generally tightening US policy towards non-proliferation, together with some degree of sympathy for the Pakistani position on Kashmir from thc carly to mid 1990s.

Over the course of the 1990s and early 2000s, particularly post-9/11, two of the three major irritants in the Indian relationship with the US declined in political significance, that is, India's continued arms supply relationship with a relatively declining Russia did not bother the US as much as it did earlier, and the US's closeness to Pakistan declined after 9/11, despite its dependence on Pakistan for its Afghanistan operations. This left only the third major irritant – India's nuclear weapons capability, particularly after the 1998 nuclear tests – to be somehow finessed, if not resolved, for the relationship to be able to move forward, something already being propelled by India's economic liberalisation and closer integration with world markets, epitomised by the information

tecture: Evolving Structures for Managing Trade, Financial and Security Relations", in Vinod K. Aggarwal and Min Gyo Koo, eds, *Asia's New Institutional Architecture: Evolving Structures for Managagig Trade, Financial and Security Relations* (Berlin and Heidelberg: Springer, 2008).

technology sector. The II-Round dialogue between Strobe Talbott, Deputy Secretary of State, and Jaswant Singh, Foreign Minister, on nuclear weapons following the 1998 tests laid the basis for what later became the Indo–US civil-nuclear agreement negotiated over 2005–8.

India has become significantly closer to the US since at least 2005, marked by not only the nuclear deal, but also by the signing of two out of three foundational agreements that enable military-to-military co-operation and arms acquisitions, that is, the Logistics Exchange Memorandum of Agreement (LEMOA) in 2016, and the Communications Compatibility and Security Agreement (COMCASA) in 2018, along with growing arms purchases. Since 2011, the country has grown significantly closer to US allies in the Asia–Pacific, such as Japan, Australia, and several ASEAN countries, reflected in growing naval co-operation and joint exercises; it needs to remembered that the overarching context for such closeness, including the Indo–US nuclear deal, has been a shift in the US Asia–Pacific security policy, driven by the rise of China. This is often understood as the formally declared "pivot", which was in 2011, later re-labelled a "re-balance", towards Asia, by the Obama Administration, whereby 60 per cent of US aero-naval assets were to be deployed in the Pacific rather than in the Atlantic. However, it needs to be understood that the pivot actually began much earlier, in ideational terms as early as 2001, and in practice from 2004, under the Bush administration.[11] The basic aim was to balance the rise of China, not through containment as was practised towards the Soviet Union during the Cold War, but rather by both internal and external balancing in order to maintain the superior strategic position of the US in the Asia Pacific, while accepting the rise of China as a given. The external balancing component of the strategy was not a new NATO-style alliance, but a shift from the

[11] See Nina Silove, "The Pivot before the Pivot: US Strategy to Preserve the Power Balance in Asia", *International Security*, vol. 40, no. 4 (2016), pp. 45–88.

traditional, hub-and-spokes pattern of defence relationships in the Asia–Pacific to a federated, network model. In this model, Asian allies, themselves increasingly concerned about China's rise and assertiveness, were to be encouraged to have stronger relationships with each other as well as have increasing interoperability of forces, something fostered by the growth of military, particularly naval, exercises among the US and its Asian allies and partners since 2001 on a multilateral basis.

The Bush administration took a key decision in 2004, which was to bring India into this federated network model as a new partner. Hence, the Next Steps in Strategic Partnership (NSSP) framework agreement of 2005, and the Indo–US civil nuclear agreement negotiated over 2005–8 to finesse the major remaining irritant in Indo–US relations over non-proliferation, brought India into the global nuclear commerce regime, while allowing India to retain its nuclear military capabilities. This would not have happened without a shift in US policy, and that can only be understood in the context of US concerns about the long term rise of China and the development of an appropriate response, which combined balancing with the continued engagement of China. The defence and foreign policies of countries in the Asia–Pacific are significantly influenced by US strategy; and it is important to understand this for it creates both incentives for behaviour as well as windows of opportunity for a range of countries in the region.

For India, the shift towards improved relations with the US, and with its Asian allies and partners, particularly since 2005, and even more since the growth of Chinese assertiveness since 2011, can be fully understood only by taking into account the context framed by this larger shift in US policy and its impact as a driver of foreign policy behaviour throughout Asia. From the US point of view, it made sense to include India as part of its federated network model of balancing China's rise. In addition, India could be an ally against post-9/11 international terrorism and the threat of further nuclear proliferation. Thus, the overarching and gradual shift in US policy, in addition to the economic rise of Asia, created opportunities for shifts in Indian foreign policy towards the US and towards its Asian allies and partners in Southeast and East Asia.

These developments gathered momentum since 2005, since the world economic downturn of 2008, after which China's relatively unscathed growth took it ahead of Japan to become the world's second largest economy, and after its growing offshore assertiveness since 2011. Thus, the US supported a Japanese proposal in 2007 to create a "quadrilateral" security dialogue among the US, Japan, Australia, and India; this led to all four states increasing their security interactions. Japan and India signed a defence co-operation agreement in 2008 and a Strategic and Global Partnership Agreement in 2014.[12] The US, Japan and India conducted their first trilateral naval exercises in the Western Pacific in 2007, and since that year, the Indo-US Malabar naval exercises were expanded to include Japan, Australia and Singapore. India–Japan bilateral naval exercises started in 2012. The quadrilateral proposal has been renewed again on the sidelines of the November 2017 East Asia summit in Manila by the Trump administration, and has been elevated to a ministerial-level dialogue in September 2019. The influence on Indian foreign policy, in terms of incentives and windows of opportunity, of the context-changing shifts in US poiicy, are clearly discernible and will have a continuing influence in the future evolution of Indian foreign policy.

On the whole, recent foreign policy changes have been slow and incremental, and they have been building on past policies without dramatic breaks, but at the same time taking advantages of windows of opportunity, such as those afforded by shifts in US policy. The Modi government's initiatives since 2014 seem to be a more energised version of earlier foreign policy changes, as one would expect from a middle power without system-shaping capabilities, but with aspirations for a bigger role and higher international status.

[12] Ibid., p. 78.

Possible Future Directions in Indian Foreign Policy: Three Broad Scenarios

What does the above discussion imply for future directions in Indian foreign policy, particularly its Asia, or Indo-Pacific policy?

From the ground covered so far, clearly there are certain constant imperatives that will continue, that is, the search for security against the felt threats of the Pakistan–China combine, as well as, more generally, the preservation and enhancement of capabilities, and the search for economic growth, and hence, for capital, technology, and partners. The aspiration, shared across political parties, to become a leading power in the world will remain, alongside the desire for strategic autonomy. At a practical level of boosting institutional capacities for foreign policy, one can expect the rectification of certain weaknesses, such as the small size of the foreign service, the relatively weak links with academia and think-tanks, and the increasingly institutionalised involvement of India's states, reflected in the creation of the States Division in the Ministry of External Affairs (MEA) in 2014, driven by the globalisation of the economies of states and their linkages with diasporas. The overall strategy – although there may be no declared grand strategy, paradigm, or doctrine – and specific foreign policies deployed to achieve these objectives will depend on the incentives and windows of opportunity offered by the global, extra-regional and regional structural context. These contexts are, in turn, shaped by the dynamics of great power interaction, specifically for the Asia–Pacific land and maritime context, the dynamics of interaction among the US, China, and Russia, and the evolution of the world economic order. While India's relationship with Europe is critical to its economic growth, the EU is not a single political entity and plays a secondary role in the Asia–Pacific landmass and waters; hence, my focus is on the overarching relationships among the US, China, and Russia in setting the geopolitical context for Indian foreign policy. One can discern the following three broad scenarios as possibilities over the next half-decade up to a decade.

First, there is a broad scenario of increased US dominance, in which the US is able to balance the rise of China, aided by the recent slowdown of the Chinese economy, aggravated by the Trump-launched US–China trade war since 2018, by a full-fledged rebalance to the Pacific, a relatively declining Russia possibly increasingly allied to China to counter US dominance. In such a scenario, one could expect India to align itself more closely with the US and its federated network of allies and partners in Asia and elsewhere. However, even in such a scenario, there will be limits to a realignment or tilt towards the US or the West. Even a slowing China will be growing faster than the US or the West in the foreseeable future, starting from a baseline of somewhat over half of the US Gross Domestic Product (GDP). Hence, it will still be narrowing the gap, albeit more slowly. And China will be impossible to isolate, given that it is already a larger trading partner than the US for almost all its Asian neighbours. Besides, if the full implementation of China's One Belt One Road (OBOR), now caled the Belt and Road Initiative (BRI) project, operational since 2013, is realised, particularly the pipelines, then it will have land connectivity with Europe, the Middle East, and much of Southeast Asia, which would reduce its dependence on seaborne trade and energy supplies.

As far as India is concerned, China will still control the headwaters of the Indus and Brahmaputra basins, and could divert the latter's waters. It will still have a clandestine nuclear and missile partnership with Pakistan, bolstering the latter vis-à-vis India; it will also have the advantage of terrain, infrastructure, and superior forces along the border, as well as be an important trading partner and potential source of capital as an incentive to shape Indian behaviour. There is nothing that the US can do to protect India in the event of a border war in which China is well positioned to grab scraps or slices of territory, or in the eventuality of a diversion of river waters. Therefore, even in this scenario, India would have incentives not to alienate China by throwing in its lot with the US, particularly if the Trump administration's increasingly transactional, as against a long-term strategic approach to foreign policy, continues. A strategic partnership with the US would be most likely, with some limits on realignment, in order to increase India's leverage vis-à-vis the China–Pakistan combine. As far as Russia is concerned, given the fact that at present something like 60 per cent of major military platforms in the Indian armed forces (combat aircraft, submarines, ships, and tanks) are of Soviet/Russian origin, and the fact that key military technologies are being shared by Russia (the leasing of a nuclear-powered submarine, reported assistance for India's sea-based deterrent, collaboration on the Brahmos supersonic missile and the fifth-generation fighter project), it will not be easy to make sudden and drastic shifts in the relationship.[13] Hence, even in a US-dominant scenario, there will be limits to a full-fledged alignment with the US.

The second possible broad scenario is the continuation of the current status quo. In such a scenario, we would expect the thrust of the Modi government's policies to continue, that is, a continuing realignment towards the US and its allies and partners in Asia, and a continuing but partial shift in defence acquisitions towards the US and Western sources, and away from Russia, while attempting to defend India's influence in neighbouring countries, the Middle East, Central Asia, and Africa, and continuing the search for infusions of capital and technology. However, in the UN and on international crises, India would make independent decisions depending on how national interest is defined from situation to situation, that is, retain its autonomy on such issues.

The third possible broad scenario is one of increasing Chinese ascendancy and US or Western decline, perhaps combined with the incoherence of US foreign policy in Asia. This is possible if a

[13] For Russian collaboration in India's submarine-based deterrent efforts, see Yogesh Joshi and Frank O'Donnell, "India's Submarine Deterrent and Asian Nuclear Proliferation", *Survival*, vol. 56, no. 4 (2014), pp. 157–74.

slowing China still manages to grow significantly faster than the US, despite the Trump-launched trade war against it, increasing its weight in the world economy and in the Asia–Pacific, given that it is starting from a baseline of over half of the US GDP and is the largest trading partner of most Asian countries. In such a scenario, if the US rebalance towards the Pacific is incomplete, if the US decides to accommodate the rise of China and its commensurately expanded definition of core national interest in the Pacific and Indian Oceans, and if China's BRI project succeeds and reduces Chinese dependence on sea routes for trade and energy supplies, then China will loom larger as both a security threat and an economic opportunity for all its neighbours, including India. Such a scenario would also probably lead to a closer Russia–China relationship, given Russia's frozen relationship with the West, following the Crimea/Ukraine crises of 2014. Given that China has an unresolved border problem with India, military advantage on the border, and a close de facto alliance with Pakistan, which is cemented by overland access to the Gwadar port, this scenario can be a threatening one for Indian security. India would then have two contrasting options. One would be an even stronger alignment with the US or West for security against China, while continuing a growing economic relationship with China to maintain a stable relationship. If this angers China and the relationship becomes confrontational, and if the US is not able to help balance China as far as the land border or possible river water diversion is concerned, India would face intensified pressure from the China-Pakistan combine all along the de facto borders.

In such a scenario, several of India's South Asian neighbours could tilt towards China. The other option would be to attempt to accommodate or appease China while attempting internal balancing by a military build-up. However, one can expect China and Pakistan to demand a very high price, possibly the formal acceptance of the LAC in the Western sector (Ladakh), concessions on Tawang, and political concessions on Kashmir, and the like. This would be almost impossible to sell domestically in India. The only situation in which India would be able to fend off pressures in such a scenario would be if its economy grows much faster than a slowing China and its military modernisation narrows the gap in the intervening period.

These three scenarios form the larger context that has framed and will continue to frame India's growing political, security, and economic engagement with the Indo–Pacific countries, ranging from the eastern rim of South Asia to Southeast and East Asia, both bilateral and plurilateral.

Index

Note: 't' next to page locators indicates tables